An Economic History of Indonesia

T0313191

Based on new datasets, this book presents an economic history of Indonesia. It analyses the causes of stagnation of growth during the colonial and independence period, making use of new theoretical insights from institutional economics and new growth theory.

The book looks at the major themes of Indonesian history: colonial exploitation and the successes and limitations of the post-1900 welfare policies, the price of instability after 1945 and the economic miracle after 1967. The book not only discusses economic change and development – or the lack thereof – but also the institutional and socio-political structures that were behind these changes. It presents a lot of new data on the changing welfare of the Indonesian population, on income distribution, and on the functioning of markets for rice, credit and labour. Concluding with a discussion on whether the poor profited from the economic changes, this book is a useful contribution to Southeast Asian Studies and International Economics.

Jan Luiten van Zanden is Professor of Global Economic History at Utrecht University, the Netherlands. He has published widely about processes of long-term economic development in Europe and Asia.

Daan Marks obtained his PhD in economics at Utrecht University, the Netherlands. He is currently working as a senior economist at the Dutch Ministry of Finance.

Routledge studies in the growth economies of Asia

An Economic History of Indonesia

1800–2010

Jan Luiten van Zanden and Daan Marks

Routledge
Taylor & Francis Group

LONDON AND NEW YORK

First published 2012
by Routledge
2 Park Square, Milton Park, Abingdon, Oxfordshire OX14 4RN

Simultaneously published in the USA and Canada
by Routledge
711 Third Avenue, New York, NY 10017

First issued in paperback 2014

Routledge is an imprint of the Taylor and Francis Group, an informa business

British Library Cataloguing in Publication Data
A catalogue record for this book is available from the British Library

Library of Congress Cataloging in Publication Data
Zanden, J. L. van.
An economic history of Indonesia, 1800–2010 / Jan Luiten van Zanden
and Daan Marks.
    p. cm. – (Routledge studies in the growth economies of Asia ; 109)
    Includes bibliographical references and index.
    1. Indonesia–Economic conditions. I. Marks, Daan. II. Title. III. Series:
    Routledge studies in the growth economies of Asia (2005); 109.
    HC447.Z36 2011
    330.9598–dc23

                                                                  2011035994

ISBN 978-0-415-67412-6 (hbk)
ISBN 978-1-138-84468-1 (pbk)
ISBN 978-0-203-12619-6 (ebk)

Typeset in Times New Roman
by Wearset Ltd, Boldon, Tyne and Wear

Contents

Figures

Tables

Preface

This book has its origins in our joint visit to Indonesia's national archive (Arsip Nasional) in 2005. In the hectic, overwhelming, but especially inviting and exciting atmosphere of Jakarta, we tried to delve further into the many mysteries that Indonesia's economic development still hides: how can a country like Indonesia, with all its human and natural resources, have such an erratic and uneven development path? And why does its growth performance display such a high degree of discontinuity? We were both already working on this project – Daan Marks as a PhD student working on the contribution of the services sector to growth in the twentieth century, Jan Luiten van Zanden as the organizer of a project to chart the dynamics of the Indonesian economy. In the midst of talks about the project – some longer than expected as it often took a while before the documents we were eager to consult were produced – we developed the idea of this book as the logical end-product of the project we were working on.

This book tries to answer the question about Indonesia's growth path through a systematic analysis of the long-term evolution of the economy of Indonesia. To this end it very much builds on concerted efforts to reconstruct Indonesia's national accounts. In this respect, we are grateful to Pierre van der Eng (Australian National University), who headed the project to reconstruct the national accounts of Indonesia for the period 1900–2000. This project was set up in collaboration with the Asian Historical Statistics project at Hitotsubashi University in Tokyo. We especially value the pioneering work under the guidance of Kono-suke Odaka, Osamu Saito and Kyoji Fukao on the reconstruction of Asian historical national accounts.

Our colleagues both at the International Institute of Social History and at Utrecht University provided us with valuable comments as well as the occasional necessary distraction. Various parts of the book were presented during seminars and conferences. We are particularly grateful for helpful comments during the Harvard–Hitotsubashi–Warwick Conference on Economic Change Around the Indian Ocean in the Very Long Run in Venice in 2008 and during the annual Economic History Society conference in Warwick in 2009.

Pierre van der Eng and Thomas Lindblad read the whole manuscript. The book has benefited significantly from their thoughtful and insightful comments, prompted by their in-depth knowledge of both Indonesia's economy as well as its history. We are also grateful to the two anonymous referees who closely read the manuscript and suggested a number of important changes. Abdul Wahid helped us to put the manuscript together, and we are particularly thankful to Connie Hopkins, whose careful language editing further contributed to the quality of the manuscript.

We hope that the book reflects the spirit of Angus Maddison, the godfather of the sub-discipline of historical national accounting, and a world scholar on quantitative economic history. Moreover, we hope that the book fits in the tradition of Thee Kian Wie's work, Indonesia's foremost scholar in the field of economic history.

1 Introduction

Indonesia between drama and miracle

The spectacular gap in incomes between rich and poor countries is the central economic fact of our time. The world is split between countries that have managed to sustain economic growth over long periods of time and those that have not. But how can we explain these divergent growth experiences? Since Adam Smith published his *An Inquiry into the Wealth of Nations* in 1776, this has been the big question in economics, a science that he more or less founded with that book. Economists have since come up with many good reasons why economies grow and become prosperous. Specialization, technological development and capital formation, factors already analysed by Smith, can be sources of economic prosperity. And it is, as he pointed out, the hidden hand of the market that can set these processes in motion. Standard growth theory predicts that if markets function properly, if institutions are efficient and distance is not a handicap, poor countries should 'catch up' with the rest of the world economy; in fact, with its productivity leader (Barro and Sala-i-Martin 1995).

Perhaps, therefore, the central problem in economics and economic history is not why some countries fared well, but why other countries have remained poor, or grown only a little, in spite of the many new opportunities created by the expanding world economy and the accumulation of knowledge. Understanding the reasons for economic failure is perhaps even more difficult than explaining economic success. One of the seminal examples of such an endeavour is the groundbreaking study published in 1968 by the Swedish economist and social scientist Gunnar Myrdal. In his *Asian Drama: An Inquiry into the Poverty of Nations* – a title that obviously mirrored Adam Smith's classic – he produced a detailed, but on the whole pessimistic, account of economic development and its prospects in South and Southeast Asia. The failure of development in post-colonial Asia was, in his view, rooted in traditional power structures that had persisted, as a result of which governments were unable to implement modern development plans. States were unable to discipline their citizens because there was no tradition of doing so. The persistent phenomenon of corruption was an important feature of these 'soft' states, which made it difficult to carry out plans consistently. This failure of development planning – of public policy – was in his view the key to understanding the *Asian Drama*. He also doubted, for example, whether rapid agricultural development, crucial for raising living standards in rural areas, could take place without a radical redistribution of lands, but such a task could not be carried out by soft states with their hands tied by the established distribution of power and wealth. He also believed that industrialization would be constrained by shortages of foreign exchange due to poor prospects for exports and the lack of inward investment. Finally, he argued that education, health and population control needed to be given greater priority than they had received so far – but again, how could a failing state manage this? On the whole, Myrdal was pessimistic about the prospect of breaking out of the 'low level equilibrium' that characterized underdevelopment. Perhaps the main theoretical contribution of Myrdal's book was his concept of 'circular cumulative causation': the conclusion that poverty created the conditions for its own continuation (Myrdal 1968; see also Lankaster 2004).[1]

Exactly 25 years after the appearance of Myrdal's pessimistic account, the World Bank published an equally famous study, *The East Asian Miracle: Economic Growth and Public Policy*, which conveyed the opposite message: large parts of Asia had found the ideal formula of 'growth with equity'. Instead of concentrating on inward-looking industrialization policies, they focused on exports of industrial commodities, making use of their surpluses of relatively cheap labour. In this way they also solved the balance of payments constraint that limited industrial growth in the inward-looking scenario. Moreover, they had invested heavily in agriculture. Most of the countries of the East Asian growth miracle had relatively equal distributions of agricultural land (sometimes the result of post-war land redistributions), which meant that large parts of the (rural) population profited from these investments. The dynamic development of agriculture was an important cause of the fact that growth occurred simultaneously with rapidly declining poverty and, sometimes, even falling inequality. In short, these East Asian countries – Taiwan, Korea, Singapore, Hong Kong, Malaysia and Indonesia – had learned from the mistakes made during the immediate post-war years, and were now doing almost everything right (World Bank 1993).

Indonesia figured prominently in both books. Although Myrdal's analysis was primarily focused on South Asia, and in particular on India, the economic and political situation in Indonesia (to which he also referred) in the mid-1960s seemed to fit it even better. As we will see, in the mid-1960s the country went through a period of political instability and economic contraction, with serious repercussions for the standard of living of large parts of the population. The development record of the newly independent country was indeed rather dismal. But this changed dramatically after 1967 – so much so that the World Bank in its 1993 study (and in many that would follow) could point to Indonesia as one of the examples of a radical turnaround of events on the basis of the medicine prescribed by the institute. From underperformer, Indonesia had emerged to become one of the brightest boys in the classroom. Therefore, Indonesia is an ideal case study for analysing the transition from 'drama' to 'miracle'.

As Myrdal did not fail to stress, the poor performance of South and Southeast Asia in the decades after the Second World War (when, to make the failure even more striking, Western Europe and Japan were catching up very rapidly with the 'productivity leader', the United States) had very deep roots. He analysed how the 'soft states' were the results of a long period of colonization, the difficult transition towards independence, and the need to stabilize new regimes and form new nation states in the post-independence period. He dealt with these 'political problems' first (in section I of his book), and analysed the economic outcomes very much as resulting from these political pressures (Myrdal 1968). In this book we will delve even further back in time, and analyse the colonial period as more than just a pre-history to the post-1945 events. This is justified on a number of grounds. The idea, for example, that 'public policy' or 'development planning' mattered was not new; the colonial state had already experimented with different sets of policies and institutions, to enhance the development of (market) production and raise the standard of living. Indonesia – and in particular Java, which was most intensively colonized – offers a series of experiments in 'development policy', the results of which can now be assessed in detail.

This debate is the starting point of this book, which attempts to explain the specific economic development of Indonesia. We believe that a careful analysis of Indonesia's development path carries the potential to offer valuable insights into the nature of long-term economic growth. Indonesia is an example of a country that did not achieve sustainable growth over long periods of time until the early 1970s. Only then did it set off on an unprecedented path of growth, which came to an abrupt end when the country was hit hard by the Asian crisis in 1997/1998. Therefore, Indonesia's growth performance can safely be characterized as erratic with a high degree of discontinuity, which makes it an interesting case to study the fundamentals of long-term growth.

In the long run, Indonesia has not been very successful in 'catching up' with the rest of the world economy, although standard growth theory more or less predicts that this is what should happen with an economy exposed to international flows of knowledge, trade and capital. Its very rich natural resources are an additional reason to expect Indonesia to have strongly profited from the growth of the world economy during the nineteenth and twentieth centuries. The principal question of this book is therefore why this did not happen – why the country remained poorer than 'average', and much poorer than the productivity leaders in the world economy.

The economic historical literature on Indonesia does not fully answer this question. Anne Booth's *The Indonesian Economy in the Nineteenth and Twentieth Centuries: A History of Missed Opportunities* is the best example of a recent study asking the same question:

> Why at the close of the twentieth century is the country still relatively poor and economically underdeveloped? What were the major policy errors of both colonial and post-colonial governments which have produced this state of affairs? Were these errors of commission or omission?
>
> (Booth 1998: 3)

But, as is clear from the second part of the quotation, she tends to focus on policy issues, and perhaps does not pay sufficient attention to the institutional structures and socio-political power relations that produced the policies chosen and implemented. Moreover, as Pierre van der Eng has argued, 'before readers can accept past decisions as "errors", they have to understand that governments indeed had different options and had compelling reasons to choose the "wrong" ones' (Van der Eng 2000: 244). We agree and try to argue that, in order to understand these 'mistakes', we will have to understand the political processes they were part of, and the institutions governing the polity involved. In this book we will of course pay much attention to policies, but we will also try to understand them on the basis of an analysis of the 'underlying' layer of institutions that tend to define the range of options policymakers can choose from.

An important aim of the book will be to explain the alternation of growth regimes that emerges from the analysis of the proximate and ultimate causes of its growth trajectory (see Chapter 2). We will argue that this was largely driven by changes in economic policies – from coercion during the Cultivation System to market-oriented policies after 1860, and from inward-looking policies during the years immediately after independence to outward-looking policies after 1982. Policy mattered, and in order to really understand the many switches in policy regime, we also pay attention to the factor-driven policy change; that is, to the factors shaping the changing political economy of Indonesia.

Finally, we are interested in the distribution of the proceeds of economic growth. Did the Indonesians themselves actually profit from growth during the colonial period? And was 'growth with equity' really the result of the growth regime under Suharto?

Compared with Anne Booth's *The Indonesian Economy in the Nineteenth and Twentieth Centuries: A History of Missed Opportunities*, which has a thematic approach, we offer a chronological account of the development of the Indonesian economy during the past 200 years. Economists who are interested in certain key developments (growth, distribution, policy, innovation) may prefer a thematic ordering of the material. We think that telling the story chronologically has certain advantages as well: it makes it easier to analyse the changes in institutions, policies and their economic outcomes in a consistent way.

There are a number of central themes in the story, and growth at the macro level and its determinants – including productivity growth – is one of them. The various chapters set out to answer why total factor productivity increased or decreased in the period concerned, in order to explain the growth performance of those years. In Chapter 2 we will present the estimates of the growth of total factor productivity that are the starting points for Chapters 3 to 9. Changes at the micro level are another; we also focus on the way in which rural credit markets and rice markets function, and try to find out what determines their efficiency and how changes in the quality of these institutions affect long-term economic growth (and again, in the next chapter we present our interpretation of the long-run changes in institutions that were conducive to economic development). Both stories are related to changes at the political and institutional level, as we hope to demonstrate. Economic policies are, we think, a very important part of the story. The fundamental changes in direction of these policies at about 1830, in the 1860s, the 1930s, the 1950s and the second half of the 1960s provide the most important breaks in our story of long-term economic change. Finally, we present much new information on the development of the standard of living and the human capital of the Indonesian population. We use new datasets of wages and prices, heights (biological standard of living), human capital (age heaping, educational attainment) and income distribution, to shed new light on what ultimately mattered: whether Indonesians improved their own condition, perhaps despite the 'drama' of their history, or thanks to the 'growth miracle' of which they became a part. There is however one topic – demographic change – that we do not discuss in detail here (a brief sketch of it is presented in Chapter 6, however); the extraordinarily rapid growth of the Indonesian population in the nineteenth century, and the spectacular fall in fertility after the 1950s, is largely taken as given. Moreover, our treatment of the most recent period, since the Asian crisis of 1997/1998, is necessarily somewhat sketchier than our analysis of previous periods – it takes a longer perspective of time to really understand what has been happening in the past 10–15 years.

In the next chapter we set the stage with a broad overview of Indonesian economic development over approximately 200 years. In that chapter we focus on the proximate and ultimate sources of long-term growth – on the growth of inputs, on total factor productivity, and on the institutional and geographic forces that shaped the process of economic growth. In Chapters 3 to 9 we continue the story with a chronological, in-depth analysis of different subperiods, with the aim of explaining in more detail why, in those different periods, growth was sometimes successfully achieved and why in other times the Indonesian economy clearly lagged behind that of its neighbours and/or competitors. The chronology of success and failure has to be established first, in Chapter 2, after which the remaining chapters will attempt to explain it.

2   Exploring the proximate and ultimate causes of 200 years of economic growth in Indonesia, 1800–2000

An important reason for focusing on Indonesia as a case study of a relatively slow process of development is that we know a lot about its economic history. Whereas the study of long-term economic growth in many other developing countries is hindered by a lack of statistical data, Indonesia, and in particular Java, is well endowed with detailed statistics on virtually all sectors of the economy (thanks to a rather efficient and relatively curious colonial administration). This makes it possible to reconstruct and analyse the long-term growth path of the Indonesian economy between 1815 and 2007 in some detail.[1] The starting points of the book are two reconstructions of the national accounts of the country: of Java in the period between 1815 and 1940, and of Indonesia between 1880 and 2007. The historical national accounts have recently been completed (for the Java project, see van Zanden 2002) or are in the process of being finished, in a project carried out in cooperation with Pierre van der Eng (see for example Van der Eng 2002, 2010). Together they offer a unique opportunity to analyse the determinants of long-run growth for a developing country over a period of almost two centuries.

When, on the basis of these new estimates, we compare the development of its GDP per capita with that of the average of the world economy (see Figure 2.1), it appears that during a large part of the period under study Indonesian growth has been relatively slow, in particular during the middle decades of the nineteenth century and again between 1940 and 1967. Catching up only started after 1967, and continued until the Asian crisis of 1997/1998. Still, at the end of the Suharto period, the ratio between Indonesian per capita GDP and that of the world economy as a whole was lower than it had been during the colonial period – and the gap with the 'productivity leader', the United States, was even larger. So in spite of the economic successes of the most recent decades, there is the problem of explaining why Indonesia has remained so poor. Was it lack of investment in human and physical capital? Or do we have to dig deeper, into the ultimate causes of economic development?

These datasets make it possible, for example, to distinguish between the 'proximate' and the 'ultimate' sources of growth (see, for example, Maddison 1987, 1988). Figure 2.2 illustrates the standard way in which economists think about the determination of income. The total output of an economy is the

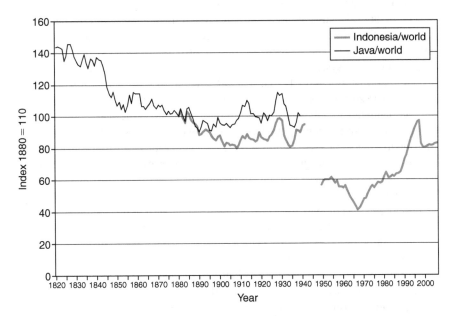

Figure 2.1 GDP per capita, Indonesia/Java compared with the average of the world economy (sources: authors' calculations from Maddison 2001; van Zanden 2002 and Van der Eng 2010).

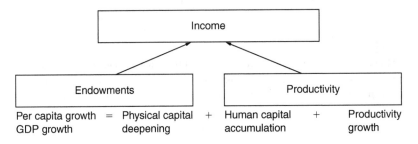

Figure 2.2 Proximate causes of economic growth (source: Rodrik 2003: 4).

function of its resource endowments (labour, physical capital and human capital) and the productivity with which these endowments are deployed to produce a flow of goods and services (gross domestic product, or GDP). The growth in per capita income can in turn be expressed in terms of three proximate determinants: a) physical capital deepening; b) human capital accumulation; and c) productivity growth.

Conceptually, this is a straightforward decomposition, and it has given rise to a wealth of literature on sources-of-growth accounting. Nevertheless, one has to be careful in interpreting such decompositions, because accumulation and productivity growth are themselves endogenous. Moreover, if we have ascertained the impact of these two on growth, the question arises as to why some countries in specific periods managed to accumulate and innovate more rapidly. Therefore it is best to think of accumulation and productivity change as proximate determinants at best. However, knowledge of the proximate sources of growth is a bridge towards a systematic study of the more ultimate factors underlying the accumulation of stocks of human capital and physical capital, knowledge and technology (Szirmai 1993: 13). Moreover, it can generate important insights that are complementary to those gained from in-depth country studies.

In the extensive literature on economic growth three possible ultimate causes of growth stand out (see Figure 2.3). First, geography is often placed at the centre of the story. Geography is a key determinant of climate, endowment of natural resources, disease burden, transport costs, and diffusion of knowledge and technology from more advanced areas (Rodrik *et al.* 2004: 132; see also Diamond 1997; Gallup *et al.* 1998; Sachs 2001). Commodities such as oil, diamonds and copper are marketable resources that can be important sources of income, but being dependent on primary resources also makes a country vulnerable to Dutch disease and the resource curse (Collier 2007). Furthermore, soil quality and rainfall determine the productivity of land.

Geography influences growth via the other two factors as well. Geography is an important determinant of the extent to which a country can become integrated with world markets, regardless of the country's own trade policies. A distant, landlocked country faces greater costs of integration (Collier 2007). Similarly, geography shapes institutions in a number of ways. The historical experience with colonialism has been a key factor in the institutional development of today's developing countries, and colonialism itself was driven in part by geopolitical considerations. Geography also dictates whether one is close to rapidly growing regions – in the nineteenth century, proximity to Western Europe or the United States – and how the 'market access' of countries develops over time.

Geography is arguably the only exogenous factor in the threefold taxonomy. Trade and institutions are obviously endogenous and co-evolve with economic

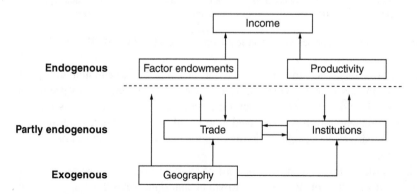

Figure 2.3 Endogenous and exogenous causes of economic growth (source: Rodrik 2003: 5).

performance. Nonetheless, it is useful to think of these as ultimate causal factors to the extent that they are not fully determined by incomes per se (Rodrik 2003: 7). Trade is shaped in large part by a country's conscious choice of policies, and institutional development is at least partly a choice variable as well.

A second strand of literature emphasizes the significance of integration in the world economy as a driver of economic growth (Sachs and Warner 1995; Frankel and Romer 1999; Dollar and Kraay 2004). The degree of openness of a country's economy – which may or may not be related to its geography – has, according to this literature, a strong impact on its growth performance. It makes it possible to profit from processes of specialization, and to increase productivity of domestic industries due to the disciplining effects of import competition.

Finally, institutions have received increasing attention in the growth literature as it has become clear that property rights, appropriate regulatory structures, the quality and independence of the judiciary, and bureaucratic capacity could not be taken for granted in many settings, and that they were of the utmost importance for initiating and sustaining economic growth. The profession's ideas have moved from an implicit assumption that these institutions would arise endogenously and effortlessly as a by-product of economic growth to the view that they are essential pre-conditions and determinants of growth (North and Thomas 1973; North 1990; Hall and Jones 1999; Acemoglu *et al.* 2001).

As the arrows in Figure 2.3 indicate, the basic framework is rich with feedback effects, both from growth back to the 'causal' factors, and among the 'causal' factors. There are reasons to think, for example, that as countries get richer, they will trade more and acquire high-quality institutions. Much of the cross-national empirical work on institutions has been plagued by the endogeneity of institutional quality: are rich countries rich because they have high-quality institutions, or is it the other way around? There are hints in the empirical literature of a mutual interaction between trade and institutions: better institutions foster trade (Anderson and Marcouiller 1999), and more openness to trade leads to higher-quality institutions (Wei 2000). These feedbacks require extreme care in laying out the hypotheses and in ascribing causality.

In-depth country studies are one way to get around these problems of endogeneity. The advantage of such case studies is that they allow a 'thick' description of the interactions among geography, trade and institutions. Therefore, let us now shift to our case study: Indonesia. In the remainder of this introduction, we will first discuss the proximate sources of Indonesia's economic growth in the period 1800–2010 by presenting a growth accounting exercise. This can help answer an initial series of questions related to the causes of its modest growth in the past 200 years: was the slow growth of GDP per capita due to insufficient investment in (human and physical) capital, or to low productivity growth? The essence of these questions is the well-known problem of (Asiatic) economic growth: the question as to whether it was perspiration or inspiration – more inputs or more efficiency – driving the process (Krugman 1994). The results of this analysis will demonstrate that it was mainly the lack of rapid technological change and efficiency, or total factor productivity (TFP) growth, more specifically, that accounts for the poor performance of Indonesia in the very long run. In the subsequent sections we will try to explain this. We will explore whether Indonesia was insufficiently exposed to market forces, where we will mainly look at openness, measured as the ratio between export plus imports and GDP. Next, we will try to operationalize the possibly problematic 'geography' of the country by analysing whether access to export markets – it is located far away from the nineteenth-century growth centres of the world economy, such as Western Europe and North America – led to less growth. Finally, we turn to institutions – is the explanation of its poor performance linked to the quality of institutions regulating market exchange?

Proximate causes of growth: a growth accounting exercise

Growth accounting: the model

Understanding characteristics and determinants of growth requires an empirical framework that can be applied to a large group of countries over a relatively long time frame. Growth accounts provide such a framework. This approach, as pioneered by Robert Solow (1956), is a sort of accounting framework based on actual data. It seeks to answer the question as to what proportion of recorded economic growth can be attributed to growth in the capital stock, growth of the labour force and changes in overall efficiency. This procedure is usually referred to as growth accounting. It starts with the basic Cobb–Douglas production function. The Cobb–Douglas production function is written as:

$$Y_t = A_t \cdot K_t^{\alpha} \cdot H_t^{\beta} \tag{1}$$

where Y is real output, A is total factor productivity (TFP), K is physical capital and H is human capital. α is the elasticity of output with respect to capital and β is the elasticity of output with respect to labour.[2] The sum of output elasticities $(\alpha+\beta)$ is the scale of returns. The Cobb–Douglas function assumes $\alpha+\beta=1$ or constant returns. Accordingly, equation (1) can be rewritten as:

$$Y_t = A_t \cdot K_t^{\alpha} \cdot H_t^{1-\alpha} \tag{2}$$

Furthermore, human capital (H) can be measured as the schooling-adjusted number of the labour force, where L is the labour force and δ is the productivity increase by each additional year of schooling, and S is the number of years of schooling:

$$H_t = L_t \cdot e^{\delta t} St \tag{3}$$

Combining equations (2) and (3) gives:

$$Y_t = A_t \cdot K_t^{\alpha} \cdot (L_t \cdot e^{\delta t} St)^{1-\alpha} \tag{4}$$

In order to transform equation (4) into the rate-of-growth form, first logarithms of the variables are taken. Next differentiations with respect to time are taken such that growth rates emerge. This gives:

$$\ln Y_t = \ln A_t + \alpha \cdot \ln K_t + (1-\alpha) \cdot (\ln L_t) + (1-\alpha) \cdot \delta_t S_t \tag{5}$$

$$\gamma_Y = \gamma_A + \alpha \cdot \gamma_K + (1-\alpha) \cdot \gamma_L + (1-\alpha) \cdot \gamma_{\delta S} \tag{6}$$

where γ stands for the growth rate.

Equation (6) shows that the real output growth rate (γ_Y) is the sum of the TFP growth rate (γ_A), the capital growth rate (γ_K), the labour force growth rate (γ_L), and the growth of labour quality ($\gamma_{\delta S}$). α is the elasticity of output with respect to capital, which means a 1 per cent increase in capital contributes α per cent to real output growth.

The concept of total factor productivity (TFP)

Technical progress represents the improvements in the production techno-logy accruing from the growth in the (stock of) unmeasured intangible investments such as human capital and R&D capital, to the extent that they have not been explicitly included in the analysis as measured by the factors of production. Moreover, it reflects improvements because of advertising, goodwill, market development, information systems, software, business methods, etc. Finally, it also reflects genuine improvements in technical and allocative efficiency.

(Lau and Park 2003: 5)

The concept of total factor productivity, defined as the ratio between real output and real factor inputs, can be traced back to Solow (1956). If we define TFP from the previous equations as:

$$A_t = A_0 \cdot e^{\lambda t} \tag{7}$$

indicating that technology would grow at a constant exponential rate of λ, then knowing λ would be sufficient to determine the contribution of technological change to the growth of output. As Chen (1997) among others points out, the problem with this λ is that it is (1) disembodied, (2) exogenous and (3) Hicks-neutral.

Disembodied technological change means that it is not yet embodied in factor inputs but takes place like 'manna from heaven' in the form of better methods and organization that improve the efficiency of both new and old factor inputs. Any technological change embodied in the factor inputs is assumed to be prop-erly specified and accounted for in the aggregation of each input.

Dowling and Summers (1998) argue that disembodied technical progress, as measured by TFP, may be lower in developing Asia than in industrial countries.

This is because investment and saving rates are so high. Since the capital stock is growing so fast, it is much newer than the capital stock of other, more slowly growing countries. Because it is of a more recent vintage and is growing faster, its embodied technological component is likely to be larger than in slower growing economies with large capital stocks. Therefore a comparable increase in productivity (γ_Y) can be achieved with a smaller disembodied TFP coefficient (γ_A), because it is already accounted for by the growth in capital (γ_K).

Furthermore, as growth continues and the capital stock grows larger along with the amount of capital per worker, the role of embodied technical progress may moderate. According to Dowling and Summers, this process of movement from embodied to disembodied technical progress as the per capita income rises will be reinforced as managerial and other organizational developments and innovations manifest themselves through the growth in foreign direct investment and as domestic entrepreneurs undertake larger amounts of research and development (R&D) expenditures.

Technological change is exogenous when its occurrence is independent of the variables in the growth model. Time is the only factor. Endogenous models, on the other hand specify, that technological change is related to R&D expenditure, learning by doing (experience), education, investment activities, etc. (see, for example, Lau and Park 2003; Robertson 2000; and Rodrigo and Thorbecke 1997).

Hicks-neutral technological change has the effect of increasing the efficiency of both capital and labour to the same extent. Thus, if through some sort of technological progress production becomes more efficient, then this affects both capital and labour equally, meaning that the ratio of capital over labour remains constant. On the other hand, Harrod-neutral technological change is labour-augmenting and Solow-neutral technological change is capital-augmenting.

Young (1995) stresses another weak point in the Cobb–Douglas production function. He points out that a relaxation of the assumption of constant returns to scale ($\alpha + \beta = 1$) could either increase or decrease the productivity estimates. If the true aggregate production function is characterized by increasing returns to scale, perhaps due to externalities among factors, then the growth of total factor productivity (γ_A) actually overstates the true degree, since it captures the increase in factors of production. Conversely, if the true production function is characterized by decreasing returns to scale, γ_A understates the degree of productivity growth.

Rodrik (1997) adds to this that capital deepening[3] probably results in the factor share of capital (α) falling over time, rather than remaining constant. For given rates of capital deepening and output growth, TFP would correspondingly increase. According to Rodrik this effect would be particularly strong in East Asian countries, as they are the ones that have experienced the most capital deepening. Consequently, the downward bias in estimating TFP would be quite large for East Asian countries.

It is also important to bear in mind that TFP as calculated from equation (6) is a 'residual', a catch-all sum indicating that part of output growth that cannot be explained by increases in input factors. TFP captures the net effect of errors and omissions in all the other data. Thus what is labelled TFP actually is a combination of errors in the data, omission of other factors that should be included in the growth equation, as well as efficiency gains and changes in technology. It is simply an 'index of our ignorance'.

(Chen 1997: 21–22)

All these qualifications show that TFP is a narrow concept of technological change and therefore the residual (γ_A) must be interpreted with some caution. Even if γ_A is small, the role of technological change could have been important because embodied technological change might have been significant. Alternatively, γ_A may be small because the production function is mis-specified, failing to take into account the endogenous aspect of technological change and alternative forms of neutrality. Conversely, a large γ_A may be due to significant effects of economies of scale and resource allocation. Another possible cause of bias is the eventuality of missing variables in the production function. Intermediate inputs, energy, experience and R&D, etc. have been considered as inputs that should be explicitly included.

Despite these drawbacks, the concept is still appealing partly because of its simplicity. Moreover, it provides a consistent decomposition of growth among its proximate sources (Collins and Bosworth 2003). Hulten (2001: 63) describes it as 'a simple and internally consistent intellectual framework for organizing data. ... For all its flaws, real and imagined, many researchers have used it to gain valuable insights into the process of economic growth.' The following section will therefore use the Cobb–Douglas function to carry out a growth accounting exercise for Indonesia.

Growth accounting for Indonesia, 1815–2007: results

Indonesia's long-term economic growth has been the subject of several studies (Booth 1998; Dick *et al.* 2002; Van der Eng 1992, 2002, 2010). Van der Eng (2010) gives a detailed growth accounting exercise for Indonesia between 1880 and 2007; we have adopted his results here. By incorporating recent work on Java's GDP in the period 1815–1939 (van Zanden 2002), we are able to cover the whole period 1815–2007. Figure 2.4 presents the results of this work. It points to a number of distinct phases in the development of total factor productivity. First, TFP declined significantly between 1815 and 1860. This decline was especially marked between 1830 and 1860. This suggests increasing inefficiencies as a result of the Cultivation System, a system of cultivation of export crops (mainly sugar and coffee) based on forced labour by the Javanese peasantry (see Chapter 4). During the 1840s and 1850s the system was gradually reformed, which led to a recovery of TFP in these years. We think this sheds new light on the drama of the Cultivation System – one of the classic themes in the economic history of Indonesia – which will be analysed in detail in Chapter 4.

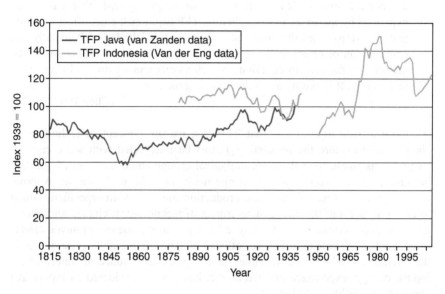

Figure 2.4 Development of total factor productivity (TFP), 1815–2007 (1939=100)
(sources: van Zanden 2002; Van der Eng 2010. The series shown are the
residual resulting from the growth accounting exercises for Java (1815–1940)
and Indonesia (1880–2007), both as indices set at 1939=100).

Second, TFP increased almost continuously, albeit initially at a modest rate,
between 1860 and 1914. During the 1860s and 1870s a new colonial regime
came into existence. With the Agrarian Law and the Sugar Law, both passed in
1870, Western agricultural enterprises were given more opportunities for expansion, signalling the demise of the Cultivation System (Booth 1998: 30). In 1901,
the ongoing debate within the Netherlands about colonial policy resulted in the
so-called Ethical Policy. This policy, which aimed at promoting the welfare of
the indigenous Indonesians, led to a series of reforms, including modern agricultural research; increased expenditure on infrastructure, irrigation and education;
medical services; and policies aimed at stabilizing rice markets and regulating
rural capital markets (Boomgaard 1986b; Van der Eng 1996). As can be seen
from Figure 2.4, TFP increased during this time, particularly on Java. To what
extent this can be attributed to these new policies will be discussed in Chapter 5.

The third period that can be discerned is between 1914 and 1939, when TFP
went through a number of cycles, but basically remained unchanged. As we will
outline in more detail in Chapter 6, following the outbreak of the First World
War, TFP declined significantly until 1923. TFP growth was positive during
1923–1928 before the Great Depression caused a major setback in efficiency.
The subsequent slowdown in gross fixed capital formation meant that the economic recovery between 1933 and 1941 was based on a more efficient use of
productive resources, assisted by economic policy and institutional change (Van
der Eng 1998).

Following the Second World War and the subsequent struggle for independence, we see a sharp increase in TFP between 1949 and 1961, followed by a drop until 1966. The increase during the 1950s can be mainly explained by the low levels of TFP as a result of the developments in the 1940s; it was hardly enough to recover to pre-war levels of TFP. Political instability and inappropriate economic policy measures taken by the Sukarno government after 1958, in our view, caused another set-back in productivity and efficiency (see the discussion in Chapter 7).

The situation in the first half of the 1960s of very low levels of income and productivity, a stagnant economy and poor public policies, was the drama analysed by Myrdal in his classic study. Soon things changed for the better, however. The fifth breaking point in the development in TFP started in 1967 and ran roughly until 1997. This period began with an unprecedented growth in TFP, which could partly be attributed to the new government, led by General Suharto, which came to power in 1966. His New Order government was oriented to the West and attracted considerable foreign investment and international aid. Moreover, his government, together with a team of experts, managed to reduce inflation and lead the economy into an impressive path of growth (see the discussion in Chapter 8).

Nevertheless, a word of caution is needed here. During the 1970s much of Indonesia's GDP growth was due to its oil and gas resources. Whereas in most countries the years 1973 and 1979 are remembered as the years of the oil crisis, for Indonesia this period is characterized as the 'oil boom'. Hence, part of the income in this period was not due to higher productivity, but to the availability of resources. Therefore it is more informative to look at TFP growth in the non-oil and gas sectors. As Figure 2.5 shows, in those sectors TFP growth was still high, but the rise in the 1970s was less spectacular.

Stagnation in oil prices reduced the income from oil considerably in the early 1980s. Moreover, the world economy suffered a recession. A number of policy reforms resulted in a reorientation of the economy towards a more diversified export economy, based on labour-intensive, export-oriented industrialization (Hill 2000: 83–84). This helps to explain the continued rise in (non-oil and gas) TFP between 1986 and 1997. It is in this period, from the mid-1980s onwards, that Indonesia joined the HPAE club (High Performing Asian Economies), which was the focus of a 1993 World Bank study. The country also shared the fate of this club in the late 1990s. The Asian crisis that hit Indonesia in late 1997, however, meant a major setback in productivity from which it is still recovering.

In sum, an analysis of levels of TFP points to a number of distinct phases in Indonesia's economic history. The basic results of our growth accounting exercise are also presented in Table 2.1. In the very long run, TFP did not contribute to the growth of output. In Krugman's words, this suggests that it has mainly been perspiration instead of inspiration that drove Indonesia's economic growth (Krugman 1994). In the next sections we will look in greater detail into the way an analysis of the ultimate sources of growth, geography, openness and institutions, respectively, can offer further insights into the story that we have presented up to this point.

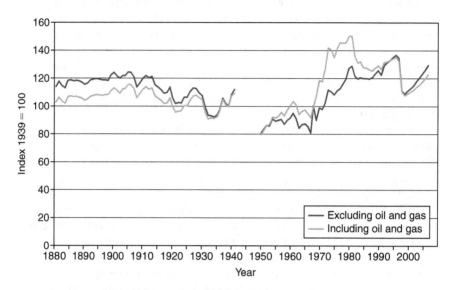

Figure 2.5 Development of TFP: including or excluding oil and gas (1939=100) (source: van der Eng 2010).

Table 2.1 Proximate sources of growth: the contribution of physical capital, labour and TFP growth to output growth

	Output (%)	Contribution of:		
		Physical capital (%)	Labour (%)	Factor productivity (%)
1815–1860*	1.7	1.0	1.1	−0.4
1860–1914*	2.4	1.0	0.9	0.5
1914–1939	2.1	1.6	0.8	−0.3
1950–1966	3.0	0.5	1.4	1.1
1967–1997	6.9	3.1	2.5	1.2
1815–1900*	1.9	0.9	1.0	0.0
1900–2000	3.1	1.7	1.5	0.0

Sources: van Zanden 2002; Van der Eng 2010.

Note
* Java only.

Ultimate causes of (poor) performance: geography

New Economic Geography analyses the effects of space on economic development at two levels. *Absolute* geography is related to truly exogenous factors such as whether the country is landlocked (which is bad for growth), whether it has natural resources (which will give mixed results – there may be a 'resource curse') and what the disease environment is. *Relative* – or second nature –

geography is about the position of a certain country in relation to other countries. Is it close to centres of economic growth, surrounded by rich countries, or at a great distance from the growth poles of the world economy? In terms of absolute geography, the story of Indonesia is rather mixed. It is rich in natural resources (oil in particular, but also mineral resources); it has an abundance of high-quality soils, which, in combination with its climate, have the potential to produce high crop yields (Buringh *et al.* 1975); and it is clearly not land-locked but has a very long coast (which may favour trade). Only in terms of disease environment is Indonesia really disadvantaged, a fate it shares with all other tropical countries. But on the whole, it would be difficult to explain its long-term economic stagnation on the basis of first order geography, although regions with a temperate climate and less volcanic activity may have been more favoured by nature than Indonesia.

A more interesting story can probably be told about second nature geography, the real subject of new economic geography (Fujita *et al.* 1999). In a nutshell, this approach argues that a country's income level is closely linked to its market access, i.e. its proximity to other high-income countries. Crafts and Venables (2003), Redding and Venables (2004) and Mayer (2008), among others, all provide empirical evidence that a higher level of market access does indeed increase a country's income level (see also the survey on NEG empirics by Head and Mayer, 2004). Nearness is, however, usually operationalized in two ways; one can look at the immediate neighbours, and one can make a comparison with the countries with which a certain nation is actually doing most of its trade, i.e. what markets this country has access to. In this chapter we try to do both.

The question is then to what extent Indonesia's geographical position affected its growth record. First we compare the development of GDP per capita of Indonesia with its direct neighbours; because for most neighbours no reliable estimates of GDP are available for the period before *c.*1900, we have to limit this analysis to the twentieth century. Figure 2.6 presents the estimates as given by the Maddison dataset. Southeast Asia is clearly a region with relatively low real income – as the comparison with Australia demonstrates. Being part of such a region therefore must have depressed incomes in Indonesia. Thus its underdevelopment may simply be linked to, and reinforced by, the underdevelopment of the region. But as Figure 2.6 also demonstrates, most countries performed better than Indonesia, with the exception of Burma and the Philippines, which both showed less growth. In the first decades of the twentieth century the differences were rather small, and Indonesia may have been at about the same level as Malaysia, Singapore and Thailand. All three countries moved ahead compared to Indonesia, however, during the post-1945 period, and although growth in the latter country during the 1970s and 1980s was relatively rapid, it was unable to really catch up during these decades. This can also be seen from a comparison between the average GDP per capita of Indonesia and that of its four direct neighbours, Australia, Singapore, Malaysia, Thailand and the Philippines (Figure 2.7). This curve shows some catching up in the 1920s and 1930s, before a huge fall of relative income levels during the 1940s and again during the first half of

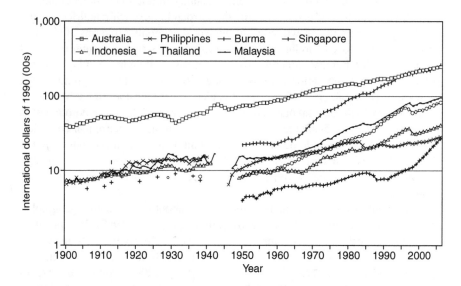

Figure 2.6 GDP per capita of Indonesia and its neighbours, 1900–2006 (source: Maddison 2003 and recent data from www.ggdc.net/maddison/).

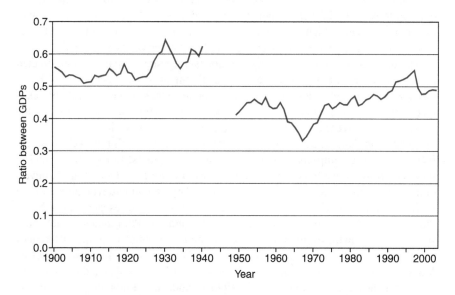

Figure 2.7 Ratio between GDP per capita of Indonesia and the unweighted average of its closest neighbours, 1900–2006 (source: authors' calculations from Maddison 2003 and recent data from www.ggdc.net/maddison/).

the 1960s, and only slow catching up during the rest of the century, which was ultimately interrupted by the Asian crisis.

These comparisons do not tell us a lot about 'market access', however, because Indonesia did not trade predominantly with its neighbours. In fact, it is striking how limited during a large part of the nineteenth and twentieth centuries trade with, for example, Australia or Thailand was (Marks 2009a: 138). Singapore, the rapidly developing hub of Southeast Asia, was the exception, but the final destination of most exports to that hub was also usually outside Southeast Asia. In order to measure the development of the market to which Indonesia had access, we have to look at the export data, which are available from the early 1820s onwards. The fact that so much trade occurred between Indonesia and the Netherlands – in the mid-nineteenth century more than 60 per cent of exports went to the 'mother country' – is also a bit problematic for such an analysis, however. This trade was to a large degree neither voluntary nor merely the result of market forces, but was directed by the state (during the period of the Cultivation System between 1830 and 1870), and/or induced by the political domination of the colony by the Netherlands. After 1870 the close links with the Netherlands gave Dutch companies, such as the oil company Royal Dutch Shell, privileged access to the colony, and may have steered its exports towards the Netherlands.

To address these issues, we have calculated the development of market access in the following way: we have compared the growth of Indonesian GDP with that of its weighted trading partners (countries to which more than 3 per cent of its exports flowed), using weights that changed every 20 years during the nineteenth century, and every ten years after 1900 (1823, 1840, 1860, 1880, 1900, 1910, 1920 etc.). To analyse the effect of its trade being perhaps too focused on the Netherlands, we have also calculated the development of its market access excluding the Netherlands (but including the other European trading partners). Theoretically, it may be expected that the growth of the Indonesian economy would be as rapid as its 'market access'; a country is relatively successful when it grows more rapidly than this benchmark, which points to improvements in its international competitiveness. Alternatively, growth that occurs more slowly than a country's 'market access' may indicate weak competitiveness.

Figure 2.8 provides the results. First looking at Java in the nineteenth century, we see that in the long run its growth was slightly less than that of its trading partners, but the difference was not very large, and from the 1850s onwards the ratio was more or less stable. Excluding the Netherlands gives a somewhat less optimistic picture. The 'Java excl. Netherlands' curve declines quite a bit (from 140 in 1820 to 80 in 1940), which demonstrates that, because growth in the Netherlands was relatively slow (the result of its high level of income at the beginning of the nineteenth century), the colonial relationship may have significantly depressed the growth of Java/Indonesia in this period. Had the UK not returned the colony to the Netherlands in 1815 – a not completely unlikely scenario as it continued to control other formerly Dutch colonies such as Sri Lanka and the Cape colony – the increase of Indonesian market access would have

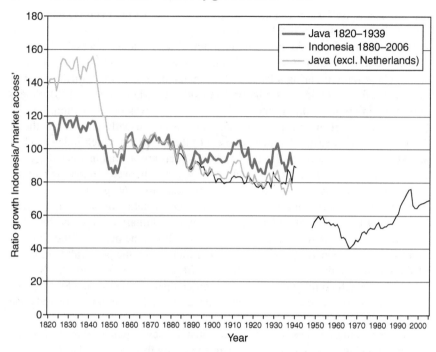

Figure 2.8 Growth of GDP of Java/Indonesia, compared with its 'market access', 1820–2006 (1880=100) (sources: GDP series: Maddison 2003 and recent data from www.ggdc.net/maddison/; export shares: Marks 2009a and Korthals Altes 1986; the series measures the ratio between the growth of GDP in Indonesia (or Java) divided by the growth of GDP of the weighted average of the export markets of Indonesia).

been more rapid during the 1820–1900 period, when growth in the UK was faster than in the Netherlands. After 1900, the Netherlands grew more rapidly than the UK, and in 1919 they were at the same parity as in 1820 – so in the long run this would not have made a big difference (all data from Maddison 2001). The decline in this relationship was almost completely concentrated in the period 1840–1860, when the problems caused by the Cultivation System led to retardation in the growth of the Javanese economy. The second period in which growth was lagging far behind market access was between 1940 and 1967. Between 1968 and 1998 Indonesia managed to regain some lost ground, but the strong upward trend was broken off during the Asian crisis, from which recovery (in 2006) still appears to be partial.

Ultimate causes: openness

A widely held idea in economics is that openness to trade accelerates economic development. Classic economic treatises by luminaries such as Adam Smith and David Ricardo showed early on the potential gains of trading between nations, and more recently advocates of globalization claim that trade promotes growth, and in turn growth reduces poverty (Bhagwati and Srinivasan 2002). Much of the evidence both in support of and against globalization has been based on cross-country growth regressions. Srinivasan and Bhagwati argue that 'In fact, while such regressions can be suggestive of new hypotheses and be valuable aids in thinking about the issue at hand, we would reiterate that great caution is needed in using them at all as plausible "scientific" support' (Srinivasan and Bhagwati 1999: 38). Therefore they call for nuanced and in-depth studies to get a better understanding of the relationship between trade and economic development.

The case of Indonesia is especially interesting. As Booth argues:

Indonesia's involvement in the world economy did transform the local economies of the producing regions through the provision of infrastructure and the growing demand for inputs and services. And yet, the transformation of Indonesia into an open export-oriented economy in the nineteenth and twentieth centuries did not lead to rapid structural change, and sustained economic development.

(Booth 1998: 203)

This observation highlights the ambiguous role that the trade sector has played in the process of economic development in Indonesia. While Indonesia's export orientation seems to have enhanced economic growth in some periods, it may have failed to do so in other periods.

Indonesia's involvement in international trade goes back to (at least) the 'age of commerce' between 1400 and 1650 (Reid 1988). Between 1823 (when the first trade statistics become available) and the present, exports and imports have grown exponentially, and the share of them in GDP has increased from about 15 per cent in the early 1820s, to 60 per cent or more in recent decades. The first phase of export expansion occurred during the Cultivation System, which led to a rise in the degree of openness of the Javanese economy from about 15 per cent to almost 40 per cent. As Figure 2.9 demonstrates, this did not lead to a rise in factor productivity – in fact, TFP went down. In theory, it is expected that openness will lead to increased exposure to (outside) market forces, inducing patterns of specialization to occur. This clearly did not happen during the 1830–1860 period, when the state regulated the export sector of the economy, exports were monopolized, and market forces were much weaker than before 1830. The decline of TFP can be seen as a direct result of this transition.

After 1860 we do find the patterns predicted by the theoretical literature: the phase of liberalization of the Javanese economy ultimately led to an increase in openness and in TFP between about 1890 and 1913. During the inter-war period these trends were less clear – violent fluctuations in both openness and TFP dominated the picture. But the turn to a more inward-looking economy after independence clearly led to very low levels of openness and productivity. Within a few years after 1949, exports and imports accounted for less than 10 per cent

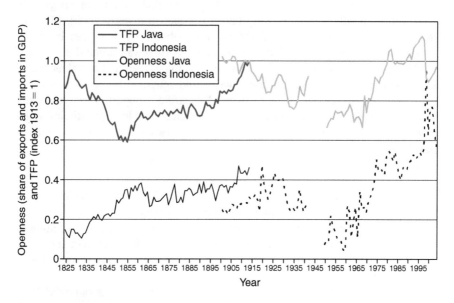

Figure 2.9 Openness and TFP (Java 1824–1913; Indonesia 1913–2003) (source: see
        Figure 2.3 and Marks 2009a).

of GDP, even less than at the beginning of the nineteenth century. The phase of
rapid growth beginning in the second half of the 1960s witnessed another strong
correlation between openness and productivity – both trends were, however,
crudely broken off by the Asian crisis of 1997/1998. What is also clear from
Figure 2.10, where we compare openness and TFP in a scatter diagram, is that
the link between productivity growth and openness in the colonial context
(between 1870 and 1913) and in the period of rapid industrialization after 1968
was different. It appears that this relationship became more 'flat' after independence; that, in other words, a larger increase in openness was needed to obtain a
certain increase in TFP after 1967 than before 1920 (we have used the non-oil–
TFP estimates here, but changing to the oil–TFP estimates does not really affect
the results).

Perhaps most remarkable is the poor performance of the export sector during
the first decades after independence, when openness fell to very low levels.
There was some growth in export volume in the early 1950s above the level
achieved in the late 1930s (Booth 1998: 205). However, compared to the dramatic expansion of world trade that occurred in the 1950s and 1960s, Indonesia's trade performance was disappointing. Whereas world trade grew by about
7 per cent annually between 1953 and 1966, Indonesian export volume grew by
less than 1 per cent per annum (Hanson 1980: 14). What caused this failure of
Indonesia to profit from booming international trade?

During the 1950s and early 1960s foreign trade was tightly controlled by the
state, which used its powers to allocate trade to its own citizens (whereas before

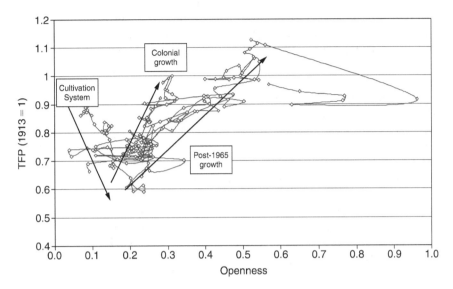

Figure 2.10 Openness and TFP: scatter diagram (Java 1824–1913; Indonesia 1913–2003)
(source: see Figure 2.9).

independence it had been monitored by Dutch firms). Therefore, exports had to be approved by and originate from state enterprises, while imports required licences that were held by state trading companies. Moreover, import and export taxes were also of fundamental importance for the financing of the new state. The importance of this kind of taxation is illustrated by the fact that government revenue from taxes on trade fluctuated between 32 and 66 per cent of total tax revenue between 1951 and 1957 (Boediono and Pangestu 1986: 3). Following the take-over of Dutch enterprises in 1957, and the subsequent period of 'Guided Democracy', trade policies only intensified, with an emphasis on indigenous Indonesian control over all aspects of economic activity. In April 1959, government trading houses obtained monopoly rights to import nine categories of goods, which comprised 75 per cent of all imports (Boediono and Pangestu 1986: 5). Private importers could import only non-essential goods and the number of importers was restricted to 400 (Paauw 1963: 212). Moreover, government intervention in the retail trade, which was traditionally handled by Chinese and Indian traders, resulted in a disruption in the distribution of goods and a scarcity of most consumer goods. The impact of government intervention in the trade sector is further reflected by the fact that in 1963 and 1964 about 70 per cent of government revenue came from foreign trade taxes (Boediono and Pangestu 1986: 6).

After the regime change of 1966/1967, barriers to international trade were quickly lowered. As a result of a series of packages introduced by the New Order government, by 1970 many of these barriers had been removed. Most export taxes were reduced, tariffs became the primary instrument of import protection and the tariff structure was simplified (Hill 2000: 114). This leads Hill (2000: 115) to conclude that 'the late 1960s ushered in a period of economic liberalism in Indonesia'. During the 1970s, this sentiment changed. Import bans began to re-appear and regulation intensified after the oil boom, mainly to protect non-oil tradable activities. The second oil boom led to further trade restrictions with outright prohibitions and an 'authorized importer system' (*Tata Niaga Impor*). However, the revenue motive of foreign trade regulations was no longer important. The contribution of taxes on trade to total revenue declined from 38.2 per cent in 1968 to only 7.3 per cent in 1982. This fall was mainly due to a significant rise in taxes on oil companies, which provided more than 70 per cent of domestic revenue in 1982 (Boediono and Pangestu 1986: 8).

The liberalization measures resulted in a dramatic increase in foreign trade as a percentage of GDP. Starting at only 14 per cent in 1965, this proportion increased to more than 20 per cent in 1970, and then more than doubled to 46.8 per cent in 1980. In 1990 the total trade as percentage of GDP reached 54.7 per cent, even rising to over 70 per cent in 2000.

Institutions

A large part of this book will be devoted to the study of changing institutions and their effects on Indonesian economic development. Here, we will sketch the long-term picture of two measures of the quality of institutions, in order to see if there is a link with economic performance. It is not easy to develop quantitative measures of the degree of efficiency of (sets of) institutions. For the case of Indonesia, which was during most of the period a rural country with a large agricultural sector, we would particularly be interested in institutions related to the functioning of agricultural markets. Rice was by far the most important commodity produced in the country, and its consumption dominated consumer expenditure. The efficiency of the rice market is therefore a first and fundamental test of the efficiency of the whole institutional framework of the country. In two earlier papers we have argued that rice prices can be used as proxies of the efficiency of rice and of rural capital markets (van Zanden 2004; Marks 2009a, 2010a).

First, we will look at the pattern of seasonal fluctuations of rice prices. As McCloskey and Nash (1984) have demonstrated, seasonal fluctuations can be used as a proxy of the interest rate on the countryside, and, as argued by van Zanden (2004), is indicative of the efficiency of rice markets as well. This also follows the fundamental insight by Douglass North's suggestion that 'the level of interest rates in capital markets is perhaps the most evident quantitative dimension of the efficiency of the institutional framework' (North 1990: 69).

Second, we will follow the changes in the degree of integration of rice markets, which is an index of the efficiency of marketing systems as a whole, and is also linked to the quality of institutions: the lower transaction costs are, the more integrated such markets will be. Reinforcing this point is a rapidly growing literature looking at Europe in the early modern period, and China and India in the eighteenth and nineteenth centuries, among others (Shiue and Keller 2004; Studer 2008).

On the basis of this literature, we have attempted to sketch the long-term development of the efficiency of rural market institutions. We collected monthly data of rice prices of the three most important rice markets of Java – Jakarta, Semarang and Surabaya – from 1825 to the present, although major gaps in the series remain. This allows us to sketch the major changes in the marketing system.

Figure 2.11 gives a summary of the development of seasonal fluctuations in rice prices in Jakarta, measured as the deviation from the 13-months moving average (see Van der Eng 1996: 191). These fluctuations reflect interest rates, storage costs and imperfections in the marketing system as a whole; for instance, local monopolies during times of scarcity. In the second quarter of the nineteenth century, when we have the first data, these fluctuations were quite strong – on average prices directly after the harvest were 30 to 40 per cent lower than in the months preceding the harvest, and this difference was much larger than found in, for example, Europe or China in the same period (van Zanden 2004). The colonial period saw a strong decline of the seasonality of rice prices. The introduction of railways and steamships in the second half of the nineteenth century had already led to a reduction (as the data for the 1880s and 1890s show), and government policies to stabilize the rice market contributed as well. In the 1920s and 1930s monthly rice prices on average fluctuated between plus 5 and minus

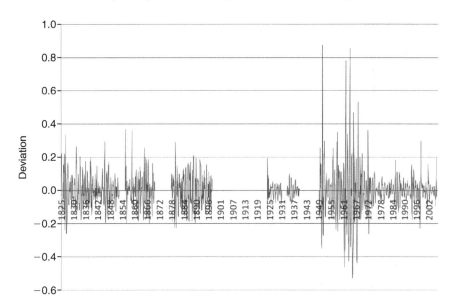

Figure 2.11 Rice prices: deviation from 13-month average, Jakarta, 1825–2006 (sources: Marks 2009a; van Zanden 2004; a working document with all the price data will be made available on www.iisg.nl/hpw).

5 per cent of the average level – these margins had been plus and minus 15–20 per cent from 1825 to 1855. The post-colonial period saw a return of instability, however. During the years of the struggle for independence (1945–1949), unsurprisingly, prices were very unstable. After 1949, seasonal fluctuations were reduced again (although not to the pre-1940 level), but the political instability and inflation of the 1960s brought a renewed period of poorly functioning rice markets (see Figure 2.11; we only present the Jakarta series, because it is the most complete, and other rice markets show very similar developments). During the Suharto regime (1967/1968–1998), seasonal fluctuations fell again to the level of the 1920s and 1930s, also thanks to the policies of the state to stabilize the market (the institution that was created to take care of this, Bulog, was probably relatively efficient).

A similar pattern emerges from the analysis of the coefficient of variation of the three rice markets, a rough proxy of the degree of integration of these markets (Figure 2.12). In the 1825–1870 period levels of market integration are extremely low, much lower than can be found in early modern Europe, or eighteenth- and nineteenth-century China and Japan (van Zanden 2004). There is a gradual fall of the coefficient during the nineteenth century, which continues into the second and third decade of the twentieth century. After 1945 rice prices in these three principal markets are diverging again, a pattern that can also be found when comparing with a much larger dataset, including other markets on Java and on the other islands (Marks 2009a). Again, the period of the independence struggle and the mid-1960s show the lowest levels of integration. Things return to 'normal' again during the 1970s and 1980s, but there is a certain increase in the coefficient of variation after the mid-1990s, perhaps as a result of the

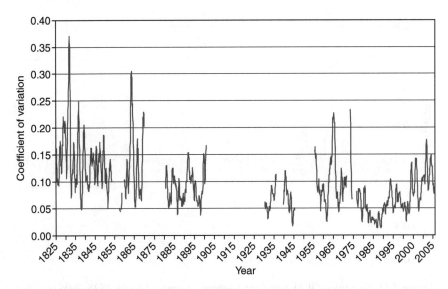

Figure 2.12 Coefficient of variation of three rice markets on Java, 1825–2006 (source: see Figure 2.11).

liberalization of rice markets and the effects of the Asian crisis of 1997/1998 (Marks 2009a).

Summing up, this attempt to quantify the efficiency of institutions leads to the following periodization. In the first six decades of the nineteenth century, rural market institutions were probably of poor quality – a theme we will develop in more detail in Chapter 4. This was also a period of stagnation and perhaps even decline with regard to total factor productivity. Between the 1860s and the 1920s institutions improved quite a lot. The level of integration of rice markets increased and seasonality fell strongly. The underlying causes and favourable effects of institutional changes in this period will be dealt with in Chapter 5. However, after 1942, institutions seem to have declined in efficiency; both indices of institutional performance reveal sharp deterioration during the 1940s, modest improvement during the 1950s, followed by another decade of institutional inefficiency during the 1960s. At the same time, levels of productivity declined sharply compared with the pre-war period. The links between these developments and their explanations will be the subject of Chapter 7. The correlation between institutional efficiency and productivity growth is confirmed by what happened after stabilization of the political regime in 1966/1967: institutions appear to have improved, and TFP began to rise (discussed in Chapter 8).

The questions we need to address in the remainder of this book are how to explain these long-term changes in the quality of institutions (measured in this, of course, highly imperfect way). Why did institutions change for the worse or for the better in the various periods discussed? What, for example, explains the worsening of the performance of markets after independence, or their improvement between 1860 and 1914? This alternation between periods of relative success and relative failure is, as was already remarked in Chapter 2, one of the main themes of this book.

Conclusion

In this chapter we have analysed the long-term development path of the Indonesian economy in an internationally comparative perspective. On the basis of partially new datasets on the national accounts of Java (1815–1939) and Indonesia (1880–2010), we could establish that its growth performance was relatively poor. Growth was almost entirely the result of factor accumulation – more labour and capital – implying that total factor productivity was nearly stagnant in the very long run. Moreover, GDP growth in Indonesia was relatively slow compared to its trading partners and its neighbours. Why? Why was the country not able to catch up before the 1968–1998 period?

A closer look at the trends analysed shows that the picture is more nuanced. There were basically two periods in which Indonesia really fell behind the rest of the world economy: between 1830 and 1860, and again between 1929 and 1967. These were also periods when institutions were relatively inefficient or even deteriorating (according to our analysis of rice markets), and when very specific economic policies were implemented. Decline in productivity was most significant during the period of the Cultivation System (1830–1870), which was characterized by coerced production of cash crops; this fall in total factor productivity occurred despite the rapid growth of exports and a marked increase in openness. Explaining what happened during this period is the main challenge taken up by Chapter 4. The interwar years constitute another rather difficult period in Indonesian economic history; it appears that the instability of the world economy in combination with an open economy in Indonesia led to the relatively weak performance of the latter's economy. The question remains whether domestic policies contributed to the relative failure of the economy in this period. The same question is relevant for the period of inward-looking policies during the 1950s and early 1960s, which resulted in low levels of openness and relatively low levels of total factor productivity. We have to explain why the first decades after independence were so difficult – culminating in the (Asian) drama of the traumatic events of 1965–1967 (see Chapter 7).

By contrast, there were also two periods in which productivity increased substantially. The first was between 1870 and 1913, during a period of colonial growth that was characterized by liberal and, after 1900, increasingly 'developmental' policies. Nevertheless, the different growth curves of Java and Indonesia in this period suggest that the positive effects were probably limited to Java. More clearly this occurred between 1968 and 1998, during the Suharto regime, which ended the period of the inward-looking policies of 1949–1966/1967, and once again reopened the economy, initially facilitated by the rapidly growing income from oil. This growth, however, continued in the 1980s, when oil income was collapsing, and became increasingly outward-oriented. This is the period when Indonesia became part of the East Asian miracle. In the following chapters we will analyse the developments in the subperiods identified above in more detail.

3 Colonial state formation, 1800–1830

Indonesia as we know it now is by and large a product of its colonial past. The current borders of the country – from Aceh in the west to Papua New Guinea in the east, as demanded by the Declaration of Independence of 1945 – coincide with the borders of the Netherlands East Indies, and are a product of a process of colonization that arguably began in 1596 when the first Dutch ships went ashore in Banten, on the east coast of Java. During the first two centuries of this colonial endeavour, until 1799, it was a private company, the VOC (*Verenigde Oostindische Compagnie*), which came to control key parts of the Archipelago and in the process began to build up a quasi-colonial state. Its first goal had been control over the Moluccas, the legendary Spice Islands, and the source of a number of extremely valuable commodities (cloves, nutmeg and mace). Next, it needed a central market to monitor its trade in Southeast Asia: Batavia (current day Jakarta) was selected in 1619 to play that role. From this basis, it extended its network by conquering large parts of Java and a few trading posts outside this island (for example, Makassar in 1666–1969). On Java it slowly developed from a trading company, interested in the commercial opportunities of the island, into a colonial state that earned most of its income from raising taxes and (as we shall see) acquiring surplus production in a number of ways, to some extent copying the practices of territorial states that were gradually marginalized by the growing power of the VOC. In 1682, for example, it conquered the sultanate of Banten, and from that moment on controlled the western part of Java. Mataram was a much stronger state, covering the central and eastern parts of the island, although its control over the port cities on the north coast was tentative. But thanks to its superior navy, army (especially artillery and the training of its soldiers) and diplomacy, and the fragmentation of political power during recurrent succession crises, the VOC slowly eroded the power basis of Mataram, first beginning to control the coastal area (which was definitively 'acquired' in the 1746, in return for an annual payment by the VOC to the sultan), and to extend its power into the heart of the neighbouring state. Another effect of the succession crisis was the splitting of the Mataram state – a solution sponsored by Dutch diplomacy – into two different states, with capitals in Surakarta and Yogyakarta.

As a result, at the end of the eighteenth century the VOC controlled most of Java and the Moluccas, as well as a few outposts on Sumatra, Borneo (Kalimantan) and Celebes (Sulawesi). The (relative and absolute) decline of the trade in spices diminished the importance of the Moluccas. The territorial expansion from the 1680s onwards had important consequences for the activities of the VOC. When it was still confined to a small land area around Batavia, commercial activities had been dominant, although the growing group of Chinese (and Indian/Arab) merchants residing in and around Batavia had already developed a thriving sugar industry there based on indigenous land and labour. But territorial expansion after 1680 meant that the VOC not only acquired land and people, but also institutions to tax and govern an increasingly large area and population. In principle, it tried to continue established practices and profit from the taxes raised by previous sovereigns, which it could 'streamline' because its power basis was much stronger than that of most 'oriental despots'. It continued to raise head taxes, land taxes, taxes on commercial traffic, etc.; but it also learned to adapt existing institutions more fully to its own goals, by, for example, demanding as taxes those commodities that could be exported (cotton yarn) or that were needed for the subsistence of Batavia (such as rice). The best example of such an adaptation of local practices was the introduction and expansion of coffee cultivation in the western corner of Java, the Priangan. From the 1720s onwards, using local modes of exploitation that implied that the sultan could claim part of the produce of the peasantry, the VOC introduced the cultivation of coffee there on a rather large scale. Local elites were co-opted into the system by awarding them a share in the proceeds. The system was so successful that from the 1760s onwards the VOC had to try to stem the rising tide of coffee production by introducing restrictions on the planting of new trees, as the market for coffee in the Netherlands could not cope with such a substantial increase in its supply.

New opportunities for raising taxes also emerged as a result of the VOC's increasing ability to monopolize the import trade of Java. In 1676 it officially acquired the monopoly of importing textiles and opium (by far the most important imported commodities) into Mataram, a monopoly that was used to cream off these lucrative trades. The VOC organized these imports (India was the main source of both commodities), but regional trade and local distribution were largely in the hands of Chinese merchants. The right to sell opium to consumers also began to be leased out by the VOC to Chinese merchants. The trade in opium was so profitable that in 1745 local VOC officials tried to increase their own share of the pie by setting up the *Amfioensocieteit* (the Opium Company). Its official aim was the elimination of corruption in the opium trade by giving the local officials (and merchants) a clear stake in the business, but soon the company shares were concentrated in the hands of a few (often retired) VOC officials, who drew a large income from them. To acquire the appropriate political patronage, some of the shares were also donated to the *stadtholder* in the Netherlands, who as a result received a huge income for free. He was allocated 30 shares, on which he earned in total about 1.2 million guilders, an incredibly large sum for this period (Gaastra 2006). Shareholders who did pay for their original share also fared quite well; in total, during a period of almost 50 years, the dividend was 863 per cent, or more than 17 per cent per annum. On top of this, the directors of the company also earned incomes well above those considered normal in comparable jobs. Attempts to reform these practices, however, failed, in part because complaints about these 'practices' fell on deaf ears – the *stadtholder* clearly had no incentive to change things (Gaastra 2006). The *Amfioensocieteit* is only one example, albeit a rather extreme one, of the gradually increasing corruption in Batavia, and more generally, in the VOC-dominated, proto-colonial society. In addition, illicit trade, which had always been suppressed by the VOC, grew spectacularly during the eighteenth century – much faster than official trade carried out by the company itself.

Partly as a result of this, while the VOC was establishing itself as a territorial power on Java, its trading empire slowly began to lose its vitality and dynamism, finding it increasingly difficult to compete with the British in particular, but also with the French, Danish and other trading companies. As the success of the VOC in the Indonesian Archipelago was largely based on its monopoly, the gradual undermining of its strength also meant that merchants from other countries were increasingly able to reap the profits that in the past were due to the VOC. Key to the gradual decline of the VOC was its inability to keep up with the British, both commercially and militarily, as a result of which the major wars between the two often ended in peace treaties transferring part of the Dutch commercial assets to the British. During the Fourth Anglo-Dutch War of 1781–1784, it became very clear that the Dutch were unable to defend their overseas possessions properly (they even needed the help of French navy to do the job). This led, a decade later, to the total collapse of the VOC after the French occupied the Netherlands in the winter of 1794/1795. Its liquidation followed in 1799. The Dutch state took over its huge debts – and its possessions: the remains of its colonial empire now reduced to a few strongholds in the Indonesian Archipelago, and the control over its richest island, Java.

Opinions about how to govern this colony differed, but there was consensus that the failure of the VOC was linked to its monopolistic nature, which had restricted trade and commercial development in the colony, harmed its economic development, and had led to the financial problems that eventually resulted in its own demise. A twofold diagnosis emerged out of the public debate about this that would direct policy over the next few decades. The strange mix between private and public in the VOC regime – as a private company that governed the island – had to be disentangled, and a more or less pure public colonial state had to be set up to remedy the many failings of the old regime. At the same time, a turn towards a more liberal economic regime was necessary in order to stimulate the general economic development of the colony (although it was not always clear if this meant stimulating private European enterprise, the economic activities of the indigenous peasantry, or both). Such a switch and its expected beneficial consequences would also create the economic basis for a 'real' state, underpinned by a 'Weberian' bureaucracy to replace the profit-hungry VOC officials (who had been, in a way, both officials and merchants). But how to achieve this transformation was quite unclear; in hindsight, we can now see that it took perhaps a century, and at least 70 years, before this transformation was completed.

Java in 1800

Java at the beginning of the nineteenth century was a highly complex, but also 'underdeveloped' society. In fact, three types of society coexisted on the island: indigenous Javanese social structures; the colonial nexus of the former VOC, essentially consisting of the descendants of VOC servants and some independent merchants; and a 'comprador' group consisting of Chinese, Arab and Indian merchants, with yet other type(s) of social structure(s). The interaction between these three groups explains much of the dynamics of Javanese colonial society and its economy in the nineteenth century. Therefore, a rough sketch of the three socio-political structures is fundamental for understanding the rest of the story.

It has been argued – by Burger (1975) in his classic study of Indonesian socio-economic history, and more recently by Talens (1999) – that the basic structure of Javanese society was feudal. This concept can probably still be used when defined appropriately, as done by Talens, who follows recent debates on this concept by Berktay (1987) in particular. The following features may be called characteristic for a feudal society:

- it is largely agricultural and non-monetarized, the majority of the population consists of peasants who are part of a (more or less) centralized state governed by an elite that draws its surplus mainly from the agricultural sector;
- this surplus is extracted using non-economic means, i.e. through labour services and claims to part of the produce of the land;
- the claims to (the produce of) labour and land of the different layers of society are overlapping: often the sovereign claims to be the sole owner of the land, but peasants have strong user rights (and a case for having certain property rights as well, for example as reclaimants of the land), and intermediate layers – the village elite, local and regional elites – have additional claims to labour services and a share in the agricultural produce;
- contracts are oral and (therefore) to some extent multi-interpretable, and without the formal and 'permanent' implications of written contracts drawn up according to (Roman/European) law.

An important characteristic of this system is its flexibility. These societies are characterized by constant switches in the relative powers of the different layers of the state. At some point in time the central authority may be quite strong, for example because a very competent king is in charge of the state. At other times – after a war, or an epidemic – peasants may have a relatively strong bargaining position and central authority may be weak. At yet other moments regional elites may be relatively effective and powerful. Because of the overlapping claims to land and labour and the flexibility of oral contracts, social relations and the distribution of the surplus can easily adjust to these swings in relative power positions because no new definitions of property rights are necessary. Socio-political structures and the distribution of the surplus can therefore adapt to changes in the power equilibrium. But it is also clear that these 'fuzzy' property rights are probably not very conducive to market exchange. Peasants, in particular in the regions close to the centre of the feudal state in mid-Java (near Yogya and Solo) had no clear property rights. They could probably claim the right to use land that they had themselves reclaimed for three to five years or, in other cases, one generation, but afterwards the *sawah* became part of the land that was controlled by the village community and redistributed at certain intervals. Hence they could not use their land as collateral for a loan and could not sell or buy it, although at the village level some 'informal' exchange of land did occur. During the first half of the nineteenth century the colonial state also favoured the system of periodic distribution of the land, because it hoped to stabilize peasant society in this way and broaden the basis from which labour services could be levied (see Breman 1980).

This 'fuzzy' set of rights to land and labour may have been a solution to the problems of organizing and maintaining a 'centralized' agrarian state in a region in which markets were extremely thin and the higher layers of society depended on direct tributes from the peasantry; it was, however, not particularly conducive to the endogenous growth of markets. The interventions by the administration of the Dutch East India Company, which during the eighteenth century became increasingly dependent on the income generated by forced export production, also tended to stabilize this system as they learned to convert their claims to land and labour into cheaply obtained export products (Nagtegaal, 1996). Moreover, the colonial administration also endorsed and, especially after 1830, stimulated the development of systems of collective ownership of *sawahs* – often in combination with periodic redistribution of land, which undermined the direct control that peasants had of this essential factor of production. After the 1850s the official policy in this field changed, and Dutch civil servants began to push for a gradual conversion of the rights to land and labour into private property rights, but the changes were very gradual and often opposed by those members of the rural elite who profited most from the old set of institutions (Boomgaard, 1987: 82).

As a result, two more or less separate systems of control over the land evolved: in the 'marginal' eastern and western parts of Java the peasants *de facto* became the private owners of the land, but local elites continued to claim part of the land and/or its produce, whereas in the central core of Java (and in particular in the *Pasisir*, the north coast), systems of communal property evolved, in which the land was often redistributed after a number of years.[1]

In the seventeenth and eighteenth centuries the VOC had already learned how to use this 'feudal' system of surplus extraction for its own purposes. It shows the flexibility of this system that the VOC – being a foreign 'capitalistic' trading body – could successfully graft itself onto these feudal structures (see Talens 1999; Nagtegaal 1996). As we have already seen, the VOC, profiting from periodic crises in the feudal states it dealt with, concluded formal treaties with the sultans ruling those states; in particular with mighty Mataram, the central state that controlled much of Java in the seventeenth century, but also with the sultanate of Banten and some lesser powers. These treaties gave the company 'sovereign' rights in increasingly large parts of the island and the privileges that were attached to them, i.e. a claim to a share of the produce of the land, to labour services, the right to levy taxes, etc. The highly successful coffee cultivation of Priangan (in the western part of Java) was developed in this way; being based on the forced cultivation of the crop by the peasants of the region in return for a quite basic monetary compensation. To 'oil the machine', members of the local elite profited from these compensations as well. During the eighteenth century the seductions of the feudal regime had changed the orientation of the VOC on Java fundamentally. It increasingly became a territorial state – which was still confined to the north and western part of the island – profiting from sources of income that were basically attached to the land. Trade itself as a source of income declined in relative importance. By and large it left indigenous social structures intact and only tended to add a few colonial administrators and advisors to their upper layers. Visitors to the island in the late 1700s saw a colonial elite – of mixed Dutch–Javanese descent – which took over many of the customs and privileges of the indigenous elite (and in the long run might have merged into 'feudal society' almost completely).

This coexistence of a Dutch colonial nexus and an indigenous feudal society was made possible by the intermediate role played by merchants from China, India and the Arab world. In particular ethnic Chinese merchants – who enjoyed a large degree of self-government in the cities on the north coast – played a crucial role as tax farmers, middlemen and entrepreneurs, but also as skilled labourers in many branches of industry (shipbuilding, metal working, etc.) (Blussé 1986). They dominated the sugar industry and the retail trade of the island (except for those parts where they were not permitted to enter) and were a major force in wholesale trade and on the informal capital market. Both the VOC and the emerging colonial state were highly dependent on cooperation with the Chinese, but the state also used its power to skim off part of the revenues the Chinese acquired as a result of their activities. Tax farming was a key instrument in this process. The state leased the farming of the most important taxes – in particular the opium tax – to competing clans of Chinese, who often could only acquire access to certain regions by renting these taxes because the state restricted the activities of Chinese in the Javanese countryside – officially in order to protect the peasants against exploitation by the Chinese middlemen (Rush 1990). The deal was, therefore, that these families acquired a near-monopoly in a certain part of Java, in return for a favourable (and perhaps in view of its intrinsic value often too high) bid for the opium tax, which also gave them access to the other taxes that were farmed out. Some of the taxes that were levied were also quite detrimental for market exchange, such as levies at *pasars* (markets) and toll-gates, as well as the monopoly on pawn houses that was also farmed out, which led to many abuses that increased costs for peasants trying to access the markets. As we will see in Chapter 4, this particular set of institutions and social-political structures resulted in poor conditions for market exchange (i.e. high transaction costs), as is clear from the existence of highly volatile, non-transparent markets and the extremely high interest rates on capital markets. Incentives for market exchange were poor, and levels of market production and specialization were relatively low. This feature of the Javanese economy would set severe constraints on the attempts to change its structure during the nineteenth century.

Another sign of the poor incentives for market exchange was the underdeveloped nature of the labour market. Labour recruitment was one of the key issues of economic development and colonial policy during the nineteenth century. According to contemporary sources and much of the economic-historical literature, wage labour was relatively marginal until well into the second half of the century. The wage labour that did exist could only be recruited using 'non-economic means', i.e. by using the coercive powers of the *priyayi*, the elite that claimed part of the labour power of the peasants (Boomgaard 1990). Moreover, Java at about 1800 was a frontier economy with a relatively low population density, in which it was relatively easy to increase the area under cultivation, either by converting extensive agricultural systems (shifting cultivation on *ladangs*) into more intensive ones (rice-cultivation on irrigated *sawahs*), or by establishing new *dessas* in almost empty areas. Nieboer's well-known theory predicts that in such a situation of absolute labour scarcity 'non-economic means' will be used to mobilise labour power in order to extract a surplus (Nieboer 1910). As discussed already, the state structures that developed on Java in the centuries before 1800 were indeed characterized by strong claims on land and labour by the elite, which in practice meant that a significant part of the produce of the land could be appropriated by them and that a substantial part of the labour of the peasants had to be supplied as labour services. In return for this the peasants were supposed to receive religious, judiciary and military services (protection) (Talens 1999: 172).

In much of the older literature the absence of free wage labour in this period is stressed. Recently Boomgaard has argued, however, that in certain commercialized pockets – in Batavia and its immediate surroundings, for example – free wage labour already existed in the seventeenth and eighteenth centuries (Boomgaard 1990). Initially this free labour market was dominated by Chinese and Dutch immigrants and their (mixed) descendants. But from the 1670s onwards, the appearance of a class of coolies (i.e. unskilled Javanese wage labourers) points to an increased participation of the Javanese in this labour market, although they were probably often bonded labourers, recruited by the VOC (or by Chinese entrepreneurs) using extra-economic means as well as economic incentives (Nagtegaal 1996: 205). It is impossible to quantify the importance of this 'free' labour market, but at the turn of the nineteenth century it was not insignificant.

Slave labour was another important source of labour in the port cities, before the British abolished it in 1815. It partly originated in the Indonesian Archipelago itself, mainly from its eastern part, where indigenous debt slavery occurred; other slaves were imported from abroad, sometimes from as far as East Africa. The abolishment may have intensified the problems of labour recruitment after 1815. Throughout the seventeenth and eighteenth centuries wages were relatively high, although they probably fell over the long run as the supply of wage labourers slowly increased and the VOC extended its control over larger parts of the island, making it possible to draw on new sources of supply of labour (Boomgaard 1990).

Java was basically a rural society with a few relatively small cities on the north coast. Batavia was likely the largest of these with an official population of 55,000 at around 1830; but in reality, the number of inhabitants was probably twice that size. Other cities on the north coast were Semarang (with an estimated population of 22,000 in 1812) and Surabaya, both somewhat smaller than Batavia (Nagtegaal 1998: 53). The other urban area was the central region of Mataram, dominated by the palace cities of Yogyakarta and Surakarta; the former city had perhaps more than 60,000 inhabitants before the Java War of 1825–1830, but this number declined to 31,000 in 1832.[2] Compared to Java's total population of about 10 million inhabitants in 1820, these cities were quite small, and only a small part of the population lived in urban concentrations. The first more or less reliable estimates of the level of urbanization are for 1850, when 8.7 per cent of the population lived in urban areas (with more than 5,000 inhabitants). As we will see in Chapter 5, levels of urbanization declined during the second half of the nineteenth century, a trend which may have started much earlier. Reid (1993) maintains that during the sixteenth and early seventeenth centuries Indonesia was quite urbanized, but there is still discussion about the size of cities in this period, which he may have significantly overstated (see Talens 1999: 46–51; Nagtegaal 1998: 49). By contrast, Boomgaard estimated the level of urbanization in 1600 at 3–4 per cent, less than half the level in 1850 (Nagtegaal 1998: 49). Moreover, a town on Java was in essence a collection of separate kampongs,

> in which the Javanese lived under conditions that were similar to those in rural areas. … To Europeans those kampongs looked like forests with houses in between. Both the coastal and the inland cities were surrounded by wet-rice fields that were worked by its inhabitants.
>
> (Nagtegaal 1998: 53)

The effect such cities had on market exchange and demand for agricultural commodities was therefore limited, and the level of structural transformation of this economy was low. The first more or less reliable data we have on the structure of the workforce are from 1880 (see Table 3.1), but change between 1800 and 1880 may have been quite limited. Three-quarters of the population earned its livelihood from agriculture, which supplied 62 per cent of GDP; when we include the 'labourers' (often working on plantations), these shares go up even more. The biggest difference with the situation in 1800 is that the share of textiles in the labour force and GDP declined since; however, at about 1800 textiles were not a typical urban industry, but carried on the countryside as a kind of putting-out system (Nagtegaal 1998: 54). The same applies to the important sugar industry of Batavia's surroundings (and the rest of the north coast); again, this industry was located in the countryside, and its spread did not really contribute to processes of urbanization and structural change.

Table 3.1 The structure of the labour force and of GDP in 1880

Sector	Share labour force (%)	Share GDP (1878/1880) (%)
Agriculture	75	62**
Fisheries	2	2
Industry	3	9
Trade	9	9
Transport (shipping and railways)	1	2
Government	2	4
Other services	2	10
Labourers and other industries*	6	2
	100	100

Sources: Labour Force: *Koloniaal Verslag* 1881; GDP: van Zanden 2002.

Notes
* Many of these labourers worked in agriculture; the other industries are forestry and salt production.
** Of which 13 per cent from export agriculture and 49 per cent from food crops.
The classification of the labour force and the interpretation of the census of 1880 followed here differ slightly from Fernando (1993).

Another perspective on the structure of the Javanese economy at the beginning of the nineteenth century can be found through looking at imports and exports (Table 3.2). The first more or less reliable data are from 1822, and nicely illustrate (to some extent) the structure of international trade just before the major changes that would occur during the second quarter of the nineteenth century. What is particularly interesting is the large role played by Asian countries. India, for example, was the 'country' with the largest share in imports, an import trade that was dominated by opium. Overall imports from Asia were larger than those from Europe. China was also quite an important trading partner in 1822, comprising almost 10 per cent of imports from outside the Indonesian Archipelago. Exports, on the other hand, were already in 1822 dominated by Europe, and more specifically by the Netherlands (with a share of more than 62 per cent of all exports) – a situation that is again typical for the seventeenth and eighteenth centuries.

Textiles were the most important item on the import side of the balance of payments (but the difference with opium was not very large); in 1822 some of this still originated from India, a trade going back many centuries, which had originally been based on the exchange of Indian textiles against Moluccan spices.[3] Traditionally, Java also exported textiles – mainly cotton fabrics to the rest of the Archipelago, the 'Outer Islands'. Rice was another important export commodity from the north coast of the island; again, a large part of these exports went to the Outer Islands. But by far the most important export product was coffee, comprising almost two-thirds of the total value of exports; sugar and spices (some of which were re-exported, and originally came from the 'Outer Islands') accounted for a large part of the rest. Sugar exports had been much higher during the final decades of the eighteenth century; they had declined by perhaps 50 per cent subsequently, and continued to do so during the 1820s

Table 3.2 The structure of exports and imports of Java and Madura, 1822–1838 (1,000 guilders)

	1822	1828	1838
Imports from			
Netherlands	3,101	6,645	12,282
Great Britain	2,512	2,167	4,509
Europe total	6,195	9,060	17,543
India	5,922	737	401
China	1,937	651	777
Japan	752	1,067	574
Singapore	775	731	1,098
Asia total	9,424	3,353	3,169
Outer Islands	2,519	7,429	10,406
Total imports	22,415	22,162	34,904
Exports to			
Netherlands	15,309	9,147	29,336
Great Britain	461	201	1,421
Europe total	16,293	9,559	32,225
India	882	95	32
China	1,404	1,698	1,779
Japan	444	291	84
Singapore	183	1,023	1,212
Asia total	2,962	3,422	3,198
Outer Islands	2,056	4,206	9,161
Total exports	24,446	18,304	47,050
Export surplus	2,031	-3,858	12,146

	1822	1828	1838
Imports from outside Indonesia			
Opium	4,019	1,012	574
Textiles	5,025	6,071	10,279
Iron	–	278	1,116
Copper and doits	1,248	1,072	2,430
Gold/silver coins	3,040	1,983	3,534
Total	19,896	14,733	24,498
Exports to outside Indonesia			
Spices	747	723	2,943
Sugar	1,034	442	9,781
Coffee	14,554	7,831	14,995
Indigo	–	94	3,170
Rice (inc. to Outer Islands)	225	1,194	3,012
Textiles (incl. Outer Islands)	518	1,153	2,687
Copper bullion	198	779	–
Gold/silver coins	2,179	814	711
Total	22,390	14,098	37,889

Source: *CEI*, vols I and VII.

(*Changing Economy in Indonesia*, Vol. 1: 63–65). The value of coffee exports also declined during the 1820s, mainly as a result of the sharp fall of prices on world markets (after the Napoleonic period, during which prices had risen substantially due to the scarcity of colonial products on European markets). The structure of exports and imports clearly reflected the 'underdeveloped' nature of the economy: agriculture dominated exports and manufactures were quite prominent among its imports.

What, in 1822, remained different from the situation of a typical 'underdeveloped' economy was that Java had a huge surplus in its trade with Europe; again, this had been the normal situation in the seventeenth and eighteenth centuries. This was solved by sending large amounts of money (mainly silver coins) to Java, a large part of which was again exported to India and China as a result of the trade deficit Java had with those countries (this is also clear from the fact that in 1822 Java was both a huge importer and a large exporter of gold/silver coins). The trade with Indonesia therefore played a role in the worldwide flows of silver that were characteristic of the world economy between 1500 and 1800. Silver began its global trek at the silver mines of Latin America, moved via Europe (Spain, the Netherlands, Great Britain), and found its 'final' destination in China and India. Java was an intermediate station in this global flow, importing silver from Europe and exporting it again to China and India.

The VOC initially found it difficult to completely understand the mechanisms behind these global flows, and tried to stabilize the value of the silver coins (guilders, rixdollars) at the same level everywhere; as this predictably led to silver scarcity in Java (and other parts of its trading empire), it unsuccessfully tried to ban the export of silver coins to China and India. The colonial expert Van den Bosch estimated that during the two centuries of the VOC period about 800 million guilders worth of coins had been imported into Java, which 'disappeared from circulation without leaving a trace of its existence' (De Bree 1928: 57). The VOC attempted to counteract this by setting the value of the silver coins at a higher level than in the Netherlands, but this only contributed to the problems with the money supply. At the same time, as the demand for small change increased, initially (in 1633) lead coins, and from 1636 onward, copper coins were introduced to fill this gap (De Bree 1928: 29). The shortage of money remained an acute problem, which led the company to introduce paper money in 1782. They were first sold as bonds with an annual interest rate of 6 per cent, but as the paper money quickly became a success, the VOC stopped paying interest on it. After a few years this resulted in a decline in the value of paper money (against coins). The company was able to stabilize paper money at about 85 per cent of its nominal value (De Bree 1928: 48). During the final decades of the eighteenth century the economic ties between Java and the Netherlands became weaker, and other (Indian, Spanish) currencies became increasingly important; for a while the Mexican dollar became the official standard coin of the colony, until it was replaced by the Netherlands Indies guilder in 1816–1818.

The British, who occupied the island between 1811 and 1816, tried to resolve some of the defects of this monetary situation by adopting the Mexican dollar – the coin then most used in international trade in Southeast Asia – as the standard coin of the colony. At the same time new copper coins (*duiten*) were minted, and the rights of the Bank van Lening (the only European bank in the colony) to issue paper money were extended. The British also tried to liberalize the trade in bullion, but had to reintroduce a ban on silver exports to China only two months after liberalization in November 1812 (De Bree 1928: 95). The continuing acute shortage of coins (and of the necessary raw material, copper) also led the British to introduce new coins, made of tin. In short, the monetary situation at the beginning of the nineteenth century was quite complex. Three kinds of money were in circulation: copper coins (and some tin and lead coins) for small change, some of Chinese origin, others being Dutch *doits*, and still others being copies of Dutch *doits*; silver coins ranging from small silver *stuivers* and *dubbeltjes* to Mexican dollars; and paper money. Moreover, rates of exchange between these different kinds of money fluctuated constantly. The mixed and complex nature of its money supply does reflect the socio-political structure of the island nicely, however.

1808–1826: reforms and their failure

The first quarter of the nineteenth century was a period of reform and experimentation aimed at the creation of a more or less 'modern' colonial state. Three stages can be discerned. The first phase consisted of reforms initiated by the new Governor-General Daendels in 1808–1811, who tried to introduce the concept of an 'enlightened' state into Java. Second, between 1811 and 1816 the British (in particular lieutenant Governor-General Raffles) controlled the colony and introduced their own ideas and practices. Third, between 1816 and 1826 the Dutch resumed their attempts at reform, now led by Governor-General Van der Capellen. Ideologically these reforms can be traced back to discussions between enlightened colonial experts about the future of the colony that started in the 1780s. The discussion intensified when the VOC was liquidated and the Dutch state (which was also reorganized at the same time – with the help of French revolutionary forces) took over its possessions in 1800. The new state the reformers had in mind – their model, inspired by Enlightenment thought, was to some extent the post-1792 French state – was highly centralized and knew only, in principle, equal citizens, and therefore abolished all feudal privileges. Moreover it had a well-defined mission: it saw itself as an instrument of progress, aiming at the improvement of the economy and society at large, enhancing infrastructure, education, industry and agriculture.

Governor-General Deandels, newly appointed in 1808, was most directly inspired by French revolutionary ideals. According to Carey's study of the causes of the Java War, 'he brought to his new post all the brusqueness and determination that had been the hallmark of his previous political and military career'. But Carey also concedes that 'the three years of his administration (1808–1811) laid the foundation of a modern colonial bureaucracy and government in Java' (Carey 2007: 131). One of Daendels' aims was to create a modern, formal (Weberian) bureaucracy, because under the old regime servants of the VOC were also merchants and therefore guarded their own mercantile interests quite closely. In fact, the fundamental difference between the private and public spheres was blurred during the VOC period, as the VOC was both the governing body and a private trading company at the same time. Daendels also forcefully suppressed (the symbols of) feudal privilege – in a way that was difficult for indigenous elites to understand – and abolished some of the labour services and forced deliveries of export products (of cotton yarn, for example). Moreover, after a rebellion at the Yogyakarta court as they were attempting to resist this attack on their privileged position, he annexed the eastern part of Java, which had previously been part of Mataram. His other claim to fame was that he designed and constructed the *Grote Postweg*, a 'modern' road that connected the major cities on the north coast of the island. Paradoxically, Daendels could only undertake this by employing extremely large amounts of labour services. At the same time, in order to finance the colonial state, he introduced the coerced culti-vation of coffee, which had been successful in Priangan in other parts of Java the Dutch controlled (Stevens 1982: 30ff.).

During the British interregnum similar policies were pursued. The key reform introduced by Raffles was the land rent, which had to replace all forced deliver-ies and other feudal duties. The juridical basis of the land rent was the claim – laid down in previous treaties between the VOC and Mataram – that the colonial government, being the successor of feudal sovereigns such as the sultans of Mataram, was the owner of all the land. All peasants, therefore, could be con-sidered to be leasers of the land, for which they were obliged to pay a certain amount of money equal to perhaps as much as one-quarter to half of its yield, dependent on the quality of the land. Perhaps paradoxically, this feudal claim to part of the produce was the basis for the introduction of a relatively modern land tax. In one stroke other feudal dues were officially cancelled and, as the tax for-mally had to be paid in cash, peasants were induced to sell a part of their crop to the market in order to pay their land rent (or – but this was considered a less desirable option – to pay the land rent in rice). In a way it was an attempt to introduce a modern, market-oriented economy in one stroke. Yet Raffles could also not do without the old structures of social control; in order to collect the land rent, local elites had to be involved. Taxation on an individual basis remained a fiction, and it became to a large extent subject to the discretionary power of local elites. Moreover, the successful system of forced deliveries of coffee in Priangan remained unchanged – the state simply could not afford to cancel this highly profitable way of taxing the population. At the same time, Raffles was forced to sell large stretches of land – including the villages that lay on them and their inhabitants – to private entrepreneurs who received almost unrestricted 'feudal' privileges on these 'private estates', including the right to tax the inhabitants and to use their labour on sugar plantations (Bastin 1954).

From 1816 onwards, after the colony was returned to the Dutch, colonial pol-icies were implemented that were to a large extent a continuation of the reforms of the previous periods. One of the modern features of the new administration, now led by Governor-General Van der Capellen, was the systematic collection of statistical data on almost all aspects of the economy and society of the island – with a focus on tax-related topics – which still forms the basis of much of our understanding of its economic and social structures (Stevens 1982: 72–94). A new generation of civil servants, some of whom had already accompanied Daendels to Java in 1808, now took over the administration of the island and, inspired by developmental ideas, began to collect information about the society they governed – or rather 'served'. Policies implemented between 1816 and 1826 were to some extent inspired by liberal ideals; nevertheless, Van der Capellen was reluctant to fully unleash the forces of the market. The protection of the Javanese population against dispossession by Western entrepreneurs or Chinese merchants was also an important policy objective. He was very critical of the situation on the 'private estates', which had been drastically enlarged by Raffles and where the fundamental rights of peasants were often ignored or suppressed. At the same time he introduced market incentives into the system of coerced coffee cultivation (still the cork on which much of the export economy floated) by linking the price paid to the cultivator to the world market price – before 1817 such a link did not exist. In this way he hoped to slowly transfer the system into one of private and voluntary cultivation (Stevens 1982: 147–149). The government also introduced the rule that contracts concerning the sale of agricultural products could no longer be concluded with the heads of villages (which had been the rule so far), but had to involve the peasants themselves. The idea was to weaken the position of the local elite and expose the peasants to some extent to the free market; nevertheless, this reform remained a dead letter.

The reforms between 1808 and 1826 were successful in one respect: in less than two decades a centralized state built on a newly created bureaucracy was set up, and started to expand its influence into the arteries of Javanese society. This was quite an achievement. This new bureaucracy, in theory, also embraced the indigenous elite; officially the 'nobility' (*priyayi*) of the island were reduced to office holders serving the interests of the new colonial state (Sutherland 1979: 7). Daendels in particular had quite forcefully acted against their feudal privileges, and Raffles and Van der Capellen followed in his footsteps (although often with more diplomatic skills than Daendels had demonstrated). The attempts to end 'feudal exploitation' by the indigenous elite had been the core of much of the reforms, which had given rise to constant frictions between the *priyayi* and the Dutch administrators.

The success of the newly emerging bureaucracy can be read from the strong increase in tax income, the result of the extension of a more or less systematic tax regime over those parts of the island that were controlled by the Dutch. Tax income grew from about 15 million guilders in 1817 (the first year for which accounts have been preserved) to more than 25 million in 1822, and continued to grow, albeit at a slower pace, afterwards (in the same years, total GDP increased from about 220 to 265 million guilders). Figure 3.1 shows the increase of the yield of a few strategic taxes, such as the opium tax and the land tax. But this 'success' had its flipside: the population did not really appreciate the increase in

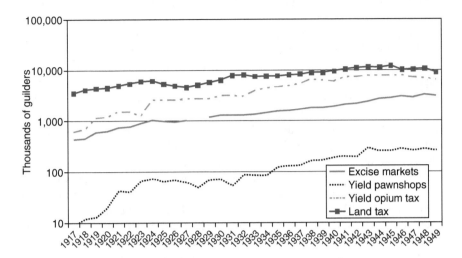

Figure 3.1 The yield of a few important taxes on Java, 1817–1850 (in fl 1,000) (source: dataset public finance Netherlands Indies available at IISH: www.iisg.nl/ indonesianeconomy/).

taxation, and taxes such as the excise on markets were hampering trade – both the retail trade of the local peasantry and the wholesale trade of the Chinese and other middlemen. Moreover, these attempts at reform were compromised by the necessity to pay for the steadily expanding and therefore increasingly costly bureaucracy. Java was considered to be a *wingewest*, which was supposed to yield profit to the 'mother country', both in terms of trade flows (which had been monopolized by the VOC, but were now liberalized and increasingly dominated by British merchants) and in terms of net income flowing into the Dutch treasury. One of the problems was the costs of the new bureaucracy. The expenses of the colonial state grew even more rapidly than its income, from about 15 million guilders in 1817 to 27 million guilders in 1824. During the first few years of Van der Capellen's regime, the budget was more or less balanced – already a disappointment, incidentally, for King Willem I, who expected profits from the colony. During the 1820s large deficits arose, however.

These deficits were the result of two developments. A large part of the income of the colonial state was dependent on exports of coffee (and other commodities), the result of the system of forced coffee cultivation in Priangan and similar 'taxes' on a smaller scale elsewhere. Van der Capellen, much like his predecessors, had been unable to abolish this system, although it was inconsistent with his general policy of liberalization, for the simple reason that it had generated a lot of money (in 1818, when this source of income peaked, it had brought in more than 10 million guilders, or 48 per cent of total revenues). But after peaking during the Napoleonic period, prices of tropical products on European markets declined between 1816 and the mid-1820s, causing the income from exports of coffee to fall dramatically (Stevens 1982: 95ff.). Low export prices meant that export production stagnated as well, and that private capital inflows from the Netherlands into the export sector were stagnating as had been expected by the colonial reformers (see also Table 3.2 for the decline of coffee income between 1822 and 1828). At the same time, the British cotton industry began to export large quantities of their products to Indonesia, undermining the (return of) Dutch trade with the colony. This 'cotton invasion', which occurred in other parts of Asia such as China and India as well, meant the end of centuries-old structure of international trade in which 'the West' had mainly exported bullion (silver) to the east, in return for the export commodities of the region. From the 1820s onwards, first Great Britain, soon followed by other countries, began to export large quantities of industrial goods to the east, as a result of which the flow of silver to that region discontinued (China, for example, began to export silver from the 1820s onwards). The immediate effect of the British 'cotton invasion' of the 1820s on the colonial economy in Java was that it undermined the recently re-acquired position of the Dutch on the Javanese market. By 1824 Van der Capellen was forced to introduce new protectionist measures to safeguard this position, and to create a more or less protected market for cotton fabrics from the Low Countries there.

What ultimately led to the demise of the liberal economic policies – and caused an enormous increase in the colonial deficit – was the Java War of 1825–1830. A large-scale rebellion against Dutch rule broke out in 1825, caused by the growing tensions between the colonial state and the indigenous elites of Java (and in particular of Mataram). It had a number of causes, but the humiliations suffered by the Javanese elite since the days of Daendels were perhaps most important. The increased exploitation of Javanese peasants by Chinese merchants acting as tax farmers for the colonial state also added to the vehemence of the revolt (of which – as so often – the Chinese minority became the first victims) (Carey 1975). The colonial army narrowly escaped defeat by Diponegoro, the charismatic leader of the rebellion who was closely related to the court in Yogyakarta. The costs of suppressing the revolt were massive and led, in combination with a decline of tax revenue due to the civil unrest, to an alarming growth of the budget deficit (which increased to about 10 million guilders in 1829, or about one-third of total expenditure). The first impulse by Willem I, the Dutch King, was to cut the ordinary budget dramatically. In particular all kinds of 'modernizing' expenditures (on infrastructure, agriculture, etc.), which had been quite important during the first ten years of the new regime, were reduced drastically. In this way some of the more progressive ideals of Van der Capellen were sacrificed. Expenditure on infrastructure, for example, was cut by more than a third between 1823 and 1828. Apparently, the attempts to reform Java in a liberal manner had failed, due to the unfavourable development of coffee prices, the lack of cooperation from the indigenous elites and the lack of response from the peasantry, who perhaps even saw their possibilities for increasing cash crop production as being reduced by the newly introduced 'oppressive' taxation. The liberal regimes of 1808–1826 had been unable to solve the two problems inherited from the VOC. They had tried to create a purely 'public' state, but this was a risky and expensive experiment. Risky because it had estranged the indigenous elite, who were not prepared to be 'degraded' to Weberian bureaucrats. Expensive because the alternative – to hire Dutch administrators – was indeed costly, and the Javanese economy was unable to carry these costs in a way that would not harm its further development. The first liberal – perhaps even 'developmental' – experiment had failed. A new approach was necessary.

4   The Cultivation System, 1830–1870

The contours of a colonial drama

A new economic approach was formulated by the high-ranking civil servant Johannes van den Bosch. In a memo that was submitted to King Willem I in 1829, he argued that because of its distant location, the resulting high transportation costs and the relatively high costs of producing coffee and sugar in Java, the island could not compete with other (Caribbean) colonies on European markets. Moreover, Javanese peasants, because of the richness of their soils and the high yields of rice cultivation, could produce their own subsistence in only a fraction of their labour time; in fact, he assumed that 120 days of labour were sufficient for the feeding of a family (Van den Bosch 1829: 304). The high productivity of rice cultivation also meant that the incentive to switch to coffee or sugar was absent; in modern terminology, peasants had a high leisure preference (Van den Bosch 1829: 305, 13).[1] The only way to stimulate export agriculture was to use the 'surplus' labour time of the peasants and coerce them to grow the crops that were demanded by European markets. This, of course, had been the traditional system of export agriculture adopted by the VOC in Priangan, among other regions.[2]

Although one can doubt the reliability of many of the statistics he used, his analysis seemed to explain why European capital and entrepreneurship were unable to develop the island (an option put forward by some reformers of the 1820s), and why at the same time, the Javanese peasants were unwilling to expand market production of cash crops.[3] Most importantly, he convinced the King, who appointed him Governor-General in 1830, that such a switch in policy was necessary. Over the next few years Van den Bosch introduced the new system he had envisaged, now (in)famously known as the Cultivation System.

The Cultivation System – its origins, functioning and the long-term impact it had on the Javanese economy and society – is one of the classic topics of the (economic) history of Java. It was an unique experiment in socio-economic 'engineering'; one can even argue that the colonial state successfully transformed the economy in a way that resembles the centrally planned economies of the twentieth century, and that the experiment ultimately 'failed' for exactly the same reasons as centrally planned economies failed to overtake the market economies in that century. Initially, however, the system worked rather well; it realized the aims of the policymakers beyond their own expectations. The early 1830s were a major turning point in export production. Exports of sugar and coffee (and indigo) went up dramatically: coffee output rose from 20,000 tonnes in 1829 to 64,000 tonnes in 1839, and sugar output from 6,700 tonnes in 1831 to 58,000 tonnes in 1840. The mechanism behind this success was that the central government allocated targets to the different residencies for the cultivation of coffee (or for the planting of new coffee trees), sugar and indigo (and a few less important crops), which were translated into targets per district and per village. Prices hardly played a role at all. Van den Bosch had already shown that export production could not take place at competitive world market prices, so the price mechanism was largely discarded. He expected, for example, quite a lot from the cultivation of indigo, in spite of the fact that peasants and administrators lacked experience with the crop, expertise about its processing was minimal, and nobody knew what the long-term consequences of growing indigo on *sawahs* were for the agricultural system and the fertility of the land. The same applied to sugar, which was also introduced in regions in which no expertise with this crop existed and where the soil was not particularly suited for growing sugar cane (although nobody knew this yet). Peasants received a certain reward for planting the new crops – the *plantloon* – that they could use to pay the land rent. They also had to supply labour services to bring the crops to the warehouses of the state, for the construction of new roads to solve infrastructural constraints, for the processing of the sugar crop in the sugar factories, etc. Monetary compensations for these labour services were extremely low (see, for example, Elson 1994 and Fasseur 1975).

Transporting the cash crops to the coast was one of the labour duties demanded from the peasantry. They were stored in warehouses there, and then transferred to the Netherlands by the *Nederlandsche Handel-Maatschppij*, a trading company set up by Willem I in 1824, which acquired the monopoly on the trade in products produced under the Cultivation System. There they were auctioned in the Netherlands with the net proceeds cashed in by the Dutch state, which in return exported large amounts of cash (*doits*) to finance the system. The net result – the difference between the net proceeds of the auctions and the costs incurred by the Dutch government – was the (in)famous 'batig slot', the surplus on the colonial budget that was transferred to the Netherlands in this way. As we will see shortly, this net surplus grew enormously during the 1830s, and became a very large part of the income of the Dutch state during the period from 1830–1870.

The initial success was the result of a number of factors. First, the colonial state recruited the cooperation of local and regional elites (village heads and 'higher' members of the *priyayi* class) by incorporating them into the system. These elites became intermediaries in the 'new' lines of communication, which again strengthened their position. Moreover, some of their former privileges were restored. An important issue was, for example, the hereditary nature of their positions. Whereas Daendels, in his drive to create a Weberian bureaucracy, had abolished this practice, making appointments that (in theory) were dependent on individual capabilities rather than inheritance, this privilege was now restored. Similarly, claims by the elites to a share of the (produce of the) *sawahs* were acknowledged (Sutherland 1979: 12). This was a radical departure from the policies that had been pursued between 1808 and 1826, which had been directed at loosening the grip of the *priyayi* on the peasant population, and disentangling the public sphere from the private interests of the indigenous elite. Moreover, local elites received a share of the proceeds of the export crops (*kultuurprocenten*), which gave them a strong incentive to cooperate with the new policies. In the regions where the Cultivation System was most successful, *regenten* became extremely rich and powerful as a result. The Dutch civil servants also received a share of these *kultuurprocenten*, which again constituted a break with the policies since 1808 aimed at creating an independent bureaucracy; in this respect, the two structures of social control converged as well. Consequently, tensions between the colonial state and the indigenous elites resulting from the 'modernization from above' between 1808 and 1826 disappeared; the state again became some kind of mix between the private and public.

Not only local elites were incorporated into the new system. Chinese merchants also played a large role, in particular in sugar processing, where they supplied much of the new entrepreneurship and expertise for the first phase of expansion. Again, the first contracts concluded between the colonial state and these Chinese sugar entrepreneurs almost completely ignored the market: the state gave them credit to establish new factories, coerced labour from surrounding villages, guaranteed that peasants would grow sugar cane on (the best) fields close to the factory, and made sure that the sugar would be bought by the colonial state for a guaranteed price (Fasseur 1975: 65). Once it became clear how profitable these contracts were, European merchants also became involved with the sugar industry, and used their political leverage to acquire similar advantageous conditions.

The initial success of the Cultivation System can therefore to some extent be explained by the fact that it reconciled the interests of the three (commercial and political) elites of the island – the colonial state/bureaucracy, the Javanese elite and the Chinese merchants. This reconciliation went even deeper: the separate identity and structure of the indigenous elite, which had not been acknowledged by the reformers between 1808 and 1826 (when it was attempted, unsuccessfully, to turn them into modern administrators), now became part of the formal structure of the administration of the island. In fact, the new structure that arose meant that two separate 'bureaucracies' co-existed: the formal administration by Dutch-born civil servants, and the 'indigenous' socio-political structures of Javanese society (with their emphasis, for example, on gift-giving, patron–client relationships, the importance of kinship and family, etc.). The highest Dutch administrator in a certain residency was considered to be the 'youngest brother' (i.e. his intimate advisor) of the local regent, acknowledging both the particular sphere of influence of the latter, and the important advisory role that had to be played by the former. This merger of two separate and in theory quite different systems of social control became one of the particular features of Javanese society during the nineteenth century. It helps to explain the remarkable stability of the colony after the violent Java War, but it also became a source of tensions between ambitious civil servants of the Weberian type (who took the 'developmental' part of their role seriously) and members of the *priyayi* class who stuck to their privileges.[4]

It is therefore clear why the Javanese elites and Chinese merchants cooperated with the new system, but why did the peasants give up their leisure and do all the hard work? Labour services were traditionally part of the institutions underpinning the state, and the degree to which they had been levied had been subject to the switching power balances in pre-colonial society. Labour services had, for example, always been more intense close to the centres of 'feudal' control – near the palace cities of Yogyakarta and Surakarta – than at a greater distance from these centres. After 1830, as the colonial state emerged as the only locus of power after defeating the last remnants of opposition in the Java War, it was in a way 'logical' that this strong state imposed its will on the population by demanding increased labour services. In sum, the colonial state acted as previous rulers would have done. An additional and perhaps even more important reason why the system functioned well initially was that the government was spending large amounts of money – mainly *plantloon* – in return for the export crops, giving peasants some kind of incentive to perform their labour services. Because of the gradual and partial commercialization of the island that had begun during the 1820s, now helped by the imposition of colonial rule on almost the whole island, there existed a large, unsatisfied demand for small copper coins, or *doits*, for small exchange on the island. By applying new industrial techniques in the Netherlands, the colonial authorities managed to produce huge amounts of cheap *doits* that could be used to pay the *plantloon*. The circulation of money increased sharply, probably lessening monetary constraints in the countryside, which had always been short of cash (Elson 1994: 261–264). At the same time labour demands on peasant households dramatically increased due to the forced cultivation of the new crops and the extension and intensification of labour services. Part of the money they received was used to buy cheap cotton textiles, which were brought to the island in increasingly large quantities and at rapidly falling prices, which were lower than those of home-produced textiles. As will be described in more detail below, the Javanese textile industry, which was still thriving during the early 1830s, suddenly contracted due to this 'import invasion' and the increased demand for labour from export agriculture (Elson 1994: 272).

The short- and long-term consequences of the Cultivation System are still the subject much debate (see Elson 1994: 301–322; Booth 1998: 93–95). There is no doubt that export production went up enormously, but the question is at what cost. Moreover, the 'prosperity' of the 1830s was followed by the famines of the 1840s; part of the debate concerns the question of whether there was a link between these two developments.

In order to analyse these issues, let us first look at the growth record (Table 4.1). A few studies have assumed that GDP per capita increased during the years

Table 4.1 The estimates of the development of real GDP, population, GDP per capita and the GDP deflator, 1815–1939 (average annual growth rates)

	GDP (%)	Population (%)	GDP per capita (%)	GDP deflator (%)
1815–1830	2.5	2.3	0.2	−0.8
1830–1840	2.1	1.3	0.7	1.3
1840–1860	0.9	1.3	−0.4	0.4
1860–1880	1.8	1.6	0.2	0.8
1880–1900	2.3	1.3	1.0	−2.3
1900–1913	3.7	1.1	2.5	1.0
1913–1921	0.8	0.8	0.0	8.1
1921–1929	3.3	1.0	2.3	−3.8
1929–1939	0.9	1.2	−0.3	−5.3

Source: van Zanden 2002.

of the Cultivation System, arguing basically that the enormous growth of export earnings from cash crops must have had a favourable impact on economic welfare (Booth 1998: 15–19). For the 1830s this is correct, but for the 1840s and 1850s the picture is much bleaker. Moreover, when we move from GDP per capita to a more appropriate measure of welfare, e.g. consumption per capita, it should also be taken into account that the level of investment during the Cultivation System went up substantially as well, and that a large share of its proceeds were skimmed off by the Dutch state.

The detailed study of the development of GDP and its components on which this book is based results in a rather different picture of what happened to income and output. First we will look at the level of colonial exploitation made possible by the system. Two sets of estimates of the size of this colonial drain are presented in Figure 4.1: the net transfers are the sums transferred to the Netherlands (according to the accounts of the Dutch government). The trade surplus, the difference between the value of exports and of imports of Java, is another proxy of the same phenomenon (the difference being approximately the net income the Netherlands received from the colony).

The estimates of 'net transfers' probably underestimate the true drain on the colony, whereas the gap between exports and imports is perhaps an exaggeration of its size.[5] In combination they show a dramatic degree of colonial exploitation, growing from close to zero in the 1820s to perhaps as much as 8 to 10 per cent of Javanese GDP in the 1850s. Even if one prefers the lower bound estimates of net transfers, they still amount to about 6 per cent of Javanese GDP during the thirty years between 1835 and 1865. Net transfers show a decline as a result of gradual reforms during the 1860s and 1870s (about which more below); the trade surplus continues to hover around 8 per cent of Javanese GDP. In terms of GDP of the Netherlands, the figures are also quite impressive. During the 1850s, when the system functioned most efficiently, the 'batig slot' contributed on average 3.8 per cent to Dutch GDP annually, and the income from Java contributed more than one-third of the budget of the Dutch state (van Zanden and Van Riel 2000:

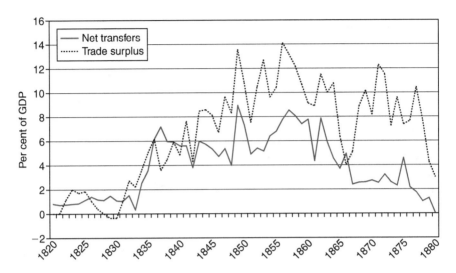

Figure 4.1 Two estimates of the colonial drain, 1820–1880 (as a percentage of the GDP of Java) (sources: Creutzberg and Boomgaard 1975–1996, Vol. 2 (*Public Finance*) and Vol. 7 (*Balance of Payments*); GDP estimates from van Zanden 2002).

223). It would be difficult to find a similar, extremely 'successful' example of colonial exploitation.

The story of economic growth is different. GDP grew rather rapidly during the 1830s, resulting in a modest increase in GDP per capita (Table 4.1). But this growth spurt was followed by stagnation during the 1840s (in particular between 1842 and 1854), when GDP per capita fell by almost 10 per cent. Bad harvests in the mid-1840s and again in 1849/1850 were part of the story, but the reasons for the deceleration of growth in this decade were much more complex. Consumption per capita fell even more in those years (Figure 4.2), because the colonial drain continued to increase, and investments as a share of GDP were much higher than before 1830. The Cultivation System led to a 'big spurt' in investment, mainly consisting of increased labour services that were invested in transport infrastructure, water management and the planting of cash crops (such as coffee trees), but also resulting from increased investment in imported machines and transport equipment (Figure 4.3). As a result, the investment ratio increased from about 5–6 per cent of GDP during the 1820s to 8–10 per cent in the 1830s and early 1840s – a level that in literature on the Industrial Revolution in Western Europe has sometimes been identified as a crucial threshold for 'sustained economic growth' (Rostow 1960). After the early 1840s it fell back to 5 per cent again, however.

Modest growth in combination with a big increase in investment (and capital stock) points to stagnating total factor productivity growth. As we have already seen in Chapter 2, total factor productivity declined almost continually during

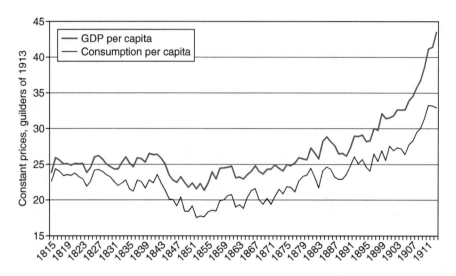

Figure 4.2 GDP per capita and consumption per capita, 1815–1913 (in prices of 1913) (source: van Zanden 2002).

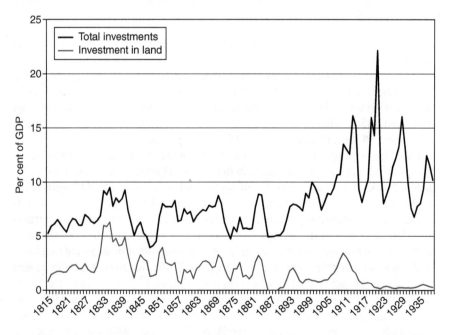

Figure 4.3 Total investments in land as a percentage of GDP, 1815–1939 (source: van Zanden 2002).

the 1830s and 1840s. Moreover, there are reasons to believe that this still under-estimates the decline. It was assumed that labour input per capita did not increase, but this is very unlikely. The rationale of the Cultivation System was to increase the labour input of the peasantry. Boomgaard (1987) presents tentative estimates of the increase of labour input per capita during the first phase of the Cultivation System. This implies that total factor productivity must have fallen even more, and fell sharply during the 1830s and 1840s – probably even in those years that are generally seen as having been rather successful and prosperous (the 1830s). This points to a strong increase of inefficiency in the new export sector created in these years, the result of the misallocation of resources on a vast scale. This is exactly what civil servants who began to criticize the system in the 1840s argued: the cultivation of indigo, for example, did not produce net profits to the state, needed extremely large amounts of labour and had negative consequences for the fertility of the soil. Similarly, the first generations of sugar contracts were so poorly designed that very inefficient forms of sugar cultivation and processing in regions that were unsuitable for this crop occurred. The avail-ability of cheap corvée labour also meant that much labour was wasted (Fasseur 1975). In sum, this 'planned' economy – as with others that would follow during the twentieth century – lacked the incentives to be efficient; capital, land and labour were squandered on a large scale, ultimately at the expense of the Javanese.

What happened from the late 1840s onwards was that these criticisms led to certain adaptations and reforms, to allow price signals to do their work to enhance efficiency. The ultimate goal was to increase the net benefits to the state because colonial administrators acknowledged that the system was not sustain-able in its initial 'crude' form (Fasseur 1975: 43). These gradual reforms were also stimulated by changes in the political situation in the Netherlands, where liberal reformers took over the state – most decisively in 1848 – and voices that pleaded for reform of the Cultivation System entered the political arena.

Initially, then, by infusing a lot of cash into the economy during the 1830s, the Cultivation System may have had some favourable effects on the living standards of the Javanese population (Elson 1994: 307), but arguably at the expense of a reasonable trade-off between income and leisure, since they were forced to work harder in return for the cash they received. But the tables turned after about 1840. A number of developments explain this change. After the long boom of the second half of the 1830s, the early 1840s were a turning point in the international business cycle, characterized by overstocking (of textiles, for instance), depressed prices for export commodities, and a general lack of demand.

To the problems of a downturn in the international business cycle should be added the fact that the monetary policies of the colonial state resulted in a break-down of the monetary system of the colony (Van Laanen 1980; De Bree 1928). During the 1830s large amounts of *doits* had been used to finance the new system, but the colonial government, believing that the demand for *doits* was extremely elastic, continued to issue these small coins even after their relative price was going down (whereas silver coins – following Gresham's insights – had almost disappeared from circulation). In the early 1840s they became convinced that this course of action led to monetary chaos, which led to renewed attempts to cut spending on the island and to increase the return flow of money into the colonial treasury by increasing the land rent (van Zanden 2007). Figure 4.4 brings together two indices of the monetary flows between the state and the Javanese population: one is the increase in the circulation of *doits*, the other the difference between the *plantloon* paid out and the land rent received by the treasury. They both show that much new money was pumped into the Javanese economy during the 1830s, but that this changed radically in the 1840s. It is therefore no coincidence that the two troughs in the latter series coincide with the two major famines that occurred in parts of Java in these years (in 1844/1846 and 1849/1850), when the money supply contracted.[6] Detailed case-studies of those famines show that the lack of purchasing power ('entitlements') was probably the most important cause of both of them (see Elson 1985; Hugenholtz 1986). The contraction of the money supply was ultimately linked to the growing inefficiency of Java's economy in those years, evident from the estimates of total factor productivity. After generating moderate but non-sustainable growth in the 1830s, the system led to the economic (and demographic) setbacks of the 1840s.[7]

Thus far, we have noticed certain similarities between this attempt at restructuring the Javanese economy through some kind of central planning by the colonial state – making use of 'feudal' means of coercion and surplus extraction – and

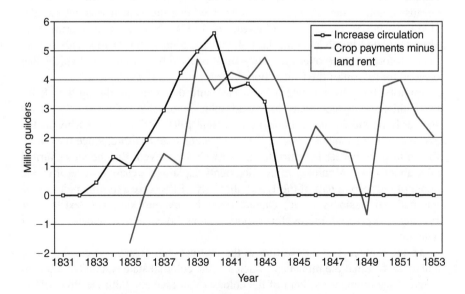

Figure 4.4 The increase in the circulation of copper coins and the balance of crop payments minus land rent in Java (in million guilders) (source: Creutzberg and Boomgaard 1975–1996, Vol. 6, Table 1; Vol. 14, Table A21).

twentieth-century examples of central planning, which often also show a combination of initial 'success' (due to the increased use of labour – also frequently coerced) and long-term problems, the results of the inefficiencies of such a system. Colonial policy, after recognizing these problems during the 1840s and 1850s, was able to adapt rather well, at the same time even increasing the size of the 'batig slot' that was channelled to the Netherlands. During the late 1840s and the 1850s the reforms were directed at streamlining the Cultivation System and at improving the functioning of markets. Examples include:

- the abolishment of the most inefficient cultures, in particular indigo, and the streamlining of the contracts with sugar factories (in order to bring their profits down to more normal levels, and increase the share of the state);
- the abolishment in 1851 of the *pasarpacht*, a tax on local markets that hindered local trade (a direct response to the harvest failures that had occurred in the previous years);
- the reform of the monetary system, involving, among other reforms, the introduction of new (small) silver coins and the intimate linking of the Dutch Indies guilder to the Dutch guilder, which stabilized the currency;
- the increase of the part of the export crops that were sold in Java itself and the re-establishing of markets in these products, resulting in the re-introduction of price signals.

An important discussion among colonial experts concerned the impact that the Cultivation System had on labour markets and the productivity of labour. As mentioned already, before 1830 there had been a small, 'free' labour market, which had nevertheless been embedded in the 'feudal' features of Javanese society; most free wage labourers were probably young men (*budjang*), obliged by village elders to perform these services for the colonial state. Under the Cultivation System the demand for labour had grown very strongly, but free wage labour by Javanese had all but disappeared (of course, Chinese and European immigrants continued to work for wages on some scale). Because of the heavy labour services demanded from households, the supply dried up, and the colonial state had converted wage labour into bonded labour because the latter was considered to be cheaper. When attempts were made, after a few decades almost entirely devoid of any free wage labour, to reintroduce it again, the extreme scarcity of it had resulted in a strong increase in wage levels; for 'coolies' – unskilled labourers – daily wages went up from 2–3 stivers in the 1820s to 4–5 stivers in the early 1850s (see Figure 4.5). This, of course, meant that a return to free wage labour was less attractive. On the other hand, liberal reformers realized that coerced labour was much less productive than free labour. In a well-known experiment carried out in Surabaya in 1849 – referred to repeatedly in the liberal colonial literature – the productivity and costs of using free wage labourers and corvée labourers were compared by the colonial authorities. It concerned the construction of defence works, which had typically, since 1832, been carried out by bonded coolies ('verplichte koelies') at a cost of 20 *duiten* per day (including

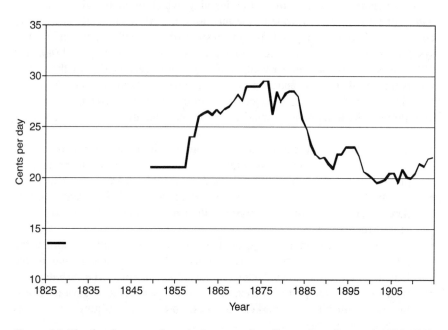

Figure 4.5 The development of nominal wages of coolies on Java (in cents) 1825–1913
(sources: Dros 1992; van Zanden 2003: 12–13).

travel costs, as they were recruited at some distance from the city). Free wage
labourers were available for 30 *duiten* per day, but because they 'worked with
much more pleasure' their productivity was much higher and the hiring of free
coolies meant a net saving of 65 per cent (this would, however, imply that their
labour productivity was about four times as high as that of bonded labourers,
which is probably exaggerated). But the conclusion from this experiment was
that, wherever they were available, the government should switch to the use of
free wage labourers again (*Koloniaal Verslag* 1849; De Waal 1865: 287). Initially this went very well and the number of free labourers increased rapidly, but
in the second half of the 1850s and during much of the 1860s free wage labour
was scarce again and wages tended to go up again (see Figure 4.5) (De Waal
1865: 287). The availability of free wage labourers in 1849–1853 may have been
a side-effect of the harvest failures and the famines that struck Java between
1844 and 1851 (Elson 1994: 100–108), and the recovery of agriculture after the
mid-1850s may initially have caused a relative decline in its supply. The long-
term effect of the Cultivation System was that it increased the scarcity of labour
and drove up nominal wages substantially.

Behind the curtains: rice markets and capital markets in nineteenth-century Java

Why did Javanese peasants not react to the new challenges of the first decades of the nineteenth century – to processes of colonial state formation and gradual commercialization – by increasing marketed output and creating a solid economic and financial basis for the newly emerging state? We argue that the lack of response is related to the quality of the institutions of pre-colonial and colonial Java. The neo-institutional approach developed by Douglass North and others maintains that the quality of the institutional framework determines the pace and the character of the process of economic development. If property rights are well protected and transaction costs are low, then markets can function efficiently, making processes of commercialization and specialization possible (North 1981, 1990). By contrast, when property rights are not well protected and institutions for market exchange are poorly developed, resulting in high transaction costs, one would expect peasants to try to keep the market 'at an arm's length', to concentrate on subsistence production and not to favour a higher degree of market production.

One of the problems of explaining long-term economic development in this way is that it is difficult to measure the quality of the institutional framework and the efficiency of markets systematically. One of the obvious reasons for this is that the institutional settings of a particular region constitute a complex phenomenon, related to property rights of labour, land and capital; government policies – in this case the political economy of the colonial state; and the efficiency of the marketing system. The literature suggests, however, a few ways to distinguish efficient from inefficient institutions and identify situations of 'institutional failure'. The bottom line of the neo-institutional approach is that institutions were important because they affected the functioning of markets; therefore, their failure should be apparent from the way in which markets worked in practice. In recent studies the point has been made that the efficiency of capital markets can be measured by the (real) interest rate: the lower it is, the greater the trust that the debtor will honour his obligations appears to be. This measure makes it possible to chart the growing efficiency of European capital markets during the early modern period (Epstein 2000: 18–24, 61–63), or to identify institutional changes – those following the Glorious Revolution of 1688, for example – that resulted in significant improvement in the efficiency of capital markets (North and Weingast 1989: 803–832).

In this chapter we take a slightly different look at this problem and focus first on the seasonal variation in the prices of the most important agricultural commodity, rice, as a proxy for the degree of efficiency of the marketing system – an approach that we already briefly introduced in Chapter 2. The fundamental importance of these markets for less-developed and largely agricultural economies is obvious: the degree to which peasants will be stimulated to increase output and market surpluses will be closely related to the functioning of the markets for their staple products. If those markets are characterized by great uncertainties, such as dramatic fluctuations in prices, it will be difficult for peasants to predict the market prices of the extra output they plan to produce, or to discover trends in absolute and relative prices that should guide them into the diversification of their activities or the development of new systems of cultivation (for example, hiring additional labour or buying manure in order to increase output). The market in such cases produces random 'noise', and the prices peasants receive for their products may appear to them to be just a matter of chance. Large, unpredictable variations in prices may therefore have a similar effect to hyperinflation: the market does not produce the appropriate information for economic decision making, and a strategy focusing on subsistence or on barter may be optimal. The net result may be under-investment (because the returns on investment are unpredictable) or investment in unprofitable activities.[8]

We first focus on one aspect of the variability of those prices, seasonal fluctuations, in order to get some grip on peasant economic behaviour. The obvious reason for the existence of seasonal variation is that harvests are concentrated in time; the increase of prices some time after the harvest is a necessary compensation for the costs of storing the crops. These storage costs consisted of the actual costs of storing the commodity, the losses that occur during storage and the interest of the capital that is invested in it. McCloskey and Nash showed in 1984 that the monthly increase of grain prices after harvest should be identical to the sum of those costs, and used this to estimate the interest rate in English agriculture during the thirteenth and fourteenth centuries (McCloskey and Nash 1984: 174–187). More recently Nick Poynder argued on the basis of independent evidence concerning interest rates on the English countryside during the period 1250–1400 that this identity may not hold. He demonstrated that the monthly increase in grain prices after the harvest was substantially larger than the sum of storage and interest costs (Poynder 1999). As we will argue here, when the assumption of a well-integrated capital market is lifted, the link between interest rates and seasonal variation becomes more complex and a broad range of seasonal variations in prices can be identified, within which actual price fluctuations will move.

One of the strong points of the McCloskey/Nash approach is its focus on the link between the capital market and the grain market. They conceptualize this link as a one-way causality: the level of the interest rate causes a certain level of seasonal variation. Recent literature on rural markets in 'developing' countries suggests that those links may be much more complex; the concept of 'interlinkage' has been coined to analyse this. 'An interlinked transaction is one in which two parties trade in at least two markets on the condition that the terms of all such trades are jointly determined' (Bell 1988: 773–830). Development economists have mainly applied this concept to the interrelationships between land and credit markets – to situations in which the landowner is also the source of capital for the peasant who leases his land. The conclusion from much of this research is that, on the one hand, interlinkage may be efficient if it reduces transactions costs, because two transactions are combined in one deal (Stiglitz 1988: 93–160). On the other hand, it may also create additional opportunities to exploit the strong bargaining position of the landowner vis-à-vis the peasant (Braverman and Srinivasan 1984: 63–81). Moreover, it can be argued that interlinkage leads to loss of information on market prices because two transactions are concluded in one deal. What follows evaluates the interlinkage between the rice market and the credit market, which means that the current literature on the linkages between land and capital markets is of limited relevance. The root cause of interlinkage is the same in both cases, however: the fragmentation of the capital market and the limited access of peasants to credit. It will be argued that market systems that are characterized by these patterns – extreme seasonal fluctuations in connection with the interlinking of crop and capital markets – probably do not produce the right incentives for market exchange.

The marketing system of Java was relatively underdeveloped. The system of weights and measures was fragmented, for example. For rice different kinds of measures were used. The weight of the most important one in wholesale trade, the *koyang* of about 1,800 kg, varied between different market towns.[9] As far as European measures were in use, they were those from before the introduction of the metric system; for example, Amsterdam pounds of 495 grams, or Rhineland rods (Korthals Altes 1994: 117). In short, the state failed to bring unity into the system of weights and measures. As we have already seen, the money supply was chaotic too, further contributing to the unpredictability of markets. Other weaknesses of the marketing system were the fact that transport costs were relatively high because of the underdeveloped nature of the infrastructure, and that at markets, city gates and bridges, taxes were levied on products that were brought to the marketplace (and sometimes, illegally, also on people moving to the town). These taxes were almost always farmed out to Chinese merchants who, according to Dutch (liberal) authors, used their position to squeeze the peasantry who came to town to sell their products. The most burdensome of these taxes was abolished in the early 1850s (De Waal 1865: 303–314; Vitalis 1851; Diehl 1993). The rice market was almost completely controlled by Chinese traders – a topic to which we will return – who in some regions had strong ties with the local elite; the *priyayi* used these ties to monetize their part of the rice harvest (Elson 1985, 1994: 257). As a result, peasants were in a vulnerable, dependent position. At the marketplace they were confronted with Chinese merchants who were backed up by the local elite and who controlled access to the market through the tollgates and other tax farms (Chinese middlemen also dominated the sale of opium). In some regions the control of the Chinese merchants on the land was even greater: in the surroundings of Batavia they rented large private estates, in which sugar and rice were grown as export crops (Boomgaard 1986a: 33–58). In other parts of the northern coast, the *Pasisir*, they acquired – through their relationships with the local elite, with whom they sometimes intermarried – access to a substantial share of the land that was claimed by this elite (Elson 1985). They were also active as moneylenders, both as the official tax farmers of the government system of pawnshops and as private intermediaries, and in this role the Chinese merchants had an important influence on the rice market as well.

The demand for rice came from the towns. As we have already seen, the urbanization ratio was relatively low, however, and appears to have declined during the nineteenth century (Boomgaard 1987: 159). Exports were another source of demand for rice; their importance increased somewhat during this period (from less than 1 per cent of net output to about 3 per cent in the mid-1850s). During the eighteenth century these were mainly destined for other parts of the Indonesian archipelago, but after 1820 exports to the Netherlands became important as well (*Changing Economy in Indonesia*, Vol. 4: Table 6). Transport costs were relatively high, and did not decline because the infrastructure remained more or less the same; the first railways (and telegraph connections) were only constructed during the 1860s. As a result, the market for rice remained rather limited and by far the greater part of the crop was consumed locally (Hugenholtz 1986: 155–188).

What kind of market resulted from these institutions? We can follow the rice market in detail, because from 1823 onwards the *Bataviasche Courant*, the official government gazette and newspaper of the merchant community of Batavia, began to publish market prices of rice (and a number of other consumption goods) on a weekly – sometimes daily – basis; a few years later it also started to publish the same prices for the two other large cities on the north coast of Java, Semarang and Surabaya. This continued until the mid-1850s, after which the number of quotations reduced substantially.

A first look at rice prices in these three market towns does not reveal a long-term trend between the early 1820s and the early 1850s. During most of the period prices fluctuated between 60 and 150 guilders per *koyang* (see Figure 4.6 for the prices of Batavia and Surabaya). There were two notable exceptions, however: during the second half of the 1820s prices were on average relatively low – between 80 and 100 guilders in Semarang and Surabaya, and about 110 guilders in Batavia – and during the second half of the 1840s, when Java was struck by a number of harvest failures (and the currency was very weak), prices moved up to much more than 150 guilders, especially in Semarang and Surabaya (Hugenholtz 1986: 159–161). It is striking that we find only weak traces (in the Semarang series) of the terrible 1849/1850 famine in Demak and Grobogan, which is consistent with the analysis of this famine by Elson, who argues that the lack of purchasing power of peasants was the core of the problem (Elson 1985).

Monthly prices of rice fluctuated strongly in the three market towns. Figure 4.7, which presents the average deviation from the centred 13-months moving average of the three market cities, clearly demonstrates this.[10] The figures show that in 'normal' years seasonal deviations from the trend measured in this way were often as large as minus 20 per cent – directly after the harvest in June/July – to plus 20 per cent in the months before the harvest, during the so called *pacek-lik* (the lean months). A more careful analysis of the average seasonal pattern shows that there were differences between the rice markets in the three cities: the peak in rice prices in Batavia (in February/March) preceded the peak in Semarang (April) and Surabaya (May), and the fluctuations in the latter two

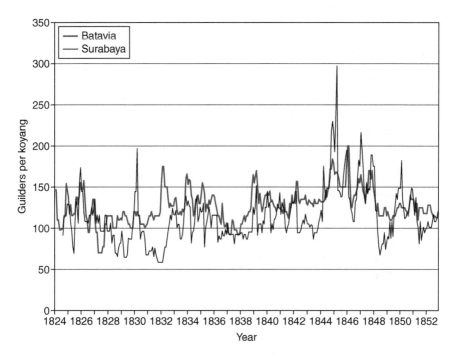

Figure 4.6 Rice prices in Batavia and Surabaya, 1824–1853 (in guilders per koyang) (sources: *Bataviasche Courant*, 1824–1827; *Javasche Courant*, 1828–1853; all prices relate to rice of average ('middle') quality).

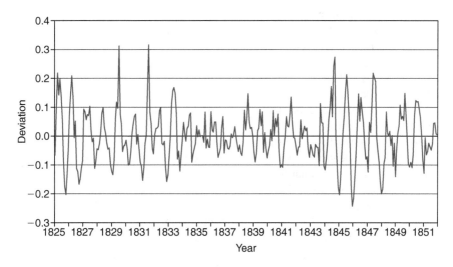

Figure 4.7 The deviation of rice prices from the 13-month moving average (average for three markets) 1825–1852 (source: see Figure 4.6).

cities were even more marked than in Batavia, the bigger market that was probably more integrated into the international trade in rice.

There is evidence that the market prices in the three cities understate the actual seasonal fluctuations in rice prices on the small rural markets where peasants sold most of their rice. In a small booklet on the Javanese rice market published in 1888 – the first significant publication on this issue – H.A. De Groot presents a table of the average rice prices in the countryside of Java, as collected by the civil servants who were involved in the cadastral survey in the late 1870s. These data show an even more pronounced seasonal pattern, in which the prices of *padi* during the *paceklik* (February/March) were more than double the prices directly after the harvest (in June/July) (De Groot 1888: 49). Other, more qualitative evidence points in the same direction. In the 'general survey of the situation of the Netherlands Indies in the year 1846', published in 1848, it is said about the (rather isolated) residency of Priangan that:

> the rice was available at fl 2.10 per picul, until the moment that the demand from neighbouring districts of Buitenzorg and Krawang, and from the residency of Cheribon, resulted in important purchases, as a result of which in the district of Soemedang fl 10 per picul was being paid.
>
> (Anonymous 1848: 7)

These and similar comments made in the 1840s, when the Dutch administrators were paying increased attention to the rice market because of the famines, suggest that the rural market was very thin, and that sudden fluctuations in demand and supply could have a large effect on prices.

In a comparative perspective those seasonal patterns stand out (Figure 4.8). Early modern European grain markets were, for example, characterized by relatively small seasonal variations. Poynder showed that the difference between the highest and the lowest average prices were in general less than 10 per cent (9 per cent for wheat in England in 1400–1539, 5 per cent in Siena in 1550–1699, and 7.1 per cent in Cologne in 1550–1699) (Poynder 1999: 7). Before 1400, seasonal variations were probably larger in Europe; the available data for English grain prices show annual variations which were similar to those found on Java (33.1 per cent for wheat in England between 1260 and 1399, for example). The available studies of some local Chinese rice prices in the eighteenth, nineteenth and first half of the twentieth centuries also indicate clear seasonal fluctuations, which are less strong than those in Java during the second quarter of the nineteenth century.[11]

According to the McCloskey/Nash approach, it can be hypothesized that the increase in price between the immediate after-harvest period and the *paceklik* is identical to the costs of storage plus the interest rate on the capital invested in the rice. The actual costs of storage were probably rather low in the Javanese countryside. Because the Javanese maintained that 'old' rice was superior in quality to the rice of the new harvest, 'old' rice even got a certain premium over the new crop, which (partially) compensated for the minimal losses that might occur.[12] The storage costs merchants incurred were rather low as well. The

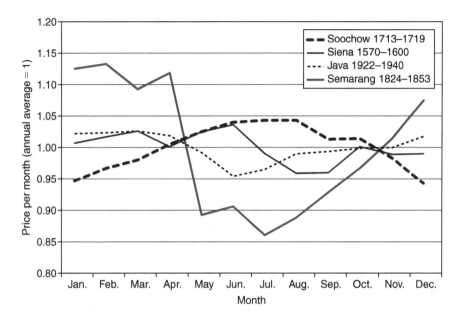

Figure 4.8 Seasonal patterns of prices of rice (on Java and in Soochow) and of wheat (in
Siena); annual average=1 (sources: Semarang 1824–1853: see Figure 4.6;
Java 1922–1940: Creutzberg and Boomgaard 1975–1996, Vol. 4; Soochow:
Chuan and Kraus 1975: 108; Siena: Parenti 1942).

annual costs of warehouses of the government salt monopoly can be estimated at
about fl 850 for a capacity of 1,000 *koyang*, and fl 1,050 for a store double that
size; per *koyang* this would mean less than one guilder per annum, or less than 1
per cent of its value.[13] The monetary expenses of storage costs were therefore
probably less than 1 or 2 per cent of the value of the product, but to this should
be added the costs of loss during storage, which are unknown. Assuming that
these costs were less than 5 per cent, we might infer that, following the McClos-
key/Nash approach, interest rates on the countryside must have been as high as
20 to 30 per cent or more; the 1870s data on small rural markets even suggest
that they may have been as high as 100 per cent. The conceptual problem with
this approach is that it assumes a more or less integrated capital market on which
peasants and merchants could borrow money at similar interest rates. In that case
it makes sense to try to establish 'the' interest rate in the countryside of medieval
England – or in rural Java. But capital markets in 'underdeveloped' countries
were often highly fragmented, and the links between capital markets and markets
for food products were often much more complex than is implied by the McClos-
key/Nash approach. We therefore turn to the concept of interlinkage to analyse
the causes of the extreme fluctuations in rice prices in more detail.

The contemporary literature that may shed some light on the seasonal patterns
in rice prices is extremely thin. Dutch administrators and scholars who studied

different aspects of the Javanese economy in the nineteenth century were much more interested in (the markets of) Javanese exports crops such as coffee and sugar. The first analysis of the rice market by H.A. de Groot (1888), however, not only contains a description of the functioning of the rice market, but also an analysis of its failures.

The first important point that De Groot makes is that the degree of integration of regional markets is very low, or even absent. This is in striking contrast to the markets for export crops, which are well integrated. He gives the example of the two markets linked by the river Brantas: Surabaya, the second biggest city of Java, and Plosso, an important regional market town. The latter town exported large quantities of rice to Surabaya, where De Groot was a civil servant for two and a half years. Transport costs between them were rather low; he estimates them at fl 0.50 per *picul*. In 1885 and 1886 market prices per *picul* in Plosso ranged from fl 3 to fl 4.50, about half the level in Surabaya (fl 6 to fl 8). The difference is sometimes more than 100 per cent of the prices in Plosso, and much larger than transport costs (De Groot 1888: 9). This is clearly in contradiction with the 'law of one price'.

Next, De Groot starts to analyse the actual functioning of the rice market. It is dominated by Chinese merchants, who in the months before the harvest advance money against extremely high interest rates to peasants, when prices are high and rice is in short supply. This 'exploitation' of the Javanese peasantry by the Chinese middlemen is a familiar subject in the writings of Dutch civil servants in this period. An earlier, anonymous paper, published in the authoritative *Tijdschrift voor Nederlandsch-Indie* of 1859,[14] distinguishes four different forms that such a transaction could take. First, peasants might borrow a certain amount of money – say fl 5 – before the harvest in return for repaying a certain quantity of *padi*, representing about fl 7.50, directly after the harvest. Second, peasants could already borrow just after the ploughing of the field, in which case a much higher interest rate would be charged. In a third form the *sawah* of the peasants would be mortgaged, implying that the merchant becomes *de facto* owner, whereas the peasants are allowed to cultivate the land for a certain share (often 50 per cent) of the crop. Finally, the peasant might receive a substantial loan from a middleman, on which he pays part of the crop as interest (the peasant would also in this case become *de facto* leaseholder of 'his' land). The interest rates that can be derived from these examples – and others in the literature – are extremely high: up to 100 per cent or more was considered normal.

These are not isolated complaints about the indebtedness of the peasantry. The literature on this period is full of examples of the capital shortage in the countryside and the fact that Chinese merchants were the sole suppliers of credit there (Elson 1994: 14–15). In fact, in the cities a similar capital shortage existed, and (expensive) credit was also vital for all commercial transactions (Hageman 1859: 137–152). The effect of the indebtedness was that peasants had to sell their crop directly after the harvest to pay their debts, or to hand in the crop to their moneylender. This depressed prices in the months directly after the harvest and made it possible for the merchants – who, according to De Groot, knew each other well – to profit from the abundant supply. After a few months the market was cleared, and prices began to rise. During the second half of the cycle, increasing numbers of peasants, who had spent their money for repaying debts and for necessary expenses, had to turn to merchants again to try to get new loans, either in the form of rice or in money. This led to the sharp increase of prices during the *paceklik* (De Groot 1888: 18).

De Groot's analysis helps to explain the strong seasonal patterns of rice prices. That markets are so poorly integrated is attributed by De Groot to the fact that the Chinese, who monopolized the local rice markets, also dominated the trade between those local markets and the cities, the main importers of the rice. His argument can be translated in the following way: the transaction costs of collecting the rice at the local level are very high; much inside knowledge is required to play the role of local moneylender; and the costs of monitoring the relatively small transactions with the peasants are relatively large. This means that it is almost impossible for outsiders to penetrate this market, and that local traders have a natural monopoly on the rice market thanks to their control of the credit market. Moreover, but this is more contentious, the Chinese have the tendency to work together, and create a virtual monopoly of the sale of rice in the import market. Both features of the rice market – its strong seasonal pattern and the lack of regional integration – are therefore interconnected.

The argument that rural markets 'failed' because Chinese middlemen had local monopolies is present in much of the colonial literature of the period. Among the causes are poorly specified property rights of peasants – often the only collateral that they could offer was their labour, i.e. their ability to produce a certain amount of rice – and the high costs of these transactions relative to the small amounts of money that were involved. To limit problems of adverse selection and moral hazard, peasants-as-debtors had to be screened and monitored carefully. This required detailed inside knowledge of the village, and often also involved cooperation between the moneylender and the village head, and perhaps also members of the higher layers of the rural elite (who had effective means to enforce the contract that was concluded between moneylender and peasant). This cooperation with the local elite could also be costly; the 'exchange' of presents may, for example, have been a normal part of this relationship. The large role that was played by inside knowledge restricted the degree of competition between merchants, and made it difficult and costly for outsiders to penetrate this market. A final and very important point is that the local monopolies of (groups of) Chinese middlemen were also embedded in the political economy of the colonial state. The state restricted access to the countryside for most Chinese traders, because it wanted to protect the peasants against becoming (too) dependent on them. Privileged groups of traders – in particular those who were farming the main taxes in the countryside – were allowed to be active there. In this way the state supported the monopoly of the tax farmers, and limited competition in the countryside. Groups of Chinese (*kongsi*) were therefore fiercely competing for the leasing of these taxes in order to get access to the countryside. In particular the lease of the most important 'tax' of all, on the sale of opium, was the main arena of competition (Rush 1990). In this way some of the surplus acquired by the local middlemen was appropriated by the colonial state.

The literature on interlinkage strongly suggests that fragmentation of the capital market is at the core of this phenomenon. It is, however, quite difficult to study those largely informal capital markets in any detail as they have not left many traces, apart from the articles written by Dutch civil servants on this aspect of rural society. And they may have been biased as reporters, because to some extent the Chinese whom they criticized were a competing elite trying to extract surplus from the Javanese peasantry in ways that were not sympathetic to Dutch administrators. One way to get some grip on the degree of fragmentation of the rural (and urban) credit markets is by analysing a particular institution, the pawn-shop. The colonial government claimed to have a monopoly on all credit trans-actions smaller than 100 guilders against a security (a valuable commodity) as collateral. Already in the eighteenth century the VOC had exploited this mono-poly for the city of Batavia, and from the early 1820s onwards the system of *pandhuizen* spread to the other parts of the island controlled by the colonial administration. This monopoly was leased out to the highest bidder, who was invariably Chinese and who paid increasingly large sums for the privilege. This leased-out monopoly was in fact one of the most 'successful' and rapidly growing taxes of the nineteenth-century colonial state (see Figure 3.1). However, in order to protect the borrower from being extorted by the leaseholder of the *pandhuis*, the pawning was strictly regulated and the interest rates on these loans were bound to a maximum, which varied from 6.5 per cent monthly for loans smaller than one guilder to 3 per cent each month for loans of fl 100. As almost all loans were very small, the average interest rate must have been close to 70 to 80 per cent on an annual basis (De Waal 1865: 337–46; Diehl 1993: 224).

One of the reasons why interest rates are often extremely high in the country-side of an underdeveloped region did not apply to the credit supplied on the basis of a pawn: the transaction costs of these loans were relatively low, because the leaseholder of the *pandhuis* did not have to incur costs in the selection and moni-toring of his clients, and his risks were very small indeed. In fact, one of the most common abuses was that the pawnbroker assessed the value of the pawn much too low, and speculated on the incapacity of the borrower to repay the loan, which made it possible for him to make an extra profit out of the sale of the pawn. It can therefore be argued that the system of pawnshops was a relatively transparent segment of the capital market with low transactions costs; normally one would perhaps expect the interest rate on these loans to be close to the opportunity costs of the Chinese pawnbroker (i.e. the rate at which he had access to capital). This was not the case, however. The financial specialist De Waal, who studied the system of *pandhuizen* in the 1850s, concluded that almost all rules were ignored by the leaseholder of the pawnshop and that interest rates were often much higher than the maximum set by the government (De Waal 1865: 344–346).

One possible reason for the failure of interest rates on pawns to come down was the monopoly claimed by the colonial government and farmed out to the

Chinese middlemen. It was argued in the 1860s that the lack of competition made it possible to keep interest rates high. If this interpretation was correct, the abolishment of the monopoly would bring interest rates down. This reasoning and the detailed report on the excesses of the system of *pandhuizen* by De Waal (1865) contributed to the end of the system in 1870. It was replaced by a system in which each citizen could buy a license (for the rather high sum of fl 50) to run a pawnshop. Their number increased sharply – from about 250 in 1869 to 998 in 1879 – but interest rates, instead of coming down, went up to 10 per cent or more per month (another element of the liberal reforms was to decontrol interest rates) (Diehl 1993: 224; Fernando and Bulbeck 1992: reprint of paper by Fokkens). In 1880 the license system was abolished as abuses had only increased and government revenues had fallen; in its place, the leasing of *pandhuizen* by the colonial government was reintroduced. The new set of rules that was introduced in 1880 was more closely geared to 'the market', which the colonial administrators had seen in action over the previous ten years. Interest rates on loans were more varied than before 1870, and on small loans they increased substantially (to 2.5 per cent per 10 days, or 143 per cent on an annual basis); only the rate on the largest loans (between fl 75 and fl 100) returned to the level that had been the norm before 1870, i.e. 3 per cent monthly. Figure 4.9 presents the new scheme that was introduced in 1880.

The failed experiment to liberalize the pawnshops suggests that the government monopoly itself was not the source of the large profits that were made on this segment of the capital market. The real problem was that the capital market was highly fragmented, and that, because of high transactions costs, interest rates

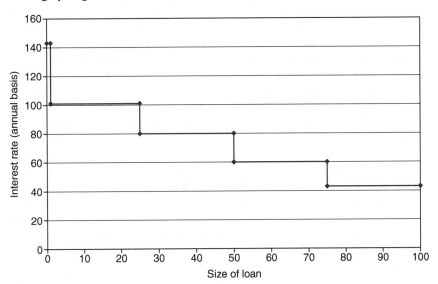

Figure 4.9 Interest rates charged on different sizes of loans (in guilders) according to the 1880 rules for pawnhouses (per cent per annum) (source: *Koloniaal Verslag* 1880: 139).

on the generally small loans on the private market were extremely high. In this particular segment of the capital market the pawnbroker could therefore profit from the large disparity between his capital costs – the Chinese had access to relatively cheap sources of capital – and the very high interest rates on the other segments of the capital market. The profits that could be made in this way were not the result of monopoly, but of the fact that this small segment of the capital market did not have the large transaction costs which drove up interest rates on the rest of the (rural, informal) capital market. The government tried to expropriate this surplus by claiming the monopoly of the *pandhuizen*, which were leased to the Chinese. The sums the pawnbrokers were prepared to pay are therefore an indication of the fragmentation of the capital market, and of the demand for this kind of credit (see their speedy increase in Figure 3.1). Unfortunately we do not know how large the volume of the loans of these *pandhuizen* was, but these sums suggest that the difference between the capital costs of the pawnbroker and the interest rate charged to his customers must have been substantial as well.

The institution of the pawnshops and the way they developed during the nineteenth century therefore provide strong evidence for the existence of a fragmented capital market, in which the peasantry had to pay extremely high interest rates, whereas the Chinese middlemen had access to much cheaper sources of capital. The 1880 rules probably give the best set of estimates of rural interest rates in this period, which varied between 40 per cent on large loans to 143 per cent on tiny ones. In a detailed study of money and credit in Buitenzorg in 1805, Boomgaard found similar interest rates on debts against collateral of land or livestock of 40 or 50 per cent annually (Boomgaard 1986a). It is not clear what the opportunity costs of the capital of Chinese moneylenders were; the literature on the networks of the Chinese does not mention interest rates, because usually members of a *kongsi* pooled resources and shared net profits. The most wealthy and creditworthy merchants had access to Dutch-owned banks, in particular the Javasche Bank, and could borrow money at 6 to 9 per cent (annually), which was probably the absolute floor of the capital market (De Bree 1928, Vol. I: 341, 351; Boomgaard 1986b). It shows how large the spread was between interest rates in the formal, western segment and the informal, rural segment of the capital market.

It has already been pointed out that Figure 4.7 suggests that there were important changes in the degree of seasonal variation during the 1825–1852 period. In the 1830s, when the Cultivation System was introduced, the degree of seasonal variation decreased – another 'proof' of the hypothesis that initially it was rather successful by infusing new money into the economy. But in the 1840s things went wrong, and seasonal variation rose sharply, peaking during the famines of the second half of that decade (after which seasonal fluctuations reduced again).

This softening of the seasonal pattern coincided with two interconnected changes, both related to the introduction of the Cultivation System in the early 1830s. The government issued large amounts of copper coins in those years, which boosted the domestic money supply. Moreover, this money was used as *plantloon* for the peasants who cultivated export crops for the colonial government. During the second half of the 1830s these payments were much larger than the land rent the peasants had to pay, which resulted in sizeable net-transfers of money to the peasantry (see Figure 4.6). In the first years of the Cultivation System there are signs that the grip of the Chinese merchants on the rice-cum-capital market declined, thanks to these injections of new money into the rural economy. To make this point Elson quotes a resident (the highest administrator in a residency) as saying that 'the increasing industry and prosperity among the people has a further consequence that they are now no longer compelled to sell a portion of the *padi* and rice product for any price in order to pay their land rent' (Elson 1994: 260). Thanks to the large amounts of money that began to circulate on the countryside, the 1830s were therefore years of relative prosperity for the peasantry.

As we have already discussed, this changed after 1840 due to a monetary crisis, in combination with a setback of the international economy. The changing effects of the Cultivation System on peasants' standards of living – after increasing purchasing power during the 1830s, the system became increasingly exploitative during the 1840s – is clearly visible in the evidence on seasonal fluctuations in rice prices (Figure 4.7). The decline of the net transfer to the peasantry in the 1840s coincided with the strong increase in seasonal variation during these years. An important implication of this is that the degree of seasonal variation can therefore be interpreted as an index of the degree of stress that peasants had to cope with: the degree to which they were unable to finance their regular expenses and had to turn to middlemen for credit. In times of stress the seasonal patterns increased markedly. In periods when real incomes and the availability of cash went up, seasonal variation went down. The consequence of this was that in times of stress, the terms of trade for peasants went down because they had to sell at lower prices directly after the harvest and buy at higher prices during the *paceklik*; during good years, of course, the opposite happened.

Summing up, we have tried to underpin the argument briefly outlined in Chapter 2 that information on the seasonal variation in prices of basic foodstuffs can be used to analyse the quality of the institutional framework of a peasant economy. It was demonstrated that the extremely large price spread of Javanese rice markets was linked to the dependence of peasants on the credit supplied by Chinese middlemen at rather unfavourable terms, with interest rates ranging from as high as 40 to perhaps 140 per cent on an annual basis. But the information on seasonal variation in rice prices cannot be directly translated into an estimate of 'the' interest rate on the countryside, as McCloskey and Nash have argued, for the simple reason that rural capital markets were highly segmented. Chinese middlemen had access to much cheaper sources of capital (with interest rates as low as 6 to 9 per cent per annum) than the peasants (who had to pay up to 140 per cent annually). The price spread on the rice market could fluctuate in between those two extremes. Moreover, the extent to which prices fluctuated during a given period was probably related to the degree of stress to which the rural economy was exposed; in times of harvest failures and shortages of money, fluctuations were much more extreme than in years of abundance.

One of the core problems of the Javanese rice market was the interlinkage between the market for this product and the credit market. Peasants, who were almost always short of money, had to borrow on the basis of their ability to supply rice after the harvest. Modern intermediation theory argues that for both lender and borrower it is efficient to establish long-term relationships in order to limit problems of adverse selection and moral hazard, which will make it possible to have lower interest rates. The interlinkage of the rice and credit markets implied, however, that the same Chinese middlemen also came to dominate the trade in rice, and were able to acquire local near-monopolies in this product (and in other foodstuffs). Commercialization, therefore, often went hand in hand with a growing dependence on local middlemen. Dutch civil servants, writing about the excesses of this system, saw that this led to the proletarianization of parts of the peasantry; they lost access to the land, and became increasingly dependent on wage labour for European sugar factories and plantations. Interlinkage also meant a loss of information. In this package deal, two transactions were combined into one, which meant that it was unclear what the interest rate and/or what the price of rice in the dual transaction was. The absence of information on prices and interest rates of course hindered the emergence of transparent markets at the local level. Moreover, the market prices that could be quoted were characterized by enormous seasonal fluctuations and probably – in view of the segmented nature of the rice market – a lot of random noise. In large regions of Java civil servants therefore had great difficulty in defining 'the' price of *padi* (which was necessary for the land rent), and reported extremely large margins within which rice prices fluctuated.

The high degree of seasonal variation in rice prices had a number of negative side-effects for the peasants. It resulted in a decline in their terms of trade, as they sold during the period of low prices, and had to buy again during the *paceklik*. Moreover, it drove up the real interest rate paid by those peasants who had an outstanding monetary loan (who received, for example, fl 5 before the harvest and had to pay back fl 7.50 afterwards).

To this combination of institutional failures of the rice-cum-credit market can be added their poor integration, already pointed out by De Groot. As is clear from the example of Plosso's rice market cited by De Groot, the poor integration of rural and urban rice markets meant that peasants received a lower price than they would get in a well-integrated market system and/or that consumers paid much higher prices for rice, keeping down demand. The failures of the rice-cum-capital market therefore strongly depressed incomes of peasants and reduced incentives to produce for the market.

In fact, from the perspective of the peasantry, market production may have seemed to be part of a system to exploit their labour and that of their families, because a greater involvement in the market appeared to result in a greater exploitation by the middlemen, who were able, through their strong control of local markets, to cream off the surplus produced by the peasants. These market failures resulted in weak incentives to increase market production, and stimulated the kind of behaviour that some economists, anthropologists and sociologists have described as being typical for peasants; for example, a strong sense of 'leisure preference' or the wish to keep the market 'at an arm's length' (Wolf 1966). In his classic books and papers on the Indonesian economy, the Dutch economist J.H. Boeke in the first half of the twentieth century developed a theory of dualism, which stressed the 'different' economic behaviour of the Javanese peasants in comparison with the (profit-oriented) Western entrepreneurs (Boeke 1910; 1947).[15] It is beyond the scope of this study to go into this debate on peasant attitudes towards the market in any detail, but the hypothesis may be formulated that the kind of market failures that are analysed here were at the root of the attitudes analysed by Boeke. The 'non-maximizing' or 'social' (in contrast to 'economic') behaviour that in his view was characteristic of Javanese peasants, may have been their rational response to the failures of the institutions of the Javanese market economy.[16]

A final point that can be made concerns a comparison with early modern Europe. The institutional framework for market exchange in nineteenth-century Java was quite different from that of early modern Europe. At first glance there appear to be some similarities, because in large parts of Europe markets were also thin and external demand for basic foodstuffs was relatively small as well. But property rights were probably much better defined in Western Europe than on Java, and dependence on middlemen appears to have been much smaller in the West. Moreover, in large parts of Europe interest rates were much lower than on Java. Clark estimated, for example, that interest rates in the English countryside declined from about 10 per cent before the 1350s to 5 per cent at about 1400, and Epstein found a similar decline of interest rates for other parts of Europe in the 1350–1550 period (Clark 1988: 265–94; Epstein 2000: 61–63). The seasonal variations in grain and rice prices tell a similar story (McCloskey and Nash 1984; Poynder 1999). Therefore, on the basis of these criteria, the preconditions for economic development were probably much more favourable in early modern Western Europe than in nineteenth-century Java.

Conclusion

In Chapter 2 we saw that the period 1830–1870 was a difficult one for the Javanese economy, because growth was slow – no catching up occurred – and total factor productivity even declined in this period. There are basically two reasons for this rather poor performance. First, institutions for market exchange were not well developed. Interest rates were extremely high, the market for rice and by implication for agricultural products as well, was quite instable, poorly integrated and in general not functioning well, as a result of which peasants – the vast majority of the population – did not have strong incentives to increase their marketed output. These relatively inefficient 'horizontal' economic institutions were, moreover, embedded in equally problematic 'vertical' or socio-political institutions. In theory, the power of indigenous rulers was almost unlimited; they could claim part of the labour and the produce of the peasantry, because well-developed 'constraints on the executive' limiting their power base did not exist.

Property rights were, in general, not well protected, although the *de facto* power of the indigenous rulers was of course much more limited than their *de jure* claims. The problem with the rise of the power of the VOC, and its transition into a colonial state, was that the imported European power structures – bureaucracies, underpinned by modern armies – were much more efficient than the indigenous means of control. The VOC, and in particular its successor, the colonial administration, were therefore much better equipped to transform these almost unlimited claims to power into real control over people, land and funds. The Cultivation System, emerging after a failed attempt to govern the colony in a more liberal way, was the most remarkable result of this process. It was a 'top-down' attempt at structural transformation of the colonial economy, almost anticipating modern forms of planning that emerged in the twentieth century, in which the state via a complex mix of coercion and monetary incentives managed to increase the export production of the colony in a dramatic way. It is arguably the most extreme example of the kind of 'extractive institutions' that have, according to Acemoglu *et al.* (2001), been introduced in non-settler colonies, to profit from the resources available there. And profit the Dutch did: we presented estimates of the extremely high shares of income that were transferred from the colony to the Netherlands, transfers that made it possible to lower tax levels and increase spending on infrastructure there. At the same time, total factor productivity declined, and fast export growth in the 1830s was followed by stagnation and even famines in the 1840s. The Cultivation System showed the same development cycle as central planning in USSR or China: in the first years it led to rapid growth – due to increased pressure on the population and the transfer of resources from subsistence production to export production[17] – but the inefficiencies inherent in the system made it unsustainable in the longer run. In the 1840s the first reforms were already being implemented by the colonial administration, and these became more radical during the 1850s and 1860s, gradually undermining the system from within. Political pressures also contributed to these changes: the sharply increased export production also led to the growth of a group of traders and planters who knew that they could grow the same crops in a much more efficient way – a group that also began to push for reforms in both Java and the Netherlands. The Cultivation System, therefore, was relatively successful in launching the export sector of Java and in creating a sound financial basis for the colonial state that had emerged after 1800, but the Javanese paid a high price for it.

5 Liberalism and ethical policies, 1870–1914

The liberal turn

The reforms implemented during the late 1840s and 1850s to streamline the Cultivation System gradually took the form of a fundamental change in the way in which export agriculture was being organized. First, a movement began to gradually abolish all forms of coerced labour, and replace them with free wage labour – a transition that was completed towards the end of the century. Second, sugar production was now gradually transformed into an industry based on (more or less) free contracts with villages and peasants, and coffee cultivation, which continued to be based on coercion, became less and less important within the agricultural economy of Java. Third, new forms of export cultivation (including tea and tobacco) were developed, using European capital and entrepreneurship; the Agrarian Law of 1870 made it possible for Europeans to rent land not in use by the indigenous population from the colonial state for a period of up to 75 years, with the aim of setting up plantations there. Finally, the colonial bureaucracy was reformed in Weberian style, the *kultuurprocenten* were abolished and salaries were again based on formal rules and hierarchies (Fasseur 1975).

As a result, during the 1860s and 1870s a new colonial regime came into existence, in which private entrepreneurs – mostly of Dutch origin – who ran large plantations and sugar factories using 'free' wage labour and 'free' land came to play a central role. To some extent, this was what liberal reformers of the 1810s and 1820s had hoped for, but it had not materialized then as a result of low agricultural prices, the poor development of institutions, and information problems. The expertise for running plantations was simply not there yet, and capital had been in short supply; both developed gradually during the Cultivation System, which can also be seen as a learning process.

There is some evidence that – in spite of the liberal rhetoric that labour and land markets were supposed to become 'free' – old mechanisms for the recruitment of labour and land continued to be important. As we shall see, the sugar industry, for example, used the power of village heads to regularly redistribute *sawahs* to claim 'their' share of the land for the growing of sugar cane (Breman 1983: 24–25). This also meant that there were limits to the conversion of village-owned land into private property in those regions in which the sugar industry retained its dominance. Coffee remained a crop for which the cultivation was based on forced labour and the income from these forced deliveries was still important to the colonial treasury, but due to a number of developments (a coffee disease, and the gradual disappearance of the upland frontier where coffee trees were grown in predominantly 'virgin' land) its importance slowly declined.

Similarly, wage labour in parts of Java continued to contain elements of coercion, although from the 1880s onwards the free labour market became increasingly important. The relatively high level of (nominal) wages in the 1860s and 1870s did not persist (Figure 4.5). Between 1800 and 1880 the population of Java had grown substantially – from about 7.5 million to more than 20 million (Boomgaard and Gooszen 1991: 82) – and the land under cultivation had probably increased by just as much. By about 1880 the frontier was more or less closed, except for a few peripheral parts of the island, and agriculture had to turn to more intensive production methods to increase output of foodstuffs and export crops (Aass 1982). According to the 'census' published in the *Koloniaal Verslag* of 1881, about 4.6 per cent of the (male) Javanese labour force was made up of wage labourers (in fact, day labourers, or *dagloners*); of the Chinese and 'other Asian' population this share was almost 12 per cent (*Koloniaal Verslag*, 1881). In the final decades of the nineteenth century the free labour market grew rapidly, stimulated also by the rapid increase of the demand for wage labour by the expanding plantation sector, which became by far the most important source of wage labour. The share of wage labourers in the total population continued to increase (Hasselman 1914). In 1930 wage labourers were thought to constitute almost 10 per cent of the population of Java, and wages had become an important source of income for a much larger part of the population (*Changing Economy in Indonesia*, Vol. 5: 96–97). Java, therefore, went through a transition from an economy in which wage labour hardly existed at all – as a result of it being crowded out by coerced labour during the 1830s and 1840s – to an economy in which, from the end of the nineteenth century onwards, 'free' wage labour was a very important means of mobilizing labour.

At the same time, the colonial bureaucracy resumed its mission to modernize Javanese society and economy, inspired by the liberal and left-wing criticisms against the 'old regime' of the Cultivation System (and in particular by its most radical critic, the former colonial servant Eduard Douwes Dekker, also known as Multatuli). For the more radical administrators this also required changes in the modes of social control practised by the *priyayi* class, who had to be trained to become members of a modern bureaucracy as well. Similarly, tensions between Dutch administrators and Chinese merchants were increasing. Attempts to reform the tax system in which Chinese tax farmers still played a big role brought these tensions to the surface. The opium farm became a constant source of experiments to control the power of tax farmers – who had a clear interest in pushing as much opium as possible – and of illegal smugglers of opium (who often colluded with tax farmers), increasingly with the aim of protecting the Javanese population against these temptations. As we already sketched above, a typical 'liberal' experiment was carried out during the 1870s, when the monopoly on pawn houses, which was farmed out to Chinese merchants, was abolished and replaced by a system of licenses in the hope that this would under-mine the quasi-monopolies these Chinese merchants had on rural capital markets.

Initially many of these experiments failed. The colonial administration still badly needed the Chinese to organize their ('dirty') business (i.e. tax collection and opium selling), as the failure of the experiment with the licensing of pawn houses demonstrates. The gradual growth of the colonial administration – its administrative capabilities and its knowledge of the Javanese society – led to a decisive breakthrough in the 1890s. Through a number of drastic reforms of the tax system, the old excises were abolished and replaced by taxes that were in fact managed – set, collected and controlled – by the colonial administration itself. The opium farm became a monopoly strictly regulated by government agencies, which, for example, registered those who bought the drug and tried to discourage consumption (Van Luijk and Van Ours 2001).[1] Regulated pawnshops and state-owned local credit banks replaced the pawn houses managed by Chinese. This was also made possible by the introduction and refinement of new direct taxes on income and property, which radically changed the structure of the income of the colonial state; again, these modern taxes were directly managed by the colonial administration. As a result, the link that had existed between Chinese community (i.e. the tax farmers) and the colonial state, which had been one of the building blocks of colonial society until the 1890s, was now severed. The decreasing importance of tax farms in colonial finance is evident from Figure 5.1, which also demonstrates that the land rent – which was to a large extent based on a close cooperation between village elites and colonial adminis-tration – also declined sharply in importance. Increasingly the Dutch colonial bureaucracy, due to its growing administrative capabilities, became independent

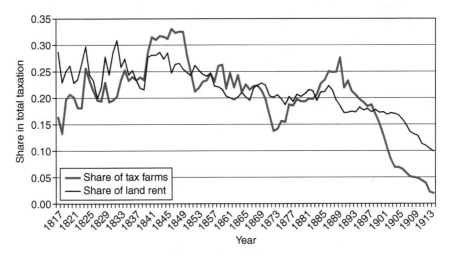

Figure 5.1 Shares of tax farms and land rent in total income, Netherlands Indies' govern-ment, 1817–1914 (sources: *Changing Economy in Indonesia*, Vol. 2; Public Finance Indonesia dataset available at IISH: www.iisg.nl/indonesianeconomy/).

of the two other systems of social control on which it had relied during much of the nineteenth century: Chinese middlemen and the indigenous elite. Consequently, it could implement its own programme for social and economic reform.

The Ethical Policy that was officially inaugurated in 1901 is often seen as the result of the ongoing debate within the Netherlands about the preferred colonial policy. The official declaration that the Dutch state regarded improving the welfare of the Indonesian population as its duty, whereas before 1901 the colony was officially considered to be a *wingewest*, is seen as a watershed in Dutch politics. It also reflected changes in domestic policies towards the working class (i.e. the gradual introduction of welfare reforms) that were consistent with changing power balances within the Netherlands (i.e. the rising influence of the middle and labour classes in politics as a result of the gradual extension of the franchise) (van Zanden and Van Riel 2000: 311–322). The point to make here is that the indigenous (i.e. Indonesian) determinants of this switch in policy have often been overlooked. The Ethical Policy was in a way the programme of the Weberian administration that in the 1890s had become the dominant force in the colony. The Ethical Policy reflected the fact that the Netherlands Indies developed into a *Beamtenstaat* (Van Doorn 1994), governed by an almost independent corps of administrators who increasingly became inspired by developmental ideas.

The 1901 address by Queen Wilhelmina was the starting point of a series of reforms focusing on the introduction of welfare services aimed at improving the economy and living standards of the indigenous population. These included modern agricultural research and extension services (already pioneered by the sugar industry, but now extended to peasant agriculture); increased expenditure on infrastructure, irrigation and education (previously focused on the needs of the European population, but now restructured and to some extent geared towards the indigenous population); medical services; and policies aimed at stabilizing rice markets and regulating rural capital markets. Recent assessments of these colonial welfare services by Van der Eng (agricultural services) and Boomgaard (all welfare services) have in general been positive, finding that they created favourable conditions for market exchange and productivity growth (in agriculture), and enhanced the general welfare level of the population (Boomgaard 1986b; Van der Eng 1996). Table 5.1 reflects these changes: the shares of civil service, education and public works in expenditure increased strongly in these years, while more basic services of the state, such as justice and defence, became less important. That the colonial state had difficulty in financing these new activities is a theme we will return to in the next chapter, but this can already be read from the increased importance of 'finance' in expenditure after 1920.

This renewed attempt to reform the colony 'from above', and to some extent at the expense of the close cooperation with former partners in the management of the colony, such as the Chinese and the indigenous Javanese elite, did not really give rise to tensions with these old 'partners'. The Chinese increasingly

Table 5.1 The structure of expenditure of colonial state, 1850s–1930s

	Justice (%)	Finance (%)	Defence (%)	Civil service (%)	Education (%)	Economic affairs* (%)	Public works (%)	Govern. factories (%)	Total (%)
1850s	3	20	25	8	1	35	4	5	100
1860s	4	10	29	9	2	34	7	6	100
1870s	4	6	30	9	2	31	10	8	100
1880s	6	12	27	14	5	20	11	7	100
1890s	5	13	29	14	5	7	20	7	100
1900s	4	17	27	13	6	4	19	10	100
1910s	4	16	20	10	8	5	26	11	100
1920s	3	23	18	10	9	4	23	8	100
1930s	3	32	18	14	10	3	14	6	100

Source: calculated from dataset Public Finance Netherlands Indies available at IISH: www.iisg.nl/indonesianeconomy/.

Note
* Includes expenditure for the Cultivation System/production of coffee and sugar.

concentrated on entrepreneurial activities; since the economy was growing rapidly after 1900, there were plenty of opportunities for them to switch from tax collection to other activities. For the Javanese elite things were somewhat more difficult. The Dutch administration in principle continued to rely on indirect rule via the *priyayi*, and respected the hereditary principle for the continuation of the internal ruling class. But some reforms were carried through: education was increasingly expected from future regents. Ability and personality were also considered fundamental, which tended to undermine the way in which regents and their dependents were being recruited (Sutherland 1979: 69). The emergence of independent voices among the Indonesian population – most clearly the Budi Utomo movement from 1908 – also put some pressure on the colonial government to consider the quality of the regents more seriously. Although the movement emerged from the Javanese ruling class, and from the still very small local intelligentsia which was arising from the *priyayi* class, its main point was that the traditional leadership was inadequate and needed to be replaced by more progressive *priyayi* who understood the new situation their society was in (Sutherland 1979: 58–60). On the other hand, the colonial administration also – at least in theory – aimed at the *ontvoogding* (emancipation) of the indigenous elite, which was to be made possible by enhancing their education (special administrative schools and training courses had to be set up), and by creating more checks and balances in the governing structure (Sutherland 1979: 70).

The long-term consequences of the market-oriented policies implemented from the 1860s and 1870s onwards, and the 'developmental' turn of policies during the 1890s and 1900s, were quite positive: economic growth clearly accelerated during the 1890s and remained relatively rapid until 1913. Per capita consumption levels also showed a continuous increase in those years, as did total factor productivity (Figures 2.4 and 4.2). Whereas peasant agriculture had – in per capita terms – stagnated in the period before 1890, it now began to contribute significantly to productivity growth, as Van der Eng (1996) has shown. We will discuss below in more detail to what extent these developments were related, and how these economic policies help to explain (productivity) growth between 1870 and 1913.

Modern imperialism

The consolidation of the colonial state on Java was another element in the transformation of Indonesia. So far this book has concentrated on Java, the core of the colonial state. During the first half of the nineteenth century a process of territorial expansion and consolidation had begun, through which Batavia increased its grip on the surrounding islands. In 1816 colonial control was limited to Java, the Moluccas and a few port cities on Sumatra, Kalimantan and Sulawesi, which had all been part of the pre-1800 network established by the VOC. Of these 'Outer Islands', as they were called in colonial terminology, Sumatra was probably the main 'prize', but in a number of steps, accelerating after 1870, all islands which were considered to be part of the sphere influence of the colonial state were brought under control. This often happened as a result of violent interventions deposing local sovereigns, and/or replacing them with princes who were more loyal to the Dutch, such as in the cases of the interventions in Bali in 1906/1908 and in Lombok in 1894 (see Van der Kraan 1980). Following the Treaty of London (1824) between the UK and the Netherlands, the latter acquired control over large parts of Sumatra, which had been partly within the British sphere of influence. This situation was confirmed by the Sumatra Treaty between the two countries (from 1871), which meant a *de facto* swap of the few Dutch colonies on the African Gold Coast for the right to fully control Sumatra; in particular, at the expense of the Sultanate of Aceh, which had remained independent before 1871. This led to the most prolonged conflict, the Aceh War that began in 1873 and continued until 1904, when the Dutch finally managed to conquer the whole territory and defeat – or at least temporarily subdue – the (guerrilla) resistance.

During the period after 1870, there was a drastic change in the way in which the Netherlands exploited its most valuable colony. Financial relations changed: during the Cultivation System, the colony had contributed heavily to the budget of the Dutch state via the 'batig slot', but the costs of the Aceh War led to the termination of the already sharply declining 'batig slot'. From the 1880s onwards the colonial state was allowed to borrow some money from the Dutch capital market, but the amounts involved were rather small. However, from the perspective of the colony, the large income transfers to the government of the Netherlands were succeeded by, after 1900, equally large private transfers of incomes to the Netherlands. The East Indies became by far the most important destination for direct investments made abroad (in 1900, for example, of the 810 million invested abroad, 750 million was in Indonesia; in 1914 the estimates are 1.68 billion out of a total of 2.27 billion) (Van der Eng 1998). Income from these investments became substantial, and covered a large part of the deficit on the balance of trade of the Netherlands (see also Figure 4.1).[2]

Following the complete elimination of restrictions on international trade with the colony in 1874, trade flows also began shifting to other destinations. In 1874, more than 60 per cent of export from the colony was destined for the Netherlands. This declined to about 30 per cent just before the First World War. Dutch exports to the East Indies remained more constant, comprising about 20 per cent of the total export of the Netherlands, but also declined if measured as the share of total imports by the colony (from 55 per cent in 1874 to 36 per cent in 1913) (Lindblad 1988: 280). Their mutual trade had therefore become less important for both economies, but at the same time the flows of human and financial capital increased significantly in importance.

During this same period, the Netherlands was involved in dividing up the world between the European powers, and in particular in establishing full control over its 'possessions' in the Outer Islands. The Dutch were relatively cautious players in the game of modern imperialism – the country lay in the shadow of the British, the superpower located just on the other side of the North Sea. Yet the Netherlands did contribute to the process of carving up the world, a fact that

is sometimes neglected in the literature about political and economic developments during this period, perhaps because the active participation of the Netherlands in modern imperialism did not fit very well with classic explanations of
imperialism. Such theories emphasized the industrialization of Western Europe,
which led to the formation of surplus capital, which then sought an outlet in the
colonies (Kuitenbrouwer 1985: 9). Because industrialization in the Netherlands
began later than elsewhere, the internal motivation for aggressive imperialism
was thought to have been absent. A more recent formulation of the causes of
modern imperialism, which emphasizes the dynamics of state formation in the
periphery and stresses the problems the colonial authorities had to deal with in
the border regions of the colonial sphere of influence, was considered more relevant for understanding the Indonesian case (Kuitenbrouwer 1985: 12, 1994). The
most important conflicts fought by the Netherlands in the colonies – the 'pacifi-
cations' of Lombok and Bali, and especially the Aceh War – appeared in various
ways to fit this theory.

In the meantime the tide has turned, and interest in the economic determinants
of modern imperialism has grown once more. Emphasis is no longer placed so
heavily on the relationship with the industrialization of countries, because
research has shown that industrial interest groups were not really involved in the
process. It was groups in the services sector especially – wholesalers, bankers,
shipping companies – that appeared to have played a crucial role in the drive
towards imperialism, during which they entered into coalitions with the largely
rural elite of England. This coalition of gentlemen from the city and the countryside was together able to control politics. They aimed to expand the role of
London as a central node in international trade and banking and used imperialis-
tic politics as a powerful means of attaining this goal (Cain and Hopkins 1993;
Kuitenbrouwer 1994).

As early as the 1850s and 1860s, companies and individuals were taking
advantage of the new possibilities that had opened up due to the expansion of
export production during the Cultivation System. Beginning in 1855, for
example, the Nederlandse Handel-Maatschappij (NHM), which saw its role as a
monopolist being threatened, rapidly began expanding its interest in various
'free' cultures. As a result, it found a destination for the enormous capital it had
acquired, which was threatening to become idle due to the gradual contraction of
the Cultivation System (Mansvelt 1926, II: 357). A serious financial crises on
Java in 1862–1863 led to immediate reactions in the Netherlands. The intense
capital scarcity in the colony led to the establishment of a number of financial
institutions, which devoted themselves to productively investing their capital in
the colony. The *Rotterdamsche Bank* and the *Nederlandsch-Indische Handelsbank* were founded to satisfy the demand for trade financing on Java
(Kymmell 1992, I: 143–149). These organizations hoped to make their capital
productive by financing new activities on Java and in the outer regions of the
East Indies. New trading firms, which were also concerned with trade financing,
were established at the same time. Therefore, even as early as 1870, parts of the
commercial and financial world in Amsterdam and Rotterdam were very anxious

to expand their activities in the colony. This pressure played a significant role in the decisive shift to liberal colonial politics in the 1860s (van Zanden and Van Riel 2000: Chapter 5). The liberal shift in colonial politics can therefore be understood from the driving force behind modern imperialism as analysed by Hobson: the plain fact that entrepreneurs were looking for new possibilities for investing their capital (Hobson 1902).

In all respects, these initiatives did not yield nearly as much as people had expected. For example, the *Rotterdamsche Bank* began focusing on domestic banking because its attempted penetration of the Dutch East Indies market quickly failed. There was a major demand for capital from the colony, and this demand would increase even more in the decades that followed, but to make successful use of this demand, good contacts and specialized information were essential. After 1870, large tracts of 'wastelands' were passed off to unwary buyers to be converted into plantations. Families in the Indies with good contacts and access to local information were especially successful, although it was quite some time before their plans began to bear fruit.

For establishing new plantations – in tea, coffee or tobacco – and for the expansion of the highly capital-intensive sugar culture, large sums of capital were required. But the growing numbers of entrepreneurs in the early 1860s who planned to make their fortunes 'in tea' or other crops often had inadequate information about the quality of the land they had purchased, insufficient technical knowledge concerning the crops they wanted to introduce and insufficient insight into the socio-economic and cultural conditions of the regions in which they were active. As a result, only a few of these entrepreneurs succeeded in realizing their plans. During the years of liberal economic politics between 1816 and 1826, these barriers had been so formidable that entrepreneurs from the Netherlands failed to play a significant role in export production. Many did not even try. The flourishing of export agriculture that began with the Cultivation System had resulted in an increase of information, trade networks and entrepreneurship. As a result, the number of attempts that were made and the chances of success were greater than they had been before 1830, but these were still extremely risky undertakings, especially when plantations were established in new regions or attempts were made to find new markets. However, some of these risks could be shared by the merchant houses that financed the operations of these entrepreneurs, with the harvest as security.

Some individuals were very successful, due to luck, skilled entrepreneurship or a combination of both. The most spectacular example was the success of *Deli* tobacco. The Dutch planter Jacob Nienhuys, by means of a clever construction in the contract he had signed with the Sultan of Deli, was able to rent 12,000 *bouw* (around 8,000 or 9,000 hectares), which would later turn out to be very valuable tobacco land, for a full 99 years. He did not have to pay actual rent for this land, only import and export duties and a certain fee for each coolie he hired (Breman 1987: 17–20). He was the first colonial to plant tobacco on these lands. To do this he had to hire Chinese coolies on contract. Locals refused to work on the plantations for the wages he offered. The tobacco he grew turned out to be of superior quality and fetched record prices in Amsterdam. This success led to the establishment of the *Deli Maatschappij* in 1869; during the first ten years of its existence it paid an average 50 per cent dividend on its share capital. Naturally, this outstanding success drew many other would-be planters. It also demonstrated the spectacular new possibilities of the 'outer regions', i.e. the islands outside Java that had previously been neglected by the colonial authorities.

However, the basis of this expansion – certainly before 1900 – was relatively weak. The chronic lack of capital in export agriculture meant that the central 'nerves' of this system – the merchant houses and *cultuurbanken* – became increasingly involved with financing the production. As a result, production and banking became closely interrelated. Even the merchant houses that were not directly involved with financing plantations still had to invest a great deal to maintain and increase their share in the affairs of the East Indies. The Chinese intermediaries, the essential links between the European wholesale trade and the rural population, worked exclusively on credit, because they in turn gave credit to their buyers in the *dessa*. In this way, Dutch capital, which was to a significant extent made up of profits originally earned in the East Indies, played an important role in the development of the colony (Van der Eng 1993).

This structure made the gradual growth of export agriculture in the East Indies possible. However, it turned out to be extremely vulnerable during years of poor harvests and/or declining prices on the world market. When the plantations were unable to pay off their credit following the harvest, the trading houses and banks were also endangered, which threatened to paralyse the entire economy of the colony. Such a crisis occurred in 1862, resulting in attempts to improve the availability of capital on Java. While this was dramatic, the sugar crisis of 1884 was significantly worse. Sugar prices and other raw material prices had been declining for several years, causing serious problems for sugar cultivation. The large trading firm Dorrepaal & Co., which was involved in no less than 22 sugar refineries, 38 coffee plantations and 53 other plantations, got into serious difficulties and almost took the *Nederlandsch-Indische Handelsbank* (NIHB) and the *Koloniale Bank* down with it. The NHM, which had taken timely precautions and had limited the amount of long-term credit it provided to plantations, escaped the crisis largely unscathed. During these years, the trading firm was in the process of transforming itself into a pure banking firm, a transition that was accelerated by this crisis in the East Indies (Mansvelt 1926, II: 415).

The logical response of the merchant houses and the East Indies banks, which experienced serious problems during the crisis of 1884, was to change the way they provided credit for export agriculture. After 1884, they therefore began to establish limited companies (*cultuurmaatschappijen*) that owned these plantations and acquired long-term finance for them on the Dutch capital market. The number of limited companies increased quickly. By holding seats on the boards of these limited companies or by taking other subsidiary posts, the directors of the trading companies and colonial banks made sure that their interests were protected. During the course of the 1880s and 1890s, a dense network of relationships developed between the *cultuurbanken*, the *cultuurmaatschappijen*, large steamship lines and other businesses that were involved in the Dutch East Indies. Businessmen also began to organize themselves in the colony itself. In 1879, the *Deli Planters Vereniging* (tobacco planters) was established, which was quickly followed by the *Algemeen Syndicaat van Suikerfabrikanten in Nederlandsch-Indië* (sugar manufacturers). The latter was the most important business organization for a long period of time (Taselaar 1998: 99).

From the above, one could perhaps get the impression that this expansion of the Dutch business community in the East Indies took place in a political/economic vacuum. The Dutch government, and therefore the colonial state, had converted to liberalism and focused as much as possible on promoting private initiative. However, nothing could be further from the truth. After 1870 the colonial government continued to play a key role in the entire process. This of course concerned traditional activities such as providing new infrastructure, i.e. roads and railways, which were also built with some delay in the East Indies.

But entrepreneurs in the East Indies, both the indigenous and expatriates, needed the government much more directly than entrepreneurs in the Netherlands. State intervention played a large role in the making of new contracts and the enforcement of old ones. The expansion of plantation agriculture and mining on Java and Sumatra was often dependent on the contracts that Dutch entrepreneurs drew up with local monarchs, who claimed the property rights to these lands. These contracts had to be certified by the colonial government to make them enforceable. Due to the information advantage of Dutch entrepreneurs and their access to markets and power, such contracts were certainly not the result of negotiations between two equal parties. After all, the local elite frequently had no idea of the value of the potential tobacco lands or of the stinking mud (oil) that bubbled up out of the ground. For the Sultan of Deli, such a contract meant that above all his own property rights, which were anything but clearly defined in his own 'feudal' society and were often only nominal in nature, had been defined and certified and that he would be able to derive a certain income from those rights. The fact that this resulted in all kinds of other property rights being violated – for example, the rights of the local population or of competing elites – was not sufficiently acknowledged by the planters and the colonial state (Breman 1987: 20). Similar problems arose during the expansion of sugar culture on Java, which used the best agricultural lands, i.e. the *sawahs*. Javanese farmers resented this. During negotiations on compensation for these lands, the entrepreneurs took advantage of inequalities in the social and political power structures. Manipulation of the regent and the head of the *dessa* was often the cheapest way to acquire good land. Workers could be pressed into service in a similar fashion. In the underpopulated areas of Sumatra, where tobacco cultivation flourished, virtually no workers were available; thus plantation owners had to import Chinese coolies, who were contracted for a specific period. After the coolies were transported to Sumatra, the plantation owners were allowed to force them to work if the coolie failed to follow the terms of his contract (Langeveld 1978: 296–298). On many plantations, these practices verged on slavery.[3]

For these reasons, the Dutch business community needed a strong state to protect its interests. The gradual consolidation of Dutch power in the outer regions of the East Indies was a second reason for entrepreneurs needing a strong colonial State. After the Sumatra Treaty of 1871, the colonial state took action against the Sultan of Deli when he revolted against Dutch authority, which led to the start of the first Aceh War in 1873. The latter is customarily seen as the beginning of a renewed ambition for territorial expansion in the archipelago of the Dutch East Indies. Economic interests clearly played a role in this process, although Dutch historians have had some difficulty acknowledging this. The great interest in Sumatra was anything but accidental. This was where extremely profitable tobacco cultivation had begun and was also where the production of crude oil started after 1890, which very quickly developed into one of the economic pillars of the Dutch East Indies. To a significant extent, the Aceh War was fought to protect and consolidate these economic interests (Kuitenbrouwer 1985, 1994).

Between 1900 and 1913, colonial development accelerated. Prices on the world market were rising almost constantly, Aceh was almost pacified and especially the outer regions profited from growing demand on world markets (Lindblad 1989: 8). Returns on capital invested in the East Indies increased more rapidly during these years than returns on capital invested in the Netherlands. This can be ascertained from data concerning the dividends of companies on the Amsterdam exchange. Dutch banks and industrial stocks paid a constant dividend of approximately 7 per cent, but the dividend of businesses from the East Indies increased from an average of 6 per cent in the 1890s (i.e. lower than the 'normal' level of Dutch companies) to 9 per cent in the following decade. It ultimately rose to around 11 per cent in the years just prior to the First World War.[4] It is significant that these high profits were almost exclusively made by companies mainly working in Sumatra and other parts of the Outer Islands – it was the expansion there that really gave the colonial economy a new big impulse.

Economic change and structural transformation during the first era of globalization

We will now take a closer look at the export expansion during the period between 1870 and 1914. The first year for which detailed export and import statistics for the whole archipelago are available is, significantly, 1874 (before that year, only similar statistics for Java have been published). In that year, exports were dominated by the traditional cash crops from Java, coffee and sugar, which together accounted for 70 per cent of the exports of the colony; the island produced almost 90 per cent of its total exports, the Outer Islands being mainly represented by spices (from the Moluccas) and tin (from Billiton and Banka) (Table 5.2). In 1914, exports had increased from 168 million guilders to 678 million guilders (the general price level had not changed much in the long run), of which almost half now came from the Outer Islands. Sugar was still the largest item on the balance of trade, with almost 23 per cent of total export value (coffee had

Table 5.2 Exports of Indonesia, 1874–1914 (in million guilders)

	1874	1880	1890	1900	1910	1914
Sugar	50	49	52	74	140	183
Coffee	68	60	37	29	12	23
Tea	3	2	2	4	12	27
Spices	6	5	7	9	14	14
Tobacco	11	15	31	74	32	64
Copra	0	0	2	10	42	61
Tin and tin ore	5	10	9	30	34	41
Petroleum	0	0	0	5	38	137
Rubber	0	0	0	0	7	27
Java and Madura	144	136	126	184	286	360
Outer Islands	25	43	51	75	166	324
Total	169	179	177	259	453	685

Source: *CEI*, Vol. 12a, Tables 2b and 6b.

dwindled to 3 per cent); oil came next, followed by tobacco, tin, tea and rubber. With the exception of tea (also grown on a large scale on western Java), these were all products that came almost exclusively from the Outer Islands.

The stories of the expansion of these export products are each quite different. Tin, for example, had been mined since 1718 on the island of Banka, east of Sumatra, where the colonial government used Chinese labourers to do the hard work. In the early 1850s, a Dutch company was set up to explore the neighbouring island of Billiton; the company was supported by Prince Hendrik, the brother of the King who was the only member of the Dutch royal family ever to visit the colony. Helped by his contacts, the colonial government was convinced to lease the island to the newly established firm, which started the exploration. When this proved a success, a joint stock company was established in 1860, the Billiton Maatschappij, in which the Prince acquired a large share, to carry out the further exploitation of the island. The first years of the company were rather difficult, but rising tin prices, lower transport costs (also of the labourforce and the necessary inputs, because almost everything had to be imported onto the small island), and improvements in the living conditions of the Chinese coolies – resulting in a sharp decline in mortality[5] – all led to improvements in the financial situation of the company, which began to pay out handsome dividends from 1866 onwards. Output of tin expanded very rapidly, and already in 1877 it exceeded the output of the government exploitation of Banka (Mollema 1927, II: 235; appendix figure 1). Its financial success (it was even able to reimburse 52.5 per cent of the nominal value of the shares, besides giving out huge dividends) also drew the attention of the colonial critics in the Netherlands, who argued for better terms for the colonial state, which did not profit much from the tin exploitation. When an extension of the concession was due, in the early 1880s, the Governor-General in the Indies cut short these discussions by unilaterally granting one. This very sensitive decision was badly timed, and led to the downfall of the cabinet that backed up the Governor-general, and eventually to the resignation of the Governor-general in 1883 (Mollema 1927, I: 32–36). The historian of the company adds to this story that the sharpness of the debate might also be related to the fact that the shares in this Billiton Company were only owned by members of the aristocracy – amongst others the heirs of Prince Hendrik, who had died in 1879. Continued high profits after 1883 (in 1887/1888 the dividend was as high as 82 per cent, the average for the 1880s was 44 per cent), and the company policy of paying out almost all profits instead of investing it in other ventures, meant that the criticism only grew (Mollema 1927, I: 49). New negotiations about its concession in 1891 and 1892 led to a formula, according to which the state would get five-eighths of the net profit made, which finally satisfied the Dutch Parliament (Molema 1927, I: 46–47). Company policy became much more expansionary, and the growth of Billiton tin production was the main force behind the expansion of tin exports in these years (Table 5.2).

The oil industry that came into existence in the 1880s and 1890s showed certain similarities with the exploitation of tin deposits on Banka and Billiton. Concessions, given by the colonial state, played a crucial role in the development of the mineral resource, and new companies were set up to acquire these concessions, as well as the necessary capital and technology. Because the drilling sites were often in nearly empty parts of the Archipelago, the oil industry was also heavily dependent on Chinese and Indian workers, who were recruited on contracts, typically for three years. The industry – in particular its most successful offshoot, Royal Dutch – made use of the same channels to get what it wanted; aristocratic colonial families such as the Loudons (who had participated in the Billiton company, and had 'produced' a number of high-ranking colonial civil servants, amongst whom a Governor-General) played a large role in its (early) history, and its network included links with the royal family, that incidentally gave the company the prestigious title of being 'Royal'. Initially, in the 1880s and 1890s, a number of companies were set up to exploit the oil resources of the different islands. Perhaps the most innovative company, the Dortsche Petroleum Maatschappij, was set up by Adriaan Stoop, who produced oil drilled on Java mainly for the local market; in these years, the main product of the industry was kerosene, or lamp oil. Sumatra was much richer in resources, and after Royal Dutch established itself, the island attracted a few other independent producers as well. On Kalimantan a British trading company, Shell, which had entered the oil trade via importing Russian oil to South and Southeast Asia, tried to produce lamp oil with the heavy oil found there, but it was only moderately successful in this respect – in fact, outlays far exceeded profits, also because the technological expertise was lacking. After the turn of the century a process of consolidation of the industry started, gently induced by the Dutch state fearing that the industry might fall into the hands of Standard Oil, the mighty American company. It led to the formation of the Asiatic Trading Company, a joint venture of Royal Dutch, Shell and the Russian oil company of the Paris Rothschilds (which produced most of the oil that was imported into the region). Together they controlled the market for kerosene in Asia – albeit that Standard was a powerful outsider with a large slice of the upper segments of the market.

Cooperation within Asiatic first of all led to a concentration of the Dutch oil companies. The independents were all taken over by Royal Dutch; the last to be taken over was the Dortsche in 1911. In 1907 – the details of this story are told elsewhere – Royal Dutch and Shell decided to merge, and form the company Royal Dutch Shell, in a 60/40 per cent combination in which the Dutch shareholders with their 60 per cent dominated. Keys to the success of Royal Dutch were that it – given its location on isolated Sumatra – had from the beginning started its own marketing organization, including an impressive shipping fleet; at the same time it had invested in technological expertise and the setting up of a professional organization. It had also profited from the fact that the oil that it acquired in Perlak was very well suited for producing gasoline (*benzine* in Dutch), produced for the rapidly growing demand for fuel for internal combustion engines, mainly those of cars. From 1902 onwards Royal Dutch made huge profits in exporting this new product to Europe. After 1907 the new combination became a real challenger to the worldwide domination of the oil industry by Standard Oil. It developed rapidly, and acquired new concessions and marketing organizations almost everywhere on the globe – in Mexico, Venezuela, the United States, Egypt, Russia and Romania – in what is probably one of the fastest growth spurts in business history. Indonesia, however, remained quite important for the company, as it was and continued to be one of the few markets it almost completely controlled, and where it had access to all the promising concessions. The spectacular expansion of Royal Dutch in the post-1907 period was therefore to a not inconsiderable extent based on the extremely large profits it made in the colony.

The oil industry, besides exploiting a mineral resource, was also a real industry (although it is usually not classified in the national accounts as such), as the refining and further processing of the crude oil took place on or near the concession, and involved highly skilled labour and sophisticated capital goods, which were both imported. Not only was the oil being produced, but linked to this there were large plants producing the tins in which the kerosene was being shipped and sold, and the industry increasingly developed new products out of the waste that was still being burned in the 1890s – gasoline, for example. The sugar industry also developed into a high-tech industry (although, again, it is usually not classified as such). Under the Cultivation System new technologies for processing the raw sugar had been introduced which already improved the yield of the crop dramatically. In the 1860s and 1870s a further transformation of the industry occurred in the sense that it officially discontinued using coercion to acquire the labour and land that were necessary to grow the crop. Sugar production had been introduced into a system of peasant farming focusing on rice as the main crop, and because of the fact that it competed with rice for the scarce irrigated land, the sugar producers had to find ways of accommodating the new liberal winds blowing in the colony. The industry never completely adapted, in the sense that it continued to use – in a far more subtle way – mechanisms of coercion to acquire a share in this land, and the labour to plant, maintain and harvest the crop. The problem was that sugar factories were highly capital intensive, consisting of large buildings and the capital goods that were being used. They could not easily be transferred to other places if the peasants no longer wanted to grow sugar on their plots, if they had ever wanted to, as they often preferred rice. On the other hand, the potential production of an acre of sugar was quite high – much higher than the alternative rice crop – and peasants could in principle profit from this, as a large part of the yield was paid out in the form of wages. However, if peasants had owned their own plots, and been allowed to decide for themselves when to work for the factory and when to plant rice or other food crops, it would have been a sheer impossibility for the increasingly large sugar plants to negotiate successfully with them and coordinate their plans. One sugar plant needed the cooperation of many hundreds – and later on in the colonial period, perhaps a couple of thousand – of peasants.

The way this was solved was, in a nutshell, rather than giving the peasants individual property rights to the land, local officials would instead rely on (a certain interpretation of) local *adat* (indigenous law) to regulate landed property. We already introduced the problem that in large parts of Java property rights were a bit fuzzy anyway – with overlapping claims of the sovereign (the sultan of Mataram, for example), local elites (who often 'rented' villages or properties from the sultan), and the peasantry (who as reclaimers of the land had some formal rights as well). In central parts of Java, where the rights of the sultans were most intense, local villages also played a large role, and there existed systems of regular redistribution of the rights to land to the class of propertied landowners (Boomgaard 1987: 64–85). This system had been enhanced by colonial authorities as it nicely solved the problem of the access to land (and labour) of the sugar industry: as part of the regular redistribution of the land, the village authorities had a good grip on the use of the land in their village, which could be used to negotiate with the owners of the sugar plants and to induce peasants to cooperate with these arrangements. In the regions where the sugar industry continued to be active after the dissolution of the Cultivation System, these systems of periodic redistribution of the land continued to function, or were perhaps even reinforced. In sum, capitalist expansion was only possible thanks to the continuation of institutions – fuzzy property rights and the periodic redistribution of land – that probably did not provide the 'right' incentives for peasants to enhance their output and productivity on this land. Because, for example, they did not own these *sawahs*, it was nearly impossible for them to use the land as collateral for loans.

In this way – using indigenous mechanisms of control in combination with arguably rather inefficient property rights – the sugar industry was able to adapt to the post-Cultivation System period.[6] International competition was the other challenge. In one respect this developed favourably, because transport costs fell dramatically (as we will see shortly), meaning that European (and Asian) markets were drawn closer together after 1870. But Europe was increasingly focused on keeping colonial sugar out for the protection of its own beet sugar industry. This led to various crises in export markets, of which the 1884 'sugar crisis' is the most notorious. It seemed, for a moment, that the Javanese sugar industry was doomed – also because of the occurrence of a new disease (*Sereh*), which led to recurring harvest failures in a period of already very low prices. The industry reacted quickly by organizing itself and by setting up – following German models – *proefstations* (experimental stations), where new breeds of sugar were developed that were resistant to the *Sereh* disease and able to produce higher yields. It was soon noticed that the disease did not strike at sugar plants in the higher regions of the island, and that plants imported from those fields continued to be resistant. Initially, in the mid-1880s, three *proefstations* were set up, funded by organizations of local factory owners in central, east and west Java; in 1907 they were united into one organization, which managed the two remaining *proefstations* (the one in central Java had been closed down in the early 1880s).

This was one of the first examples of the systematic application of science to the problems of 'tropical agriculture' (as it was called in those days), and it was quite successful in the medium- to long-run. Yields went up, diseases were successfully eliminated, and the sugar industry continued to contribute substantially to exports and GDP, in spite of the fact that it was competing with the increasingly dense population on Java for the island's best land. (Table 5.2 demonstrates the rapid growth of the industry after 1900 – it continued to be the largest producer of exports goods). This was not without certain tensions; especially when the price of rice was high and the peasants needed the land the most, they could react via the 'spontaneous' burning of the canes, which to some extent reflected their discontent (Elson 1979). In other industries, such as tea and rubber, similar problems related to the coexistence of Western plantations and indigenous agricultural interest arose. Tea was a relatively new export crop, which only became more important towards the end of the nineteenth century. The western part of Java, the Priangan – before the 1830s the most important producer of coffee – developed into the main tea production area, where large plantations were set up by mainly European entrepreneurs on land leased (for 75 years) from the colonial government. This led to commercialization of the countryside, and local farmers increasingly learned – by working on the Western plantations – how the crop was planted, harvested and processed. At the end of the nineteenth century, this led to the rise of the indigenous production of tea on small plots of land often reclaimed by the local population. Plantation owners stimulated this process by handing out seed to their employees and potential tea planters, and by buying up the harvested leaves, which were then processed and sold by the plantation (Van Doorn 1994: 203–205). It seemed as if a happy cooperation between Western-style and indigenous entrepreneurship was feasible. The position of the Javanese farmers in this coalition was very weak, however, because they did not have access to market outlets and did not own the equipment for processing the tea leaves. Attempts sponsored by the colonial administration to organize them and form cooperatives (following European models of, for example, milk factories) turned out to be unsuccessful – even a government-owned factory for the processing of the tea leaves failed (Van Doorn 1994: 207). Other attempts to raise production standards of the indigenous tea were also not very successful; one of the limitations was that tea production continued to be one of the many activities peasants carried out – often in combination with rice cultivation or other forms of subsistence farming. The absence of specialization meant that the skills and technologies necessary for increasing the quality of the product were not acquired; the peasant never developed into a specialist tea planter (Van Doorn 1994: 208). And the lack of quality control of the tea produced in this way to some extent harmed the reputation of the Javanese tea industry. The debate about the advantages and disadvantages of indigenous tea production continued into the 1920s – when they became even sharper as prices fell and markets were much less willing to absorb low quality tea – but the sector continued to enjoy the support of the colonial administration in the region.[7]

The rapid expansion of exports and successful integration of parts of the Outer Islands into the international economy was made possible by radical changes in transport systems. First and foremost, international distances were being shortened by the introduction of new technologies and the sharp reduction of transport costs. The costs of transporting a tonne of goods from Java declined radically, a process that had already started in the 1820s and 1830s, but accelerated in the second half of the century. The Suez Canal, which shortened travel times dramatically, and the almost simultaneous construction of a network of telegraph lines connecting Southeast Asia with the rest of the world – even more dramatically reducing the travel times of information – were crucial changes inaugurating a new era of 'globalization'. It brought the Netherlands Indies much closer to the world market and the 'mother country', with major consequences for economic relations between the two. It became, for example, much easier to manage a company from its head offices in Den Haag or Amsterdam – as the ease of communication enabled major business decisions to be made there now, which had been quite impossible before 1870 due to the long time it took to consult each other.

Internally, the Netherlands Indies also profited from the transport revolution of the nineteenth century. It was rather slow in constructing a network of railways; the first track, 25 km between Semarang and the Principalities, was only constructed in 1867 (when, for example, British India already had a well-developed network of 6,400 km). Initially (as in the Netherlands itself), the state tried to leave this to private initiative, but from the 1880s onwards it began to play a more constructive role, integrating the existing (few) lines into one network, and broadening the network to include all major regions of Java (and later on, constructing a few lines on Sumatra as well). This resulted in a major decline in transport costs. The transport system on Java had been quite inefficient. The roads had been few and rather poorly maintained, with the exception of the main road connecting the ports along the north coast – Daendels' infamous *Postweg* – mainly making use of coolies for transport. During the period of the Cultivation System, peasants had been obliged to deliver their products at the warehouses of the NHM along the coast, so the incentive to improve the transport system had been limited (although a great deal of coerced labour was in fact invested in the job). Inland transport meant the hiring of coolies who could transport one *picul* (circa 60 kg) on their back, and were paid 2.5 to 3 cents per *paal* (mile) – or the equivalent of 35 to 40 cents per tonne-km. In Sumatra, in 1890, transport costs were at the same level, even when using oxen and cart. The new railways operating in the 1880s lowered this to 8 to 16 cents per tonne-km, dependent on the product being transported (the more expensive the product was, the higher the rate), but this was still quite high compared with, for example, internal transport costs in the Netherlands, which were as low as 3 to 6 cents per tonne-km. In 1905, rates had been lowered to 4 to 6 cents per tonne-km, or 10–15 per cent of the level of the 1860s (by comparison, the price level had hardly changed at all in these years) (De Waal, 1865: 330; Hasselman, 1914: 192). This decline in fact still underestimates the real fall in transport costs, because railways were much faster than oxen and coolies, not to mention the enormous gains in terms of comfort enjoyed by travellers; before 1860, large parts of Java could only be reached by walking on very poor roads, if there were roads at all.

A similar revolution occurred in shipping between islands. Again, it had a dual face: the number of connections and their intensity increased tremendously, from only a few lines connecting Java with a few outposts in the 1850s to a very intensive network of dozens of nodes on the various islands, which were serviced regularly, in the post-1900 period. At the same time, transport costs went down, but not by that much. The colonial state had in the first half of the century maintained a network of shipping services between (mainly) Java and the Outer Islands – including Singapore – and, to a lesser extent, between the different port cities on the north coast. This overseas transport was already much cheaper than overland; the average rate in 1848 (for which the rates set by the Government's Pakketvaart are available) was about 25 cents per *koyang* per mile (or about 8 cents per tonne-km) (Campo, 1992: 642). In the 1850s the mail services were privatized, which initially led to an increase in prices despite the generous subsidies the private companies received from the colonial state (in 1861 the average tariff per *koyang* per mile had increased to 28 cents, but the general price level also had risen a little). To the dismay of Dutch entrepreneurs, between 1865 and 1890 the contract was even awarded to a British-owned company, which was marginally cheaper than the Dutch alternative; the NISM (*Nederlandsch-Indische Stoomvaart Maatschappij*) was, however, able to lower the freight rates substantially (to 16 cents per *koyang* per mile, or 5 cents per tonne-km) (Campo 1992: 46, 642). The Dutch shipping companies operating the line between the Netherlands and Indonesia discovered, however, that they could not coordinate their activities with those of the NISM (which was oriented towards the traffic on Singapore and India), and therefore lost a lot of potential cargo. In 1890 they decided to put in a bid for operating the inter-island services, and set up the *Koninklijke Paketvaart Maatschappij* (KPM) to acquire the bid. The taking over of the inter-island traffic by the KPM resulted in a very rapid expansion of transport services; transport of goods and of passengers increased sevenfold between 1891 and 1913, whereas in the 1880s it had stagnated (Campo 1992: 644). This was also induced by the colonial government, which relied on the KPM for (amongst others) the transport of military to the battlefields of Aceh, Lombok and Bali. As Joep á Campo has demonstrated in a classic study on the KPM, it was as much an instrument of economic expansion (as it made possible the opening up of new ports and their hinterlands) as of colonial state formation (as it assisted in the consolidation of the colonial state in the Outer Islands). Transport prices were not, however, further lowered by the KPM – they remained at 16 cents per *koyang* per mile until the mid-1920s.

Indonesian producers were therefore increasingly drawn into the market due to the sharply declining transport costs, more reliable infrastructure and institutional changes that were favourable for market exchange and trade. As we saw in Chapter 2, market integration increased considerably during these years, and seasonal fluctuations in rice prices declined strongly, all indicating that markets were becoming more efficient (Figures 2.11 and 2.12).[8] Both Western and Indonesian entrepreneurs reacted by increasing their participation in the market, and by specializing, which resulted in productivity gains. This led to modest changes in the structure of the economy. For Java, we can follow this structure during the nineteenth century (Figure 5.2). The share of smallholder agriculture declined from about 60 per cent of GDP at about 1815 to 40 per cent a century later; the largest gains were made by export agriculture, which grew from a miniscule percentage in 1815 to around 20 per cent in 1913. Other sectors increased their share as well, but at a much more modest pace – or, as was the case with transport, the growth of output was accompanied by a strong decline in output price, almost stabilizing its share in GDP.

One of the most spectacular examples of structural change was the almost complete disappearance of large parts of the textile industry from Java. As we saw in Chapter 3, before the 1820s Java was home to a relatively well-developed textile industry, which exported part of its produce to the Outer Islands. The sharp decline of this industry had begun in the 1820s and 1830s, with the 'cotton invasion'; first from the UK, and later from Belgium and the Netherlands as well. Java (and the rest of Indonesia) increasingly relied on imported cottons, a trend that did not change fundamentally during the second half of the nineteenth century. It was a rational response to changes in relative prices because prices of cash crops went up in the long run, whereas prices of cotton textiles fell dramatically as a result of industrialization in Western Europe and the decline of transport costs. Figure 5.3 shows how the supply of cotton textiles was taken care of: which share was produced locally (and which share imported). It clearly shows the strong decline of the industry – according to late nineteenth- and early twentieth-century sources, almost no spinning was taking place on Java anymore (and also on the Outer Islands it had become quite rare); the weaving of textiles too had become a small industry. Only the last stage in the production process – the batik industry, an indigenous technology to add layers of colour – was growing rapidly from the 1840s onwards, thanks to the cheap supply of cotton fabrics. Nevertheless, the growth of batik production could not compensate for the decline in the rest of the industry. Figure 5.3 also demonstrates that the main driving factor behind the shrinking of the textile industry was the strong decline in the prices of cotton textiles – indigenous producers were simply unable to

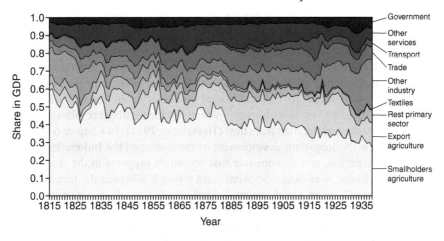

Figure 5.2 The structure of Javanese GDP, 1815–1939.

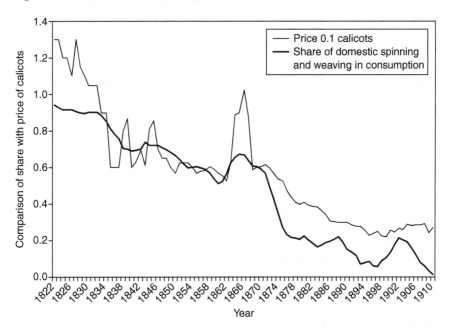

Figure 5.3 Share of domestic textile production in total consumption (five-years moving average) compared with the price of calicots, 1822–1910.

continue competing with the very low prices made possible by mass production in British and Dutch factories.

Improved institutions and better access to markets therefore produced the expected results: total factor productivity went up during these years (see Chapter 2). This was not only happening in the export sector of the economy – in oil, or sugar – but also in smallholder agriculture, where, as Van der Eng

(1996) has demonstrated, the decades between 1890 and 1920 were a period of productivity growth. Yet, the Indonesian economy did not embark on a process of 'modern economic growth'. Before 1900 growth was sluggish and did not lead to a strong improvement in the standard of living – contemporaries in the early twentieth century were concerned about the slow development of the Java-nese economy, and the government issued an inquiry into the welfare of the population – the first one in its history – which produced mixed results (apart for many interesting and detailed statistics) (Hasselman 1914). In Chapter 6 we will briefly review the long-term development of the stature of the Indonesian popu-lation in this period, and demonstrate that not much progress in the 'biological standard of living' was made. So what went wrong? Why did the turn to more market-oriented – even developmental – policies not result in major improve-ments in the lot of the Indonesian population?

Failure, like success, often has many fathers. One of the most significant dif-ferences between the process of economic change that occurred in Java/Indonesia in this period, and what we see happening in Western Europe at the same time, is the absence of real structural change in the economy. One feature was the decline of urbanization; as we saw in Chapter 3, Java was a very rural island in 1800 (and 1850), with only a few relatively large cities. The share of the population living in cities with more than 20,000 inhabitants was 6.8 per cent in 1850, but fell to about 3 per cent in 1890 (Boomgaard 1987: 159). None of the industries that expanded rapidly in this period – such as oil, sugar, tobacco and tin – were urban based, and their links with urban activities were often rather weak. The oil industry exported its main products directly via its own ports, and the same more or less applies to other mining activities as well (tin and coal in Kalimantan). Impressive new man-ufacturing facilities related to the processing of the raw sugar arose in Java and near the oil fields of Sumatra and Kalimantan, but these all used foreign techno-logy and imported skilled labour – they were classic enclaves of 'Western' tech-nology and institutions. Unskilled labour in these growth industries largely came from Javanese peasants (who worked the fields for the sugar mills) and Chinese and Indian contract labourers who were active on the oil fields and plantations of the Outer Islands. The impact of these new sources of employment on labour markets was limited; nominal wages, which peaked in the 1870s, declined over the following twenty years. Real wages followed in their wake, also falling between the mid-1880s and 1910, which contributed to the diagnosis of the declining welfare of the Javanese peasantry (Figures 4.5 and 6.5). The tendency of real wages to stagnate was, of course, also related to the continuing strong growth of the labour force and the population in these years – a trend that will be discussed in more detail in the next chapter.

The only industry that might have supplied a significant amount of employment for unskilled labourers – which often lay at the basis of a process of industrializa-tion with its foundation in low-wage costs – was textiles, which, as we have already seen, was almost continually shrinking in (relative) size. In another large country that suffered from the 'cotton invasion' of the 1820s and 1830s, India, this was fol-lowed by the emergence of a local factory-based cotton industry in the 1850s and

1860s, but we do not find traces of such a development in Indonesia. This may imply that the country was simply too successful as an exporter of cash crops and minerals that this crowded out industrial activities – a kind of 'Dutch disease' effect. Industrial production and employment outside the export sector (the sugar factories and the oil refineries), and in particular the textile sector – which would have been the logical candidate for export-oriented industrialization – may have been depressed by the successes of export agriculture. The industries that did perform well, those related to sugar and oil, were moreover not spatially concentrated, but located in faraway places on the Outer Islands (the oil wells were in Sumatra and Kalimantan), or in the Javanese countryside. One of the keys to 'modern economic growth' appears to be that movement away from agriculture is accelerated by the cumulative effects of industrial and urban growth, but this was lacking in Indonesia in this period; as we saw already, the level of urbanization even went down.

Exchange rate policies may have contributed to the 'Dutch disease effect'. After a few years of hesitation, the (rudimentary) central bank of the colony, the Javasche Bank, decided in 1877 to follow the Dutch central bank in switching to the gold standard instead of sticking to silver, which had traditionally been the basis of the currency (Prince 1989). This was criticized by part of the colonial commercial elite, as major competitors did not do this. Malaysia and Singapore, for example, only made the move in 1906; due to this, they may have profited from the decline in the value of silver. Indonesia, on the other hand, was drawn into a process of deflation in the 1880s and 1890s that probably harmed its economy. The main consideration for moving to gold was that this would enable the colonial government to borrow cheaply on the Dutch capital market.

The picture of economic change between 1870 and 1914 is therefore mixed: the move to more market-oriented policies certainly helped to stimulate economic development in this period, and was one of the factors behind the growth of per capita output and total factor productivity. The switch to developmental policies during the 1890s and early 1900s seemed promising. We will review their impact in more detail in the next chapter, and also point out the limitations of these policies. For one, the funds invested in welfare services were quite small, and the colonial state was unable to generate more money to realize its ambitions. Another equally important cause of growth was the improvements in infrastructure, such as railways and shipping between the islands, which greatly reduced transport costs. These changes, in combination with the improvements in international transport infrastructure (such as the Suez Canal), led to the rapid integration of Java and parts of the Outer Islands into world markets. European entrepreneurs were not the only ones to profit from these changes – Indonesians managed to increase their shares in various exports as well. Growth was, as a result, to a large extent export-led. Its impact on the domestic market – on the real incomes of the Indonesians – was limited (as we will show in the next chapter), and it did not result in the kinds of cumulative processes of structural change, urbanization and industrialization that, according to Kuznets (1966), are the core of the process of 'modern economic growth'.

6 The constraints of a colonial economy, 1914–1942

Riding the waves of the international economy

The nineteenth century had been an exceptional period of stability and peace. The first half of the twentieth century would be quite different, and the consequences of the Great European Civil War that went on between 1914 and 1945 would also be felt in 'distant' Indonesia. As we saw in the previous chapter, the years immediately preceding the First World War had been very dynamic for the export economy of the country. International markets were booming, and the Indonesian output of sugar, oil, tobacco and rubber had grown rapidly (Table 5.2), as a result of which the openness of the country had increased markedly (see Chapter 2, Figure 2.9). Indigenous, small-scale agriculture also contributed greatly to the revival of the economy, as Van der Eng (1996) has demonstrated. For the first time there had been a substantial increase in total factor productivity, which continued into the war years (Chapter 2). Both Java and the Outer Islands contributed to the growth spurt (Figure 6.1). The Indonesian export economy was now dominated by commodities produced in Sumatra and Kalimantan, such as oil and tobacco, but Java's economy was even more dynamic in this period, thanks to the revival of peasant agriculture, the growth of transport and trade, the expansion of government services, and a slow process of industrialization that began to take shape. Textiles still stagnated, but a number of other industries saw their output increase by on average 5 per cent in these years (Table 6.1).

The First World War (1914–1918) dramatically changed this picture of a rapidly developing economy realizing substantial growth. The export sector went through two cycles of 'boom and bust' between 1914–1921, before settling into somewhat calmer waters. During the first two to three years of the war, the enormous increase in world market prices, combined with the fact that the Dutch economy more or less remained outside the war – which meant that business could be continued 'as usual' – brought high profits and high demand to the export sector of the Indonesian economy. Oil, for example, became a highly strategic commodity during these years, when the fleets of the main warring states were increasingly using oil for their motive power (instead of coal). Most spectacular was the development of rubber, which also suddenly became a highly strategic good for which demand skyrocketed; its exports rose from 7,100 tonnes in 1913 to 45,700 tonnes in 1917, and further increased to 89,700 tonnes in 1919 (*Changing Economy in Indonesia,* Vol. 12a: 160). What put an end to the boom in the Indonesian economy in these years was the heightened shortage of shipping capacity (due to the German unlimited submarine warfare), which made it, from early 1917 onwards, much more difficult to ship the goods out of the country, and at the same time caused increased scarcities of imported commodities. As a result, in late 1917 and 1918 exports shrank seriously, despite skyrocketing prices on world markets. After peace returned, another, even more extreme cycle set in: initially high prices of export commodities and a renewed supply of shipping capacity resulted in an unprecedented boom, which, however, was followed after 1920 by an equally deep recession – the result of falling prices on international markets. On balance, the period between 1914 and 1921 of war and recovery did not bring much economic growth, as Figure 6.1 and Table 6.1 demonstrate; only the government sector expanded rapidly, but this was not unproblematic, as we shall see shortly.

The 1920s, however, were in many respects a continuation of the growth trends that had set in between 1900 and 1914. Exports boomed, domestic agriculture also grew substantially (although output growth was just as fast as population growth), and industrial output continued to expand (as it had also done during the war years), albeit from a very small base. The international sector of the economy recovered from the bad times it had gone through during the previous decade, and the sharp expansion of government services came to an end.

What was different in the 1920s was that the honeymoon of the Ethical Policy was over. Between 1900 and 1920 government expenditure had increased enormously, partly as a result of the ambitious welfare programmes that were carried out. This not only included the welfare services as such (education, agricultural

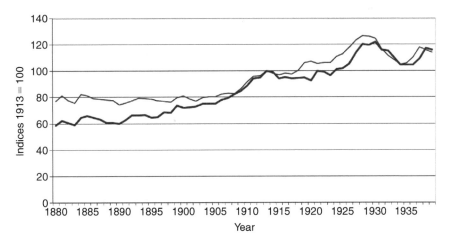

Figure 6.1 GDP per capita of Java and Indonesia (1880–1939) (1913 = 100) (sources: van Zanden 2002; Van der Eng 2002).

Table 6.1 The growth of real value added of the various industries on Java and Madura, 1816–1938*

	Agriculture		Other primary	Textiles	Rest of industry	Trade	Transport	Other services	Government	Total
	Foodstuffs	Exports								
1816–1830*	0.68	-0.36	3.61	2.34	6.29	6.97	2.78	5.16	3.56	2.14
1830–1840	1.01	18.57	0.57	-1.19	-0.03	5.73	3.68	0.07	-0.32	1.90
1840–1860	0.50	1.01	0.38	0.66	1.50	3.10	2.20	0.88	2.10	1.01
1860–1880	2.16	2.66	-0.26	-0.03	1.22	3.27	5.28	0.66	0.32	1.90
1880–1900	1.01	4.08	0.52	0.75	2.99	2.92	11.63	2.68	0.65	2.20
1900–1913	1.84	4.66	2.05	0.16	5.19	4.46	6.99	2.16	4.40	3.43
1913–1921	0.34	0.97	0.63	-2.01	4.25	-2.00	-0.69	-1.37	8.46	0.66
1921–1929	1.44	6.60	7.21	0.83	4.20	4.58	2.62	-0.08	0.76	3.70
1929–1938	1.98	-3.46	2.36	2.83	5.37	-3.42	-5.63	1.25	2.23	0.63

Source: van Zanden 2002.

Note

* All indicated years are averages of three years, implying that 1816–1830 is the growth rate between 1815/1817 and 1829/1831.

extension, etc.), but also large-scale public works (irrigation) and transport infrastructure. The government was increasingly involved in financing and running the railways and in improving the ports, and had become much more active in stabilizing the rice market. Total expenditure increased from less than 150 million guilders in 1900 to more than 1 billion guilders in 1920 and 1921 (Figure 6.2). To some extent the state managed to finance this via the introduction of new taxes, and in particular a few war-related levies brought in a substantial amount of money. But the end of the war meant that the rationale for these special taxes disappeared, and prices were decreasing regardless, which depressed the profits that formed the basis of this special taxation. A gap had opened up between expenditure and income that had to be narrowed somehow – the colony had already become too dependent on the Dutch capital market for financing the huge deficit (Figure 6.2). The new Governor-General Fock (1921–1926) inaugurated a period of severe budget cuts, aimed at balancing the budget, and welfare services such as education were among the first casualties of these measures. His successor, De Graeff, a staunch conservative, continued the cautionary policies of Fock, as a result of which government services received much less attention than before 1920. Education more or less maintained its share in public expenditure, but in particular the share of public works (such as irrigation) declined sharply (Table 5.1).

Despite the budget cuts in the first half of the decade, the 1920s were still years of growing prosperity. The tide turned in the early 1930s, when the Indonesian economy was badly hit by the international depression. Again a source of

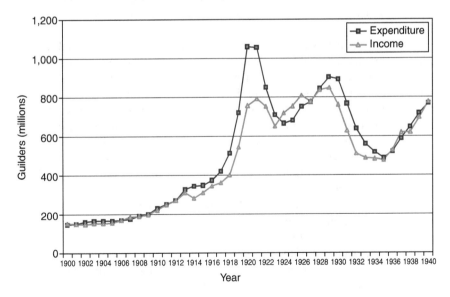

Figure 6.2 Income and expenditure of colonial government, 1900–1940 (sources: *Changing Economy in Indonesia*, Vol. 2; dataset Mellegers 2004 at www.iisg. nl/indonesianeconomy/).

instability was the world market: world prices of export commodities fell enormously in these years. Almost all markets for primary commodities – including those for oil, which had previously enjoyed a rapidly growing demand – were characterized by huge surpluses.

Among the main victims of the depression was the sugar industry, which until the early 1930s had handled the most important export product of the colony. Its position had always been rather weak, in the sense that it met stiff competition from abroad – not only the cane sugar industries of the Caribbean or India, but also the beet sugar that was being produced in Europe itself. This had traditionally enjoyed the protection of major European states (Germany, France); it was only the Brussels Sugar Convention of 1902 that had inaugurated a brief period of free trade in the commodity, which led to a renewed growth of the industry in Indonesia. This came to an end in 1931, however, when collapsing prices and increased international protection (which had returned after 1918) brought the colonial government to join an international agreement to ban overproduction and divide international markets. It is rather ironic that in 1930 even the Netherlands – one of the few free markets to which the Javanese sugar could be exported – increased its import levies on the product in order to protect its own agriculture (Taselaar 1998: 438). The Indonesian position in the international agreement concluded in 1931 was very weak, as it was dependent on export markets it could not get access to anymore. Japan, for example, closed off the market of Taiwan and began growing sugar cane there itself, and the major market of India was also increasingly protected. As a result, production had to be curtailed – the colonial state had to step in impose such a policy – and remained much below the level attained in the late 1920s (Van der Eng 1996: 202).

Problems in other export industries were similar, and led to comparable interventions by the colonial government. Indonesia participated in international agreements to restrict the output of both tea and rubber, both somewhat more successful than the sugar agreement. Intervention in the rubber market was complicated by the fact that increasingly rubber was the product of small-scale farming, and could therefore not be controlled like the plantation sector, which dominated the production of sugar (and, to a lesser extent, of tea). The other main export product, oil, was regulated by a cartel set up by the large oil companies themselves, who drew up the famous Achnacarry Agreement of 1928. The Indonesian market would become one of the 'best' examples of the successful functioning of this cartel. This was relatively easy, as Royal Dutch controlled 80 per cent of the market, and could fix the price at the desired level – making it possible for the others to follow its lead (Jonker and van Zanden 2007).

Due to the openness of the Indonesian economy and the conservative monetary policy aimed at sticking to the gold standard, the extreme fall in world market prices immediately translated into a lowering of prices domestically; this deflationary impulse was very sharp and, moreover, continued until 1936/1937. In total, Indonesian prices almost halved in the 1929–1936 period (they declined by 47 per cent). No other country for which similar statistics are available saw its price level decline so much, and during such an extended period. In India, for example, a country in a rather similar situation, prices declined by 'only' one-third; and in Germany, probably the industrial country worst affected by the depression, they declined by 23 per cent. The causes of the prolonged and deep nature of the depression were as follows: Indonesia had a relatively open economy, dependent on exports of primary products. The prices of those products fell much more than the prices of manufactured commodities, and the depression was therefore much more severe in countries specializing in those goods. Independent primary producers – in particular those in Latin America – reacted to the depression by drastically changing strategy: they shut their markets to imports of manufactured goods, which they were unable to afford to buy at world market prices in any case, and developed an import substitution strategy focused on industrialization. This strategy was often relatively successful, in particular in the medium to long run. For Indonesia, being a colony, this was not a real option, however, although some import substitution did take place. This was partly induced by the rapid growth of Japanese industrial exports to Indonesia, which competed heavily with the 'traditional' Dutch supply of those commodities. Dutch industry, already in bad shape as a result of the Great Depression, started to lobby for more protection on the Indonesian market, which it did receive from 1933 onwards, when the Crisis Import Ordinance was introduced (Van Oorschot 1956). It is typical for the fate of a colony that this U-turn in Dutch policy did not result from a different perception of the interests of the Indonesian manufacturers – or other 'indigenous' causes for a change of policy – but was instead due to the deteriorating position of Dutch textile industry on the Indonesian market (Taselaar 1998: 432–440). This also led to the increased protection of Indonesian industry in its home market. For the first time, textiles were a source of economic growth, and the rest of industry also expanded relatively rapidly in these years (Table 6.1).

Being a very open economy dependent on primary products is part of the story explaining the intensity of the depression of the 1930s. Monetary policies also contributed to the problems, and in particular led to a continuation of the depression during the period from 1933–1936. The Dutch guilder was not pushed from the gold standard – as happened to the British pound in September 1931 – nor was there a conscious devaluation of the currency, as many countries, including the United States, carried out after 1931. Instead, the Dutch monetary authorities preferred to stick to the gold standard, which meant that the level of prices and wages in the economy became much higher than that of its competitors (van Zanden 1997). As a result, in the Netherlands the depression lasted longer than elsewhere – until September 1936, when the gold standard was finally abandoned. Because the Netherlands-Indies guilder was linked to the Dutch guilder, this policy had similar implications for price levels in the colony and for its exports, and resulted in a continuation of the depression in 1933–1936, when elsewhere the worst was usually over.

The only 'bright' side to this story was that, as a result of radical changes in relative prices – those of export commodities fell much more than prices of

products produced for the domestic market – and the tentative protectionist policies that were enacted from 1933 onwards, a process of industrialization began.
This process ended the long period in which the secondary sector had declined
relative to other sectors of the economy, which had accelerated. The industrial
sector's share in GDP of Java, which had fallen to as low as 15 per cent in the
late 1920s, increased to 28 per cent in 1938/1939. The depression, therefore,
induced the first wave of industrial growth since the beginning of the nineteenth
century. The textile industry, which was among the first industries to receive
protection, grew rapidly – output doubled in the second half of the 1930s – and
went through a process of mechanization, although the number of power-looms
remained much smaller than that of handlooms, and yarns continued to be
imported (Dick *et al.* 2002: 160–161). But overall growth was very modest in
these years: during the first four to five years of the depression, GDP per capita
fell dramatically, by almost 20 per cent, making Indonesia one of the worst
victims of the Great Depression; only Spain and Austria appear to have done as
poorly, but in both cases political circumstances played a role as well. Indian
GDP per capita declined by 'only' 7 per cent in the years between 1929 and
1936 (Maddison 2001). Linking the fate of Indonesia's economic and monetary
policies so closely to that of the Netherlands was therefore a major mistake, and
the disadvantages of being so closely tied to the Dutch economy soon became
quite clear.

Small-scale agriculture to some extent also profited from the problems in the
export sector of the economy. The output of sugar contracted enormously –
exports declined by almost two-thirds between 1929 and 1936 – but because
sugar competed with rice for the high-quality *sawahs* on Java, rice production
could be increased substantially. This, in combination with years of good crops
and the gradual introduction of the first generation of high-yielding varieties,
caused rice output to expand rapidly (Van der Eng 1996: 202). As a result, Indonesia once again became self-sufficient in rice, mainly thanks to the increased
production on Java. The gains made by industry and small-scale agriculture were
not large enough to compensate for the contraction of the agricultural export
sector and the related service industries (trade and transport) (Table 6.1). Only
after 1936 did the tide really turn; the abolishment of the gold standard in September of that year was the beginning of a brief period of recovery that would
continue into 1940/1941, when, after the occupation of the Netherlands by
Germany, the government became even more active in stimulating the Indonesian economy.

Welfare policies in action: the example of the reform of capital markets

From the 1890s onwards, the colonial state developed a broad range of welfare
policies aimed at improving the fate of the indigenous population. The debate
about the 'diminishing welfare' of the Javanese population that began in the
1880s was at the background of this policy change, as a result of which most

policies were directed at the population of Java, where the standard of living was considered to be lower than elsewhere. Economic historians have been relatively positive about the long-term consequences of these policies. As pointed out in Chapter 2, the efficiency of the rice market greatly improved in the late nine-teenth and early twentieth centuries: seasonal variation of rice prices fell mark-edly, and the degree of market integration increased at the same time. We speculated that this was due to improved networks of communication overseas and over land, in which the state began to play an increasingly large role, and to the direct effects of welfare policies, for example, those aimed at stabilizing the rice market. The efficiency of institutions, we showed, improved markedly in the late colonial period, and the economy reacted positively to this (as economists would expect). Moreover, growth occured not only in the 'capitalist' part of the economy, but also in small-scale agriculture, which was the focus of the welfare policies.

In 1905 the Department of Agriculture was created as a separate entity, which became the key player in a newly emerging system of agricultural research and extension services (Boomgaard 1986a). In export agriculture – in particular the sugar industry – much experience had already been accumulated through agri-cultural research into improving the yields of crops and suppressing diseases. In the Netherlands a similar system had been set up, heavily subsidized by the state, which was also increasingly successful in furthering agricultural development. The same model was applied to Indonesia, and in particular to Java, with, under-standably, a certain focus on rice cultivation. Systematic research into the socio-economic and technical aspects of rice farming was undertaken; experimental plots were used to test ideas about new methods of cultivation and to develop new varieties; and village farming schools (*desalandbouwschooltjes*) were set up to diffuse the new knowledge among the peasant population (Van der Eng 1996: 73–76, 83–97). In the 1920s this led to important breakthroughs in the develop-ment of new rice varieties, which increasingly found their way into small-scale agriculture. One new seed variety developed in the 1930s, the so-called 40c population obtained through the crossing of Chinese and Indian varieties, was eventually adopted in large parts of Indonesia and the Philippines, and was used in the latter during the 1960s and 1970s in the famous experiments by the Rice Research Institute (Maat 2001: 194–195).

Related to these research and extension services were policies aimed at stabi-lizing the rice market. Indonesia, and in particular Java, had since the 1860s become increasingly dependent on imports of rice from Thailand, Vietnam and Burma, among other countries. During the 1910s, war, the scarcity of shipping capacity and crop failures in mainland Southeast Asia caused severe disruptions of the market for rice, which the government initially tried to cope with by banning exports (parts of the Outer Islands were still net exporters of rice). When this did not have the desired effects and the scarcity of rice increased – undermining the standard of living of the population, and perhaps leading to social instability – the government, between 1917 and 1920, took the rice market into its own hands: it began to buy rice in the surplus areas of the Archipelago and sell it in the deficit regions. Moreover, it set maximum retail prices and limited the output of the competing sugar industry (Boomgaard 1986b: 69). These were bold measures to stabilize the rice market and protect the consumers; that the efficiency of rice markets increased in these years of high instability is perhaps proof of their effectiveness (see Chapter 2, Figures 2.11 and 2.12). At the same time, investments in irrigation – another important welfare policy – were stepped up in these years, leading to a rapid growth of the irrigated area in the interwar period; the sugar industry profited from these investments as well (Boomgaard 1986b: 71–72).[1]

International pressure sometimes also played a role in moderating the policies of the colonial government. Labour conditions on the large-scale plantation, particularly in Sumatra, had always been problematic: wages were relatively high (by Indonesian standards) as these places were highly dependent on migratory labour from China and India, among other countries, as well as Java. These 'coolies' were hired on the basis of a contract for a number of years (often three), but in order to be sure that they would really work hard during this period, employers were allowed to sanction them – and, more generally, act as court and judge at the same time in case of labour conflicts. This *'poenale sanctie'* (penal clause), officially introduced in 1880, often resulted in the exploitation of Chinese labourers, who were dependent on their employers. They remained indebted, and therefore could not terminate their contract (Touwen 2001: 111–113). As part of the new start made by the Ethical Policy, an in-depth study of labour conditions was carried out, but the results were so problematic that it remained unpublished. Commercial interests were apparently so large that in reality little was altered during the first decades of the twentieth century, although some planters and their companies attempted to change things for the better on a voluntary basis. The creation of a Labour Inspectorate and its increased activities during the 1910s and 1920s meant that some measures were taken to improve the position of the coolies, but, as Lindblad concluded in a detailed study on the topic, 'the Labour Inspectorate did possess the capacity to alter labour conditions for coolies, but its scope of action remained very limited' (Lindblad 1999: 235). Only pressure by the United States and the International Labour Office (in 1929–1930) resulted in the abolishment of the penal clause in 1931; not accidentally, in a period when the labour scarcity that was the root cause of the problem turned into large labour surpluses as a result of the world depression (Touwen 2001: 117).

Another element of its policies for which the colonial administration was relatively sensitive to (foreign) criticism was its role in the opium trade. Before the 1890s, the opium monopoly, leased out to Chinese farmers, was one of the most important sources of finance, supplying about 12 per cent of net income. As we saw in Chapter 5, increasing criticism of this situation led to the introduction of the *regie*, a system completely managed by (Dutch) civil servants. It was more expensive to run and not geared to the maximization of consumption. Instead, the new *regie* incorporated such goals as controlling consumption levels and addressing the worst problems of addiction. The new system was much more expensive, but initially also generated much more income; whereas before 1900 gross income had fluctuated around 18 million guilders, it increased to almost 42 million in 1913 and 62 million in 1920 (but costs as a share of proceeds increased from about one-tenth to one-third). In the interwar period, however, the goal of restricted consumption became increasingly important, also due to international pressure (again, mainly coming from the United States). A system to license consumers and monitor their intake was introduced, which, in combination with the raising of the price level of opium, proved to be very effective: the level of consumption still rose until 1913, more or less stabilized from 1913–1920, and began to fall quite strongly in the 1920s and 1930s. On Java, per capita consumption fell by almost 50 per cent between 1920 and 1929; on the Outer Islands the decline was about one-third; the depression and even stricter controls on consumption resulted in another decline by about two-thirds between 1929 and 1937 (Van Ours 1995; Van Luijk and Van Ours 2001). As a source of public income, opium was also becoming more marginal: it contributed less than 3 per cent to government income in these years.

We will look a bit more closely at welfare policies geared towards the capital markets, because of the key role these markets play in economic development. Colonial officials had already in the nineteenth century identified the problem of the malfunctioning of rural capital markets, although they had a rather one-sided interpretation of its cause, which they often attributed to the exploitation of the peasants by Chinese middlemen who monopolized rural markets (see Chapter 4). In response, colonial administrators developed an innovative package of measures combining both 'traditional' and 'new' forms of credit supply and intermediation, which seemed to be relatively well adapted to societal structures and local circumstances. These new policies are a good example of the work carried out by the more enlightened members of the colonial administration, some of whom began to see themselves as 'development workers' *avant la lettre*, carrying the 'white men's burden' (see for example Van den Doel 1994).

The first reforms of the credit system, already underway in the late 1890s, were to a large extent inspired by similar initiatives in Western Europe aimed at solving market failures in the countryside. The most important source of inspiration was Friedrich Wilhelm Raiffeisen (1818–1888), who in the 1850s developed the concept of the cooperative bank. Put simply, this bank collected the savings of the rural residents with the aim of providing credit to the farmers. In this way farmers could be freed from their dependency on external sources of credit. The idealistic character of the bank was much emphasized by its founder. Raiffeisen viewed the founding and administration of the bank as an act of Christian charity for which no compensation could be expected. According to this same principle, profits could not be distributed among the members, but were to be deposited in a central fund and used to support farm credit. It was also essential to create reserves to cover the unlimited liability of the members of the cooperative as much as possible. Partly due to Raiffeisen's initiatives, the first cooperative banks were established in Germany as early as the 1860s. In the 1890s this movement also spread to the Netherlands, where it became a big success, particularly after the establishment of central cooperative banks in 1898 (Sluy-terman *et al.* 1998).

It was only natural for the Dutch colonial administrators who wanted to reform rural capital markets in Indonesia to copy this model. The problems were similar. One of the key problems was that outsiders – for example moneylenders from the city – could not assess the creditworthiness of farmers, because they lacked necessary information about the quality of their entrepreneurship and assets. Because of this information problem, if no collateral in the form of land were available, outsiders would not lend money to farmers, or only lend at very high interest rates to cover the high risks involved. The Raiffeisen model was based on the idea that within the village community this kind of information was freely available: all farmers and many non-farmers (shopkeepers, for instance, or the local notary or schoolmaster) knew quite well who was to be trusted and who was not, or who would use new credit in a careful way and who would waste it. By setting up a cooperative – an in principal democratic association of farmers 'guided' by a few members of the rural elite – this 'inside' knowledge could be used to direct credit policy. In order to create trust, the unlimited liability of the members of the cooperative was introduced as a rule; this meant that the wealth of the local landowner and the notary who joined the cooperative backed up its solvency as well, and that those members of the local elite had a strong incentive to monitor its activities, for example by becoming members of the board that governed the cooperative (Sluyterman *et al.* 1998).

The pioneer of this model on Java was the civil servant W.P.D. de Wolff van Westerrode, who after a visit to Europe during which he came in contact with the ideas of Raiffeisen, tried to put them into practice in 1897 in the district where he was stationed, Purwokerto. In a way the model appeared to be ideally suited to Javanese conditions: it appealed to non-economic motives – many civil servants strongly believed that the behaviour of the Javanese peasant could not be explained from economic motives alone – and in particular to a spirit of coop-eration among the peasantry; both of which civil servants saw as being charac-teristic of Javanese society (Henley 2004). In a few parts of the island rudimentary cooperative institutions already existed. Amongst them were *priyayi* banks that catered to the needs of the indigenous elite (the *priyayi*), and the *lum-bungs*, or village rice barns, to which wealthy peasants brought their surplus rice and from which poor peasants could borrow rice during the planting season or during the period just before the harvest when rice was scarce, the *paceklik*. Both *priyayi* banks and *lumbungs* were heavily dependent on the protection provided by Dutch civil servants – at least that is the picture that emerges from the literat-ure written by the Dutch civil servants themselves – and most led a marginal existence if this support was unavailable (Cramer 1929: 17–25).

The new inspiration offered by the Raiffeisen model meant that this support became much stronger after 1896, in particular when in 1901 the Ethical Policy was proclaimed. De Wolff tried to breathe new life into the two types of coopera-tive institutions that already existed. He formalized the structure of a *priyayi* bank by setting up the *Poerwokertosche Hulp-, Spaar- en Landbouwcredietbank*.

By pushing hard, and thanks to the support of increasing numbers of other civil servants who shared his concerns, the number of *volksbanken* (popular banks, as the banks modelled after the *Poerwokertosche* were named) and *lumbungs* increased rapidly in the years after 1901. In between these two models – the simple *lumbungs* administered by the village elite and the formal *volksbanken* governed by Dutch civil servants – a third model developed, of the *dessabank*, often growing out of the *lumbungs* by accepting savings and supplying small cash credits (instead of rice). A threefold structure of credit came into existence, of which the *volksbanken* catered to the needs of the upper echelons of Javanese society, and the *lumbungs* and the *dessabanken* supplied the needs of the peasantry for cash and credit.

What is most striking, however, is that not much remained of the cooperative ideals that were behind the first new initiatives. Most banks – small or large – were tightly monitored by Dutch civil servants. The surplus rice for the *lumbungs*, for instance, was often acquired through coercion – by using the proceeds of local (religious) taxes, or simply by ordering the peasants to store part of their harvest in these common storage bins, which were controlled by the village's head. Or to quote Cramer (1929: 20), they were 'voluntary ... on the instigation of the regent'. The problem of corruption in the management of the *lumbungs* was never really resolved, and complaints about abuses continued to resurface.

At the other end of the spectrum similar problems arose. Attempts failed to turn the first *volksbanken* into real associations with a vigorous membership, comparable to the way in which the European cooperative banks were governed by their members, who met regularly, discussed strategic issues and elected the board. Members of the local elite refused to become members of the *volksbanken* and to subject themselves to these kinds of procedures, with which they were unfamiliar. They only became members when this was a condition for getting a loan (Cramer 1929: 22). As a result, Dutch civil servants dominated the *volksbanken*, and administrating such a bank became an integral part of their work (Cramer 1929: 42).

An additional problem was the lack of (voluntary) savings by the Javanese. The Raiffeisen model was based on the idea that at least some, relatively wealthy farmers would save voluntarily and that members of the rural elite would contribute their savings. But this had been a major problem during the first decades of the cooperative movement in Europe, which only took off in a big way during the 1890s and 1900s, when the prices of agricultural products (after having been at a low ebb during the agricultural depression of the 1870s and 1880s) went up again and rural prosperity increased. Javanese peasants were much poorer than Dutch or German farmers – a factor which in itself already explains a large part of the difference in savings behaviour – and they may have had less trust in these associations (which never became 'their own'). We have already seen that most of the savings in rice that formed the basis for the *lumbungs* was at best quasi-voluntary – or not voluntary at all. The *volksbanken* received most of their deposits from Europeans and from the government; only a small fraction came from the Javanese population.

The result was that the credit system (the *volkscredietwezen*) became part of the government welfare services, whereas in Western Europe the cooperatives were and continued to be part of the private sector, keeping the state at an arm's length. This happened in a few steps from 1906 onwards, a process that was concluded with the establishment, in 1912, of the *Dienst van het Volkscredietwezen*, a formal governmental body that was put in charge of the *volksbanken* and the *dessabanken*.

A second, perhaps equally important part of the reforms implemented in the early 1900s was the replacement of the leasing system of the pawnshops by a government monopoly. In the 1890s, criticism of the system of pawnshops was again on the rise; in 1900 the government decided to survey it, and De Wolff van Westerrode was asked to direct the survey. The recommendations that followed from it were to abolish private pawnshops and introduce a government monopoly. The decision to implement these recommendations was carried out very swiftly; in 1904 all pawnshops on Java and Madura became part of the Government Service (with the exception of pawnshops still licensed in Surakarta). At the same time interest rates were lowered substantially. Figure 6.3 illustrates the magnitude of the change, which, for the smallest loans, declined from 143 per cent annually before 1901 to 72 per cent after that date. They were lowered further in 1920, to 48 per cent for the smallest loans, which usually dominated the business. It took some time for the government monopoly to establish itself – between 1901 and 1910 total lending by the government monopoly was probably less than the sums handled by the private pawnshops before 1900.[2] But in the long run these reforms resulted in a strong expansion of credit supplied by the pawnshops.

What was the impact of these reforms on the Javanese peasants' access to credit? In order to answer this question, we first compared the amount of credit supplied by the four institutions discussed previously (on the basis of data on loans outstanding at the end of the year to eliminate double counting, as far as these are available) with the development of the value added of the agricultural sector (excluding export crops, which were mainly produced by Western plantations – although there were of course many exceptions to this rule).[3] The reason for making such a comparison is that prices fluctuated enormously between 1905 and 1940: strong inflation during the 1910s was followed by deflation during the 1920s and first half of the 1930s. Moreover, the value added of food production by smallholders seems to be the relevant measure to compare with as many of these policies were aimed at facilitating access to credit for the peasantry. But it would be wrong to assume that only peasants profited from the expansion of government-sponsored credit. In fact, more than half (and in a few years almost 70 per cent) of the credit supplied by the *volksbanken* did not find its way to 'villagers', and perhaps as much as 50 per cent of the loans pawnshops made went to shopkeepers, craftsmen and other small businessmen (Van Laanen 1980: Table 6). Yet, a comparison with total GDP seems to be even more off the mark, because that includes the large Western sector of the economy, which had other sources of credit, such as the colonial banks, which supplied at least four to five times more credit between 1910 and 1940 than the institutions discussed previously.

Figure 6.3 shows the strong expansion of these welfare services between 1905 and about 1930; while it is assumed that in 1910 the 'old' level of the credit supply of the pawnshops was again reached, it still appears that the amount of credit increased substantially in the 1910s and 1920s. The decline of the ratio between credit and value added in the second half of the 1910s is probably not related to diminishing supply, but rather to declining demand for credit. Prices were very high in those years, which made it possible to pay back loans and borrow less, whereas the size of value added in agriculture exploded due to inflation. After 1921, when times were more difficult, however, the credit supply continued to grow until 1929, albeit at a rather low level in nominal terms. The expansion was almost completely dominated by the reformed pawnshops and the *volksbanken*, with both catering to the needs of the Javanese and non-Javanese middle classes. The institutions most clearly linked to small-scale agriculture, the *lumbungs* and the *dessabanken*, were much less successful; their combined loans increased from about 1.7 per cent of value added in agriculture in 1910 to a peak of 2.3 per cent in 1929. This shows, on the one hand, how difficult it was to reach out to the poorest strata of rural society, to create and manage institutions that were trusted by and accessible to the peasantry. On the other hand, the peasants must also have profited from the reform of the pawnshops (which they often used), and, to a lesser extent, by the more elastic supply of capital on rural and urban markets due to the rise of the *volksbanken*.

Another measure of the success of these reforms is the decline of interest rates. This is easiest for the pawnshops: as already mentioned, their rates declined strongly from 143 per cent for the smallest loans under the pre-1901 regime (as set by the government), to 72 per cent in 1901 (following the

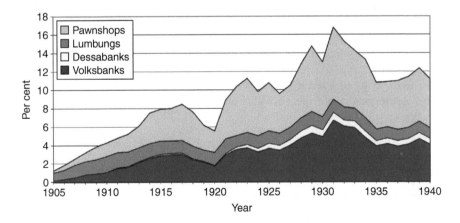

Figure 6.3 The ratio between credit supplied by four welfare services and value added of agriculture (excluding export agriculture), 1905–1940 (sources: Van Laanen 1980: Table 5; van Zanden 2002).

introduction of the monopoly) and finally to 48 per cent in 1920. This lowering of interest rates in 1920 was a response to the large profits made during 1915–1919; in 1915–1918 profits were on average five million guilders, and they increased to an embarrassing 17 million guilders in 1919 (van Zanden 2009a: 170). After 1920 profits turned into losses, however, and this contributed to the already large deficits of the colonial state in those years. So in 1924 policy was again changed, and interest rates returned to their pre-1920 level of 72 per cent for the smallest loans (and almost all loans were very small). Finally, in 1928, after years of high profits, interest rates on the smallest loans were again reduced to 48 per cent; other interest rates were kept at the prevailing level. One can argue that this increase in interest rates in 1924 was the result of a significant change in policy. Before the mid-1920s, the costs and revenues of the govern-ment monopoly had been more or less equal (van Zanden 2009a: 170). This changed in the mid-1920s, however, and the pawnshops became – again – a significant source of net income to the colonial state. This change is perhaps indicative of the development of the Ethical Policy in general, which lost much of its appeal and dynamism during the first half of the 1920s.

The *volksbanken* began operations with an interest rate on loans of 12 per cent (and 6 per cent on savings), but already in 1910 this was considered too low, and raised to 18 per cent (Table 6.2). The interest rates of the *lumbungs* were related to the extra amount of rice borrowers had to return after the harvest; because prices after the harvest were much lower than before it, the nominal interest rate in terms of the amounts of money borrowed and repaid was lower, perhaps by as much as 15 to 20 per cent. The rates shown in Table 6.2 were much lower than rates in the private market before the rise of the Welfare Serv-ices. Hasselman (1914: 12), in his review of the Inquiry into the Welfare of the Javanese of 1905, estimated interest rates on loans in rice (to bridge the gap between the time before and after the harvest) at 100 per cent per year. For loans in cash, 50 per cent was his estimated average, which is not that much higher than the rates which became usual in the *dessabanken* (see also Cramer 1929: 11). With the possible exception of loans by the *dessabanken*, interest rates on loans supplied by the welfare services were generally (much) lower than in the private sector.

The lowering of interest rates was to a large extent the result of the fact that the state stepped in and spent sizeable amounts of resources on the newly estab-

Table 6.2 Estimates of interest rates of loans supplied by the Government Credit System, 1905–1937

	Volksbanken	Dessabanken	Lumbungs
1905–1913	12–18	24–45	–
1913–1926	13.5–18.8	40–60	30–50
1929–1937	8–15	30–40	25–30

Source: Van Laanen 1980: 41.

lished or reformed institutions. In order to make the new situation sustainable, the new institutions had to induce the population to bring their savings to them, which would result in a rise in the (visible) savings ratio of the population. This did not happen, however. As Van Laanen (1980: 40) already estimated, only a small fraction of the loans supplied by the new institutions could be financed from savings they mobilized themselves. Before 1930 this ratio fluctuated between 10 and 13 per cent when the pawnshops are included in the estimates; without the pawnshops, the ratio was about 20–25 per cent. After 1930 this share became larger (up to 27–28 per cent), but it continued to be much below parity.

The following reasons may help to explain this. At first glance the stagnation of savings can be considered the logical result of lowering interest rates, as lowering a price would normally – at least in the short run – result in a decline of its supply. Institutional factors may have also played a role. A significant difference with post-Raiffeisen Europe is that the new institutions set up after 1900 did not become independent cooperatives for which the farmers themselves were responsible and which they could therefore trust, but part of a colonial state distrusted by most of them (and by many members of the rural elite). This limitation was stressed (amongst others) by Djojohadikoesoemo (1943: 180–181) in his study of the credit system in the 1930s, and the discussion on the reform of the government credit services focused on ways to turn it into a true cooperative system (Djojohadikoesoemo 1943: 185–188). This appears to have been a very general problem, associated with introducing the 'European' model of the cooperative into very different socio-political settings in the 'Third World'. The lack of popular, 'democratic' backing of cooperatives had been a major problem limiting their success in stimulating development in these countries; often they became instruments in the hands of small elites to exploit the rural population and/or redistribute government funds to the advantage of the few (see Van Roosmalen and van Zanden 2001 for a review of these problems).

Finally, one can also argue that the ultimate failure of these policies was linked to the fact that the colonial government was unable, and perhaps unwilling, to reform the basic institutional setting of the economy by introducing a clear system of formal property rights, which would have made it possible to use land and buildings already owned by the peasantry as collateral for loans. As argued by De Soto (De Soto 2000), such a failure is the main reason for the stunted development of capital markets in developing economies, a point that likely can also be made for colonial Java. Land owned by Javanese peasants could be sold to other Javanese, and probably even mortgaged, but it could not be bought by Chinese and other 'Foreign Orientals' (Arabs, Indians),[4] nor Europeans, which restricted the value of a mortgage on this land. Middlemen and local moneylenders used this 'gap' in the institutional framework (which made it nearly impossible to use land as a collateral for loans at the *volksbanken*) to find other ways for 'mortgaging' land in a more informal way, for which different indigenous institutions were developed. The fact that land could be used as a source of credit 'outside the government services' was an important factor behind the increased dynamism of the private capital market in the 1930s

(Djojohadikoesoemo 1943: 174–175 gives a number of examples); but this did not occur as a result of the new welfare services, but more or less in spite of them.

A related question is whether the peasants who received loans via this system were actually using this to buy inputs (new rice varieties, fertilizer) to increase their productivity. Again, this question was asked by colonial administrators, who tried to analyse the purposes for which the loans were used. In practice, it was very difficult to monitor the farmers who had received a loan, because 'there [was] so little personal contact between the bank management and the clients it [was] easy to obtain a loan for consumption purposes under the guise of a pro- ductive loan' (Penders 1984: 2). Moreover, there was no coordination between this welfare service and the agricultural extension officers who were also active in the countryside – most *dessabanken*, for example, only supplied money for very short periods of time, whereas the agricultural extension service wanted the peasants to invest in the (medium) long term. In a recent survey of the activities of the VCW (the *Volkscredietwezen*), one critic surmised that 'it would seem reasonable to conclude that generally the VCW had not been able to cope to any appreciable extent with the problem of chronic rural indebtedness and failed to help increase the rate of indigenous agricultural specialization' (Penders 1984: 4).

This review of late-colonial policies to restructure local capital markets in order to improve their efficiency and increase access to them for local farmers has shown that, on the one hand, the colonial state and its administrators worked outelatively modern developmental ideas and implemented equally modern reforms. They tried to introduce the Raiffeisen model for cooperative banking – which at the time was becoming a success story in Western Europe – to stimu- late local forms of 'cooperative' or indigenous banking, and did reform the system of pawnshops by introducing a government monopoly. They were clearly aware of the importance of 'micro-finance' – to use the term that has become fashionable more recently. These reforms, which were part of the Ethical Policy initiated in 1901, were moderately successful in the sense that in the parts of the capital market that were monitored by the state, interest rates went down sub- stantially and access to relatively cheap capital must have increased for those villagers who gained access to this segment of the capital market. But as other development efforts since 1901 have demonstrated, the key problem was the lack of 'self-help' or 'auto-activiteit' (as contemporary critics called it – see Penders 1984: 3). Yet, to some extent the new institutions seem to have worked: output and productivity of Javanese agriculture did increase strongly in this period, whereas it had been more or less stagnant during much of the nineteenth century (Van der Eng 1996).

But the success of this part of the new welfare services was mixed: savings by the local population did not increase (enough), and the local banks remained dependent on the savings of Europeans and subsidies from the colonial state. The new banks remained under the tutelage of the colonial administration, which not only helped to finance them, but also monitored their activities closely as a guarantee against corruption and mismanagement. The human capital and 'civil society' necessary for the 'bottom-up' running of such a bank was simply not present on Java, and it is still an open question as to whether the local power structures and institutions facilitated such cooperative efforts (as many colonial officials thought, but also as Sukarno and other nationalist thinkers have maintained since), or in fact obstructed them (see the discussion in Henley 2004).

In the long run, these reforms failed to really change conditions on rural capital markets. They were already put to the test in the 1930s, when the system more or less continued to function, but the private sector (middlemen supplying credit to peasants) became increasingly important again, and many of the old abuses (which had of course not disappeared in the 1920s) returned, also due to the fact that private sector credit was often more flexible (Djojohadikoesoemo 1943). These welfare services did not survive the war and the struggle for independence, and in the 1950s the problems that had plagued local capital markets in the nineteenth century returned.

The balance sheet of colonial rule: demographic change, the standard of living and human capital formation

One of the striking features of Indonesian development in the colonial period was the very rapid growth of its population. Economic growth was not slow, thanks to the expansion of export agriculture and mining activities, but this was to a large degree 'extensive growth', linked to the strong expansion of the Indonesian population. In 1820, Java had probably about 10 million inhabitants, and Indonesia as a whole may have had about 15 million, or less than 1.5 per cent of a global population of slightly more than one billion (Boomgaard 1986b for Java; Maddison 2001 for the global population). By 1900, when the data are somewhat more reliable, the population had tripled to about 30 million in Java and 45 million in Indonesia as a whole; the total population of the world increased by 'only' 50 per cent in these 80 years, as a result of which Indonesian share in it increased to about 2.9 per cent. Forty years later, Indonesia's share had grown to 3.2 per cent (its total population had grown to about 75 million), at which level it more or less stabilized during the rest of the twentieth century. To put this into perspective for Asia, whereas the total population of Indonesia increased fivefold between 1820 and 1940, the population of India or China did not even double (India: from 209 to 390 million, China: from 380 to 520 million), or, to make another comparison, whereas in 1820 Japan had about twice the population of Indonesia, in 1940 they were about the same size. Indonesia's direct neighbours – the Philippines, Malaysia, Thailand and Burma (and *a fortiori* Singapore) – had a similar or sometimes even higher rate of population growth, however. Strong demographic growth clearly was a feature of Southeast Asia (Maddison 2001).

To some extent the rapid growth of population can be seen as the result of the success of colonial policy. After the end of the Java War in 1830, a long period of relative social and political stability followed, in which 'law and order' was maintained through the growing power of the colonial state. Moreover, except from the late 1840s, the food supply seems to have been sufficient as no major famines occurred. The gradual integration of regional markets, making it possible to increasingly import large quantities of rice and other foodstuffs, may also have enhanced the robustness of the food supply. Compared with colonial India, where at times millions died as a result of disastrous famines, and China, where similar major crises happened – the result of bad harvests and deteriorating public infrastructure – Indonesia was almost a haven of stability and of cheap food (Hugenholtz 1986: 155). Colonial administrators were very much aware of the need to secure the food supply, as famines could be sources of unrest and instability. They intervened frequently when harvests failed and the danger of a severe famine emerged, and were, with a few notable exceptions (central Java in 1900–1902) quite successful in their policies (Hugenholtz 1986). These policies became more systematic after 1911, when the government began to intervene more regularly in the import and export trades of rice and other foodstuffs to stabilize the food supply (Hugenholtz 1986: 180).

Another relatively successful welfare policy was health care. This had started in the 1820s, when inoculation against smallpox was organized by the state; after which it remained a feature of the medical system, and may have been a major cause of the decline in (infant) mortality in the nineteenth century (Boomgaard 1987). Malaria, traditionally another major killer, could gradually be pushed back in part thanks to the large-scale production of quinine starting in the late nineteenth century. Java became the world's most important producer of the product with a market share of more than 90 per cent in the 1930s (Taylor 1945). After 1900 even more ambitious reforms were introduced to improve the sanitary and health situation of the population, such as the training of (indigenous) medical staff, the building of hospitals (which had already began much earlier), and the setting up in 1911 of a Public Health Service (Boomgaard 1986b). It is unknown to what extent these reforms led to a decline in mortality and to an increase in life expectancy, however.

Increased fertility may also have played a role in the population surge. The Cultivation System created a situation of labour scarcity; the huge demand for labour by the colonial government may have induced households to increase the birth rate, as Boomgaard (1987) has argued, leading to a further acceleration of population growth in these years. The information that is available on wages and prices allows us to reconstruct what happened to the development of real wages in this period. To put real wages – an important index of the standard of living – into international perspective, we have applied the methodology developed by Allen (2001) and Allen et al. (2011) to compare levels of real wages internationally. The starting point is to construct for each country a more or less similar 'barebones' basket – a minimum subsistence basket of goods necessary for survival – consisting of a large quantity of cheap staple food (rice in this case), combined with small quantities of other foodstuffs (oil, meat, fish), textiles and a few other necessities (5 per cent of the budget is also allocated to housing). The Javanese basket is modelled after studies from the 1920s and 1930s into the structure of expenditure of Javanese households (Van der Eng 2001). The main ingredients are 175 kg of rice (similar to the baskets of other Asian countries), 3 kg of meat or fish, 3 kg of (coconut) oil, 3 m of calico, and small quantities of firewood and salt.[5] What gives these budgets a certain uniformity is that they allow for almost the same intake of calories (around 1,940) and proteins (50 grammes) per day, on the basis of the goods that are actually consumed in the countries concerned. Moreover, it is assumed that a single male, unskilled wage earner has to earn an income that is sufficient for a family of three adult consumers (two adults and two children). Finally, 250 work days per year are assumed. The 'welfare ratio' that is estimated is the (annual) real wage divided by the costs of the basket of feeding and clothing this family of four; when it is below one, then a wage labourer can hardly maintain his family, whereas when it rises to more than two or three, real wages are relatively high.

Figure 6.4 shows the estimated real wage (as a welfare ratio) on Java between the 1820s and 1930s. In the long run it fluctuates around one, which is more or less the minimum that is sustainable. For the middle decades of the nineteenth century – with short breaks during the mid-1840s (harvest failures) – real wages are relatively high, consistent with the notion of labour scarcity in this period. In the late 1890s and 1900s – when the discussion about the declining welfare of the Javanese population is going on – real wages are indeed declining strongly, a trend that continues into the 1910s. Wage stickiness probably helps to explain these trends: prices declined between 1880 and 1895, and increased strongly between 1895 and 1920, leading to the fall in real wages in this period. Nominal wages clearly lagged behind prices during the First World War, but the recovery after 1920 was very limited – real wages do not seem to have returned to the

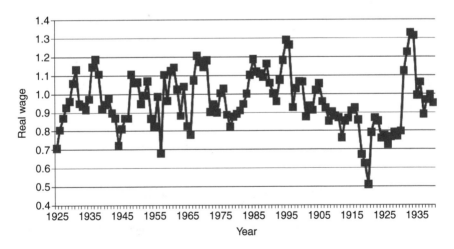

Figure 6.4 Real wages of coolies expressed as welfare ratios, Java 1825–1940 (sources: *Changing Economy in Indonesia*, Vol. 13 (Dros 1992); *Changing Economy in Indonesia*, Vol. 15 (Korthals 1994); the dataset rice prices of Figure 2.11).

pre-war level rapidly. This only happened during the 1930s, when strong deflation in combination with sticky wages led to a sharp increase in real wages. In
the second half of the 1930s they returned to parity again, however, showing that
in the long run the gains in real wages were extremely limited.[6]

Figure 6.5 demonstrates how real wages on Java compared with those in
China (Beijing) and Western Europe. The Chinese series is more or less representative for the most advanced parts of Asia: the level of real wages in Japan
and in India was about the same (Allen *et al.* 2011). In these parts of Asia,
including Java, real wages were close to the minimum as estimated here. In
China, for example, they decreased substantially during the wars of the middle
decades of the century (Opium Wars, Taiping Rebellion), but recovered rather
well after about 1870. The gap with Western Europe is huge; at the beginning of
the nineteenth century (and, as Allen *et al.* 2011 demonstrates, also in the eighteenth century), there was already a large gap between the high-wage region
around the North Sea (London and Amsterdam) and Asia. Amsterdam real
wages declined considerably during the first half of the nineteenth century, and
thanks to the ongoing industrialization process, German real wages caught up.
At the end of the nineteenth century the gap between Europe and Indonesia (and
China) had widened substantially.

Real wages are, however, not an ideal guide to the long-term evolution of the
standard of living of the population in a society where only a small share of the
labour force is dependent on a wage income. Moreover, the GDP figures used at
various places in this book also do not tell us much about what happened to the

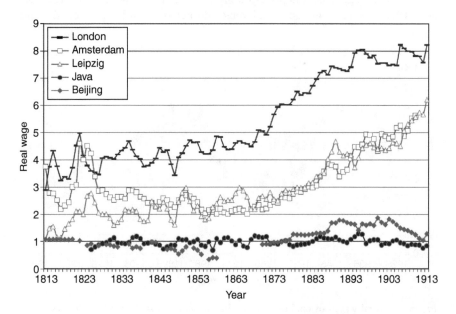

Figure 6.5 Real wages as welfare ratios, Java compared with Beijing and Western
Europe, 1813–1913 (sources: Allen *et al.* 2011; Figure 6.4).

standard of living of the 'average' Indonesian, as income inequality may vary tremedously. For two years, at around 1880 and 1925, and for Java only, we can reconstruct the distribution of income over various ethnic groups as they were distinguished by the colonial administration (Indonesians, Foreign Asiatics and Europeans), and within these groups, which gives us a unique picture of the changes in income inequality in the late-colonial period. The two benchmarks are during periods of relative prosperity – just before the 'sugar crisis' of the mid-1880s and the Great Depression of the 1930s – and therefore give us some insights into the question of who profited from the expansion of the economy in the years in between. Let us first concentrate on the differences between the three ethnic groups: income per capita of the Indonesian population increased by about 38 per cent between 1880 and 1925, but inflation in this period was almost as large (27 per cent), leaving almost no room for an increase in real income (plus 8 per cent). Foreign Asiatics did much better, and increased their average income by almost 90 per cent, and by 48 per cent in real terms. Europeans, who had by far the highest incomes in 1880 (on average more than 30 times the average income of an Indonesian), more or less stabilized their income in real terms. Only the Chinese and the other 'Asiatics' increased their real income, but equally significant is that the share of the non-Indonesian population in total population and in total income increased quite a bit. The European population in particular grew much more quickly than the total population, and their share in total income went up from 6 to 20 per cent. These changes help to explain why Indonesians profited so little from economic growth: whereas GDP per capita increased by about 50 per cent in this period and real incomes (as estimated here) on average went up by 30 per cent, the real income of the average Indonesian increased by only 8 per cent, and a large part of the increased income was 'eaten up' by the growing real incomes of the 'Foreign Asiatics' and the growing population of Dutch and other European inhabitants.

Within the different income groups, income inequality did not increase dramatically. The Gini coefficient of the Indonesian population stabilized at 0.32 (which is rather low), and the Ginis of the two other groups in fact declined somewhat (from 0.64–0.63 to 0.54–0.53), but note that income inequality within the group of 'Foreign Asiatics' was higher than within the group of Europeans, although their average income was much lower (among the European group we find a lot of civil servants forming a solid 'middle class'). The Gini coefficient of the total population does increase substantially however, from 0.39 to 0.48, as a result of the growing importance of the non-Indonesian population in the total. It reflects the fact that Indonesians hardly profited at all from the economic expansion of this period.

There is, moreover, evidence that these trends towards a substantial increase in income inequality did not end in 1925. The share of the richest 1 per cent of the population increased quite dramatically in the following years (from 14 per cent in 1925 to 17 per cent in 1930 and 22 per cent in 1933), and remained at this very high level during the 1930s. Other measures of inequality show a similar tendency (Leigh and Van der Eng 2009).

Table 6.3 The distribution of income among households and social groups on Java, 1880–1925

	1880				1925			
	Number (000)	Average income (fl)	Share income	Gini	Number (000)	Average income (fl)	Share income	Gini
Indonesians	3,939	146	0.88	0.32	7,114	201	0.72	0.32
Foreign Asiatics	57	629	0.05	0.64	129	1,179	0.08	0.54
Europeans	9	4,598	0.06	0.61	63	6,150	0.20	0.53
Total	4,006	163	1.00	0.39	7,306	270	1.00	0.48

Sources: 1880: van Zanden 2003; 1925: the basic source is Meijer Ranneft and Huender (1926) for the Indonesian population, and for the rest of the population income tax records taken from *Indisch Verslag, 1931–40*, Vol. VII: 118–119.

To further analyse the links between growth and inequality, the concept of extraction ratio has been introduced by Milanovic *et al.* (2007). They argue that some kind of upper limit to the level of inequality in a relatively poor society exists, because part of the income is necessary for subsistence, and only 'the rest' – the surplus in Marxian terms – can be appropriated by the elite. A certain level of the Gini coefficient – 0.50 for example – in an economy with a low income level therefore has other implications than in the same Gini for a relatively prosperous country. The extraction ratio is then defined as the ratio between the actual Gini and the maximum feasible Gini (given a certain level of GDP per capita). When this extraction ratio is close to 100 per cent, then the vast majority of the population survives on a subsistence level, and the elite gets the entirety of the surplus; when it is much lower than 100 per cent, it means that the majority of the population has a more comfortable level of income and/or that there exists a relatively large middle class, which also gets part of the surplus. The extraction ratio can thus also be seen as a (inverted) measure of the quality of institutions in a society: if the elite is unconstrained and appropriates the whole surplus, incentives for economic development will be relatively small. A low extraction ratio, on the other hand, points to the fact that the middle classes do profit from economic growth, and therefore have positive incentives to invest into the economy. To return to the case of Indonesia: using the Milanovic *et al.* (2007) framework makes it possible to estimate that the extraction ratio in Indonesia between 1880 and 1940 was more or less constant at about 100 per cent, which is a clear sign of the poor quality of its institutions. In other words, Indonesia did have some economic growth, but it moved along the maximum-Gini curve (as shown in Figure 6.6); whereas the Netherlands, for example, moved away from this curve. In the latter, inequality (although high at the beginning of the nineteenth century) did not increase with economic growth, but large parts of the newly created surplus went to the middle classes and even the working class (after about 1860).

There is independent, anthropometric evidence confirming that the Indonesians did not profit from the process of growth that occurred during the colonial

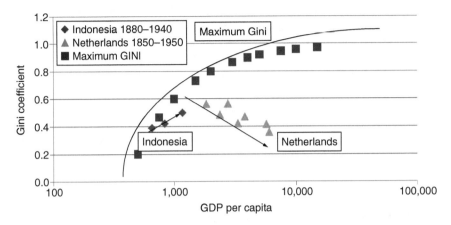

Figure 6.6 The relationship between GDP per capita and the (maximum) Gini (sources: Milanovic *et al.* 2007; Baten *et al.* 2009a (for the country-Gini's)).

period. A number of studies have documented the long-term development of the heights of Indonesian males and females from the mid-nineteenth century onwards (Baten *et al.* 2009b; Földvari *et al.* 2010). As is well known, the height of a population is largely dependent on the level of food consumption (and in particular of proteins) and on its health, in particular during the first five years of life. When the stature of a population increases, it points at improvements in health and diet; conversely, a shrinking population is generally considered to be a sign of a deteriorating 'biological standard of living'. Indonesians were relatively small during the nineteenth century. Cohorts born in the 1850s and 1860s probably measured only about 160 cm (for males);[7] heights then slightly fell in the 1870s and 1880s, recovered afterwards, and remained at about 160–161 cm in the interwar period. Only after 1950 did an increase in the average height set in – to about 165 cm in 2000. It is interesting to note that differences within Indonesia were rather small: males born on Java were on average somewhat smaller than inhabitants of Sumatra and the other Outer Islands, but the difference was less than 1 cm in the case of Sumatra and about 1 cm in the case of the Outer Islands (Földvari *et al.* 2010). Peasants were – again on average – no taller than people with professions outside agriculture.

There is little evidence that colonial rule in the long run brought about a real improvement in the standard of living of the Indonesian population. It may have led to a modest decline in death rates and a related rise in life expectancy, due to the imposition of the *Pax Neerlandica* and introduction of medical services such as smallpox inoculation, but this also led to a strong increase in population growth that tended in the long run to undermine part of these gains. Another part of the story concerning the very rapid population growth is that fertility levels in Indonesia were quite high, and remained so for a long period. One of the most important determinants of fertility is the age of women at first marriage. This was relatively low in large parts of Indonesia, and the share of the population that did not marry at all was equally small. In the 1920s girls on Java married shortly after menarche and sometimes even earlier and the average age of marriage was probably about 15–16 years old in large parts of the Archipelago (Gooszen 1999: 146). In a few parts of the country, in particular where Christianity was influential, marriage sometimes occurred later; in Aceh, on the other hand, very early marriage also was the rule (Gooszen 1999: 146–147). Child marriage had already become an issue during the colonial period, and the 'Mindere Welvaarts' Commission (the Committee to study the lesser welfare) from 1904/1905 paid attention to it in its report. They demonstrated that early marriage was basically a strategy of parents to select the 'right' marriage candidate for their offspring. This is suggested by the following quote:

> Poor people with attractive daughters ... try to bring them to the attention of the wealthy. And should the wealthy choose one of them, then the marriage must be concluded as quickly as possible...., for postponement might lead to cancellation.... If these daughters become the wives of moneyed folk, then there is a good chance that their parents will be given support when times are hard.
>
> (Gooszen 1999: 146)

Early marriage also had the function that the girl could not oppose it, or in the words of the regent of Banten:

> If you allow a girl to grow up freely until she has reached the age when her passions are aroused, you run the risk ... of her choosing a person with whom she will never enjoy a happy marriage. You can prevent this by compelling her to marry another man, but as they say in North Banten: 'when the heart is baked, don't try to knead it' ... you increase the chance of destroying marital fidelity.... It's completely different story for girls between the ages of seven and ten, who have yet to experience the feeling of love.
>
> (Gooszen 1999: 147)

This was the pattern in Java, where parents clearly dominated the decision-making process and seem to have had an interest in early marriage. This was not the case everywhere. In the south of Sumatra, for example, the boy and the girl were main actors in – or even initiators of – the process, as a report from 1852 already makes clear:

> It takes a long and tedious delay in the Lampongs before a marriage is brought about. If a young man is in love with a girl, he makes her proposals in writing and sends love letters to her, writing on lonthar leaves. From the time he becomes a declared suitor, he no longer repairs to the village where his bride lives, but does everything by writing and leaves his relations and

friends to act for him. They require not only to obtain the consent of the
bride's parents, but also in the first place with them the amount of dowry
(*jujur*).... It often happens that a long time elapses before the suitor has collected the whole sum, and even that many never attain the whole and consequently die unmarried. This is the reason why such a large number of
unmarried persons are found. Perhaps in this also consists one of the causes
of the small population of the country.

(Zollinger 1847/1851: 697)

This practice still existed in the 1920s; the Census of 1930 (volume VIII: 29) for
example writes, when noting the high level of literacy in this region:

> In the Lampong districts the high level of literacy has a special cause in the
> village game of young men and women, who court each other via writing
> letters ('*die met briefjes elkaar het hof maken (mandjau)*').

An interesting aspect of this procedure is that the boy had to let the girl know 'in
writing' that he was interested in her, which presupposes that both were able to
read and write. We will see shortly that indeed in this part of the Archipelago the
level of literacy was strikingly high – among men and, in particular, among
women. It demonstrates that such customs had an impact on the interest in
reading and writing skills, or alternatively, that in parts of Indonesia at an early
stage the level of literacy was high enough to result in customs like this.

Fertility is strongly affected by the age at first marriage of (especially)
women. In the long run, most developed societies have gone through a process
known as the 'demographic transition': the decline of the death rate (which may
already have started on a modest scale in nineteenth-century Java) was after a
few decades followed by a fall in the birth rate, resulting in a new equilibrium of
lower birth rates and a more elevated life expectancy. This transitory phase was
one of rapid population growth, but this ended as a result of the decline in fertility during the process of demographic transition. One of the central issues in the
debate about this is what forces were causing the decline in fertility (the birth
rate) in the long run – given that the decline of the death rate has clear socio-
medical and economic causes (improvements in diet, better medical care, etc.).
Perhaps the most convincing interpretation of the causes behind the second part
of the demographic transition is that it is linked to the choice between 'quantity'
and 'quality' of offspring. Because parents have resource constraints – in terms
of time and money – they have to either try to have as many children as possible,
or to concentrate all their time and money on a few children, who will be given a
lot of human capital (many years of education). Looking at data from post-1950
developing countries, there appears to be a strong link between the level of
education of the women involved, and their fertility (Figure 6.7). Women
with (almost) no human capital will on average have between six and eight
children, whereas women with on average eight to 10 years of education will
prefer to have many less children: only one to three. Econometric analysis has

demonstrated that the link between female human capital and fertility is very strong. Well-educated women marry relatively late (which suppresses their fertility), and also have fewer children within marriage; both of which lead to the relationship demonstrated in Figure 6.7. The economic rationale is that increasing the human capital of women means that their work will become more valuable, and the opportunity costs of having children – which will be raised mainly by the mothers – will increase considerably. Therefore, a woman in such a household will have a strong incentive not to devote all of her time to the getting and raising of offspring. On the other hand, the level of education of men tends to have a (weak) positive effect on fertility, implying that if men are highly trained – much more than their spouses – the distribution of labour within the household will probably induce women to concentrate on reproductive activities, and have more children as a result. To stop a population from growing, the best remedy seems to be to educate the women.

The continuing relatively rapid increase of the population of Indonesia suggests that (female) human capital formation may have been a crucial problem. Before 1900 the colonial administration had only a very limited interest in educating the population of Indonesia, and almost no money was spent on this. The money that was spent, was restricted to the schooling of the Dutch (and other European) children living in the colony, and of the children of the small ruling elite – the *priyayi*. This underinvestment in human capital is the most obvious example of a 'missed opportunity' as described by Booth (1998) in her study of Indonesia in the nineteenth and twentieth centuries. In the 1890s only 4–5 per cent of the adult population had enjoyed primary education, a percentage that

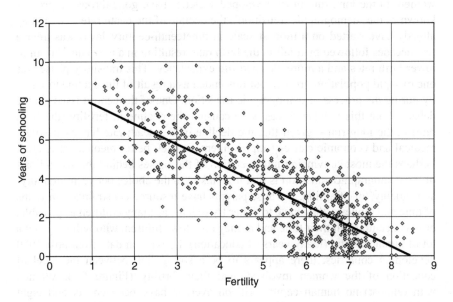

Figure 6.7a Fertility and average years of education of women, 1950–2000 (developing countries, general trends).

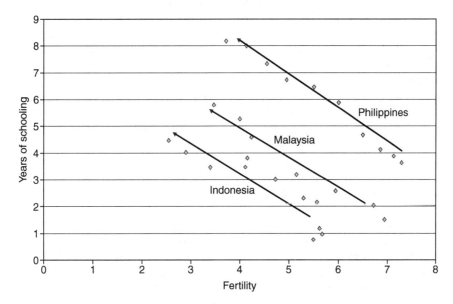

Figure 6.7b Fertility and average years of education of women: specific patterns of Philippines, Malaysia and Indonesia, 1950–2000 (sources: dataset derived from
Schultz 1997).

would rise to 10–12 per cent in the early 1920s and 15–17 per cent in the 1930s.
This was, as Bas van Leeuwen (2007) has demonstrated, comparable with India,
but much lower than Japan, where a quarter of the population had had access to
primary education in the 1890s. What was even more striking was the insignifi-
cance of secondary and higher education in Indonesia, again in comparison with
Japan and with India, where a relatively large group of Brahmans had gained
access to these forms of education. As a result, in terms of average years of education, Indonesia lagged far behind India, and even further behind Japan.

This is also reflected in levels of literacy. According to the census of 1920,
only 6.52 per cent of male Indonesians (older than 15 years) were able to read
and write, and only 0.46 of the women; these shares were much higher for
'Foreign Asiatics': 58.09 and 8.55 per cent, respectively.[8] Familiarity with
Dutch, the language of the colonial administration, was even rarer: among the
Indonesian population only 0.24 per cent of men and 0.03 per cent of women,
and only 1.98 and 0.81 per cent of the 'Foreign Asiatics', had 'knowledge of
Dutch'. There were, as mentioned already, a few regions with much higher
levels of literacy. Lampong (western Sumatra) is the best example; here, among
the Indonesians, 48 per cent of men and a staggering 35 per cent of women were
literate in 1920. The (partly) Christian regions of Manado (northern Sulawesi)
and Ambon also stand out, with similar or even higher levels of literacy
(Menado: 53/35 per cent, Ambon 36/37 per cent – on the latter island women
were, according to these statistics, even slightly more literate than men). These

high levels of literacy reflect the activities of missionaries there, and the access people in these regions had to employment in the colonial army (and administration). Islam as such did not play a large role, however, as Hindu Bali also had relatively low levels of literacy (8/0 per cent). By 1930, levels had increased a bit, with literacy among male Indonesian adults at 13.17 per cent; for females this percentage was 2.27, showing that the policies to increase the supply of education were at least partially successful. But an overall level of only 7 per cent literacy was still extremely low.

Literacy is only one index of human capital; recent literature suggests that numeracy, using age heaping as a proxy, may also be quite important for economic development (A'Hearn *et al.* 2009). Age heaping is the tendency of people who are not very numerate and who are not used to working with (large) figures to 'heap' their age when asked about it. When this occurs, many more people are 30, 40 or 50 than is statistically likely to be the case – and almost nobody is 39, or 41. This over-representation of numbers ending on 5 and 0 can be calculated. The Whipple index, which is 100 when there is no age heaping and 500 when all ages end in 5 and 0, is often used as a proxy of the phenomenon. The Indonesian data on this are rather scarce, however, as the census takers in 1930 concluded that the data on ages that they had collected were dominated to such an extent by what had to be misrepresentation of the actual ages of the population, that they decided not to publish these results! Only for a few selected groups were the data considered good enough to publish them. We present the Whipple indices that can be estimated for these groups: for the inhabitants of the Moluccas (as we saw already, a relatively highly educated group), the Whipple indices are 175 (men) and 189 (women). For three largely Christian parts of Sulawesi they are in Minahassa 137/163 (again, men/women); in Sangihee 160/190; and in Talaud 200/238 (the latter are two islands near Sulawesi with a predominantly Protestant population).[9] Interestingly, data for the Chinese and the other Asiatics were also published, which makes it possible to make a distinction between those born in Indonesia, and those who immigrated during their lifetime. Such a comparison demonstrates the generally high level of numeracy among the Chinese: those born in Indonesia have Whipple indices of 145/160 (again, male/female), those who immigrated 150/146 – the low level among the female Chinese immigrants may be related their relatively small number. Other 'Foreign Asiatics' had much higher Whipple indices, with those born in Indonesia of 288/364, and immigrants of 340/417. Levels higher than 300, indicating a very limited familiarity with numbers, were probably also 'normal' for the Indonesian population (see Chapter 9 for the post-independence development of age heaping).

Thus we may conclude that at the end of the colonial period Indonesia had a very low level of human capital, with only small pockets of higher training and education: among the Chinese and the Europeans, and among small groups of Indonesians who were either deeply involved in the colonial administration and the army, affected by missionary activities, and/or had developed an indigenous demand for literacy and related skills (as in parts of Sumatra). Not only were levels of primary education very low, perhaps even more striking is the – by relative standards – miniscule level of participation in secondary and tertiary education. This is also true in comparison with colonies such as India, which possessed a much larger (potential) 'intelligentsia' of relatively highly educated men.

The limits of the colonial project

To what extent can we blame the colonial state for failing to invest sufficiently in education? The relatively high levels of education found in a few pockets of the Archipelago where inhabitants had close links with the colonial state (such as the Moluccas), demonstrate that Indonesian households were probably ready to invest more in education, if possibilities for getting access to jobs that required such skills were available. This was, clearly, one of the major problems during the colonial period; many government jobs, especially the medium and highly skilled ones, were reserved for European (Dutch) employees. Dutch was the language of the administration (although Malay was used as well, in particular in contacts with the Indonesian population), and only they had the appropriate diplomas for it. The famous scholar of the Islamic religion and community, Snouck Hurgronje, pleaded in 1911 for reorganizing the division of official functions in such a way that many more Western-educated Indonesians could have access to those jobs (Lindblad 2008: 149–178). Reforms in this field were slow, however, to the great disappointment of the rising number of Indonesians who finished secondary or tertiary education, but were given jobs well below their abilities (Kahin 1952: 48–49). Moreover, discrimination in the job market was not limited to the public sector. Social segregation based on ethnicity was even stricter in private business (Lindblad 2008: 33). To make matters worse, during the depression of the 1930s, it was the Indonesian employees who were fired first, and whose employment declined strongest, whereas most large companies tried to cushion their (highly skilled) European employees from the worst effects of the crisis (Jonker and van Zanden 2007: 434). It was only after independence that these companies really started to work into the direction of *Indonesianisasi* of their workforce (Lindblad 2008).

Discrimination in the job market reflected a more fundamental characteristic of the kind of colonial society that had emerged. It was based on formal distinctions between classes of people: indigenous Indonesians (not called that yet), 'Foreign Asiatics' (subclassified into different groups), and Europeans, all of whom had separate sets of rights and duties. Segregation was the fundamental principle of the colonial state. Each group paid, for example, different (direct) taxes – and there is some evidence that the tax burden shifted towards the Indonesian population during the 1920s and 1930s (Kahin 1952: 26–27). A typical example is the export tax on rubber, introduced to restrict the output of the rubber industry as part of an international consortium aimed at stabilizing the rubber market. This tax was levied on the indigenous (small-scale) producers, but not on the Western (large-scale) plantations, who were supposed to pay income tax (Touwen 2001: 189). The different 'ethnic' groups had their own schooling systems – the colonial government, for example, paid much larger subsidies to the 'European' schools than to their Indonesian counterparts. They were also subject to different legal systems. Western, mainly Dutch law governed the relationships of Europeans, while indigenous common law (*adat*) formed the basis for court rulings among Indonesians. They had different political rights as well. The *Volksraad* (People's Council) that was established in 1918, consisted of 'ethnic' groups of representatives: Indonesians had 30 representatives (of which 10 were appointed by the Governor-General), Europeans 25 (10 appointed), Chinese 4 (one appointed) and finally there was one appointed Arab (Gouka 2001: 284). The 'Foreign Asiatics' were supposed to be on the side of the colonizers, as were the often rather conservative representatives of the indigenous elite (but at times more radical voices were also heard there). Moreover, the body had very limited rights, and only played a role in consultations on policy – the Governor-General and the Parliament in the Netherlands still had the right of veto.

Yet, the *Volksraad* of 1918 can be considered a major step forward, responding to the first stirrings of the nationalist movement at the time. Those years saw the flowering of the *Sarekat Islam*, an organization originally set up in 1911 by Javanese merchants (to protect themselves against increased competition from Chinese merchants), which quickly became a quasi-independence movement; first, in 1916, pleading for a gradual evolution towards self-government, but gradually, also as a result of the increased importance of communists within its ranks, becoming more radical in its political and social programme (Blumberger 1987: 56–70). At first, the government more or less accepted this radicalization of the movement – during the 1910s it was to some extent moving in the same direction. This changed in the early 1920s, however. In a way, the ensuing crisis marked an end to the honeymoon years of the welfare policies of the 1910s and 1920s, and signalled a turn towards the more conservative policies that would be dominant in the rest of the interwar period.

The financial crisis of the early 1920s was, to some extent, inevitable. As we have already seen, during the war and the inflationary boom of the post-war years (1919–1920), expenditure had increased enormously and tax income did not grow to the same degree. This was, however, also due to the fact that the colonial state was unable to tap into some of the huge incomes that were being earned by the big international companies working in the colony. The story of the taxation of the profits made by Royal Dutch Shell illustrates the point. Oil prices and profits had increased dramatically during the 1910s. We know from internal sources, which have recently been analysed as part of a business history of the company, that even the board of directors was quite embarrassed by the enormous profits they made in these years. It can be estimated that during the peak years these profits amounted to about 400 million guilders, an incredibly large sum when compared with, for example, the national income of Indonesia of about five billion guilders. The board of Shell did everything possible to hide the magnitude of the profits and became extremely secretive in its financial reporting, but still they paid out dividends up to 100 per cent of the nominal value of the shares in these years (part of which were bonus shares). Which part of this huge profit income came from the cheap oil the company produced in Indonesia is not completely clear, however. At some point Marcus Samuel, the chairman of the board of Shell Transport and Trading company (the London-based parent company), stated in public that '95 per cent of the profits of our group are made in the Dutch Indies', but this is an exaggeration; 40–50 per cent is probably a much better estimate (Jonker and van Zanden 2007: 267). At the end of 1920 the government of the Netherlands East Indies had begun to scrap some of the export levies introduced earlier that year to tax the excess profits made in the major commodity export sectors because of high world prices. However, the oil levy remained in force and in May 1921, with world oil prices falling, the government even proposed a substantial increase to help solve the colonial budget deficit. Sir Henri Deterding, the CEO of the company, was furious and ranted that the decision spelled 'the beginning of Bolshevism in the Dutch Indies' (Jonker and van Zanden 2007: 267–269). He started a full-scale political campaign against the export tax, mobilizing support both within and outside the Netherlands. In August 1921 the Royal Dutch board issued a sharply worded request to the Minister of Colonial Affairs De Graaff warning of the imminent, near complete ruin of the oil industry in the Netherlands East Indies if this policy continued; the company also announced cutbacks in production there because operations were becoming too expensive (Taselaar 1998: 226–227). Moreover, members of the board of directors such as Hendrikus Colijn had easy access to Parliament (Colijn was, oddly enough, at the same time the political leader of the orthodox Protestant party), whilst Deterding had an audience with Queen Wilhelmina to discuss the export tax. Deterding also began mobilizing his relations outside the country, trying to convince the Rothschilds and Deutsch, a French oil company associated both with the Rothschilds and with the Group, to ask the French government for a *démarche* with the Dutch government. In addition, he decided to cancel the Royal Dutch interim dividend for 1922 as an effective protest if the export tax remained in force (Jonker and van Zanden 2007: 268). These and similar threats were effective. The Second Chamber approved the proposed increase of the export tax, but the First Chamber rejected it after having secured from De Graaff a promise to abolish the tax in 1923. Some of Shell's most intimate business partners, such as the legendary Armenian oil magnate Calouste Gulbenkian, agreed that the company had overreacted, as the total yield of all export taxes of the Netherlands East Indies in 1921 amounted to slightly less than eight million guilders, against a total dividend paid out by the Group of as much as 163 million guilders (or an estimated total profit of about 400 million guilders). Even if we assume that oil generated all export tax revenues, which was definitely not the case, then the export tax cannot have lowered the Group's total profits by more than 2 per cent.

This story is significant because it illustrates the problems faced by the colonial state: it could not simply tax its citizens and companies as it thought was justified, but had to deal with supervision from the 'mother country', and was therefore – in this case in particular – severely constrained in its actions. Many Dutch citizens, for example, owned shares of Royal Dutch, and therefore did not want the company to pay extra taxes in Indonesia. And board members of Royal Dutch Shell such as Colijn and Deterding could use their influence at the Dutch Parliament and even with the Queen (who supposedly owned many shares of Royal Dutch as well), to affect opinions 'at the highest level'. It therefore was not possible for the colonial state to tax the large profits that were made by the company; only when new concessions were granted could it introduce more stringent profit-sharing agreements, as happened with the new Jambi-fields (Jonker and van Zanden 2007: 431). The colonial state, in short, could not develop the kind of '*contrat social*' that formed the basis of modern citizenship in the democracies of Western Europe, because its actions were constantly monitored, if not completely controlled, by the 'outside' interests of the 'mother country'.

As we have already seen, the financial crisis of the early 1920s put an end to the strong growth of expenditure on education and other welfare services. At the same time, the climate within the country changed as well; whereas the colonial government had been relatively tolerant towards the emerging independence movement – Sarekat Islam – and had also tolerated the growth of a trade union movement, often linked to Sarekat Islam, it became much more reserved towards further developments. That after 1918 part of Sarekat Islam came under the influence of the communists certainly played a role; the growing influence of the communist party (PKI) led to a short-lived rebellion on Sumatra in 1926/1927, which demonstrated the increased strength of the movement. In 1927 a new party, the PNI (Indonesian Nationalist Party), was attempting to breathe new life into the debate on independence, this time from a secular point of view. Its leaders – a young engineer called Sukarno in particular – could not, however, count on the sympathies of the colonial administration. When PNI became too influential, its leadership was simply detained; first in 1929, when they were sentenced to three years imprisonment for 'the disturbance of public order' and, after being released in 1931, again in 1933, this time without being brought to court (Sukarno remained detained until he was freed by the Japanese in 1942) (Kahin 1952: 90–94). Sukarno's fate characterizes the defensive, conservative mode Dutch colonial policies had entered into in the late 1920s. A very moderate attempt by the *Volksraad* to discuss plans for the evolution of the administration of the colony towards self-government (modelled after similar proposals discussed in the Philippines), the motion Sutardjo from 1936, was flatly rejected by the Dutch political elite and the Parliament (Gouka 2001).

This turn towards conservatism in the late 1920s is quite striking, given the trends set in motion with the Ethical Policy of 1901. Whereas in India and the Philippines serious negotiations about independence were going on, which slowly prepared both the colonial elite and the 'mother country' for the changes that were inevitable, the Netherlands and the Netherlands Indies were stuck in a negation of these developments – as least, that is how we, with the benefit of hindsight, can now asses what was happening. Part of the explanation for this conservative turn is probably that Indonesia was extremely important for the Netherlands: the latter could not imagine itself without the vast colony. Many more Dutchmen, relatively speaking, lived in Indonesia than, for example, British citizens in India (or Americans in the Philippines). And – perhaps even more importantly – a large share of Dutch income was earned in Indonesia. Royal Dutch Shell was only one, however formidable, example of the very close links between the two countries. It was estimated that, in 1938, Indonesia was the destination of about 40 per cent of Dutch investments abroad, or about 22 per cent of total wealth of the Netherlands in 1938; moreover, this brought in about 8 per cent of national income in these years (van Zanden 1997: 44). This also had, as we have seen, political implications. It is typical that the dominant Dutch statesman of the 1930s, Hendrikus Colijn, who had made his career in the Dutch-Indonesian army (he had helped conquer Lombok in 1894) and was a director of Royal Dutch Shell between 1913 and 1921, held very conservative views on the relationship with the colony.[10] He was, moreover, supported by a strong and equally conservative colonial lobby, in which large colonial companies such as Royal Dutch Shell and the large colonial banks played a decisive role (Taselaar 1998).

The strength of the colonial lobby of Western – mainly Dutch – business was not only the consequence of the importance of the colony for the Netherlands, but was also due to its high level of organization. We saw already that groups of entrepreneurs in different export industries had organized themselves – the sugar industry is perhaps the best example of this. This organization was based on common interests: in the development of new technologies (such as more productive varieties of sugar cane), but also to defend their political interests. The large colonial banks that were active in Indonesia formed a crucial link in this network. Whereas in the Netherlands itself commercial banks were slow in developing long-term relationships with industry, as industry did not really need long-term financing from them, in Indonesia these ties between banks and the main export industries had become very close, mainly due to the scarcity of capital there. The NHM, the trading body that had played a key role in the Cultivation System, had been transformed into a major bank with long-term interests in many 'cultuurmaatschappijen'. Similar banks had emerged from the 1860s onwards, which all had close ties with parts of industry and export agriculture. The high level of organization of the colonial lobby, which was able, to a large extent, to dominate policy making in the 1920s and 1930s, was therefore based on a tight network of interconnection between banks and (export) industries. The various lobbying groups for Dutch enterprise were extremely active in the 1920s and 1930s – many an initiative resulted from growing concerns about the 'left' welfare policies enacted by the colonial state in the previous period – both in the Netherlands and in Indonesia (they, for example, set up their own training programme for colonial servants in Utrecht, because they considered the Leiden programme to be too 'ethical'). The *Ondernemersraad voor Nederlandsch Indie*, the top-lobbying organization established in 1921 – which was, significantly, set up in the Netherlands and consisted mainly of entrepreneurs active in that country – became extremely influential, and in due course had its own (four) representatives in the *Volksraad* (Taselaar 1998).

The conservatives could also continue to dominate, however, because the 'countervailing power' was relatively weak. The movement for independence was dependent on a few intellectuals who could easily be imprisoned – because, ultimately, the level of education of the masses was quite limited, which kept political participation at a minimum. This also created the impression that this movement was not well-rooted in Indonesian reality, and could therefore simply be ignored (as happened in the 1930s). It was a vicious circle: because of low levels of human capital formation the movement remained relatively weak, but its weakness also meant that its wishes to improve the economic and social possibilities of the Indonesian population – to be treated equally – could be ignored, and therefore prospects for social mobility remained limited, which restricted the number of people who could be recruited by such a movement.

Conclusion

In many ways, Indonesia was slowly awakening in this period, in a manner that colonial reformers should have been able to appreciate. Bottom-up processes of institution building – the first societies, unions, political parties with a mass following that were able to organize themselves effectively – were beginning to fill the gap of the absent 'civil society'. Western education, however limited its spread still was, played an important role in the process. This should have all been good news. Yet these developments, which began around 1900 and accelerated in the 1910s, did not get enthusiastic support from the colonial state. On the contrary, in the mid-1920s the relationship between the new social and political movements and the colonial state became very strained. This was partly due to what colonial administrators considered to be the major threat of communist involvement in the movements, and partly because they were unable to appreciate the political programme that emerged, in which independence became – inevitably – a priority. So what began as years of high expectations, after the programme of the Ethical Policy of 1901 had been launched ended in a kind of stalemate. The Dutch in power became increasingly entrenched in a conservative, backwards-looking position, aimed at consolidating their privileged position – at times even determined to roll back some of the gains made since 1901. The immobility of the Dutch position led to a widening of the gap between them and the independence movement. The latter was successfully repressed: no large rebellions occurred any more after the Sumatra rising of 1926 and, to outside observers, on the political front everything seemed to exemplify peace and quiet in the 1930s.[11]

At the same time, however, the mixed blessing of being so closely linked to the Dutch economy was again clearly evident in the 1930s, when misguided monetary policies – the defence of the gold standard – led to the continuation of the depression until 1936. The Indonesian economy, which had become quite open and dependent on a few export products, was extremely vulnerable to the large swings in export prices and market conditions during the 1914–1942 period. It also could not opt for a systematic policy of import substitution, being closely linked as it was to policy making in the 'mother country'. The colonial state was only prepared to end the liberal regime of free trade when the interests of Dutch industry were at stake. During the early 1930s, this resulted in the increased protection of Dutch cotton textiles on the Indonesian market, against Japanese competition. This protectionism was broadened to other industries as well, but only in the late 1930s did this begin to include a more conscious attempt to further industrialization on Java. The unbalanced character of the measures is also illustrated by the fact that the Dutch export interests received protection on the Indonesian market, whereas the most important Indonesian export product, sugar, was almost banned from the Dutch market (as part of the policies to protect its agriculture). The unbalanced character of trade policies in the 1930s reminded some observers of the days of the Cultivation System in the 1830s, when the Javanese economy had been fully exploited to the Dutch advantage (Taselaar 1998: 460, citing the specialist on trade policy Blaisse). It was the – perhaps rather predictable – result of the fact that Dutch (industrial and agricultural) interests were well organized, and that decision making took place in the Parliament in The Hague, where politicians had a '*contrat social*' with the Dutch, and not with the Indonesians. This was, we argue, the fundamental reason for the ultimate failure of the Ethical Policy: the limits of that policy were dictated by the interests of the Dutch economy and society. When conflicts between those interests and that of the Indonesian population arose, the latter had virtually no means of affecting the outcome of the decision making process.

This is, however, only part of the story. As the example of the attempt to introduce Western models of cooperation into rural credit markets demonstrates, colonial reformers also discovered how difficult it was to reform the institutional framework of Javanese society. Local power structures, long traditions of clientelism and patronage, and the low level of education of the peasantry – making them dependent on political and economic brokers – made it impossible to introduce the models of cooperation that were being developed in Western Europe to break through the constraints of agricultural development there. Micro-finance was understood to be a key element in such a development process, but it had to be organized 'top-down', controlled by European civil servants, and supplied through state funds, instead of being based on locally generated savings. Moreover, peasants had reasons to mistrust colonial administrators – even if the intentions of the latter may have been good. In the long run, the peasants had not profited from agricultural modernization; their living standards had remained the same at best, and the gains of growth had gone to the Chinese merchants and the Dutch capitalists (and administrators), who did profit from the changes. Inequality had increased as a result.

Indonesia was also caught up in one of the famous vicious circles of underdevelopment, characterized by low levels of human capital, early marriage, high population growth, and low 'quality' of the offspring (meaning low investment in children), which resulted in a perpetuation of this state of affairs. The colonial state was unable to break through the vicious circle; for example, a more rapid *indonesianisasi* of public administration and Western enterprise might have created better incentives for Indonesians to invest more in their children. This was all going to change in the post-independence period, however; but, as we will demonstrate, it took quite some time before this meant that the vicious circles were indeed broken. Moreover, the stalemate between Indonesian intelligentsia and colonial administration that had emerged in the 1920s and 1930s had serious consequences for the way in which the country was to gain its independence.

7 The lost decades?

From colony to nation-state, 1942–1967

Introduction

In both Latin America and in Africa, the post-independence decades were periods of dramatic falling behind caused by violence and instability on the one hand, and poor growth on the other (Bates *et al.* 2007: 925; see also Easterly and Levine 1997; Bertocchi and Canova 2002; Artadi and Sala-i-Martin 2003). Therefore Bates *et al.* (2007) label this period the 'lost decades' – a period lost for economic development due to the problems of independence and the instability of the new, post-colonial regime. The key element in their argument is that political, fiscal, currency and market fragmentation created economic balkanization in post-independence Latin America and Africa, which in turn resulted in stagnation. This chapter will argue that the Indonesian case in certain respects resembled the Latin American and African experience (see also Marks 2010b). However, in order to do justice to the achievements that were realized, it might be more appropriate to call these years transitional decades for creating a nation-state, albeit initially at the expense of economic integration and development. But before we deal with the story of post-independence Indonesia, we will briefly sketch the political and economic developments in the 1940s.

1942–1949: conflict, independence and economic stagnation

1942–1945: the turning tide?

The Japanese occupation of March 1942 to August 1945 is widely regarded as a watershed in modern Indonesian history. Reid (1980: 18), for example, argues that the Japanese occupation brought 'such profound change that it is not inappropriate to regard 1942 as the beginning of the whole revolutionary upheaval which gave birth to modern Indonesia'. Whereas this notion may indeed be true for the political developments that were yet to come, the Japanese invasion also marked the beginning of a period of economic hardship, instability and disintegration.

Economic performance during the Japanese occupation was weak at best. Initially the reason for the Japanese invasion was to secure the supply of strategic raw materials to Japan, such as oil, rubber, tin and other metals (Booth 1998: 47; Reid 1980: 19; Brugmans *et al.* 1960: 253). The Japanese formulated their policy as follows:

> Efforts will be made for developing Malaya, Sumatra, Java, Borneo, and Celebes as the sources of supply for important resources and for winning their political support. The native populations shall be granted political participation according to their standards; however, the military administration will be continued for the time being.
>
> (Nishijima and Koicho 1963: 123)

By the middle of 1943, however, damage to Japanese shipping by Allied submarines forced the Japanese administration to place emphasis on economic self-sufficiency in the different regions so that demands on imports and shipping were minimized (Brugmans *et al.* 1960: 494; Nishijima and Koicho 1963: 263). This had devastating consequences for the Indonesian economy, which by 1942 had achieved a high degree of regional specialization (Booth 1998: 48; Touwen 2001). The so-called cultivation crops, such as rubber, coffee, tea and quinine, which had been directly connected with the world market, were cut off from their traditional export markets.

Unfortunately, available statistics make it difficult to come up with a meaningful estimate of total economic activity, and for this reason economic historians usually deal only summarily with this subject (Booth 1998; Dick *et al.* 2002). Van der Eng (2002) did estimate that by 1949 national income had dropped to less than half of the level in 1941. Figures on the production of the six main food crops on Java also give a hint about the economic stagnation between 1942 and 1945. Table 7.1 shows that, except for sweet potatoes, production of Indonesia's main food crops fell significantly between 1942 and 1945. According to Van der Eng, this can mainly be attributed to the reduction in harvested areas.

Table 7.1 Harvest of six main food crops in Java, 1940–1946 (in 1,000 tonnes)

	1940	1941	1942	1943	1944	1945	1946
Irrigated paddy	8,491	8,459	7,853	7,654	6,620	5,495	5,157
Upland paddy	493	525	436	449	259	169	171
Maize	1,904	2,430	2,170	1,595	1,175	967	725
Cassava	8,411	8,736	8,735	7,524	5,264	3,240	3,518
Sweet potatoes	1,407	1,472	1,314	1,082	1,484	1,511	992
Peanuts	196	210	207	210	109	55	81
Soybeans	293	339	351	273	107	71	128
Total output food crops	100	104	99	91	73	72	74

Source: Van der Eng 1996: 303, 1998a: 195.

Note
Harvest has been calculated by multiplying the harvested area (Van der Eng 1998a: 195) by the average yield (Van der Eng 1998a: 193) of the different crops.

Other scattered sources also suggest that production fell significantly. By 1944 sugar production fell to less than one-third of the level in the late 1930s, when the industry had still not fully recovered from the depression. By 1943 rubber output in Sumatra and Java had dropped to one-fifth of what it had been in 1941, and in the 1945–1946 harvest year, the total output of tea fell to less than one-tenth of what had been harvested in 1942–1943 (Lindblad 2008: 53). The main reason for these large drops was that the production of plantation export crops that were not deemed essential for the war efforts was terminated under the Japanese (Booth 1998: 49). Many of these plantations were converted to the cultivation of foodstuffs or war materials (Van der Kerkhof 2005: 185).

Production in the non-agricultural sector also stagnated. Even the oil industry, which was an important sector for the Japanese, showed a large drop. The damage caused by the Dutch scorched-earth policy resulted in output in 1942 that was less than half than that of the 1938 level. And while in 1943 production increased to 6.5 million tonnes (90 per cent of the 1938 level), it fell again to only 850,000 tonnes in 1945 (Booth 1998: 49; Hunter 1966: 61).

Some industries that were considered essential for producing war materials might have grown a little. In the textile sector, for example, the Japanese authorities brought about 10,000 modern looms from Japan and 150,000 old looms, together with a number of technical experts. However, the shortage of raw materials and spare parts resulted in very low production levels (Booth 1998: 50).

Another major problem during the Japanese occupation was the situation in the transportation sector, which disturbed the smooth circulation of commodities (Kurasawa 1997: 115). On 1 June 1942 the Japanese established the *Rikuyu Sokyoku* (Land Transportation Board) with the aim of taking care of non-military land transportation. But this state organization faced a number of problems. First, the *Rikuyu Sokyoku* was to administer civilian transport only. But military demands were given priority in transportation, meaning that a large number of wagons were set aside for the transport of troops and military supplies. Second, the war disrupted all export and imports. In the Dutch period the main commodities requiring transportation were the goods for export, so that the direction of trade was from the inland production areas to the nearest port on the coast. But since under Japanese rule commercial trade was suspended, the flow of commodities changed direction from East to West, which disturbed the smooth allocation of wagons (Kurasawa 1997: 118). Third, there was a drastic shortage of fuels during the Japanese occupation. In the Dutch period, coal imported from Sumatra and Borneo was used for the main railway lines, and timber was used for the other trains. As a result of the shortage of ships, it was impossible to transport coal to Java, and consequently timber had to be used as fuel. Ironically, to obtain fuel and thus build up the transport capacity, wagons had to be allocated daily for the transport of timber, which could severely disrupt the means of transporting rice and other commodities (Kurasawa 1997: 118). Moreover, demand for timber was so high that increasingly undried timber and other kinds of trees, such as rubber, had to be used. This meant a less efficient use of energy.

Fourth, the Japanese tried to unify the two different railway gauges that were laid down in Java into a single narrow gauge of 1.067 metres, which was the same as the railways in Japan. This required the replacement of the wide gauge railways. But at the same time rail-building materials were sent to Thailand to construct the infamous Burma–Siam Railway (Kurasawa 1997: 118). This resulted in non-functioning railway sections.

The general picture of economic development under the Japanese is thus appalling, especially when taking into account the suffering of millions of Indonesians who were subjected to forced labour by the Japanese, combined with a terrible famine in 1944/1945 (Lindblad 2008: 54). By the end of the war, the lack of maintenance and Japanese damage, including the removal of equipment, formed the worst problems (Dick *et al.* 2002: 68). Large parts of the railway network had been demolished and material had been shipped to Malaya and Thailand; bridges were broken into pieces and sold as scrap iron; and ports and river mouths had not been dredged (Brugmans *et al.* 1960: 283). It was estimated that for the rehabilitation of the railways 300 carriages for passenger transport, 3,000 carriages for goods transport, 150 locomotives and 55,000 tonnes of rail were needed (CBS 1947: 121). Total loss and damage to the economy was estimated at 2.3 billion guilders (in 1942 prices) (Fruin 1947: 47).[1] This was roughly 50 per cent of total GDP in 1941, and thus it would require a substantial period of rehabilitation to restore the economy to normal peacetime conditions.[2] But the next four years were far from normal or peaceful.

Struggle for independence, 1945–1949

On 15 August 1945 Japan surrendered unconditionally. Two days later, on 17 August, the Indonesian leaders Sukarno and Hatta proclaimed the Republic of Indonesia 'in the name of the people of Indonesia' (*atas nama bangsa Indonesia*). However, the Netherlands was in no way prepared to accept an independent Indonesia. They regarded the Republic as a state run by collaborators with the Japanese and were therefore planning their arrival to accept the Japanese surrender and to restore the colonial regime, which they believed that they had built out of 350 years of effort (Ricklefs 2001: 260, 262).

The Indonesian Archipelago during the years of Indonesian struggle for independence was divided into two countries. The territory controlled by the Republican government initially embraced all of Java and Sumatra, although the Dutch established control over a number of cities and surrounding areas in Java and Sumatra in the course of 1946. Both sides faced a similar problem. The Republican government had very limited sources of income, but at the same time a great need for funds to build up a state apparatus and, above all, to wage a guerrilla war against the returning Dutch colonial forces. The Republican government's budget deficit amounted to Rp.1.6 billion in 1948 and Rp.1.5 billion in 1949 (Lindblad 2008: 58). But the Dutch were also in financial need after being impoverished as a result of the Second World War and at the same time having to maintain a large military force with more than 150,000 soldiers in

Indonesia by July 1947 (Feith 1964: 201; Ricklefs 2001: 276; Dick *et al.* 2002: 169).

These circumstances were an important incentive for the Dutch to launch a first military offensive (*Politionele Actie*) in July 1947, which they gave the meaningful code name 'Operation Product'. During this operation the Dutch gained control of all the deep-water ports in Java. In Sumatra, plantations around Medan, oil and coal installations around Palembang, and the Padang area were secured. Because the attack was so sudden and swift, most infrastructure and crops were captured without damage, although some Republican forces retreated destroying what they could (Dick *et al.* 2002: 169; Ricklefs 2001: 277).

After having conquered large parts of the Archipelago, the Dutch found the economic apparatus in shambles. Export volumes were at a fraction of pre-war levels: 12 per cent for oil, 5 per cent for estate rubber, and less than 1 per cent for sugar and palm oil (Lindblad 2008: 65; Booth 1998: 49–51). Estates were in a deplorable condition, with many having been unproductive for several years. Although conditions were better among smallholders, whose modest production facilities had remained largely intact, their exports remained far below pre-war levels, as they were severely hampered by the slow recovery of transport and trading networks.

But relatively rapidly the Dutch succeeded in rehabilitating the vital export economy (Dick *et al.* 2002: 169). Foreign trade expanded dramatically during the years 1947–1949, although admittedly from a very low level (Lindblad 2008: 224). Production by Indonesian smallholders contributed significantly to this. In 1948, nearly three-fifths of all rubber exported came from smallholders in Sumatra and Kalimantan, and virtually all copra exports from Sulawesi consisted of deliveries from indigenous cultivators (Lindblad 2008: 69). Moreover, a good harvest brought down rice prices, rice mills resumed operations and rail services were gradually restored. However, whereas during a second 'Police Action' the Dutch succeeded in seizing all remaining Republican territory, the Indonesians put more effort into sabotage this time. Many mills and plantations suffered damage, but road and rail traffic also became targets (Dick *et al.* 2002: 169; see also De Bruin 2003).

Eventually the Dutch, forced by American threats to suspend NATO aid, reluctantly conceded Indonesia's independence. From 23 August to 2 November 1949, negotiations finally took place that settled the terms under which the Netherlands would acknowledge Indonesian independence. These negotiations, called the Round Table Conference, resulted in a financial and economic agreement (Finec), which more or less guaranteed unrestricted operations by Dutch business enterprises in an independent Indonesia. Article 1 of this agreement ordered the full restoration of legal rights as laid down under colonial rule, with article 3 offering guarantees against nationalization, unless deemed to be in the public interest, in which case adequate compensation had to be paid. Under article 5 Dutch enterprises promised to participate in economically viable joint ventures with Indonesian capital. Moreover, article 19 stipulated the obligation of the Indonesian government to consult the Dutch government on matters of financial and economic policy with a bearing on Dutch interests (Lindblad 2008: 73). It seems justified to conclude that 'Finec contained the maximum attainable guarantees for the unhindered continuation of Dutch business' (Baudet and Fennema 1983: 213).

The size of debt to be taken over from the colonial government was a matter of profound disagreement. Accumulated debt to the Netherlands rose from 2.6 billion guilders in March 1942 to 3.2 billion guilders in December 1945. By March 1947 the colonial government's internal debt to the Netherlands amounted to a massive four billion guilders, and this sum would be further increased by deficit spending in 1947 to cover the costs of the first military campaign. The final estimate of the colonial debt, as of September 1949, reached a staggering 5.9 billion guilders. Negotiations during the RTC reduced this sum to three billion guilders, although another 1.5 billion was added from the external debt of the Netherlands Indies government (Lindblad 2008: 74). Despite resentment at the huge inherited debt, the Indonesian government faithfully fulfilled its international obligations. When the Harahap cabinet in 1956 revoked the economic and financial agreement as a result of the protracted dispute over West Irian, only US$171 million of the original US$1.13 billion, or 15 per cent remained to be repaid (Thee 2009: 21). No other former colony was obliged to take over such a large debt from its colonial ruler. Indonesia thus paid a high price for its independence, quite apart from the physical damage and loss of human lives during the Revolution. At long last, the Netherlands formally transferred sovereignty on 27 December 1949.

Case study: the rice market, 1942–1949

The Japanese military government recognized the importance of the colonial system of price control, in which the so-called *Voedingsmiddelenfonds* (VMF, Food Supply Fund) tried to stabilize rice prices by purchasing or selling rice. The Japanese tried to continue this system of control. Therefore they established the Office for Food Supply (*Syokuryoo Kanri Zimusho*, SKZ) to take over the functions of the colonial VMF and the Corporation of Rice Wholesalers (*Beikoku Sho Dogyo Kumiai*, BSDK) to which all rice had to be sold. The BSDK then took care of the distribution of rice to retailers in the city.

When the Japanese forces occupied Indonesia in March 1942 it was a seasonally marginal period for rice. Because of the breakdown in traffic due to the occupation, difficulties arose in the rationing of rice and shortages occurred. There was a shortage of rice for civilians, especially in Jakarta and Bandung. To alleviate the situation in the cities the Japanese army released 6,000 tonnes of rice from the stocks that were taken over from the VMF. Moreover, troops were mobilized to transport foodstuffs by boat, truck and train (Sato 1994: 115–116). Food supply should indeed not have been a problem, since in 1941 the Netherlands Indies had been self-sufficient in rice and Java produced a considerable surplus. Also during 1942 there was no reason for concern about the food situation, because the harvests were good and the stocks abundant (Van der Eng

1994: 10). In 1943, however, the production of rice started to fall. Since farmers were forced to distribute part of their harvest to the Japanese administration, there was little left for self-consumption. In some cases the amount that remained was hardly enough to sustain a family for two or three weeks. The black-market price for rice in 1942 ranged from 30 cents to one guilder per litre. Only the middle class could afford to pay these prices (Nishijima and Koicho 1963: 284–286).

A drought in 1944 made the situation worse. Rainfall during the dry season only amounted to 27 per cent of the average dry season rainfall (Sato 1994: 121). Yet the low rainfall was not the main problem. Total rainfall during 1944/1945 was actually not extraordinarily low. It was rather the length of the dry season – of course combined with transport problems – that caused a harvest failure. This had severe consequences for the Indonesian population. Distribution of rice was aggravated by the shortage of petrol and spare parts, which affected milling capacity, and the fact that transport facilities were insufficient. The effects were very much felt by the population. A Dutchman in hiding wrote in his diary that Indonesians had displayed a poster in Batavia with the text: '*Nippon mesti mati, kita lapar!*' [Nippon must die, we are hungry!] (Brugmans *et al.* 1960: 499). Another Dutchman reported that 'all private food transmission has been forbidden, which has created a desperate situation in regions with a habitual food shortage as for instance Madura [...]. Several people have reported from Madura that they have seen people dying on the streets' (Sato 1994: 133).

That the Japanese policy of rice distribution indeed failed is reflected by estimates of average daily caloric intake, which supposedly fell from 2,000 kcal in 1940–1943 to 1,500 kcal in 1944–1945 (Lindblad 2008: 53; Van der Eng 1994: 81). Moreover, unofficial prices varied significantly throughout Java, indicating that transport impediments and controls made it increasingly difficult for the black market to allocate rice supplies from surplus to deficit areas. As a result, retail prices in December 1944, a month for which the official distribution price was raised from 8 to 10 cents per litre, black market prices ranged between 3.25 guilders in Jakarta en Bogor, 1.50 guilders in Semarang and Kediri and even 1.20 guilders in Bojonegoro (Anderson 1966: 92). The Japanese were very well aware of the problems in the supply of food, and also its consequences for the common people. The malnutrition caused severe health problems, which were aggravated by the shortage of medicines. As a result of this there were two million excess deaths, and in many residencies the death rate exceeded the birth rate.

Soon after the surrender by the Japanese, the Republican government established the Agency for the Supervision of the People's Food Supply (*Jawatan Pengawasan Makanan Rakyat*, or the PMR). Basically the PMR continued the work of the SKZ during the Japanese occupation and the VMF during the colonial period. But unlike the VMF, the PMR did not function on the basis of the voluntary purchase of rice via the rice mills. It followed the procedures of its Japanese predecessor, where farmers were obliged to hand over 20 per cent of the rice harvest (Van der Eng 1994: 42–45). However, in the areas under

Republican control the system of rice purchase and supply did not work very well. There was a chronic shortage of capable personnel and of money to finance the purchase of rice. Moreover, transport of foodstuffs was often disrupted by private gangs who tried to seize commodities for the black market trade. This was one of the reasons behind the famines reported in 1946 in several parts of Java and Sumatra, while stocks in Besuki were immobilized because of transport problems (Van der Eng 1994: 47). Overall per capita food supply in 1946 was not much higher than in 1944 and 1945.

For the areas under Allied control the situation was different, but not the outcome. Since the colonial government had no control over the rural areas, it depended largely on rice imports. However, in 1946–1947 rice was so difficult to obtain on the world market that the Combined Food Board in Washington determined the allocations of food products on the world market. Because in 1945 all countries represented in the board assumed that after the Japanese surrender Dutch colonial government would be restored in Indonesia, the Dutch representative could claim amounts of rice for the whole of Indonesia. But expected stocks in mainland Southeast Asia turned out to be much smaller, and consequently in 1945 Indonesia was allotted only 56,000 tonnes, while the original claim was for 153,200 tonnes (Van der Eng 1994: 49–50). During 1946 the area under Allied control gradually increased, but only about 3 per cent of the area harvested with the main food crops in Java was controlled by the Dutch. This meant food supply remained very much dependent on imports from abroad or from areas under Republican control. Moreover, due to the inflow of large number of refugees from the unsafe rural areas, the situation in cities like Jakarta, Surabaya, Semarang and Bandung deteriorated rapidly (Van der Eng 1994: 56–57).

In July 1947 the Dutch launched their first military action. This attack was partly inspired by a Republican food blockade, the meagre prospects for food supply in the areas under colonial control and the possibility of capturing stocks of rice in the territory under Republican control. The action was successful from a military point of view, but the Republican forces employed a scorched-earth strategy and 40 per cent of the rice mills and rice stocks went up in flames. The recovery of large parts of Indonesia – in particular those parts that were considered to be valuable for export production – did mean that the food supply of Jakarta and other cities improved dramatically. Rice prices in the capital, which had been extremely high during the first half of 1947 (peaking at 3.71 guilders per litre in February 1947), fell by almost 75 per cent between April and September (when they reached 80 cents per litre – still 10 times as high as in 1941).

After the military action the Dutch controlled the pre-war surplus areas in North and East Java, and the Republican government controlled the areas in Central and the far end of West Java. As a result, the decline of rice prices that had begun in summer 1947 (and was interrupted by the usual scarcity during the *paceklik* just before the harvest) continued in 1948, when prices in Jakarta were on average half of their level in the previous year. The situation in Republican territory became more difficult after June 1948. During the 1948 main harvest, farmers had been obliged to hand over about 30 per cent of their paddy harvest against fixed, but – due to the Republican policy of monetary financing of the budget deficit – rapidly depreciating prices. Moreover, in combination with a relatively poor harvest, this resulted in rapidly increasing prices (Van der Eng 1994: 62). In late December 1948 the Dutch army launched its second military action, in another attempt to break through the stalemate. Its economic consequences were limited (rice prices, for example, did not show a renewed decline anymore), but its political consequences were disastrous: its very success – the leaders of the independence movement were, for example, captured – led to renewed pressure on the Dutch government to accelerate negotiations and acquiesce to the independence of the new country. It took another year to finalize the process and hand over sovereignty to the new state.

1949–1966: from democratic experiment to 'guided democracy'

From the transfer of sovereignty in December 1949 to the military coup in 1965, which was the prelude to the fall of President Sukarno, Indonesia was preoccupied with politics (Dick *et al.* 2002: 170). It had its first experiment in parliamentary democracy (1950–1958), its first general elections (in 1955), a transition towards 'Guided Democracy' (in 1958), and, in particular from that point onwards, a gradual but unstoppable disintegration of the political system that had been established in the late 1940s, resulting in the military coup d'état of 1965. The early and mid-1950s were years of relative peace and prosperity, but gradually political instability increased, and, linked to this, economic performance deteriorated, in particular during the years of Guided Democracy between 1958 and 1965. We saw already in Chapter 2 that this led to the falling behind of the Indonesian economy compared to its direct neighbours and compared to the world economy as a whole. Levels of total factor productivity fell strongly in the 1940s and also did not recover in the 1950–1967 period. Only the mid-1950s were relatively peaceful and prosperous, but this period was too short to have a major impact on overall trends (and, as we will argue, even in the mid-1950s structural problems were not addressed fully). In short, we need an explanation as to why the performance of the Indonesian economy was so poor in these years, and why, after a perhaps promising start, the period ended in political chaos and economic contraction.

Part of the explanation of the ′failure′ of the 1949–1965 period is simply that the challenges were too immense, and that, due to Dutch 'negligence' and lack of anticipation, Indonesians were unprepared for this big job. To begin with, the new regime inherited an economy and infrastructure that were severely damaged, and in which the potential to export commodities was sharply reduced. This was the result of years of depression, warfare, prolonged neglect and guerrilla sabotage; this applied not only to transport and communications, but also irrigation and power supplies. But these physical problems were relatively small compared to the challenge of setting up a new state, and reorganizing the economy. The guerrilla warfare of the 1940s had been financed by printing money – or simply taking the things that were needed. How to finance the new state was among the many urgent problems that had to be solved. Printing money had led to widespread inflation, which had to be brought under control. A new state apparatus had to be set up – building on the bureaucracy introduced by the Dutch, but replacing expatriates with Indonesian staff. Moreover, the economy also had to be 'nationalized', because major functions had been dominated by Dutch and other European companies and expertise (Lindblad 2008). The question was how to do this: gradually replacing the Dutch was considered too slow of an option, but what were the consequences of more radical actions for the production of export commodities and the level of services supplied? On top of this, the newly independent state had to 'deliver' – to demonstrate that it could supply more and better services to its citizens than the colonial state. Increasing mass literacy, for example, was high on the agenda. Finally, following the aims of the independence movement, some kind of Indonesian democracy had to be developed, to stabilize the new relationships within the country.

It is therefore perhaps no surprise that things did not develop smoothly. One of the striking features of the experiment in democracy that was carried out in the 1950s was that in certain respects it looked so similar to the Dutch example (Feith 1962: 122). The Dutch Parliament consisted of many, often quite small parties, who after elections had to form a coalition in order to govern the country. The provisional Indonesian parliament that came into existence in the late 1940s, and the new parliament elected in 1955 – the latter as a result of elections based on proportional representation (as was the rule in the Netherlands) – were also made up of a large number of parties, which necessitated complex and never-ending bargaining between the leaders of those parties in order to ensure the support of a parliamentary majority. This weakened the position of different cabinets succeeding each other in the 1950s; no cabinet, nor any minister, had a really secure majority in parliament. It is significant that all cabinets were only in office for less than one year, with the exception of the relatively strong first Ali Sastroamidjojo cabinet, which broke the record by lasting almost two years (Table 7.2). Foreign observers noted that the sharp conflicts between parties in the coalition, and also between different fractions inside these parties, had a negative effect on Indonesia's development process (Feith 1962).

The large number of (small) parties was already in the 1950s seen as a weakness of the Indonesian version of parliamentary democracy, but the political elite that crafted the constitution had introduced the system of proportional representation because it was afraid of being dominated by the Islamic party Masjumi, which would probably, given the fact that more than 90 per cent of Indonesians were Muslims, dominate election results if the alternative 'district' ('winner takes it all') system used in the UK and introduced in British colonies had been tried.[3] Moreover, the new Republican elite that was responsible for independence was already divided among a number of parties, which all wished to survive under the new circumstances.

Table 7.2 Cabinets and political parties, 1949–1959

Period	Prime minister	Political parties
19 December 1949–6 September 1950	Hatta	PNI, Masjumi
6 September 1950–21 March 1951	Natsir	Masjumi, PSI
18 April 1951–23 February 1952	Sukiman	Masjumi, PNI
30 March 1952–2 June 1953	Wilopo	PNI, Masjumi
31 July 1953–24 July 1955	Ali Sastroamidjojo	PNI, NU
August 1955–3 March 1956	Harahap	Masjumi, NU, PSI
March 1956–14 March 1957	Ali Sastroamidjojo	PNI, Masjumi, NU
9 April 1957–9 July 1959	Djuanda	*Kabinet kerdja*
9 July 1959–	Sukarno	*Kabinet kerdja*

Source: Lindblad 2008: 223.

The other fundamental idea underlying the political system as it was introduced in 1950 was that the president – 'father of the fatherland' Sukarno – had a largely representative position within the new political structure. The first constitution, drafted in 1945, had a strong presidential system, which had given much power to the president, but in the 1950 version that formed the basis of the experiment in democracy of these years, this had been radically changed out of fear that Sukarno would become too powerful. At the same time, he was by far the most charismatic leader of the new country. He controlled the selection of parties and of ministers that would be part of new cabinets, and therefore at crucial moments could influence policy making, sometimes formally, often informally. Nobody could monitor him, however, and he had only a limited interest in daily politics and in economic matters. Through his travelling and his role in the movement of non-aligned countries (that had its first highly successful meeting in Bandung in 1955) he became aware of the role politicians such as Mao Ze Dong could play in the shaping of their societies. In fact, he launched the idea of Guided Democracy directly after visiting Russia and China, and was already at the time accused of being influenced too much by the Chinese experiment (Legge 1972: 270–271). He gradually became more of a fan of the Chinese experiment, which drew him closer to non-democratic ways of governance, and towards the Communist Party. Political rights were gradually suppressed under Guided Democracy: political parties were banned (Masjumi and the PSI in 1961) and the free press limited. The movement from parliamentary democracy towards some kind of authoritarian regime therefore did not happen during the Suharto years, but between 1958 and 1965.[4]

Political instability is perhaps almost inevitable for newly emerging states, as new rules of the game and a new political equilibrium have to be developed and accepted by a new political community. In the economic sphere two problems were part of the same package: how to balance the government budget (and end the printing of money, which led to inflation), and how to balance the external account. Most newly independent countries after 1945 found a dual solution for both problems: state income could be boosted by heavily taxing imports (via the introduction of new tariffs and surcharges), which, by lowering imports, also helped to reduce the current account deficit. Moreover, such a conscious – or often perhaps rather accidental – strategy of import substitution also helped to set up new industries which produced for the home market, and in the 1950s and 1960s industrialization was seen as a key element of any development strategy. An overvaluation of the currency was also frequently part of the formula, in this way penalizing exporters, as often exports were in the hands of old colonial or comprador elites. Again, it is not always clear if it was conscious strategy of overvaluation, or simply the result of the fact that prices on the domestic market – due to political instability and the problems of financing the budget – were rising more rapidly than on world markets, and that for reasons of prestige, devaluation of the currency was kept to a minimum. Part of the solution was often to introduce a system of multiple exchange rates to fine-tune the system (punishing exporters of certain commodities, or transfers of capital more than other transactions).

This is, unsurprisingly, also the road Indonesia took in the 1950s. Basically, after 1952 different cabinets dealt with the possible imbalances by restricting imports (increasingly using licenses to allocate them to favourite entrepreneurs), trying to cut expenditure, and, when all else failed, printing money. To begin with, the share of tariffs in total government income increased strongly. In the 1920s this had been less than 12 per cent; it increased somewhat during the 1930s (12–15 per cent), but in the 1950s it went up to more than 40 per cent, and became by far the most important source of government income (Boediono and Pangestu 1986: 3). The increased importance of these policies was also related to the policy of 'nationalizing' strategic parts of the economy.

The task the new government faced in the 1950s was to stabilize and expand an economy that was foreign-dominated and largely privately owned. In 1952 it was estimated that 50 per cent of all consumer imports were still being handled by four Dutch firms, and 60 per cent of exports by eight firms. Moreover, private banking was largely in hands of seven foreign banks, three of which were Dutch (Glassburner 1971: 79–80).

The cabinet that was led by Mohammed Natsir of the Masjumi party was dedicated to changing this situation (and to economic reforms as such) (Glassburner 1971: 84). This cabinet came to power when the so-called Korea boom was in full swing. The Korean War resulted in strong export demand and hence a rising source of government revenue. The resulting budget surplus was merely the result of high export incomes, directly through export duties and indirectly through the effect of higher incomes on income taxes and import duties. Thus the budget surplus was the result of an exogenous shock rather than of a clearly formulated fiscal policy (Higgins 1957: 1). Nevertheless, the cabinet did react to this situation, by liberalizing imports as means of keeping domestic prices down, raising standards of consumption and encouraging the development of indigenous enterprise. It also designed the so-called Economic Urgency Plan. As in other developing countries emerging from colonial rule, the Indonesian government attributed the country's backwardness to the colonial government's lack of interest in developing manufacturing industries, resulting in a largely agrarian economy (Thee 2003a: 15). To achieve a more balanced structure, high priority had to be put on industrialization in the first years of independence. Therefore Sumitro Djojohadikusumo launched his Economic Urgency Plan (*Rencana Urgensi Perekonomian*), in which the manufacturing sector would play a crucial role as the engine of growth. Unfortunately, with only six months in office, this cabinet could make little genuine progress.

The cabinets that followed could no longer profit from the 'Korea bonus', and were therefore in a much more difficult position. The peak of the Korea boom had passed by mid-1951, and Indonesia's exports began to decline. The 1952 budget deficit was nearly three billion rupiahs, as compared with a surplus of 1.7 billion rupiahs in the preceding year (Glassburner 1971: 86). In early April 1952 the Wilopo cabinet was formed with austerity as its initial economic theme (Glassburner 1971: 86), since by the middle of 1952 it was apparent that Indonesia was facing 'a first-class financial crisis' (Higgins 1957: 2). This fiscal stringency was, however, promptly abandoned by the first Ali Sastroamidjojo cabinet. From a fiscal point of view, this cabinet's first nine months were catastrophic. The government's debt trebled and foreign exchange reserves were depleted.

Another way to manage the balance of payments problem was to manipulate the exchange rate and to introduce different exchange rates for different

Table 7.3 Expenditure and receipts of the Indonesian Government, and the money supply, 1950–1968 (in million Rp)

	Receipts	Expenditures	Balance	Money supply
1950	6,990	8,726	−1,736	4.30
1951	11,811	10,625	1,186	5.00
1952	12,247	5,025	7,221	6.60
1953	13,591	15,659	−2,068	7.52
1954	11,789	13,391	−1,602	11.12
1955	14,227	16,317	−2,090	12.23
1956	18,452	20,015	−1,564	13.39
1957	20,571	25,610	−5,040	18.91
1958	23,273	35,313	−12,040	29.37
1959	30,571	44,350	−13,780	34.88
1960	53,648	60,544	−6,896	47.84
1961	62,218	88,522	−26,304	67.65
1962	74,020	122,078	−48,058	135.90
1963	162,130	329,800	−167,670	263.36
1964	283,386	681,330	−397,944	725.00
1965	960,766	2,526,320	−1,565,554	2,572.00
1966*	13,142	29,433	−16,291	22.20
1967	84,900	87,555	−2,655	51.50
1968	185,283	185,283	0	113.90

Sources: *Statistical Pocketbook of Indonesia*, various issues.

Note
From 1966 on calculated in million of new Rp. (1,000 Rp. old=1 Rp. new).

commodities (and for imports and exports). Table 7.4 gives an idea about the degree to which the official rate and the black market rate, which probably reflected more closely the market value of the rupiah, diverged. Despite attempts to bring them closer together by devaluing the currency, the rupiah continued to be extremely overvalued, which meant that exporters were severely taxed because they received only a fraction of the market value of their commodities. This made importing goods very lucrative, but the import business was concentrated in the hands of a few large Dutch companies and groups of Chinese merchants. To foster indigenous entrepreneurship, in the early 1950s the Benteng programme was introduced, which aimed at giving import licenses for certain commodities to Indonesian citizens ('national importers') only. The programme led to large-scale corruption and seriously undermined political practices – as every party tried to get its share of the pie – and was only moderately effective in enhancing the growth of entrepreneurship. Many licences were, for example, re-sold to Chinese or Dutch importers, and the Indonesians often only acted as fronts for those more experienced parties (the so-called 'Ali Baba' companies) (Lindblad 2008: 125–136).

Cutting expenditure was a much more difficult task. Creating employment for part of the political clientele had already become part of the 'normal' process of policy making in Indonesia, which meant that cutting expenditure was unpopular with all political parties. In fact, there were many urgent reasons for increasing expenditure. One was to foster closer bonds with its citizens. Investing more in education – and trying to raise the still very low level of literacy to 100 per cent within one generation – was one of the keys to the increased legitimization of the new state. As we will see in more detail in Chapter 9, it was very successful in this respect. According to the population censuses, the share of literacy increased from less than 10 per cent in 1930 to 39 per cent in 1961 and 61 per cent in 1971 (Van der Eng 1996: 113); this was a massive increase by any standard, and mainly due to the policies pursued in the 1950s and 1960s. The level of enrolment in primary education, which had been only 15–18 per cent in the

Table 7.4 Exchange rate of the Rupiah against the US dollar

	Official exchange rate	*Black market rate*
1951	3.8	16.5
1957	11.4	45.8
1960	45	150
1962	45	850
1964	250	7,200
1965	10,000	36,000
1966	10*	122*
1967	235	290

Source: Dick *et al.* 2002: 192.

Note
* In 1966 the new Rupiah 1/1,000 was introduced.

1930s (meaning that only one out of six boys and girls in the relevant age group went to school), increased dramatically to 40 per cent in 1955, 50 per cent in 1960 and 65 per cent in 1965, although the quality of education probably did not improve accordingly (Van Leeuwen 2007: 268).[5]

The new state faced large backlogs in the maintenance of infrastructure – much new investment was needed – and had enormous ambitions concerning education, health care and other welfare reforms. International aid could help to soften some of the choices to be made – in 1955, for example, Indonesia received a large loan of US$55 million from the IMF – but this was clearly not sufficient to solve its problems (after 1967 Indonesia would start to profit much more from development aid; see Chapter 8). The only item on the budget that offered room for strong cuts was the military. As in other newly independent countries after their independence struggle, expenditure on the military had increased enormously, but now that things were calming down again it should have been possible to downsize the army. This was much discussed in the 1950s, and some measures were implemented; according to the official figures, the share of defence in the budget fell from 31 per cent in 1951 to 24 per cent in 1955, and 22 per cent in 1956 (after which an increase set in again, to 32 per cent in 1959, and 38 per cent in 1961) (Paauw 1960: 436–437; and BPS 1961–1963).[6] These policies did not make parliament and the governing political parties very popular among the military, however, and tensions between the latter and the political establishment – sometimes mitigated by Sukarno – increased strongly.

'Printing money' by borrowing from the Central Bank was the third option, which was used increasingly during the rest of the decade. Table 7.3 gives an overview of the government deficit and the development of the money supply, which demonstrates the way in which things spiralled out of control. In 1952 there was even a surplus on the government budget (but these statistics have certain margins of error, and expenditures are surprisingly low in that year). Between 1953 and 1956, the high point of the democratic experiment, budget deficits were quite small, and the money supply grew only at a modest rate. But in 1957 the budget deficit tripled, and in 1958 and 1959 it doubled again. What went wrong in these years?

One of the key problems of the new Indonesian democracy that we have not discussed so far was the balance between the regions. This concerned in particular the way in which the Javanese, who represented two-thirds of the population (and an even larger share of income) and could therefore easily dominate the political landscape, would be willing to take the interests of the inhabitants of other islands into account. This had been a concern of the Dutch, who had preferred to set up, as their legacy, a federation of Indonesian states instead of a unified and centralized state. But they were at the time, of course, not the right party to convince the Indonesian elite that this would be a good idea. Instead, Indonesia became a unified state, in which almost all political decision making occurred in Jakarta. In the provisional parliament that was formed after independence, the 'Outer Islands' were strongly overrepresented, but the elections of

1955 changed the balance. The dominance of Java in policy making became much more visible as a result.

This might not have been a real problem, if the distributional consequences of government policies had not been so dramatic. The system for regulating foreign exchange set up in the early 1950s – of high import tariffs, export levies and an overvalued currency – redistributed a large part of the income from the outer provinces to Java, and especially to Jakarta. The main exports came from the 'periphery': oil, rubber, copra, tobacco and tin, which were all produced in Sumatra, Kalimantan and other 'outer islands'. The production of sugar, once the huge contribution of Java to exports, had collapsed in the 1930s and 1940s, and never recovered. The 'peripheral' centres of export production, in Sumatra in particular, were, given the geography of Indonesia, often much closer to actual world markets – in Singapore – than Jakarta. Entrepreneurs there knew what the prices on world markets were, and how big the gap was between these prices and what they received for their export products. Selling on the domestic market, where prices of certain commodities were highly regulated, was often also much less attractive than smuggling the produce to the 'free' world market (Bevan *et al.* 1999: 327 give the example of the prices of petroleum products, which remained constant between 1950 and 1965 – they were even lowered just before the election of 1955[!] – and of which the black market price was 20 times the official price).[7] Given the short distances to Singapore, the incentive to smuggle these products out of the country and to return with illegally imported consumption goods became quite strong. The 'authorities' who could easily do this were the military governors (and other military personnel) of the districts involved, who were at the same time struggling with budget cuts that made it necessary to fire part of their personnel; since the latter was often considered to be part of their personal clientele they could not easily be 'disposed of'.

The outer provinces that contributed most to exports were penalized by the new policies, which were, it should also be added, also directed at the old colonial – mainly Dutch – elite that had dominated export production. Java, and Jakarta in particular, profited most from the new system; as we shall see below, its population grew very rapidly in these years. Overvalued exchange rates meant that imports were heavily subsidized – and Jakarta was not only the centre of the import trade, but also the main destination of many imports. Here the new 'Indonesian' import firms were set up, thanks to the licenses granted by the government, and made huge profits, which were often channelled to the real Chinese owners of these firms. In short, the new system systematically transferred funds from exporters to importers, and – in what was a quite sensitive matter in the Indonesian situation – from the Outer Islands to Java.

These problems really came to the surface after 1955. In December 1956 the regimental commander in West Sumatra took over civil government, a takeover in North Sumatra was announced, and the commander in South Sumatra forced the civilian governor there to begin introducing autonomy measures. The army councils in Sumatra rapidly acquired support by introducing reforms, repairing schools and roads, and reducing corruption. Furthermore, on 2 March 1957, the commander of East Indonesia proclaimed martial law in the whole of his region – the start of the Permesta rebellion. Theoretically this meant that he took over all civil authority from Bali through Nusa Tenggara, Sulawesi and Maluku.

Sukarno used the occasion to re-establish some kind of presidential system in which he controlled the political process in much greater detail. In a speech on 28 October 1956, Sukarno called for the parties to be buried, and two days later he said that he had an idea (*konsepsi*) of a new system of 'Guided Democracy' (*Demokrasi Terpimpin*). Only in February 1957, in the middle of the Sumatra rising, did Sukarno implement this new form of government, which he argued would be more suited to the national character. It would be based upon a 'mutual cooperation' (*gotong royong*) cabinet of the major parties, advised by a National Council of functional groups (youth, workers, peasants, religions, regions and so on) (Ricklefs 2001: 309). *De facto* this meant that the power of the old political parties and of the elected parliament became much more limited – and over the next few years was gradually phased out.

Although from a political perspective Sukarno managed to keep Indonesia united, the 'Guided Democracy' and the accompanying principle of 'Guided Economy' led Indonesia into one of the most dramatic economic crises in its history. Whereas the cabinets in the 1950s had tried to make choices – difficult choices in many cases – which had gradually undermined their position, Sukarno's Guided Democracy was characterized by the desire to make no choices at all – and leave the economy more or less to itself. Budget cuts on the army were ended and the share of defence in total expenditure rose again, as we have already seen. This was linked to the confrontational style of his international 'diplomacy'. First, in 1958/1959, the assets of the Dutch companies still active in Indonesia were nationalized, as part of an offensive to force the Dutch to hand over West Irian to Indonesia. It had been held separate during the negotiations about independence in 1947–1949, and became a bit of an obsession for Dutch policy makers, who did not want to transfer sovereignty to Indonesia – a conflict that erupted in 1958/1959. This was, on the one hand, a big blow to the Indonesian economy (which began to slide into depression in these years), but with the benefit of hindsight can also been seen as an inevitable part of the decolonization process. As a result of this confrontation with the Dutch over Irian Jaya, the military could again claim the highest priority (they started, for example, to infiltrate the island), and, consequently, an increase in their share of the budget.

Following the takeover of Dutch enterprises in 1958/1959, and the subsequent period of 'Guided Democracy', trade policies only intensified, with an emphasis on indigenous Indonesian control over all aspects of economic activity. After the takeover of Dutch estates, 2,300 Dutch managers were replaced by Indonesian military men, who often had no management skills at all. In April 1959 government trading houses obtained monopoly rights to import nine categories of goods which comprised 75 per cent of all imports (Boediono and Pangestu 1986: 5). Private importers could import only non-essential goods and the number of importers was restricted to 400 (Paauw 1963: 212). Moreover, government intervention in retail trade, which was traditionally handled by Chinese and Indian traders, resulted in a disruption of the distribution of goods and a scarcity of most consumer goods.

Table 7.3 demonstrates how the problem of the public deficit was 'solved' in these years: basically by letting it run rampant. Only in 1959/1960 were there signs of a certain restraint – the budget deficit declined sharply in these years, and a partial monetary purge was implemented, which reduced the money supply – but again after 1960 we see a classic case of government finances fuelling the money supply, leading to increased inflation, which gradually spun out of control. The confrontation with Malaysia and with the United Kingdom in the same years, as well as the increased political isolation of Indonesia, cutting it off from development aid – the country even withdrew from the United Nations in early 1965 – all contributed to the deterioration of the situation. Sukarno remained 'unconcerned' about the economy, however, and continued dreaming about the revolution. In a famous speech on Independence Day, in August 1960, he stated:

> I belong to the group of people who are bound in spiritual longing by the Romanticism of Revolution. I am inspired by it, I am fascinated by it, I am completely absorbed by it, I am crazed, I am obsessed by the Romanticism of Revolution.
>
> (Legge 1972: 350–351)

This was not the right spirit in which to deal with the basic economic problems of the country. At the same time, he probably thought that his position was so strong that he would survive any economic or political change; in this, history would prove him wrong.

Economic developments, 1950–1967

Recent literature has been relatively favourable in its assessment of the 1950s. Lindblad (2008: 38), for example, argues that we should not paint too bleak a picture of economic development during the Sukarno period. And Dick *et al.* (2002: 170) stress that 'the phases of parliamentary democracy (1950–1958) and Guided Democracy (1959–1966) were as distinct as their different constitutions'. These reassessments are based on the claim that GDP growth was reasonably good up to about 1958, with an average annual growth in total GDP between 1949 and 1957 of 4.3 per cent, and in per capita GDP of 2.9 per cent (see Table 7.5; also Van der Eng 2002: 171–173). However, looking at the early independence period in isolation and ignoring the sharp decline during the 1960s seriously blurs the picture.

During the period from 1949–1961, the country recovered from the setbacks of the Japanese occupation and war of independence. As a result, growth rates look promising for these periods, but in reality represent nothing more than making up for the lost ground. On balance annual average GDP growth was a mere 1.0 per cent during 1929–1967, while per capita growth was –0.6 per cent.

Table 7.5 Growth of GDP and its components, 1939–1966

	Agriculture	Manufacturing	Oil and gas	Trade	Transport	Government	Other services	Total services	Total GDP	Non-oil and gas GDP	GDP per capita
1939–1949	-1.0	-5.0	-3.6	-2.7	-5.5	-5.5	-1.1	-2.7	-2.3	-2.2	-3.3
1949–1966	2.5	5.1	8.4	3.8	2.4	0.4	3.0	3.0	3.5	2.2	1.0
1949–1957	2.4	10.9	12.9	5.9	7.3	6.8	4.5	5.5	5.5	4.3	2.9
1957–1966	2.7	0.3	4.5	2.1	-1.7	-4.9	1.8	0.9	1.8	0.4	-0.6

Source: Van der Eng 2010.

At the end of the Sukarno era (or at any point during the that period), GDP per capita was still substantially lower than in the 1920s (or the late 1930s); in 1953, total GDP was back at its pre-war level, but GDP per capita only returned to its pre-war level in 1970 (see Figures 2.6 and 7.1).[8] As we saw in Chapter 2 (Figure 2.8), the relatively poor performance in these years is particularly striking when compared with its 'market access', the export markets for which Indonesia was producing. Whereas between 1860 and 1940 Indonesian growth had been more or less comparable to that of its major export markets, it now fell back considerably compared to this benchmark – which is often seen as a sign of failing policies or bad institutions.

Because the share of the labour-intensive sectors in total output increased while that of the modern, capital-intensive sectors declined, the 1960s in particular can even be characterized as a period of structural retrogression (Booth 1998: 70–71). Industrial output had fallen sharply during the 1940s; after independence a rapid recovery followed, but that was short-lived, and in fact ended with the collapse of the Korea boom in 1952 (manufacturing output increased at 20–30 per cent annually between 1949 and 1951, but afterwards the growth rate fell back to 5.5 per cent). After 1957, when the transition towards Guided Democracy ensued, the growth suddenly ended – 1958 was the first year with a contraction in both manufacturing output (–10.5 per cent) and GDP (–1.2 per cent); an even sharper contraction followed in 1962/1963, during the confrontation policies directed at Malaysia (GDP: –5.3 per cent; manufacturing output: –10.7 per cent). On balance, the share of GDP accounted for by the manufacturing sector fell from 12 per cent in 1939 to only 7 per cent in 1965 (Booth 1998: 87–88). Similarly, the population

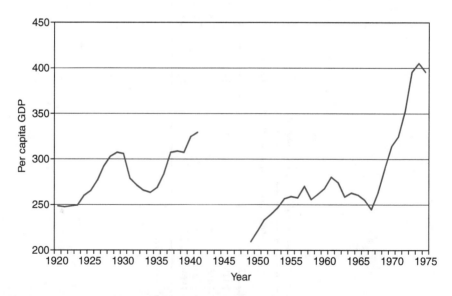

Figure 7.1 Per capita GDP (in billion 1983 Rupiahs), 1920–1975 (source: authors' calculations from Van der Eng 2002: 171–173).

censuses from 1930 and 1961 show that the manufacturing share of the labour force fell from 10.6 per cent in 1930 to 5.7 per cent in 1961. This demonstrates that the aim of rapid industrialization was not realized, in spite of the protectionist policies aimed at greater self-sufficiency in industrial production.

Fortunately, the agricultural sector was somewhat more robust – its decline during the 1940s was limited, but as we have seen, food production per capita went down quite a bit because population continued to increase. Agricultural growth during the 1950s and 1960s was relatively stable, but the gap between the demand and the supply of rice that had opened up in the 1940s continued to increase, and Indonesia was forced to import a growing share of its needs, which put more pressure on the (already very weak) balance of payments (Van der Eng 1996: 170).

Trade and transport were important sources of growth and employment, which were increasingly taken over by Indonesians. We have already discussed the way in which the state tried to take over these sectors of the economy from foreign (largely Dutch) control, a policy that was more or less successful, but came at a price (as we will demonstrate in a case study of the inter-island traffic below). At the same time, the overvaluation of the currency and the sharply increased tariffs on imports implied that international trade grew very slowly, if at all, and that the economy became much more inward-looking. The ratio of international trade (exports plus imports) to GDP was already at a historically low level in 1949, but declined even further during the 1950s (see Figure 7.2).

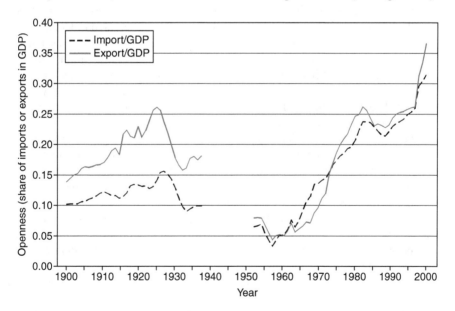

Figure 7.2 Indonesia's openness to foreign trade, 1900–2000 (sources: import and export figures: Marks 2009a; GDP figures calculated in current prices from Van der Eng 2002).

Note
5-year moving averages.

The literature on openness that we briefly discussed in Chapter 2 has also tried to quantify the effects of changes in openness on GDP. Frankel and Romer (1999), for example, find that a 1 percentage point increase in the share of exports in GDP raises per capita income by up to 1 per cent. If this is correct, the halving of the export share between the late 1930s and early 1950s (from 18 per cent to 8 per cent) must have depressed real incomes by about 10 per cent; the further decline of this share in the 1950s to about 5 per cent must have further contributed to the low levels of income in these years.

In Latin America, during the 1930s and 1940s in particular, or in India during the 1950s and 1960s, import substitution had been a relatively successful strategy for building up an industrial basis. Why did this not work in Indonesia? Perhaps the single most important cause of its failure is that different cabinets did not develop a consistent strategy towards industrialization, but carried out ad hoc plans to deal with the crises they faced. Sumitro's Economic Urgency Plan, arguably the only consistent plan developed in these years, is perhaps the best example. In his memoirs he writes about the background of the plan:

> Then I became the Minister of Trade and Industry in the Natsir cabinet. There were two main jobs. The first was to dismantle all the puppet states which the Dutch had bequeathed to us and establish a unified trade policy.... Then I was up against the monopolies of the Dutch, the so-called 'big five' trading companies. The whole point of the Urgency Plan was not to protect the Indonesian industries but to abolish the protection granted to Dutch concerns.... So the point of the so-called Benteng Policy was to try and set up a counter-force to Dutch interests. I had no illusions about what might happen but I thought that if you gave assistance to ten people, seven might turn out to be parasites but you might still get three entrepreneurs. I saw my role very much as helping the small producers – that was a legacy from my childhood experiences and from my thesis work on rural credit. I wanted to help the farmer move into non-farm activities – processing, transport etc. I didn't believe in policies such as quotas and quantitative restrictions, but neither did I believe in leaving the market as it is. That is the best recipe for political suicide for any regime. You have to ask what can be done to rectify the distortions created by the existing power relations in the market. Unless we made an effort in education, training, vocational guidance, cooperatives and strengthened their bargaining power, the small producers would remain poor. This has been my concern since the 1930s. The Industrial Plan was an outgrowth of these concerns.
>
> (Sumitro 1986: 35)

This did not mean, however, that these inward-looking policies were without their effects on the economy. One important change starting in this period was the process of urbanization: the rapid growth of cities, and in particular of Jakarta. The urban system of the Netherlands Indies had been relatively balanced at a low level; in 1930, only 5 per cent of the population lived in cities with more than 20,000 inhabitants, and the largest city, Jakarta, with 435,000 inhabitants, was only marginally larger than the second-largest, Surabaya, with 342,000 (Semarang was third with 218,000) (*Changing Economy in Indonesia,* Vol. 11: Table 15). This began to change immediately after independence; in 1950 Jakarta had already tripled in size to 1.5 million, and it would almost double during the 1950s (to 2.7 million in 1960, and then to 3.9 million in 1970); other large cities grew much less, and no other city had more than one million inhabitants in 1960 (Surabaya: 962,000, Bandung: 902,000; Semarang: 485,000). The urbanization ratio had increased in 1961 to 14.8 per cent for Indonesia. Almost 70 per cent of the urban population lived in Java.

It is clear that Jakarta really took off as a primate city in these years, claiming an increasingly large share of the total urban population. In 1961 more than 20 per cent of the total urban population lived in Jakarta. This was probably not unrelated to the changes in the political economy of the country. Ades and Glaeser (1992) (see also Galiani and Kim 2008) have demonstrated that for areas with a large primate city a typical feature is inward-looking development policies with a strong concentration of political power in the capital city – an analysis that completely fits the facts of the process of Indonesian urbanization, where large groups of migrants flowed to Jakarta (Marks and Van Lottum 2010). At the same time, the process of urbanization accelerated; in 1950, 12.4 per cent of the population lived in cities (as opposed to 5 per cent in 1930), which increased to 14.6 per cent in 1960 and 17.1 per cent in 1970. But in this respect the real acceleration would happen after 1970, when it increased by 5 percentage points within a decade (to 22.1 per cent in 1980), by more than 8 per cent in the next decade (to 30.6 per cent in 1990), and by more than 11 per cent over the next 20 years (42.0 per cent in 2000 and 53.2 per cent in 2010) (United Nations 2004).

The highly concentrated urban activity in Jakarta was partly a result of underinvestment in interregional transport and telecommunications, thus favouring producers, consumers and investors in Jakarta over those in other parts of the nation. As Krugman and Livas (1992) have shown for Mexico City, in such a situation net transport costs are lower for domestic goods in the central city because firms are located in that city. Using data for many countries, Henderson (2003) found that the degree of urban concentration, rather than urbanization, contributes to economic growth. He asserted that over-concentration would be very costly to economic growth of the country. Hence, the increasing dominance of Jakarta over other cities in Indonesia had a negative effect on economic growth. It created regional imbalance, resulted in large-scale smuggling in the 'periphery' and later, open revolt. Thus, in line with Henderson's findings, Jakarta's urban primacy hampered sustainable development in Indonesia in the 1950s.

Rice markets and cooperatives

Increasingly inward-looking policies, to some extent a by-product of the need to finance the new state, and to some extent the result of deliberate choices, contributed significantly to the poor performance of the Indonesian economy in the 1950s and the first half of the 1960s. The institutional context also deteriorated during these years, further undermining its recovery. In Chapter 2 we introduced two indices of the behaviour of rice markets – measures of price instability and of market integration – as proxies for market efficiency. Considering the importance of rice in the Indonesian economy, we argued that a well-functioning rice market is a precondition for economic development.

Looking first at seasonal fluctuations in rice prices, we saw that markets began to perform much better in the late colonial period, due to improvements in the marketing system, better infrastructure and transport facilities. But the gains between 1850 and 1920 were largely undone during the 1940s: prices fluctuated enormously in the late 1940s, 1950s and 1960s, as Figure 2.11 demonstrates. The high volatility in rice prices in the 1950s and 1960s partially reflected the inflationary pressures resulting from the way in which the state 'solved' its financial problems. In a few of the years (1961, for example) price instability was also the consequence of a bad harvest.

An underlying goal of efforts at price stabilization was to integrate Indonesia's rice markets, since integrated markets can contribute in an important way to stable prices (Timmer 1991: 239). A harvest failure in market A would in case of autarky cause an extreme supply shock and a sharp increase in price. If markets are spatially integrated, however, this effect will be mitigated by an influx of rice from market B. But spatially integrated markets also enhance productivity growth because of economies of scale and division of labour. Our second index of market efficiency is the degree of correlation between 'different sets of' rice markets.[9]

In Figure 7.3 price fluctuations between markets are illustrated by the so-called coefficient of variation (CV). This coefficient is obtained by dividing the standard deviation of the different market prices by the mean of these market prices. The rationale behind this variable is that in perfectly integrated markets the Law of One Price holds. Thus, in this case the price of rice would be the same in all markets resulting in a standard deviation of 0. In Figure 7.3 a CV is computed for three groups of cities (dependent on the sources that were available), but they show very similar developments.

In the years following independence, spatial price differences were, compared with the interwar period, extremely large and, although falling around 1953, they remained highly variable and at a much more elevated level. This suggests that Indonesia in the period following independence was a 'balkanized' country with a poorly functioning marketing system, whereas in the colonial period it apparently formed a much more integrated economy. This latter finding confirms the conclusion of De Vries (1941: 31) who wrote:

> It is already apparent that Java, Sumatra, Borneo, and Celebes form an economic whole since these regions complement each other; it is a matter of vital importance for the people of these regions that the leading central apparatus intervenes to promote further integration.

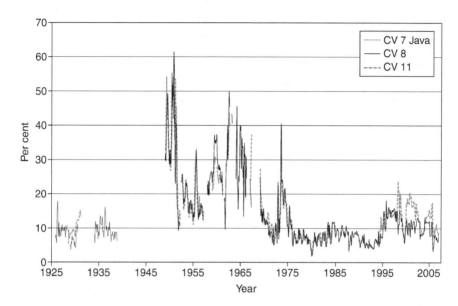

Figure 7.3 Coefficients of variation of rice prices, different groups of markets, 1925–2006 (sources: Marks 2009a; van Zanden 2004b; a working document with all the price data will be made available on www.iisg.nl/hpw).

Notes
Fluctuations measured by coefficients of variation.
cv 7 Java: Weltevreden (Jakarta), Bandung, Semarang, Surabaya, Yogyakarta, Surakarta (Solo) and Malang.
cv 8: Jakarta, Bandung, Semarang, Surabaya, Palembang, Medan, Pontianak and Makassar.
cv 11: Jakarta, Bandung, Semarang, Surabaya, Palembang, Padang, Medan, Pontianak, Makassar, Manado and Banjarmasin.

This economic integration was considered essential to progress of the Archipelago. However, during the Japanese occupation and the subsequent Revolution this system where Java 'was becoming the managerial nucleus of the whole system' fell apart (Paauw 1963: 157).

This is not a surprising conclusion. An integrated economy, especially in a large archipelago like Indonesia, depends very much on efficient transport and distribution networks. These were destroyed during the Japanese occupation and the Revolution. As discussed before, during the Japanese occupation inter-island trade was halted by the loss of transport facilities and by Japanese policies preventing the movement of regional surpluses. After independence, shipping availability for the domestic transport of goods between islands was still below pre-war volumes, since Dutch shipping was first thwarted and after 1958 banned from Indonesian waters (see below). Moreover, harbour facilities worsened, and the small volume of inter-island trade that moved was handled inefficiently, with delays and losses. The network of roads severely deteriorated between 1939 and 1959 as well (Leinbach 1986: 193; Leinbach and Chia 1989: 66). Not only were roads vulnerable to rapid deterioration from monsoon rains, but bridges were not rebuilt and roads were reclaimed by the rainforest. This lack of rehabilitation and maintenance had devastating consequences for road transport. Most of this deterioration took place during the Japanese occupation and Indonesian revolution, so that growth rates in the number of vehicles from 1949 onwards look quite impressive. But this is only because the road system had to start from a very low level. In 1949, for example, the number of passenger cars was only one-third of what it had been in 1939, and the total number of cars was halved during this period.

At the end of the Old Order, the road transport system of Indonesia was in a deplorable state. In 1967, less than 20 per cent of the length of national roads and only 15 per cent of provincial roads were assessed in good condition. Of the *kabupaten* roads, which constituted 60 per cent of all roads, none were reckoned to be in good condition (Dick and Forbes 1992: 260). This meant that transportation between village and market town was difficult, and sometimes, especially in the wet season, impossible.

The poor functioning of the marketing system was not only limited to the development of the agricultural sector (as the study by Van der Eng [1996] shows, agricultural productivity declined sharply in these years). Local specialization of production within a national economy required a widening of the reach of the local market. Village markets had to be linked together by transport and larger distributive organizations. But in newly independent Indonesia, neither transport facilities nor distributive channels expanded rapidly enough to promote the growth of national markets and to encourage regional specialization, despite Java's surplus of labour and the Outer Island's surplus of land, which should have provided a comparative advantage for inter-island trade. The pattern of specialization and resource use that had emerged in the interwar period was one in which Java produced an increasingly large volume of manufactured consumer goods, distributed partially outside Java. At the same time the growth of Javanese manufacturing was hampered by lack of market opportunities and supplies of raw materials (Paauw 1963: 166).

A poorly functioning infrastructure and inefficient transportation networks thus translated into fragmented markets, which harmed economic growth. It not only resulted in a loss of specialization and economies of scale, but also in extreme temporal price fluctuations, which an integrated market could have cancelled out. These unstable prices had a number of ensuing consequences.

First, unstable prices resulted in displaced investments in physical capital, because investments became riskier. With unpredictably fluctuating prices an investment is too risky, because whether the investor will profit from it depends on the (uncertain) future price. Second, price instability led to transaction costs for consumers in reallocating their budgets. For example, if a food crop constitutes 20–30 per cent of a consumer's expenditure, then a doubling of prices required a reallocation of a quarter of total expenditure. A third reason why unstable food prices influenced economic growth was the inter-linkage with macroeconomic factors. In Indonesia in the late 1960s, rice accounted for one-quarter of GDP and one-third of employment. In such an economy, instability in rice prices caused macroeconomic instability, which in turn lowered economic growth.

One of the ways in which the colonial state had tried to improve rural markets, in particular credit markets, was through the setting up of local banks – often (more or less) cooperative in nature, but also monitored strongly by the colonial administration (see Chapter 6). Indonesian nationalists had already in the 1920s and 1930s adopted the idea that cooperation could be a 'typically Indonesian' way of realizing development. In 1929 they organized the first Cooperative Congress, and leading nationalists such as Mohammed Hatta considered cooperatives as a way to put into practice some of the principles of Pancasila, the official state ideology, developed by Sukarno, stressing (among other ideals) social justice and democracy (Hatta 1957: 14). The Japanese occupation had ruined the existing cooperatives, however, and after independence they had to be set up again from scratch (Hatta 1957: XXV). Hatta, who became vice-president of the new republic, was the main initiator of the movement, which grew rapidly in size: at the end of 1955, there were more than 11,000 cooperatives with almost two million members (of which 404,325 were women) (Hatta 1957: 110–111).[10] At the same time the activities of the local banks and the *Bank Rakyat Indonesia* (BRI), the successor of the central bank of the local banks (originally set up in 1934), rapidly expanded. As part of the Benteng-development programme, the new bank received 200 million rupiah for the 'community approach to rural development', amongst others for restoring the village banks that had survived the Japanese occupation (Schmitt 1991: 90–91). This brief period of increased attention to the countryside – of 'balanced development' as it was termed at the time – ended in the second half of the 1950s. Hatta resigned as vice-president in 1956, because his views were no longer compatible with those of Sukarno; he was, however, also disillusioned by the growing corruption in the cooperative movement (Schmitt 1991: 91). Balanced development was replaced by Sukarno's 'Guided Democracy', which implied in this case that the BRI and the cooperative movement was mainly 'used' to realize objectives such as self-sufficiency in rice and clothing, in order to further limit the influence of foreigners – and of international trade – on the economy (Schmitt 1991: 92). This also implied a new approach to the cooperatives; a distinction was made between 'Western', voluntary forms of cooperation, and 'Eastern', collective types, which needed the kind of leadership and guidance that Sukarno thought was necessary for the Indonesian economy as a whole (the essence of the Guided Democracy and Guided Economy ideas) (Sukarno 1967: 279). The rice and clothing self-sufficiency policies did not succeed, however. Farmers mistrusted the new organization of the banks, and the new 'Rice Centres' that were set up to implement the new policies were bureaucratic and inefficient; moreover, these new centres found it difficult to find the necessary funds for their activities (Schmitt 1991: 97–101). The functioning of rural markets was also hindered by the sudden ban on Chinese businesses in the countryside in 1959, which resulted in a mass emigration of these merchants (Lindblad 2008: 145).

The poor management of the agricultural sector was among the main causes of the sharpening of economic problems in the mid-1960s. The balance of payments problems of these years meant that there was an increased scarcity of fertilizers, which had to be imported on a large scale. Imports of fertilizers, which had increased to more than 130,000 tonnes in the early 1960s, suddenly fell to 95,000 tonnes in 1963/1964, 33,000 tonnes in 1964/1965 and 24,000 tonnes in 1965/1966; moreover, due to the high prices of imported goods, farmers were not stimulated to use such inputs (and others, such as pesticides)[11] (Bank Indonesia 1960–1965: 156).[12] This was one of the main causes of the poor harvest results of the mid-1960s (Bank Indonesia 1960–1965: 146). A contributing factor was that, because rice prices were to some extent controlled by the state, farmers preferred to switch to other crops for which the prices were not monitored. Rice imports increased dramatically in these years, whereas at the same time the price of rice on international markets was rising rapidly, resulting in a strong decline of the country's terms of trade, which had decreased substantially since the Korea boom. Set at 1950 = 100, the barter terms of trade had declined to 56 in 1963, and went down even further to 41 in 1965, 44 in 1966 and a staggering 31 in 1967 (Bank Indonesia 1966–1967: 125). While the differentiated exchange rate system reduced the consequences of this decrease, this all put enormous pressure on the balance of payments, and contributed to the inflationary problems of these years. All of this illustrates the severe limitations of the inward-looking strategy Indonesia followed in these years.

Case study: the decolonization of inter-insular traffic[13]

The preceding paragraphs have described how Indonesia struggled after independence to organize the country and its economy. Political and economic considerations were often conflicting. A case study of the *Koninklijke Paketvaart Maatschappi* (KPM), the company that had acquired the quasi monopoly from the colonial state to carry out most of the transport between the islands, offers a more detailed view of how the problematic economic decolonization significantly affected Indonesia's growth performance.

Losses incurred by KPM during the war had been very severe, resulting in acute tonnage shortages in the immediate post-war period. Whereas in 1939 the KPM fleet comprised 136 ships, at the end of the war only 26 remained, scattered across the Pacific and Indian Oceans. The initial impulse was to reconstruct the fleet completely and to resume all former operations. The colonial government in fact stated that priority should be given to the reconstruction of shipping 'above any other single sector of the economy' (Campo 1998: 13). At the end of 1946, KPM operated 22 regular lines, a number that doubled within five years, while total route mileage rose from 46,000 to 160,000 geographical miles (Campo 1998: 6).

After the refusal by KPM to set up a mixed enterprise, jointly owned by KPM and the Indonesian government, in 1952 the latter established a shipping company of its own, PELNI (*Pelayaran Nasional Indonesia*). Its ultimate aim was to usurp the role of KPM in inter-island and short-distance sea transport. PELNI started operations with 13 ships, but within five years its fleet had grown to 38 ships totalling 38,000 tonnes. As most vessels clearly were too small for long-distance shipping, PELNI incurred heavy losses, which contrasted painfully with KPM's continuing profits (Campo 1998: 26; Dick 1987: 17). Freight rates were set by the government and PELNI tended to conform to KPM's levels – undercutting would increase losses and overcharging would reduce its market share – but it did not enter into arrangements on routes or schedules. PELNI usually consigned new ships to existing KPM routes without prior notification, which resulted in a sub-optimal allocation of tonnage. The Indonesians did not accept offers for advice or support. 'They prefer to take their own line. In the Asian perception consultation [with] the Dutch seems to amount to loss of face' (Campo 1998: 27). It had become sufficiently clear that cooperation between PELNI and KPM was not the Indonesian goal.

KPM continued reducing its Indonesian activities by laying off personnel, transferring dispatch from its own agencies to commissioned agencies, and contracting out other activities. Unprofitable lines were discontinued, while the government no longer allowed KPM to operate foreign charters on regular lines. Despite lavish profits, hardly any investment was made in Indonesia. Investments that KPM did make in new ships were for trade outside Indonesia (Dick 1987a: 15). The KPM–PELNI competition rested on the opposing interests of a large, profitable 'colonial' firm and an undercapitalized, poorly performing national company. With the substitution of KPM by PELNI being only a matter of time, KPM's attitude towards the Indonesian economy became 'to get as much out of it [as it could] as long as it lasted' (Campo 1998: 29).

In February 1956, strained by social unrest and political tensions, the situation was becoming rather paradoxical. The Indonesians wanted to get rid of KPM, yet feared its departure. KPM wanted to stay, but was prepared to relocate. KPM calculated that strong measures against it would do much more harm to Indonesia than to itself. At least until the middle of 1957, KPM remained confident that the Indonesian government assessed the situation the same way. Still, it took two important precautionary measures. First, it insured its entire fleet with Lloyds against seizure. Second, in November all captains received a sealed letter containing instructions in case of emergency to be opened when they received a coded message.

The breakthrough was triggered by a wave of political protest and trade union action. The refusal of the Netherlands to relinquish sovereignty of Dutch New Guinea brought matters to a head. On 1 December 1957 Dutch aircraft were prohibited from landing, Dutch-language newspapers and magazines were banned, and an official national strike was called for the following day (Dick *et al.* 2002: 184). On 3 December 1957 local trade union representatives occupied KPM's head office in Jakarta. Having lost effective control the directors immediately instructed all ships to flee to foreign ports; 34 escaped, but 29 were held in Indonesian ports by crews or military guards. Another 11 were seized on the high seas.

The Indonesian government, which most likely had approved and, according to some, even coordinated the action, legalized the takeover in retrospect (Dick 1987a: 24). On 7 December KPM held the government responsible, and gave 'notice of abandonment' of 40 ships to Lloyds in London. The huge claim for 114.5 million guilders, which would have to be paid if the ships were not released within four months, was a great shock that might have serious consequences for Lloyds, as British ambassador McDermott made clear to the Indonesian government. In February 1958 Lloyds sent its representatives to Jakarta for direct negotiations with the Indonesian government. They put the Indonesians under great pressure by threatening to raise insurance rates or even to withdraw all ship insurance, which would have raised food prices or even caused shortages. Prime Minister Djuanda decreed that all ships be released on 20 March 1958, while forbidding KPM to re-enter inter-insular shipping. All ships had to leave Indonesian waters on short notice (Campo 1998: 34–35).

In the period immediately following the expulsion of KPM, it seemed that water transport was not as negatively affected as might have been expected. The vacuum that had been created was filled quite swiftly (Ali 1966: 35). Within three years total shipping capacity (PELNI and private enterprises) was at a level comparable to that before the expulsion of KPM (Tables 7.6 and 7.7).

However, productivity of water transport declined quite sharply in these years. Whereas KPM had productivity rates – as measured by tonnes of goods transported divided by total gross tonnage – of around 20, this fell to levels below 10 for the total Indonesian fleet in 1960. Given the scarcity of capital and the abundance of labour in the new post-colonial context, using capital goods in such a relatively inefficient way was clearly 'counterproductive'. This decline is

Table 7.6 Inter-island freight (in 1,000 m³) and productivity of KPM and PELNI, 1950–1960

	KPM			PELNI		
	Transported goods	Total gross tonnage	Productivity	Transported goods	Total gross tonnage	Productivity
1950	3,610	176.6	20.4			
1951	4,079	185.9	21.9			
1952	3,835	178.5	21.5		20.5	
1953	3,630	170.1	21.3		36.8	
1954	3,312	184.9	17.9	437.7	51.1	8.6
1955	3,176	187.3	17.0	720.2	36.4	19.8
1956	2,999	190.5	15.7	968.4	46.3	20.9
1957				1,006.4	58.0	17.3
1958				808.2	89.7	9.0
1959				1,254.7	134.6	9.3
1960				1,514.9	154.2	9.8

Source: *Statistical Pocketbook of Indonesia*, 1958 and 1961.

Note
Productivity is measured by dividing transported goods by total gross tonnage of the fleet.

Table 7.7 Tonnage, cargo and productivity of inter-island fleet, 1957–1964

Year	Tonnage owned (in 1,000 tons)			Tonnage chartered (in 1,000 tons)			Total tonnage in 1,000 tons	Total cargo in 1,000 tons	Fleet productivity
	PELNI	Private	Total	PELNI	Private	Total			
1957	30.5	21.1	51.6	18.9	28.3	47.2	98.8	n.a	n.a
1958	57.7	28.0	85.7	38.4	24.8	63.2	148.9	n.a	n.a
1959	80.8	58.8	139.6	61.1	47.2	108.3	247.9	2,797	11.3
1960	93.4	71.1	164.5	77.6	56.1	133.7	298.2	2,713	9.1
1961	108.8	125.7	234.5	116.1	60.9	177.0	411.5	3,027	7.4
1962	132.1	113.2	245.3	100.8	43.5	144.3	389.6	2,281	5.9
1963	154.0	158.9	312.9	90.2	43.9	134.1	447.0	2,800	6.3
1964	144.2	191.5	335.7	29.6	20.6	50.2	385.9	3,300	8.6

Source: Dick 1987: 28.

Note
Productivity is measured by dividing transported goods by total gross tonnage of the fleet.

unrelated to a fall in trade, because domestic trade still increased (slowly) in these years (Sulistiyono 2003: 237). Dick (1987a: 26), quoting an unpublished UN report, shows that it was not so much lack of capital in the form of ships that slowed down developments in the water transport sector. It was a lack of organizational knowledge and skills, combined with the elimination of efficient networks between traders and shipping companies. These were lost as a result of the troubled nationalization of this important sector. He notes that 'by eliminating the KPM the Indonesian Government achieved a symbolic political victory, but at the very high cost of destroying the inter-island transport system' (Dick 1987a: 25). Inter-island shipping services that had facilitated economic growth for years now became an obstacle to further development. This obviously had repercussions in other economic sectors, and in particular for the patterns of specialization between Java and the Outer Islands that had come into existence in the colonial period.

These findings directly link the troublesome economic decolonization and the deterioration in macro-economic performance during the 1960s.[14] This link, we believe, is not sufficiently acknowledged in the literature concerning the economic development of Indonesia.[15] Dick is a notable exception, although he actually blames KPM's monopoly position rather than the difficult decolonization process:

> It is unfortunate that the aggressive use of monopoly power by the KPM denied Indonesians access to modern shipping until 1941.... This undoubtedly contributed to the problems encountered after Independence and must be set against the very substantial economic benefits brought by the KPM.
>
> (Dick 1987a: 11)

Conclusion

The first 20 years of independence ended in a nightmare: the economic and political instability of the mid-1960s resulted in the military coup of 30 September 1965, Suharto's counter-coup, and the massacre of hundreds of thousands of (alleged) communists that followed the success of that move. Many countries found it difficult to develop new, stable institutions after independence, but Indonesia was certainly not among the more successful ones. What were the causes behind these 'lost decades'? Part of it can be explained by the attitude of the Dutch colonizers; they ignored the 'writing on the wall' during the 1920s and 1930s, and did not start thinking seriously about independence, let alone making specific preparations for it. They persisted in this attitude after the war, and it took them a long time to really understand the new situation that had emerged after August 1945. And finally, they maintained their hold on Irian Jaya, the only major territorial concession they had been able to get from the negotiations over independence, further increasing tensions between them and the new state in the 1950s and early 1960s. Dutch presence in the economy – although gradually declining due to the process of *Indonesianisasi* – continued to be a source of problems and tensions in the 1950s, until the final nationalization of Dutch assets in 1958–1959.

It would be too easy to hold only the Dutch responsible, however, even if we add to this that the generally very low level of education – another part of the colonial heritage – did not enhance the functioning of parliamentary democracy in these years. Policy decisions by the new political elite, and in particular Sukarno, partly explain the poor economic development as well. When Sukarno held more or less absolute power during the years of Guided Democracy between 1958 and 1965 things really got out of hand. The budget deficit, the money supply and, predictably, the price level all spun out of control. These economic problems culminated in the disastrously bad years of 1965–1967, when the economy went into decline – and without a doubt these economic problems contributed substantially to the political drama of these years. Sukarno severely misjudged the consequences of the economic downturn.

What happened between 1958 and 1965 partly explains why the political elite preferred, in 1945/1946, a constitution in which the political parties and parliament would have a great weight in policy making, over the presidential constitution that had been proposed earlier. Yet the first experiment in constitutional democracy failed after eight years. It is not easy to identify the reasons for this.[16] Feith (1962), in his classic study of the subject, saw the drama of the democratic experiment as a confrontation between a group which was loyal to Western-style democracy and its values – of which Hatta was the leading figure – and a group, headed by Sukarno, who did not share these beliefs. Hatta lost, democracy became discredited, and Sukarno emerged as the sole leader of the new nation. We have stressed the inherently unstable character of politics in a new nation. The bottom line seems to be that the challenges that had to be met, both in the political sphere and in the economic domain, were so overwhelmingly large that the relatively weak cabinets that had to deal with them found only partial solutions, which at times created more problems than were being solved. The economic policies pursued did not produce economic growth, which would have enhanced the authority of the elected cabinets, but instead – because they were strongly inward-looking and undermining the current market institutions – often increased the economic problems the country faced. Indonesia rapidly fell behind its neighbours and the markets to which it had access – in relative and absolute terms – in these years (see Chapter 2). The problem that finally undermined the democratic experiment was that the inward-looking strategy – aimed at establishing a commercial elite among the Indonesians, at restricting imports and raising public income – also led to a strong redistribution of income from the Outer Islands, from Sumatra in particular, to Java, and especially to Jakarta. This led to large-scale smuggling and other insubordinate activities in the 'periphery', which undermined the authority of a central government that was already losing its popularity with the military, because it tried to cut the huge defence budget. This eventually led to open revolt in 1957/1958, which ended the democratic experiment and inaugurated the period of Guided Democracy.

These findings lead to the conclusion that Indonesia's early independence period can be in many respects almost considered as 'lost decades' (see also Marks 2010b). We should not paint too bleak a picture, however. There were achievements as well – the rise of mass education being one of them – on which the new regime could build. As we shall see in the next chapter, the Indonesian elite – and in particular Suharto – had learned many lessons from the mistakes and failures of the 1945–1965 period. Things would be approached very differently by the new 'strong man'; the contrasts between Sukarno and Suharto could not be more dramatic. Thanks to the different approach after 1965/1966, compared to Latin America and Africa, Indonesia's 'lost decades' were relatively short.

8 Success and failure of the 'new order', 1967–1998

Introduction

In the three decades after the publication of Gunnar Myrdal's *Asian Drama* (1968), Indonesia was one of the fastest-growing economies in the world, which was able to narrow to gap with the rest of the world economy substantially (Chapter 2). By all standards, growth was remarkably rapid: its GDP per capita increased more than that of its neighbours (Figure 2.7); growth was also much faster than its 'market access' (its weighted export markets), pointing to strong improvements in its international competitiveness (Figure 2.8); and the quality of institutions, as measured via the functioning of rice markets, also improved dramatically (Figure 2.11 and 2.12). In the 30 years between 1967 and 1997, GDP and GDP per capita grew, on average, 6.8 and 4.6 per cent per year, respectively. In 1972 GDP per capita at last exceeded the peak reached in 1941, and by 1997 it was almost three times that of 1941 (Van der Eng 2002: 144; 2010: 304–306). This was not only due to more labour and capital – to 'perspiration' – but also to productivity growth as another important source of income growth (Figure 2.5).

Indonesia's achievement is even more impressive if we consider its initial condition in a comparative perspective. As can be seen in Table 8.1, in 1965 Indonesia was among the poorest economies in the world, with a low share of trade in GDP, a (very) large agricultural sector and a (very) small manufacturing industry. From a political perspective, too, the starting point was highly problematic. The last years of the regime of Sukarno were chaotic and extremely unstable. Yet it seems as if Indonesia did almost everything right over the next thirty years. Suharto and his staff implemented a set of policies that were directed at stabilizing the economy and the political system; increasing output and productivity in the agricultural sector; attracting foreign investment (at least, initially) and foreign aid; eliminating artificial, overvalued exchange rates; and strongly improving incentives for export production. The central issue of this chapter is therefore to explain the successes of this period: was it good luck, because, for example, oil and gas income exploded during the 1970s, or because the new technologies of the 'green revolution' were just becoming available in the same years? How important were the lessons learned during the Sukarno

Table 8.1 Indonesia in 1965 in a comparative perspective

	Population (in millions)	GDP per capita (in 1990 international dollars)	Trade share (share of GDP)	Agriculture (share of GDP)
Indonesia	106	983	0.24	0.53
South Korea	29	1,436	0.27	0.36
Malaysia	10	1,804	0.80	0.29
Taiwan	13	1,810	0.41	0.24
Thailand	32	1,308	0.35	0.32
South Asia*	477	763	0.21	0.40
Sub-Saharan Africa**	259	1,099	0.43	0.39
Latin America***	745	3,709	0.36	0.21

Sources: Population and GDP estimates: Maddison (www.ggdc.net/maddison/); trade share and agricultural share: Temple 2003: 155.

Notes
*   India, Pakistan, Bangladesh and Nepal.
**   Angola, Benin, Botswana, Burkina Faso, Burundi, Cameroon, Cape Verde, Central African Republic, Chad, Comoro Islands, Congo 'Brazzaville', Côte d'Ivoire, Djibouti, Equatorial Guinea, Eritrea and Ethiopia, Gabon, Gambia, Ghana, Guinea, Guinea Bissau, Kenya, Lesotho, Liberia, Madagascar, Malawi, Mali, Mauritania, Mauritius, Mozambique, Namibia, Niger, Nigeria, Rwanda, São Tomé and Principe, Senegal, Seychelles, Sierra Leone, Somalia, South Africa, Sudan, Swaziland, Tanzania, Togo, Uganda, Zaire (Congo Kinshasa), Zambia and Zimbabwe.
*** Argentina, Brazil, Chile, Colombia, Mexico, Peru, Uruguay and Venezuela.

years? How vital was good economic advice from the 'Berkeley Mafia', a team of economists who were in charge of important policy areas in these years, or was it much more important that good advice found the right ear?

It would, however, be wrong to see the period from 1967–1997 as monolithic, because the regime and its basic economic policies went through a number of important changes. We will deal with them briefly.

1967–1970: stabilization and rehabilitation

After the disastrous last years of the Sukarno regime, which ended in economic chaos, the first mission of the Suharto government was to stabilize the economy (Thee 2009: 55; Dick *et al.* 2002: 194). To this end, Suharto turned to a group of economists from the Faculty of Economics at the University of Indonesia for advice. These economists (Widjojo Nitisastro, Ali Wardhana, Sadli, Emil Salim and Subroto)[1] were appointed by Suharto to form a 'Team of Experts in the Field of Economics and Finance' with the assignment of drawing up a 'Programme for Stabilization and Rehabilitation'. This programme provided guidelines for Indonesia's economic recovery and specific policies on a balanced budget, the balance of payments, rehabilitation of the physical infrastructure and agricultural development (Dick *et al.* 2002: 196, see also Thee 2003b: 200, 231). Throughout the New Order, this group of technocrats and their affiliates were able to determine key features of economic policy in relative isolation from day-to-day politics (Hofman *et al.* 2004: 13–14). The importance of this group is also stressed

Table 8.2 Growth of GDP and its components, 1967–2007

	Agriculture	Manufacturing	Oil and gas	Trade	Transport	Government	Other services	Total services	Total GDP	Non-oil and gas GDP	GDP per capita
1967–1996	4.1	10.8	3.7	7.6	7.1	10.7	6.8	7.4	6.9	7.4	5.2
1967–1972	5.5	12.7	16.5	8.9	5.8	20.5	5.7	7.7	10.2	8.0	6.5
1972–1980	4.7	10.3	4.8	7.8	7.3	17.5	5.7	8.0	6.8	7.3	4.7
1980–1986	3.3	9.1	-3.7	4.4	6.4	6.2	5.6	5.4	3.5	5.3	2.8
1986–1996	3.5	11.3	1.6	8.9	8.1	3.7	8.9	8.0	7.6	8.4	6.5
1996–2000	1.0	0.7	-1.5	-2.4	-0.5	-0.8	-3.9	-2.6	-1.2	-1.2	-2.6
2000–2007	3.1	5.0	-2.3	6.1	11.5	2.1	6.6	6.6	5.0	5.6	4.1

Source: Van der Eng 2010.

in the World Bank study about the East Asian Miracle: 'each [of the High-Performing Asian Economies] boasts at least a small ideologically consistent technocratic core that answers directly to the top leaders and therefore has some independence from the legislature and other sources of political pressures' (World Bank 1993: 170). To some extent this might indeed explain Indonesia's success. Suharto brought political stability, albeit of a repressive nature, and with the help of the technocrats Indonesia embarked on a high growth path.

By the late 1960s the orthodox monetary and fiscal policies proposed by the technocrats had already brought inflation down. Moreover, ties with the international donor community had been re-established, reversing Sukarno's policy to cut links with the capitalist world. These measures subsequently attracted both domestic and foreign investors (Hill 2000: 15). In a survey on the Indonesian economy, the late Heinz W. Arndt, a leading scholar on Indonesia's economic development, wrote in 1969: 'The Indonesian economy has turned a corner. The first objective of the Suharto government, stabilization, has been achieved' (Arndt 1969: 1).

1971–1980: rapid growth

Between 1972 and 1980 real GDP grew at an annual rate of 6.8 per cent (see Table 8.2). This was in a large part due to the rise in oil prices. In 1973 international oil prices quadrupled, resulting in windfall revenues for Indonesia. In addition, Indonesia benefited from substantial volume increases thanks to earlier exploration efforts. The volume of crude oil exports rose by 55 per cent between 1972 and its peak in 1977 (Bevan *et al.* 1999: 244).[2] But non-oil exports also did well. Timber and coffee exports increased in volume, and world prices for rubber, palm oil and tin rose substantially in 1973 and 1974, and for coffee in 1977. As can be seen in Table 8.2, all sectors showed a marked increase, but especially the 'modern' sectors (manufacturing and services) grew rapidly.

The rapid growth in manufacturing can be attributed to new investments, following the reversion of the rigid investments controls of the Sukarno era. Growth in the textile sector was especially impressive with a growth in output by 36 per cent in two years. The rapid growth in government was a result of the decision to raise the government take to 85 per cent of the foreign oil companies' net operating income. Government salaries were subsequently raised substantially. The increase in the share of routine expenditures in GDP was modest (8.6 per cent in 1972/1973 to 11.5 per cent in 1979/1980); development expenditures rose more significantly (from 5.8 per cent to 11.4 per cent). This reflected a large increase in social expenditure, largely for irrigation, rural water supply and schools.

In 1979, the Iran–Iraq war caused another round of large oil price increases. Between 1978/1979 and 1981/1982, oil and gas taxes as a proportion of government revenue increased from 53 to 70 per cent and foreign exchange from oil and gas rose from US$7.4 billion to US$19 billion (Robison 1986: 377). Immediately prior to the second boom the government had devalued the currency and it had increased tariffs to improve the competitiveness of non-oil exports.

Initially the government was slow in spending these new oil revenues. In 1980 part of it was spent on subsidies for fuel oil, rice and fertilizer. Expenditure of oil revenue accelerated in 1981. The fuel and food subsidies were the fastest growing part of the budget, mainly because of the unusual behaviour of world prices for these products. The expansion of the development budget also enabled the government to further promote industrialization. To this end, the Indonesian government aimed at the processing of primary products. For example, in 1980 log exports were limited to 32 per cent of total output, and in 1981 they were banned unless companies had investments in processing. As a result, plywood manufacturing investment increased substantially under joint ventures, particularly with the Japanese.

1982–1986: re-orientation

Falling oil prices, followed by a sudden decline in economic growth in 1982, indicated the end of oil-financed growth and abundance (Figure 8.1). At the same time, trade was still highly regulated. There were extensive restrictions on foreign trade, including high tariffs and a multitude of non-tariff import barriers (Bird and Manning 2003: 77). Moreover, import quotas increased mainly to the benefit of cronies close to the 'first family' who sought to capture monopoly profits (Basri 2001). When world oil prices fell and slower world economic growth depressed commodity prices in the early 1980s, this also heavily affected Indonesia. Growth slowed, trade and investment fell, debt increased and the government faced a major fiscal challenge due to the falling oil revenues. These developments provoked discussion about the 'high-cost' economy and the uncompetitive nature of many Indonesian industries. The onset of crisis once again enhanced the role of the technocrats, who urged extensive deregulation to

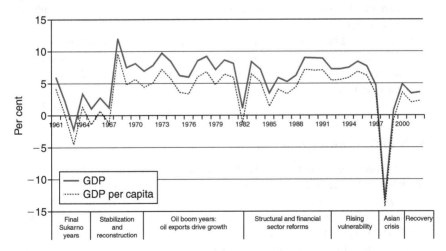

Figure 8.1 Annual GDP growth, 1961–2002 (sources: World Bank, WDI; see also Hofman *et al.* 2004: 15).

get the Indonesian economy back on its growth path (Hill 2000: 116; Lewis 2007: 113). When, in 1983, a number of exogenous shocks led to a crisis (bad weather hit the rice harvest and then the oil price slipped from US$37 to US$30 a barrel), the government was forced to react.

At the end of March 1983 the rupiah was devalued by 28 per cent (from Rp.703 to Rp.970 per US$). Moreover, 47 major capital projects, worth US$14 billion, were deferred and military expenditure was cut. The government also implemented financial deregulation measures. The objective was to mobilize private savings now that public savings were reduced by the drop in oil prices. At the same time, however, a high-cost and inefficient industrial sector was only kept alive by excessive non-tariff barriers. Only in 1986, when oil prices fell sharply again (from US$28 to US$12 per barrel), was this interventionist trend reversed (Hill 2000: 17).

The most important measures taken during this period were another devaluation of the rupiah in September 1986 by 31 per cent (from Rp.1,134 to Rp.1,664 per US$), and a series of trade and investment deregulation packages, which substantially reduced tariff rates and eliminated most quantitative import restrictions (although these were replaced by tariffs). In October 1986, 165 import monopolies were abolished and replaced by tariffs. Average tariff rates fell from 27 per cent in 1986 to 20 per cent in 1991, 15 per cent in 1995 and only 7.3 per cent in 2001 (Bird and Manning 2003: 78). Furthermore, Fane and Condon (1996) found that the average Effective Rate of Protection (ERP) for the non-oil manufacturing sector declined from 59 per cent in 1987 to 16 per cent in the early 1990s. Moreover, the number of areas in which foreign companies were allowed to invest was doubled. Before this more than 1,000 products were subject to import regulation and license. Hill argues about this period:

> There can be little doubt that the packages transformed Indonesian industry from a protected, inward-looking sector to one which is increasingly outward-looking and internationally competitive.... The reorientation of thinking over this period within the Department of Industry, extending up to the Minister, from protection and control to promotion and export, was clearly evident.
>
> (Hill 2000: 117)

1987–1997: growing into trouble?

Annual growth between 1987 and 1996 was similar to that of the 1970s, but this time it was achieved without buoyant oil revenues. Macroeconomic management was praised and economic reforms and a resurgent investment boom at the beginning of the decade spurred growth, especially in the manufacturing sector (World Bank 1993: 139).

At the same time, however, the period of far-reaching trade reforms during the late 1980s slowed down in the early 1990s. A number of policy measures taken in the preceding years were reversed, and crony capitalism became more widespread again. Suharto had frequently reconciled pressures from cronies with technocratic direction. But, whereas technocrats, economists and business analysts criticized the high-cost economy (a term that encompassed corruption, nepotism and collusive behaviour), a cluster of prominent interests created obstacles to further liberalization and competitiveness (Lewis 2007: 206). The influence of the technocrats was especially undermined by the so-called 'technologists', who saw aggressive industrial policy based on increasingly high-tech projects as the best way to develop Indonesia. But army generals – who provided the political backbone of the Suharto regime and who were long accustomed to arbitrary rent-seeking – and other 'cronies' were using the state more and more for personal gain.

Therefore it is not surprising that many government monopolies and cartel arrangements remained relatively untouched. For example, a clove monopoly was granted to a private–state joint venture in 1991, tariff protection was granted to a large petrochemical plant in February 1995, and tax exemptions were granted to an automotive company in 1996 (Bird and Manning 2003: 79). Not surprisingly, all three companies were partly owned by the then President Suharto's children.

The strong performance of the economy diminished Suharto's attention to needed policy and institutional reforms. Moreover, with the economy rescued from the troubled state of the mid-1980s, the technocrats had lost some leverage to push through difficult and fundamental reforms. Schwarz (2000: 52) therefore concluded that: 'In times of economic distress [...] [the technocrats] have enjoyed a broad mandate to determine policies. At other times, their influence has been more restricted'.

Despite these developments, Indonesia's economy continued to perform well during the 1990s. Foreign investors remained optimistic about Indonesia's prospects and a series of reform packages further lowered tariffs, removed non-tariff barriers and opened up new areas for foreign investment. But behind this macroeconomic success lay a number of worrying developments. With nearly 2,000 products still facing some kind of export restriction by 1996, protectionist measures remained widespread. At the same time numerous new banks opened in an environment of financial deregulation, far outpacing the capacity of regulatory authorities to monitor them. The high costs resulting from corruption and market-distorting measures began to affect the competitiveness of some key non-oil exports. This is reflected by the fact that the growth rate of textile exports declined from 6 per cent in 1993 to a negative 7.2 per cent in 1996. Moreover, a considerable portion of new foreign investment went into unprofitable areas such as real estate.

The political economy of the Suharto regime

Why was the Suharto regime so successful in generating economic growth and in spreading its benefits to large parts of the population? How could the economy grow so fast, whereas at the same time Indonesia was one of the most corrupt countries in the world (in 1997, at the end of the Suharto regime, it was indeed leading international lists of corruption), in which a small elite systematically plundered its riches? This is the paradox we want to explore: how fast economic development could occur in a country plagued by 'massive, systematic, and endemic corruption and rent-seeking', which must have undermined the working of the market economy substantially (Rock 2003).

Part of the answer is that Suharto had learned from the failure of the Sukarno regime, which had ended in economic chaos. The basic lesson was that the economy mattered; that a stable regime had to be based on a stable, growing economy. Whereas Sukarno had concentrated on the building of a nation state, and believed that political success would ultimately solve the country's economic problems, the fundamental mission of the Suharto government was economic development (Thee 2009: 55; Dick *et al.* 2002: 194). As we have already seen, he put together a team of 'technocrats', which was very successful in stabilizing the economy.

Another part of the answer is that economies with unsophisticated structures can grow quickly, even if they are not managed in a very efficient way. Soviet-style economic planning that generated fast economic growth from the late 1920s to the 1960s is an example of such a relatively inefficient way of producing rapid growth and structural change. One of the keys to understanding such a process is the fact that this economy could draw upon a large reserve of labour from the people working in agriculture, whose marginal labour productivity was very limited, if not close to zero (Allen 2003). By transferring these labourers from agriculture to industry, the economy could grow rapidly, even though 'static' efficiency may have been low, due to the fact that price signals did not play a role in the planning process. To realize such a development process, however, one needs the means to finance the growth of the industrial sector. In socialist planning this is realized – at least in theory – by exploiting the peasantry, after abolishing private property through the collectivization of agriculture. Here the parallel with economic development during the Suharto years ends; his regime was able to generate other means of investment into the newly expanding 'modern' sectors of the economy.

One of the key problems that the Sukarno regime was unable to solve was the financing of government expenditure; rampant inflation, the result of inflationary financing, did in fact contribute significantly to his downfall. Another way to phrase the question about the resources for industrialization is: how did Suharto manage to finance this? Where did he get the resources from to balance the government budget and to modernize the economy at the same time? Analysing the finances of the state often tells us a great deal about the political economy underlying it. In the Indonesian case this is a bit problematic, because a large part of 'public' income and expenditure was carried out via other channels than the 'official' state. Army commanders generated their own sources of income, members of the Suharto clan raised their own 'voluntary' contributions to finance their schemes, and the activities of large state institutions such as Bulog (in charge of rice policy) and Pertamina (mainly oil) were less than fully integrated in the government administration. At the very start of his career Suharto realized that he needed such discretionary funding to stabilize his regime, and he appointed a member of his clientele (Ibnu Sutowo) as the director of Pertamina to take care of this (Elson 2001: 151). But even if we look at the official figures, the changes between the Sukarno and the Suharto years are quite striking.

A first, very important change in government funding was linked to the international orientation of the regime. Suharto's rise to the presidency began with his anti-communist counter-coup, and he continued to play the anti-communist card with gusto. More generally, his pro-Western political ideas and the pro-market economic ideas of his 'technocrats' meant that international aid agencies and donors were more than willing to supply Indonesia with development and/or military aid. In the early 1960s Sukarno had also received some development aid (mainly from Japan, as part of compensation for war damages), but it did not contribute greatly to the financing of public expenditure (only in 1961 did its share increase to 16 per cent, but it was less than 2 per cent in 1963–1965). Whereas Sukarno had told the West to 'go to hell with your aid' (Hill 2000: 79), the New Order government initially relied heavily on foreign aid from Western countries (and Japan) and multilateral aid agencies to provide the necessary funds for rehabilitation of the obsolete infrastructure (see Figures 8.2 and 8.3). In 1967, during the first attempts to stabilize the economy, the share of development aid in total government income increased to 29 per cent, and it continued to fluctuate around 20 per cent during the rest of the Suharto era (Figure 8.2). This obviously still strongly underestimates the importance of international aid, because a large part of it was spent directly on projects, and did not enter into the government budget. Moreover, and this is perhaps surprising in view of Myrdal's notion of a soft state, detailed research has established that development aid was relatively well spent in Indonesia; it was not only spent on the items that it was supposed to be spent on, but it also did not displace domestic expenditure on the same items (Pack and Rothenberg Pack 1990; Burke and Ahmadi-Esfahani 2006).

A second, even more important source of income that began to flow from the late 1960s onwards were the proceeds from oil (and natural gas). In the 1950s and early 1960s the sector had been neglected; for example, important oil wells had not been returned to Royal Dutch Shell because of the political sensitivity of such a decision. In 1965 Shell was so exasperated by the problems of working in Indonesia that it decided to withdraw and sell its possessions to the Indonesian state. A reorganization of oil policy followed in 1966; to break through the stalemate, production sharing agreements were concluded with the major oil companies, which meant that in the future the country would benefit from increases in oil prices. In 1968 the state oil company Pertamina (successor of the smaller Permina) was set up. Only a few years later, in 1973, oil prices began to increase very strongly, further enlarging the profits made. Oil proceeds dominated public income in the 1970s and 1980s: their share increased from 9 per cent in 1967 to 25 per cent in 1971/1972 and 48 per cent in 1974/1975, to a peak of 62 per cent in 1981/1982 (see Figure 8.2). Again, the total bonus from oil must have even been much larger, as a large part of the income of Pertamina was spent on ambitious development projects, such as the Krakatau steel works, and a large part of the oil money never went into the coffers of the state. But, directly or indirectly, a substantial amount of the oil proceeds were used by the state and its institutions to carry out development projects.

An important part of the explanation of the success of the economic policies of the New Order was the close cooperation with Sino-Indonesian businessmen, who could mobilize large amounts of capital and had the skills and the knowledge to develop new projects and enterprises. During the 1950s and early 1960s, policy making had been geared towards establishing an indigenous *pribumi* entrepreneurial class, which had antagonized the Chinese community. The Benteng programme had been clearly focused on discrimination against both European and Chinese entrepreneurs, and in 1959, this hostile attitude culminated in the (renewed) banning of Chinese merchants from parts of the Indonesian countryside, after which about 100,000 Chinese inhabitants left the country (Lindblad 2008: 139–147). Relationships with them improved considerably during the Suharto years, and he increasingly worked closely with them in initiating large 'developmental' projects.

Finally, Indonesia was also able to attract foreign direct investment. When Suharto took power, his economic policy makers realized that Indonesia was in urgent need of new capital and technical and managerial skills to rehabilitate and modernize the economy. To attract new foreign investment they drafted a new Foreign Investment Law in 1967, which ushered in a brief period of an

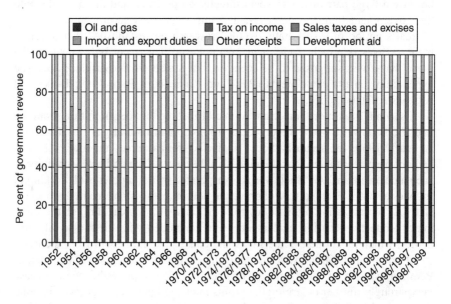

Figure 8.2 Structure of government revenues, 1952–2000 (source: *Statistical Pocketbook of Indonesia*, various issues).

open-door policy towards foreign investment (see Figure 8.3). As early as 1970, however, this policy was already becoming more restrictive when a number of fields were barred to foreign investment. Growing dissatisfaction with the extent of foreign ownership and control in the Indonesian economy erupted in January 1974 into demonstrations in Jakarta. The demonstration broke into violent riots, with Japanese cars and a substantial number of buildings being burnt, and an official death toll of 11 people shot by the security forces (Cribb and Brown 1995: 127). These riots,[3] which were nominally directed at the perceived over-presence of Japanese investments in Indonesia, eventually resulted in a significant plunge in FDI, followed by a more restrictive foreign investment policy (Thee 1987: 383) (Figure 8.3). The reason that this shift did not have major impact on economic development was that the windfall government revenues, from resource-rent taxes as a result of the two oil booms, enabled the government to finance investments on its own. Moreover, oil proceeds made it possible for the government to renegotiate the original terms of entry to enhance the benefits for the national economy by placing more restrictions on the operations of foreign-controlled firms. These restrictions basically involved more 'Indonesianization' with regard to equity ownership, management and local content, and an increase in the number of fields closed to new foreign investment (Lindblad 1991: 198–199; Thee 1996: 7). The restrictiveness in Indonesia's foreign investment regime came to an end because the government had to introduce a series of policy reforms following the sharp drop in oil prices in 1982, and again in early 1986. The aim of these reforms, mainly deregulation measures, was to restore macroeconomic stability and to promote a more efficient private sector which would be able to generate more non-oil exports, particularly manufactured

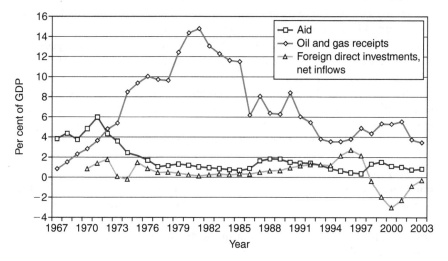

Figure 8.3 Foreign aid, oil proceeds received by state and FDI, as share of GDP (sources: Aid and FDI: World Development Indicators; oil and gas receipts: Bank Indonesia, annual reports, various issues).

exports. Initially these measures had only limited impact on the ratio of net FDI inflow to GDP. Only with the introduction of a new investment deregulation package in June 1994 did FDI really start to flow into the country. This deregulation package contained further significant relaxations of the remaining regulatory controls, such as the divestment rule (requiring foreign investors to divest to a minority position within a specified period of time). But this surge in FDI inflows was nullified as a consequence of the Asian crisis. Overall, despite periods of openness to foreign investment, the inflows have never loomed large in the aggregate picture (Hill 2000: 78).

These fundamental changes, resulting in large transfers to Indonesia, solved the dual problems – of finding equilibrium both on the balance of payments and of the public budget – that had plagued the Indonesian economy between 1950 and 1966, and made it possible to develop and implement plans to transform the economy. Moreover, the development strategy that was carried out was more than adequate. The team of technocrats helped to introduce market-oriented policies, which put an end to the large distortions characteristic of the import-substitution strategy of the 1950s. The exchange rate was brought into line with the actual value of the currency (see Table 7.4); from 1978 onwards, the exchange rate was increasingly used to further the interests of exporters, instead of trying to tax them as much as possible. Deficit financing was ended and the money supply reformed (1,000 rupiah were transformed into 1 in 1966). All of this created the right incentives to increase export production again.

A key characteristic of the development effort was that it focused on the countryside – on the agricultural sector in particular. One of the most ambitious aims of the new regime was to realize self-sufficiency in rice, because output of the food crop had lagged behind population growth, and the huge deficit in rice had greatly contributed to the problems of the 1960s. The question remains why the country adopted a strong rural development strategy. Many scholars refer to Suharto's rural background (Dick *et al.* 2002: 216). Woo (1991) suggests an alternative explanation for Indonesia's pro-rural strategies (see also Hill 2000: 134). He argues that support of the peasants was necessary for long-term stability. Therefore, the emphasis on agricultural development was a rational choice, rather than being ideologically driven. Suharto himself was convinced that increasing the welfare of the rural population would be one of the keys to the success of his regime, and he therefore steered a large part of the developmental efforts in that direction. He began to promote (rural) cooperatives in a more vigorous way than had been done previously, and developed a variety of other means to improve incentives for peasants to increase their market production and use more purchased inputs. On the other hand, efforts to increase rice production were actually nothing new; these had already started in the colonial era. Therefore, it can be argued that the earlier efforts accumulated, and with new technologies everything came together in the 1970s.

The increased support of the rural population was also linked to the political 'reforms' Suharto introduced in these years. The multiparty system was reshaped into a system with one dominant party (Golkar), which was supported by the government and its many allies. These included the military and a number of official opposition parties, which were allowed to participate in elections and in deliberations in parliament (the few times they occurred), but whose role was limited by their lack of power, funds and access to the media (or, when the media became too critical of the New Order, by simply banning them). The strength of Suharto's political machine, Golkar, was that it was also used as a mechanism to distribute favours in return for political support, such as votes at election time; an important part of these favours consisted of inputs into agriculture, such as fertilizers, pesticides and credit (Schmitt 1991: 107–110).

Another key element in the success of the development strategy was the stability of the regime. For slightly more than 30 years – between March 1967 and May 1998 – one person dominated the state and the country, and, more importantly, there was a high degree of continuity in the aims and instruments of government policy (although some major changes occurred, as we have seen). This stability was based on the alliance crafted by Suharto and his skilful manipulation of that coalition. He came to power as an army general. As we saw in the previous chapter, the army played a large role in Indonesian politics and society, and was also increasingly active economically, in particular after the seizure of the possessions of the Dutch companies in 1957/1958, which usually led to a taking over of their management by the army. After the 1965 crisis, the army further enlarged its role, both in the economy and, obviously, in the political process. During the late 1960s and 1970s it was the most important instrument of rule – and army generals, such as Murtopo, Soejono and Sutowo, played a key role in political and economic development. The problem of the Indonesian state being 'soft' – unable to implement its development plans – was to some extent solved by the strong hierarchy of the military. Suharto and a small group of military 'entrepreneurs', who managed Golkar, Pertamina, Bulog, state banks and much more, transformed this 'soft' state into a relatively focused 'machine' aimed at political stability and economic development.[4] As a group these 'patrimonialists' formed an activist counterbalance to the 'technocrats' – the free-trade oriented economists – who controlled macroeconomic and monetary policy. In the late 1960s Suharto leaned mainly on the economists, but after the successful stabilization of the economy, and the start of the inflow of foreign aid and oil money, the patrimonialists got the upper hand, and they dominated policy making in the 1970s. At the same time, however, Suharto developed his ties with the Sino-Indonesian community, and the business concerns of his family (initially of his wife Ibu Tien, and later of his sons, daughters and other relatives) began to expand. During the 1980s he gradually managed to limit the importance of the military in the regime, and began to lean increasingly on his Sino-Indonesian network and his family. Only in times of crisis – during the mid-1980s – were the technocrats again called in to solve problems. The radical change towards export production in the 1980s, which after the stabilization of the late 1960s was perhaps the most important policy change during these 30 years, was of their making.

As a result, the regime consisted of what was perhaps a relatively good mix between 'activism' and 'laissez faire' economic policies. One of the dangers of being a large exporter of oil in the 1970s and 1980s was the 'Dutch disease', the crowding out of other exports due to the enormous increase in income from oil. The 'solution' to this was to spend it all – and perhaps waste part of it – on economic development projects, often initiated by the patrimonialists. Some of these projects may have been too ambitious (such as the Krakatau steel mills), but others were quite helpful for the development of the economy (as, in particular, the policies towards agriculture). A dependency solely on market forces – without the optimistic plans of the patrimonialists – would perhaps have thrown the country back into the niche it had occupied before the 1930s, of being an exporter of primary products only. In the 1980s and 1990s, when the role of the military contracted, the role of 'activists' was taken over by members of the Suharto clan, Sino-Indonesian businessmen related to them, and newcomers such as Habibie, who made the case for an even more offensive industrial policy (moving into the manufacture of cars and even planes).

This is not to deny that economic development was severely handicapped by the enormous growth of corruption during these years. Between 1967 and 1998 the key to economic success was being close to the Suharto clan – first the military, later on his family and friends. This clan plundered large parts of the economy. The oil and gas sector is the most infamous example. Pertamina became the cash cow of the clan and its projects, and as a result went bankrupt in the mid-1970s, when oil prices were at a historical high (as a result of which Ibn Sutowo had to withdraw). This did not stop the renewed, often illegal, use of oil funds for 'development' purposes. After 1998 the company started to clean up the mess: it cancelled or re-tendered over 152 contracts that had formerly been with Suharto's family members and associates, and ordered them to sell their stakes in oil and gas projects. An audit sponsored by the IMF showed that between 1996 and 1998 Pertamina alone had misappropriated 1.5 billion dollars annually through corruption and inefficiency (Hertzmark 2007). Moreover, the large-scale mismanagement of this sector had had a number of severe consequences. Whereas in other countries the national oil companies, such as Malaysia's Petronas, had developed into strong businesses that were gradually able to compete on international markets, Pertamina had remained a very weak business partner, unable to play such a role (the irony is that Petronas had initially been modelled after Pertamina, but has since clearly overtaken its Indonesian 'sister'). Domestic policies towards the oil industry had been dominated by the desire, in order to buy popular support, to keep petroleum prices as low as possible (as happened during the Sukarno years), which meant that consumption was growing much more rapidly than production (Hertzmark 2007).[5] On the other hand, after about 1980 output began to contract (oil production was falling already, but the output of natural gas was still increasing), because the company and/or the Indonesian state were unable to develop policies to attract investment in the relatively small oil fields that still remained. As a result of these policies, in the late 1990s Indonesia became a net importer of oil.

The reserves of oil and natural gas were not the only natural resources 'pillaged' by the New Order. Indonesia possessed very large and valuable forests, which had to some extent been preserved by previous regimes (*Changing Economy in Indonesia*, Vol. 16). The exploitation of these forestry reserves only started in earnest after 1967, and was in a similar way embedded in the power structure of the Suharto regime: the military often received concessions for services rendered, which were (often) sold to Sino-Indonesian or Japanese businessmen, who used local power structures and their contacts with the military to guarantee a smooth 'harvesting' of the timber. Usage rights of local communities were often ignored, not to mention the intrinsic value of these forests for biodiversity. The government only focused on earning as much as possible from these reserves. As a result, in the 1970s Indonesia became the world's largest exporter of tropical timber, which contributed a great deal to export income. What changed in the 1980s was that the government induced the businessmen involved to increasingly saw the timber on the spot and, instead of exporting the raw timber, export plywood or paper. This resulted in another boom in forestry exports, which consolidated Indonesia's position as one of the world largest – if not the largest – exporter of these products (Christanty and Atje 2004).

As the examples of oil and forestry products show, Indonesia's rapid growth in the Suharto years was strongly dependent on the exploitation of national reserves, and therefore, it could be argued, non-sustainable. In a seminal paper Repeto *et al.* (1989) have analysed what the implications of 'green' national accounting would be for the growth rate of its economy (it was in fact one of the first studies in this field). For the period of 1970 to 1984, they estimated 'net domestic product' (defined as GDP minus estimates of net natural resources depreciation which covers timber, petroleum and soil). The result suggested, among other things, that while GDP over the period of 1970 to 1984 had increased by 7.4 per cent per year, 'net' domestic production had increased by only 4.0 per cent per year. In 1984, for example, the entire depletion of resources from the three natural resource sectors comprised about 17.9 per cent of GDP (see also the overview of this literature in Alisjahbana and Yusuf 2003). The gap between 'actual' and 'sustainable' growth did, however, diminish after 1984, when growth became more dependent on exports of manufactured commodities.

Economic developments: structural change?

Having reviewed the political economy of the New Order, we now switch to an analysis of the economic achievements of the period. One of the questions that should be asked is whether the Suharto regime has generated a process of what Kuznets called 'modern economic growth', i.e. sustained increase in per capita income combined with rapid population growth and sweeping structural changes (Kuznets 1966: 1). According to Kuznets this process is the result of productivity gains in all sectors of the economy and an increase in the scale of production and consumption. Therefore it is informative to explore to what extent 'sweeping structural changes' took place in the occupational structure and assess what happened to labour productivity in the different sectors. This is followed by an analysis of developments in agriculture, industry and services respectively.

Developments in employment and labour productivity

According to Kuznets (1971), an indicator of economic development is the share of agriculture in employment and output. He found that, as countries develop, the share of the labour force working in the agricultural sector falls. At first this is due to an increasing share employed in the industrial sector. In a later stage of development, economic theory predicts that the share of employment in the service sector will start to rise.

As can be seen in Figure 8.4, in 1961 employment in agriculture was still dominant. What is striking, though, is that also in relative terms employment in this sector was even larger than in 1930. Because of this pattern, in which the share of the labour-intensive or traditional sectors in total output increased while that of the modern, capital-intensive sectors declined, Anne Booth (1998: 70–72) calls this a period of structural retrogression.

After the 1961 population census we see some signs of what Kuznets would call modern economic growth. The share of agricultural employment decreases to 39.3 per cent in 2000. Between 1980 and 1990, a period that was characterised by relatively slow economic growth and a re-orientation of the economy, this share remained almost constant. The share of industry in total employment increased only slowly from 7.9 per cent in 1961 to 13.7 per cent in 1990 and 16.9 per cent in 2000.

Figure 8.4 also reveals that already in an early phase of development service sector employment was significant and (much) higher than industrial employment (see also Marks 2009a). Horlings (1995) found that the Netherlands did not

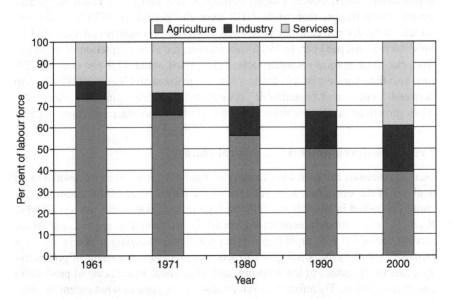

Figure 8.4 Occupational structure, 1961–2000 (sources: *Sensus Penduduk 1961*, 1961; *Sensus Penduduk 1971, Seri D*, 1971; *Hasil Sensus Penduduk 1980, Seri S*, 1980; *Hasil Sensus, Seri S*, 1990; *Statistik Indonesia*, 2000).

follow the 'sectoral model', which is characterized by shifts in employment from primary to secondary to tertiary. He argued that, 'instead of transfers of labour from agriculture into industry and then into services, the structure of the Dutch economy became more advanced without significant growth of industry' (Horlings 1995: 107). This scenario seems to hold for its former colony as well. In the case of the Netherlands, Smits attributed this development path to important linkages between agriculture and the service sector, especially distributive services (Smits 1990: 90). The story in Indonesia is rather different. It is not so much linkages between agriculture and services that are responsible, but rather the failure of the industrial sector to absorb the large group of labourers pushed out of the agricultural sector and trying to find work in the urbanizing regions. A large number of these labourers ended up in low-productivity service sectors, in the 'informal sector', a theme to which we return below.

The employment figures can be combined with GDP estimates. This makes it possible to draw some conclusions about developments in labour productivity. The labour productivity estimates are presented in Table 8.3. A number of interesting observations can be made.

To begin with, labour productivity in the service sector turns out to be, as expected, higher than in agriculture. Labour productivity in industry, however, is significantly higher than in services. This suggests that the shift in labour to services that has been taking place raises the overall performance less than a shift to manufacturing would have done. These findings support similar conclusions drawn by Alexander and Booth (1992), and suggest that the service sector in Indonesia accounts for a much greater share of the non-agricultural labour force than was the case in countries such as France, Italy, Japan or Taiwan at a comparable stage of development (Alexander and Booth 1992: 285).

The findings above are strengthened if we look at growth rates in labour productivity. As can be seen in Table 8.4, growth in labour productivity in industry was especially high in the 1970s, when industrialization took off in Indonesia. The decrease in labour productivity in trade between 1961 and 1971 and again between 1990 and 2000 is likely because the labour surplus that occurred as a

Table 8.3 Labour productivity in Indonesia's service sector, 1961–2000 (in 1993 Rp. per labourer)

	Agriculture	*Industry (excl. oil and gas)*	*Trade*	*Transport and communications*	*Total service sector*	*Total labour productivity*
1961	814.2	3,690.8	2,410.6	3,227.2	1,699.4	1,210.2
1971	996.8	3,877.7	1,982.0	3,233.9	1,480.0	1,403.9
1980	1,337.2	5,260.3	3,428.8	5,125.7	2,633.8	2,254.9
1990	1,530.8	7,010.2	4,391.2	6,266.3	4,117.1	3,313.2
2000	2,009.4	9,472.5	3,255.7	6,165.0	4,213.0	4,341.5

Sources: employment figures: Timmer and De Vries 2007; GDP estimates: for agriculture and industry: Van der Eng 2002; other sectors: Marks 2009a.

Table 8.4 Average annual labour productivity growth, 1905–2000 (%)

	Agriculture	Industry (excl. oil and gas)	Trade	Transport and communications	Total service sector	Total labour productivity
1961–1971	2.0	0.5	−1.9	0.0	−1.4	1.5
1971–1980	3.3	3.5	6.3	5.3	6.6	5.4
1980–1990	1.4	2.9	2.5	2.0	4.6	3.9
1990–2000	2.8	3.1	−3.0	−0.2	0.2	2.7

Source: see Table 8.3

result of the crises that took place in these periods was mainly absorbed in this sector.

With this information it is possible to estimate the contribution of structural change to productivity growth. This method is usually called the shift-share method and was introduced by labour economist Solomon Fabricant (1942). The shift-share methodology is still popular in decomposing aggregate productivity growth (see Syrquin 1984 for an overview; for more recent applications, see Van Ark 1996; Mulder 1999; Timmer and Szirmai 2000; Lains 2004). The formula is:

$$LP_t = Y_t / L_t = \sum_{i=1}^{n} (Y_{(t,i)} \times L_{(t,i)}) / (L_{(t,i)} \times L_t) = \sum_{i=1}^{n} L_{(t,i)} \times S_{(t,i)}$$

where LP denotes labour productivity, Y output, L the labour force and S the share of labour in each sector.

The difference in aggregate labour productivity levels at time 0 and t can be written as:

$$LP_t - LP_0 = \sum (LP_{(t,i)} - LP_{(o,i)}) \times S_{(o,i)} + \sum_{i=1}^{n} (S_{(t,i)} - S_{(o,i)}) \times LP_{(o,i)}$$
$$+ \sum_{i=1}^{n} (S_{(t,i)} - S_{(o,i)}) \times (LP_{(t,i)} - LP_{(o,i)})$$

The first term on the right-hand side represents the intra-sectoral productivity growth, and corresponds to that part of the productivity change which is caused by productivity growth within the sectors. The second term is referred to as the static shift effect, and represents the effect of the change in sectoral employment shares on overall growth. This effect is positive when labour moves to branches with relatively high productivity levels. The third effect measures the dynamic shift effect, and is positive when labour shifts to sectors which improve their productivity performance. The sum of the second and third term is referred to as the total structural change effect.

The results of this exercise are given in Table 8.5, which shows that between 1961 and 1971 productivity growth was limited, with only 1.5 per cent average

Table 8.5 Decomposition of labour productivity growth, 1961–2000

	1961–1971	1971–1980	1980–1990	1990–2000
Labour productivity growth per year	1.5	2.5	3.9	2.7
Intra-sectoral growth	55.9	75.3	75.1	59.4
Structural change				
Total	44.1	24.7	24.9	40.6
Static	55.4	14.5	16.6	35.1
Dynamic	−11.3	10.1	8.3	5.6

Source: author's calculations from Table 8.3.

annual growth. Structural change accounted for 44.1 per cent of this labour productivity growth, although it has to be noted that the dynamic effects were negative. Between 1971 and 1980 labour productivity growth is mostly explained by productivity growth within sectors. Only in the final decade of the twentieth century do we see signs of structural change again in which the static effect is dominant. This means that a shift of labour took place to more productive sectors, not accounting for the changes in productivity in these sectors.

Agriculture in transition

Until the 1970s the prevailing impression of the Indonesian agricultural economy was one of pessimism (Booth 1989: 1235). In the literature it was stressed that Indonesian cultivators were unable or unwilling to absorb modern production techniques, and few observers saw any prospect of rapid agricultural development in the early years of the New Order. In this respect David Penny wrote:

> The reluctance of farmers to buy fertiliser, modern tools, etc., is still so great that it is unlikely that any substantial modernisation of Indonesian peasant agriculture will take place in the next decade or two.
>
> (Penny 1969: 264)

This negative assessment was proven wrong in the decades that followed. Agriculture became a central focus of the New Order's development strategy. In the 1950s and 1960s the typical approach to economic development for a less-developed country emphasized exploiting agriculture to generate the surplus that would make it possible to make a fast transition to industrialization. For most countries development planning was synonymous with industrial planning (Prawiro 1998: 127). From the beginning of the Suharto regime, however, Indonesia gave first priority to agricultural development, which became a highly successful part of the development policy.

The success of the New Order's agricultural policies was the result of a large package of measures. First, and perhaps foremost, was the stabilization of the economy, which meant that agricultural markets began to function more or less properly after the chaos of the mid-1960s. The measures of market efficiency presented in Chapter 2 – the seasonal variability of rice prices and the degree of integration of rice markets – both returned to much lower values, indicating that markets became much more reliable and predictable. Equally important was the fact that the government began to invest heavily into this sector. In the 1950s and early 1960s projects had been developed to promote the package of fertilizers, pesticides, new rice varieties and extension services to the population, but for a multitude of reasons these projects had failed. The New Order was much more successful in this respect because it had more resources (to, for example, subsidize fertilizers and make huge public investments in irrigation structures), and because it was able to end the organizational disorder of the extension services and impose more efficiency. As we saw in Chapter 7, fertilizers had become notably scarce in the mid-1960s and their prices had gone up relative to the price of rice; this changed radically after 1967, when large subsidies were introduced to stimulate their use. As Van der Eng (1996: 110) has shown, relative prices of nitrogen and phosphor declined rapidly after the mid-1960s, to reach the levels that were normal in (for example) Japan. The size of subsidies is also clear from the fact that after-retail prices of these fertilizers were only 25–50 per cent of their actual prices on the world market – the difference being the subsidy, which apparently also covered the costs of distribution and sales (Van der Eng 1996: 112). The promotion of the use of fertilizers was part of a series of measures to further the intensification of, in particular, rice cultivation; the main target of the policy was to make Indonesia self-sufficient in rice again. The intensification policy also predated the New Order, but had been relatively unsuccessful before 1967, when less than 9 per cent of the area cultivated with rice was covered by the programme of BIMAS, the central agency in this field. This increased very rapidly after that date; in 1971 it had gone up to almost 40 per cent, in 1979 to 75 per cent and in 1987 to more than 90 per cent (Van der Eng 1996: 100). In this way, Indonesia could profit from the start of the 'green revolution': BIMAS was one of the first to introduce the new high yielding varieties from IRRI in the Philippines, and the long-term success of the intensification policy was to a large extent also dependent on these inputs.[6]

The supply of rural credit was another key area in which the New Order government invested heavily. Rural credit was taken up by BIMAS, which was the main agency in this field until the early 1980s. BRI, the central 'developmental' bank, which had played a role in this field in the 1950s, but had also diverted most of its funds to the trade sector (as part of the Benteng programme), resumed its role for the agricultural sector after 1967; the bank concentrated on the top layers of the peasantry, however. The cooperative movement, which had expanded strongly in the early 1950s, had been more or less dormant during the years of Guided Democracy, when their capital had been eroded by the strong inflation in these years. Suharto attached great importance to the cooperatives, however, and after a reform of the system in 1967/1968, when those that existed only on paper were liquidated, the movement started anew (Van der Eng 1996: 125–128).

The ups and downs of the cooperative movement in these years show how dependent it was on the changing political leadership of the country – it seemed to lack the 'bottom-up' strength that would allow it independent from such influences. Two forms of cooperatives were set up after 1967: Village Unit Activity Centres (*Badan Usaha Unit Desa*, or BUUD), which had a certain degree of 'bottom-up' monitoring (via elections of the leadership), and the Village Unit Cooperative (*Koperasi Unit Desa*, or KUD), which were only cooperatives in name, but in practice were government institutions, embedded in 'top-down' organizations led by the state. Initially the BUUDs were more successful (they could often build on earlier experiments in cooperative action), but after 1974 they were discouraged and gradually all cooperatives were transformed into KUDs (Van der Eng 1996: 125–129). They played a large role in supplying inputs – credit, fertilizers, new varieties of rice, etc. – to the farmers; in 1990, 78 per cent of the males employed in agriculture were a member of such a 'cooperative'. The KUDs were clearly part of the larger political economy of the New Order regime; they were governed 'top-down', could use coercion to carry out their plans, and recruited the political support for Suharto's Golkar party whenever this was required (Suradisastra 2006).

Besides BIMAS and the BRI, other sources continued to play a role, some of them with origins in the colonial period, such as the Lumbung Desa (rice banks), pawnshops, and the *dessabanken*. Interest rates on the non-subsidized loans remained at a high level; whereas at about 1980 the interest charged by BIMAS was only 12 per cent per year, and branches of BRI set similar rates (12–21 per cent), local *dessabanken* charged 48–72 per cent, and pawnshops about 60 per cent (Mears 1981: 323). The latter probably reflected the scarcity of local credit more effectively than the rates set by BIMAS and other government agencies.[7] In the 1980s interest rates on BRI loans were raised, to bring them closer to the prevailing market rates – in the 1990s the successful KUPEDES programme of BRI charged about 30 per cent on their loans (Patten *et al.* 2001). In real terms, this was still quite high, given an average inflation rate of 8 per cent during this period, pointing to the fact that Indonesia continued to be a country of capital scarcity, and perhaps rather inefficient capital market institutions (see Boomgaard and Henley 2009).

Returning to agriculture, its central importance in development policies in the Suharto years is also clear from its high share in government expenditure. Total expenditure on agriculture was about 8–11 per cent of value added of the sector (during the colonial period this was less than 1 per cent), as (again) Van der Eng (1996: 148) has demonstrated.

Rice has been the success story of Indonesia's agricultural development. In 1979 Indonesia had been the world's largest importer of rice, yet, only six years later, in 1985, the country had reached self-sufficiency in rice. Of the major Asian rice producing countries, only Burma's rice production grew more rapidly from the mid-1970s to the early 1980s (Booth 1989: 1240). This is a remarkable achievement since other oil-exporting countries saw a stagnation or decline in agricultural growth as a result of the adverse effects of the so-called 'Dutch disease'. This theory predicts that a dramatic improvement in the price of oil in an economy would lead to a marked shift in the structure of production away from the non-booming tradable goods sectors towards the non-tradable sectors. But whereas the other countries tended to invest their windfall gains in large industrial projects and ambitious construction projects, Indonesia devoted considerable budgetary resources to improving infrastructure serving smallholder agriculture, to the development and dissemination of new seed varieties and to subsidising inputs such as fertilizer resulting in a 'green revolution' (Booth 1988: 2; Dick *et al.* 2002: 217). The height of this revolution was in the period 1978–1981, during which agricultural output, especially rice output, grew at the extraordinary rate of 6.1 per cent. The combined effect of depressed markets for agricultural products, slowdown in the expansion of the land frontier, ecological limits on further increases in cropping intensity and exhaustion of 'green revolution' advances for rice caused a slowdown in the growth rates to a still respectable 3.1 per cent during the period 1982–1988 (Dick *et al.* 2002: 219; Tabor 1992: 162).

Industrialization

Compared to Malaysia, the Philippines, Thailand, South Korea, Hong Kong and Singapore, Indonesia had one of the smallest manufacturing sectors in the region in 1965, and perhaps one of the smallest among the world's largest developing countries (McCawley 1981; Soehoed 1967); by 1996, however, it had the second-largest manufacturing sector after South Korea (Dick *et al.* 2002: 221). This was achieved by the double-digit growth of the sector, which implies a doubling of real output about every six years (Hill 2000: 156). Since 1965, Indonesia has gone through four phases of development in the manufacturing sector, each corresponding to a specific policy emphasis and to international developments (Aswicahyono 1997: 2; Hill 2000: 157). The first phase was the period of very rapid growth between 1967 and 1973, driven largely by liberalization and the restoration of macroeconomic stability. Falling inflation, the reopening of domestic and international markets, and an increase in consumer demand and spending spurred these developments. Moreover, following the Foreign Investment Law of 1967 and the Domestic Investment Law of 1968, foreign and domestic investment rose rapidly, bringing not only capital but also valuable managerial, organizational and technical skills, as well as new industrial technologies (Dick *et al.* 2002: 222). Furthermore, the import licensing system was dismantled in 1967 and export bonus schemes were introduced in 1967 and 1968.

The second phase of industrial development can be characterized as one of inward-looking and import substitution, following the oil boom in 1973. Introduction of new tariffs and widespread use of non-tariff barriers enabled light consumer goods and consumer durables to replace imported products. According to Hill (2000: 158–159) this state-directed industrialization led to high, yet inefficient growth.

The decline in oil prices after 1981 prompted a third phase of policy reappraisal. Initially the response was limited to prudent macroeconomic management and a large devaluation in 1983. However, when oil prices started to fall sharply in the mid-1980s there was an unambiguous change of direction, leading to the fourth phase of industrial policy and development aimed at liberalization and promoting manufactured exports. The deregulation measures involved reductions in tariff and non-tariff barriers, liberalization of foreign regulations, financial sector reforms and efforts to reduce the monopoly power of the big businesses. This phase resulted in greater independence of the private sector firms and generated substantial increases in foreign investment (Pangestu 1991; Thee 1991). A point to bear in mind is that in all phases of industrial policy Indonesian manufacturing experienced considerable sectoral variations in the degree of protection and monopoly power (Basri and Hill 1996; Thee 2002; Widodo 2008).

As Table 8.6 shows, the structure of production in Indonesia changed markedly during the Suharto era. While manufacturing's share in value added was only slowly increasing during the period 1975–1985, it increased to 27 per cent by the year 2000. The resource-intensive industries have traditionally been the leading contributors to manufacturing value added. Although their contribution to the total economy value added increased marginally, their share in the total manufacturing output declined from almost 70 per cent in 1975 to roughly 43 per cent in 2000. In this category, food, beverages and tobacco have always accounted for most of the value added.

The industrial policy during the New Order placed a lot of emphasis on the development of large-scale industries – the projects of the patrimonialists – utilizing the revenues from oil and gas. Nevertheless, the contribution of these industries to total value added increased only marginally between 1975 and 1985. Growth accelerated after the liberalization of the economy, with textiles, paper and printing, and iron and steel responsible for most of the growth.

The rapid increase in the share of manufacturing in the total value added of the economy is mirrored in Indonesia's exports, increasing fivefold from 9.4 per cent in 1975 to 55.1 per cent in 2000. The initial increase in manufacturing exports in the 1980s stemmed mainly from the resource- and labour-intensive industries, such as wood products and garments and leather. The increase in the export share of wood products can be attributed to the ban on log exports in 1981 and the consequent increase in the exports from the plywood industry. Consumer electrical and electrical and non-electrical machinery showed rapid increases in their shares, especially during the latter half of the 1990s (Jacob 2005: 433).

An important reason for the increase in exports from the late 1980s onwards was the export-oriented investment from the four Asian newly industrialized countries (NICs) (i.e. South Korea, Taiwan, Hong Kong and Singapore) and Japan (Jomo 1997: 27–55). Relocation of industries from those NICs and the strategy of the international buyers to disperse production locations were a major reason behind these investments. Moreover, in textiles and garments, unfulfilled market quotas under the Multi-Fibre Agreement (MFA) provided the bulk of foreign investment and export growth.

Table 8.6 Pattern of structural change, 1975–2000

Sector	Sectoral composition of value added						Sectoral composition of exports					
	1975	*1980*	*1985*	*1990*	*1995*	*2000*	*1975*	*1980*	*1985*	*1990*	*1995*	*2000*
Primary (1)	**27.7**	**20.6**	**22.2**	**16.7**	**11.6**	**7.9**	**6.0**	**6.7**	**6.1**	**2.3**	**1.1**	**0.8**
Oil, gas, mining (2)	**20.5**	**26.3**	**14.2**	**14.6**	**9.8**	**17.6**	**73.9**	**70.8**	**40.6**	**27.9**	**17.3**	**16.2**
Petroleum refinery (353)	**0.6**	**0.3**	**5.0**	**3.2**	**2.0**	**5.5**	**1.0**	**6.8**	**23.7**	**14.4**	**7.5**	**13.3**
Manufacturing (3)	**10.9**	**11.1**	**13.0**	**19.1**	**24.6**	**27.0**	**9.4**	**7.4**	**17.9**	**38.4**	**51.1**	**55.1**
Resource-intensive manufacturing	*7.5*	*7.0*	*7.3*	*10.2*	*11.9*	*11.6*	*5.4*	*4.9*	*9.9*	*19.0*	*16.4*	*12.8*
Food, beverages and tobacco (31)	6.3	5.1	4.7	6.7	8.7	7.9	2.5	1.4	1.3	5.0	4.2	3.8
Wood products and furniture (33)	0.2	0.6	1.2	2.2	1.7	1.7	0.0	0.8	4.8	10.3	8.8	6.1
Rubber and rubber products (355–356)	0.7	0.8	0.7	0.8	0.8	1.1	2.9	2.6	3.7	3.1	2.9	1.8
Non-metallic mineral products (36)	0.3	0.5	0.7	0.5	0.7	0.9	0.0	0.1	0.1	0.6	0.5	1.1
Labour-intensive manufacturing	*0.9*	*1.0*	*1.3*	*2.6*	*4.0*	*4.7*	*0.0*	*0.3*	*2.7*	*10.7*	*16.5*	*15.3*
Textiles (321)	0.4	0.5	0.9	1.6	2.5	2.5	0.0	0.1	1.1	3.9	6.7	7.3
Garments and leather (322–323)	0.5	0.5	0.4	1.0	1.5	2.2	0.0	0.2	1.6	6.8	9.8	8.0
Technology-intensive manufacturing	*2.5*	*3.1*	*4.4*	*6.3*	*8.7*	*10.7*	*4.0*	*2.2*	*5.4*	*8.7*	*18.2*	*27.0*
Paper, paper products and printing (34)	0.3	0.2	0.4	0.9	1.3	1.6	0.1	0.0	0.1	0.7	2.2	3.9
Industrial chemicals (351–352)	0.5	0.5	0.8	0.9	1.2	1.2	2.8	0.2	1.0	1.6	2.1	2.6
Iron and steel (371)	0.0	0.2	0.5	0.6	0.9	0.5	0.0	0.0	0.1	0.5	0.5	0.5

Non-ferrous metals (372)	0.1	0.1	0.4	0.6	0.7	0.5	0.7	1.4	2.9	3.7	4.3	2.9
Shipbuilding and repairing (384)	0.1	0.1	0.2	0.1	0.1	0.1	0.0	0.1	0.2	0.4	0.3	0.2
Motor vehicle (384)	0.6	0.6	0.1	0.7	1.1	1.8	0.0	0.0	0.0	0.1	0.5	0.5
Other transport (384)	0.0	0.0	0.1	0.1	0.1	0.0	0.1	0.0	0.0	0.1	0.1	0.1
Other manufacturing (mainly electrical and non-electrical machinery) (381–383)	0.9	1.4	1.9	2.4	3.3	5.0	0.3	0.5	1.1	1.6	8.2	16.3
Electricity, gas and water (4)	**0.3**	**0.3**	**0.4**	**0.6**	**0.6**	**0.5**	**0.0**	**0.0**	**0.0**	**0.0**	**0.0**	**0.0**
Construction (5)	**5.0**	**5.0**	**6.6**	**5.8**	**6.7**	**4.0**	**0.0**	**0.0**	**0.0**	**0.0**	**0.0**	**0.0**
Finance and insurance (8)	**2.4**	**2.0**	**2.6**	**3.8**	**4.1**	**4.1**	**0.0**	**0.2**	**2.3**	**3**	**3.3**	**1.3**
Other services (6, 7, 9, 0)	**32.6**	**34.4**	**36**	**36.2**	**40.6**	**33.4**	**9.7**	**8.1**	**9.3**	**14**	**19.7**	**13.3**
Total	**100**	**100**	**100**	**100**	**100**	**100**	**100**	**100**	**100**	**100**	**100**	**100**

Source: Jacob 2005: 429–430 (based on input–output tables).

Notes

Bold and italic type indicate that, for example, the sub-category resource-intensive manufacturing consists of food, beverages, and tobacco, wood products and furniture, etc. In the input–output tables economic activities are subdivided into nine main categories and many other subcategories. These are given in brackets. For example, manufacturing is category number 3, and food, etc. is number 31 (3: manufacturing, subcategory 1).

Clearly, rapid industrialization has generated far-reaching structural change in Indonesian manufacturing, yet not always in the direction posited by economic theory (Hill 1992: 209). The 'typical' pattern of industrialization involves an evolution from simple, labour-intensive activities towards more skill- and technology-intensive industries. Indonesia was in the first phase until around 1970, but then departed from the model of export-oriented, labour-intensive growth due to the country's resource endowments. Indonesia only began to exploit its strong potential comparative advantage in labour-intensive manufactures in 1985. This was soon followed by the rise of more technology-intensive industries in the 1990s, illustrating that Indonesia rather quickly ascended the technology ladder by learning to produce goods of increasing value, sophistication and complexity (Jomo 1997: 28). An important feature of Indonesia's industrialization is that the export of manufactures is strongly consistent with its comparative advantage (Hill 1992: 219). Initially this was in natural resources, followed by labour-intensive activities, and since the 1990s also in basic technology-intensive sectors.

Service sector growth

The service sector played a crucial role in the economic development of Indonesia during the Suharto era, not only in underpinning the growth of tradable goods in agriculture and industry, but also in generating employment opportunities (Marks 2009a). The contribution of the service sector to GDP has consistently been more than 35 per cent, while average annual growth in output was 7.4 per cent between 1967 and 1997.

Within the service sector trade has always been the dominant subsector, producing on average more than 40 per cent of sectoral value added. The question remains, however, to what extent foreign trade has actually functioned as an engine of growth. In Chapter 2 we already discussed the literature suggesting a strong link between openness and economic growth, pointing out that such a relationship was also quite strong in the Indonesian case, with the exception of the period between 1830 and 1870, when increased openness did not lead to higher incomes. Perhaps the most important switch during the (early) New Order was from inward-looking policies – which had clearly been unsuccessful – to outward-looking ones. This suggests that foreign trade – by facilitating international exchange – indeed played an important role in economic development in these years. Hanson (1980: 51; see also Booth 1998: 227) elaborates on the relationship between trade and growth; he lists three conditions which need to be fulfilled in order for trade to contribute significantly to a country's economic development:

1   a large export sector;
2   rapid export growth, especially in per capita terms; and
3   a comparative advantage in products with growth-promoting or at least non-growth-retarding production functions.

Figure 8.5 summarizes the links between growth of GDP and openness in Indonesia during the twentieth century. It shows that in the period 1900–1929 the export sector accounted for a growing proportion of GDP. Moreover, export volume growth per capita accelerated after 1900, and the direct contribution of exports to GDP growth was high. Booth, however, argues that the third factor was not met in this period. Indonesian export staples – sugar, tobacco, tin, rubber and palm oil – lacked 'growth-promoting production functions' (Booth 1998: 228), so that international trade failed to generate a broadly based development.

This changed, however, in the period 1967–1997. During this period growth in the volume of exports and the contribution of exports to GDP were both high. What is more important, though, is that the composition of export products also changed. Whereas in the colonial period agricultural products and petroleum dominated exports, in particular since the 1980s the role of oil has been over-taken by manufactured exports (Van der Eng 2002: 155; Hill 2000: 82). Through their backward linkages, these products have had a much greater impact on eco-nomic development in Indonesia (Athukorala and Santosa 1997: 89).

Throughout the twentieth century, the trade sector has also become increas-ingly important as an employer. Especially in the 1960s and 1990s, the growth of the number of people working in trade was significantly higher than in other sectors. Table 8.3 revealed the effect that these changes in the number of people employed in the trade sector had on labour productivity. In the 1930s labour pro-ductivity in trade was high: almost four times as high as labour productivity in agriculture and considerably higher than that in industry. However, whereas

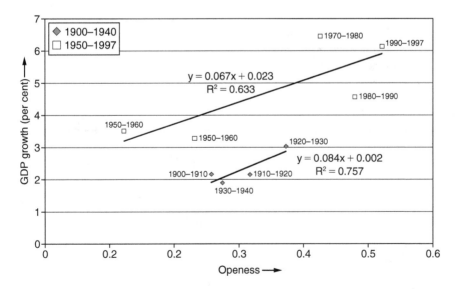

Figure 8.5 Openness and growth, 1900–97 (source: Marks 2009a: 144).

Note
Decadal averages for growth and openness. Openness is measured as imports and exports divided by GDP.

labour productivity in those other sectors increased, productivity in trade fell dramatically up to 1971. During the 1970s the trade sector clearly benefited from the profitable exports of oil. During the 1980s productivity growth slowed down and even fell in the 1990s. Strikingly, only in 1990 was productivity in trading higher than it was in the 1930s. These developments in labour productivity in trading reflect how the Indonesian trade sector has been transformed from one dominated by merchants to one in which peddlers are predominant.

This is supported by an indirect estimate of the size of the informal sector which can be arrived at by using an estimation method devised by the International Labour Organization (ILO) (see also Frankema 2008: 171–172). The method basically involves a decomposition of the economically active population by employment status. First, the labour force is split up into the categories of own-account workers (self-employed workers and employers), wage earners (including salaried employees) and unpaid family workers. Then the category of own-account workers is further subdivided into self-employed working in agriculture (farmers), professional and technical self-employed (i.e. lawyers, technicians, supervisors, etc.) and other self-employed. The combined share of the non-agricultural, self-employed and unpaid family workers in the total economically active population, corrected for the share of professionals, technicians and employers, is taken as a proxy for the size of the urban informal sector (PREALC 1982; ILO 1993). For Indonesia these figures can be retrieved from annual issues of BPS, Statistik Indonesia and the ILO, Yearbook of Labour Statistics.

The time series for the years 1965–2003 are displayed in Figure 8.6. It shows that the share of urban informal sector workers in the total labour force almost

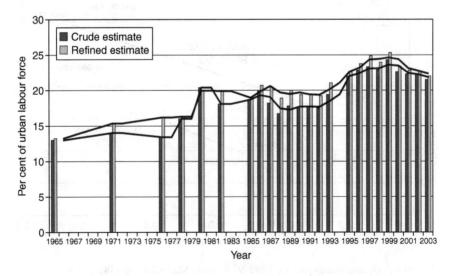

Figure 8.6 Share of urban self-employed in the total labour force, 1965–2003 (sources: BPS, *Statistical Yearbook of Indonesia* (*Statistik Indonesia*), various issues 1975–2003; ILO, *Yearbook of Labour Statistics*, various issues 1966–1995).

doubled from 13.8 per cent in 1965 to a maximum of 25.0 per cent in 1999, in the wake of the Asian crisis. Since 1999 the share has declined to 22.0 per cent. If we look at this long-term trend in more detail it appears that it was particularly in the economically difficult years of the early 1980s, and the final years of Suharto's presidency before the Asian crisis, that the urban informal sector expanded most rapidly. It is also noteworthy that from the 1980s until the early 1990s the trend line appears to be more or less horizontal, fluctuating around 20 per cent. In this same period the share of the trade sector in total employment did not change much either (see Table 8.3). The overall trend for Indonesia is very much in line with the literature that states that the urban informal sector has expanded considerably since the 1960s (Thorbecke 1991: 1596; Manning 1998: 103; Booth 2000: 81; Butzer *et al.* 2003). This strong rise contrasts sharply with what we find in the OECD countries, where the share of self-employed has declined significantly since the 1930s, typically to a level between 7 and 10 per cent of the total labour force (Frankema 2008: 172).

Despite the dominant position of the trade sector, the expansion of services is nowhere better illustrated than in the case of transport and communications, although performance has been somewhat mixed in the different subsectors (Hill 2000: 184, 187). The Suharto government inherited a transport network that was in a ramshackle state, and large investments, but also policy changes, were needed to counter this problem. In the mid-1960s the Indonesian government became aware that inefficiencies in inter-island shipping threatened the Indonesian economy in general. After 1970 inter-island shipping was brought back onto a moderate, although far from impressive growth path. Between 1970 and 2000 the total Indonesian merchant fleet increased from 642,530 gross rate tonnage (GRT) to 3,394,000 GRT, or on average 4.5 per cent annually. The composition of the fleet did not change much. Growth in loaded cargo was more volatile. However, average annual growth for the entire period was at 4.6 per cent, quite similar to that of the merchant fleet.

That growth in water transport was only moderate is a consequence of improvements in road transport (discussed below) that have shifted general cargo to road transport. This is especially the case for short distances. At the same time, road/ferry links have enabled road transport to erode what formerly was the preserve of sea freight (Dick and Forbes 1992: 272). Examples are ferries across the Bali Strait between Ketapang (Java) and Gilimanuk (Bali), and across the Sunda Strait between Merak (Java) and Bakauhuni (Sumatra). These developments shifted freight between Java and Bali and between Java and Sumatra from water to road. Road transport is often preferred by traders because door-to-door consignment eliminates double-handling.

Yet it is not so much growth, but rather efficiency and low transportation costs that matter. Regulation measures resulted in a rather competitive market that was quite easy to enter. For example, under the second Five-Year Development Plan (*Rencana Pembangunan Lima Tahun*, REPELITA II 1974–1979) the emphasis was on replacement and expansion of the fleet. To this end the government established a National Fleet Development Corporation (*Pengembangan*

Armada Niaga Nasional, PANN). PANN provided both rehabilitation loans and new and second-hand dry cargo tonnage. Dick (1985) notes that this moderniza-tion and expansion of the inter-island fleet led firms in the inter-island shipping industry to engage in both price and non-price competition. This increased com-petition resulted in a significant fall in water transportation costs. From 1971 onwards transportation costs in constant prices were at least half of those in 1939 (Marks 2009a: 111). Moreover, productivity was also quite high. In 1982 the majority of shipping firms had a productivity of more than 10 tonnes of cargo per year per deadweight tonne of capacity (Dick 1985: 101). Yet this was still only half of KPM's productivity in the 1950s. In the mid-1990s productivity had increased to levels comparable to that of KPM in the 1950s. However, inter-island transport continued to be hampered by irregularity in service, which from a development perspective is rather important (Leinbach and Chia 1989: 125).

Rail transport went through difficult times as well. In 1963 all public railways in Indonesia had been unified under a new administration, *Perusahaan Negara Kereta Api* (PNKA). In 1973 the PNKA was renamed PJKA (*Perusahaan Jawatan Kereta Api*). Dieselization and the abandonment of most unprofitable lines improved PJKA's financial position, but it continued to require subsidies from the government.

These organizational changes could not prevent rail transport from experienc-ing a significant decline during the 1970s. In this period tramway lines were abandoned, as they were no longer economically viable. By the mid-1970s, in the face of vigorous bus competition, passenger traffic had collapsed to only 22 million.[8] The rehabilitation of Jakarta's metropolitan network and the introduc-tion of fast intercity trains eventually helped to revive passenger transport from 58.2 million in 1990 to 191.6 million in 2000. Dick states that this is 'impressive enough by pre-war standards, but at [current levels] of population and mobility [it is] no more than a niche operation' (Dick 2000: 195).

During the New Order investments in road transport were significant. About 55 per cent of expenditure in transport had been allocated for the development and maintenance of the road system (Leinbach 1986: 196; Dick and Forbes 1992: 264). This high proportion reflects both the size of the task of repairing the road network and the importance of it: the restoration of commerce was believed to depend essentially on improvements to the transport system (Leinbach 1986). Initial investments were directed at emergency repairs in West and South Sumatra as well as in East and West Java (Leinbach 1989: 469).

In the 1970s the total number of motor vehicles increased from 0.8 million to 3.9 million, an average annual growth of 15.4 per cent. In the 1980s growth was 7.9 per cent. This trend was dominated by motorcycles, for which the share rose to 70 per cent of all motor vehicles (Marks 2009a: 115). Some of the rapid growth in vehicle numbers is due to road improvements. The length of roads increased between 1968 and 1985 by some 2.5 times as much, and between 1985 and 2000 by about 1.7 times as much. In the late 1970s Indonesia was still well behind comparable countries, such as India, which had three times the road length per capita and almost eight times as much road per unit of area (Dick and

Forbes 1992: 267). Probably more important has been the improvement in the condition of roads. The proportion of asphalted roads rose from 24 per cent in 1970, to 41 per cent in 1985 and 57 per cent in 2000 (Marks 2009a: 125).

The most significant growth took place in air transport. With an average annual growth of more than 18 per cent both in passenger-kilometres and tonne-kilometres during the 1970s, one could speak of an air transport revolution. In the 1980s growth was moderate compared to earlier periods, but still significant with almost 8 per cent annually for passengers and nearly 10 per cent for freight. This growth path more or less continued until the Asian crisis in 1997. Air transport was severely hit by this crisis. Between 1997 and 1999 both passenger-kilometres and tonne-kilometres halved. It is interesting to see that this did not affect the load factor. Apparently, airlines cut back on (unprofitable) routes. Moreover, since 2000 a spectacular growth in air transport can be seen due to the proliferation of low-cost carriers.

In conclusion, significant investments in roads, the re-organization and deregulation of the water transport sector, and repair of the railways, combined with continuing growth in air transport caused what Dick and Forbes (1992) call 'a quiet revolution' in this sector.

Conclusion

Let us return to the questions asked at the start of this chapter: how did Indonesia recover from the 'Asian Drama' that was unfolding in the mid-1960s, and develop quite successfully, despite the fact that it was one of the most corrupt countries in the world? First the good news: in spite of its poor institutions, Indonesia was a highly successful economy in the period between 1967 and 1997. From being one of the least-developed economies in the world, with a very small manufacturing sector, it developed into a major exporter of manufactured goods with a sizable share of its population active in the industrial sector. On average, GDP per capita increased by 4.6 per cent annually, much faster than its market access, pointing towards structural improvements in its international competitiveness. Finally, the country was able to start catching up with the productivity leader in the world economy.

One of the keys to this success was that the state, in contrast to Myrdal's expectations, transformed itself from being 'soft', to a relatively efficient apparatus able to carry out a more or less consistent set of developmental policies. Suharto crafted 'a pro-growth political coalition' that enabled the state 'to use selective policies in a wide range of areas to meet its development objectives while simultaneously meeting its economic objectives' (Rock 2003). This increased capacity was not unrelated to the leadership qualities of Suharto, who had learned from the mistakes of his predecessor, and was much more interested in solving economic problems and realizing economic development. Moreover, whenever the economic machinery ran into troubles – such as happened in the mid-1980s – he was flexible enough to try new approaches and new policies. In the long run, however, a high price was paid for the dependence on one leader, as Suharto was uncritical about the way in which power was being used and abused by his clientele and family. Corruption, large-scale inefficiencies and massive failures such as the bankruptcy of Pertamina in 1976, were to some extent the price paid for the rapid structural transformation that occurred in Indonesia. One of the paradoxes of Suharto's long reign is that, although it started as a military dictatorship, it led – from the early 1980s onwards, when his rule became more 'personal' – to a gradual lessening of the role of the military in economy and polity (Elson 2001: 235ff.). This 'unintended consequence' probably eased the transition towards democracy after 1998.

Good luck played its part in the 'success story' of the New Order as well. The 1950s and 1960s were a period of strongly declining terms of trade for the Indonesian economy. Suharto's regime profited from the enormous bonanza of the oil boom of the 1970s.[9] At the same time, he could reap the benefits of the 'green revolution', the high-yielding varieties of in particular rice, which had been developed in the 1960s. Development economists also paid much more attention to the rural sector in these years, after the failure of much of the large-scale industrialization planning which had dominated thinking in the 1950s and 1960s. The growth pattern that can be observed is therefore one of relatively balanced growth: agriculture received a large share of development funding – favoured by Suharto because success there was seen as inevitable for the political stability of the country. The services sector showed rapid growth as well, and contributed, via increased openness and improved transport facilities, strongly to economic growth. The industrial sector was the one most strongly affected by the favourable climate; first, resource-intensive industries (based on oil and forestry products) dominated the picture, but from the mid-1980s onwards, labour-intensive and technology-intensive industries have come to the fore, and begun to contribute significantly to growth of output and exports.

9 Crisis, recovery and the evolution of living standards since independence

Crisis and *reformasi*

> Indonesia is in deep crisis. A country that achieved decades of rapid growth, stability, and poverty reduction, is now near economic collapse.
>
> (World Bank 1998: 1)

Unlike the crisis of the mid-1960s, which many people had predicted due to the reckless disregard of sound economic policies, the financial and economic crisis of the late 1990s was unexpected. As we saw in the preceding chapter, Indonesia grew rapidly between 1966 and 1996, backed by political stability, competent macroeconomic policy, rapid productivity growth and a relatively efficient use of the oil windfall. At the eve of the crisis most macroeconomic indicators, such as fiscal deficit, foreign exchange reserves and inflation, were still sound. Therefore the Asian crisis caught Indonesia by surprise. Few predicted the Indonesian crisis, and certainly none its severity (Hofman *et al.* 2004: 49). As it turned out, Indonesia was the worst affected Southeast Asian economy (see Table 9.1).

Course of the crisis

The trigger for the Asian crisis was clearly Thailand. Forced by a speculative attack, Thailand unexpectedly withdrew its support from the foreign exchange market on 2 July 1997, and the Thai baht dropped dramatically in price relative to other currencies. The 'contagion effect' led to similar currency depreciations in neighbouring countries, like Malaysia and the Philippines. Indonesia relaxed its support for the rupiah in mid-August. Despite this measure, the mood in Indonesia was still cautiously optimistic (Hill 1999: 15; Sadli 1999: 16). The country's economic and financial indicators still looked good, as reflected by single-digit inflation, a balanced budget, a manageable current account deficit and buoyant savings and investment (Dick *et al.* 2002: 232; Hill 2000: 262). However, the floating of the rupiah did aggravate the crisis. With a depreciating rupiah, investors tried to get out of the currency as soon as possible to minimize their losses (McLeod 1997: 43–44). Moreover, trying to put a halt to the continuous depreciation, the government tightened monetary policy by steeply raising

Table 9.1 Southeast Asian economic indicators, 1991–1998

	Indonesia	Malaysia	Philippines	Singapore	Thailand
GDP growth					
1991–1995	7.8	8.7	2.2	8.5	8.6
1996	8.0	8.6	5.5	6.9	5.5
1997	4.7	8.0	5.1	7.8	–0.4
1998	–13.6	–6.7	0	1.3	–6.5
Inflation					
1991–1995	8.9	3.6	10.5	2.6	4.8
1996	6.5	3.5	8.4	1.4	5.8
1997	11.6	2.6	5.1	2.0	5.6
1998	65.0	5.4	9.0	–0.2	8.1
Current account/GDP					
1991–1995	–2.4	–7.0	–3.6	12.9	–6.2
1996	–3.3	–4.9	–4.5	15.0	–7.9
1997	–2.9	–5.2	–5.2	15.4	–2.0
1998	5.4	7.5	1.2	17.8	8.1
Government balance/GDP					
1991–1995	–0.2	0.3	–1.6	12.4	2.8
1996	1.2	1.1	–0.4	13.9	2.4
1997	1.2	5.5	–1.8	6.0	–0.9
1998	–5.5	–1.0	–3.6	–1.0	–4.5

Source: Hill 1999: 24.

interest rates. This weakened the fragile banking system and led to a contraction of the real economy.

Unable to deal with the crisis, Indonesia turned to the IMF for 'consultation' and signed a rescue package by the end of October. At the same time Indonesia realized that it could not even hold the relaxed version of the exchange rate, so it effectively withdrew from the foreign exchange market in October before exhausting its reserves, which led to a further fall of the rupiah. As part of the first IMF package, Indonesia had agreed on the closure of 16 banks on 1 November. The rationale was to demonstrate the government's determination to deal directly and decisively with financially troubled banks (World Bank 1998: 1.6). Instead, this triggered widespread uncertainty in the rest of the banking system. In early December rumours spread that Suharto was very ill. The combination of a financial crisis, an upcoming election and an aging, sick president led to increasing uncertainty. As a result, the exchange rate depreciated in the first three weeks of January from Rp.4,850 to Rp.13,600 to the dollar (Figure 9.1).

Between February and April 1998 trends were mixed. Plans were announced to restructure financially troubled banks, and on 8 April a third IMF package was signed with comprehensive coverage of virtually all major issues (World Bank 1998: 1.7). As a result, exchange rates and stock markets even began to pick up a little. Nevertheless, the exchange rate continued to fluctuate. May 1998 turned out to be a watershed in Indonesian history (Hill 1999: 20). Rising fuel prices in

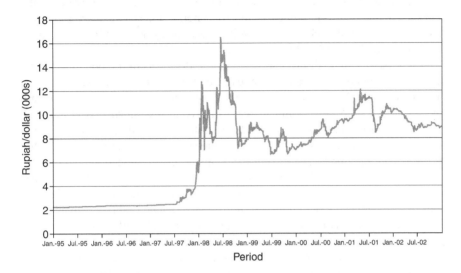

Figure 9.1 Rupiah/US$ exchange rate, 1995–2002 (source: Bank Indonesia).

early May resulted in a wave of protests. During those demonstrations four students were killed at Jakarta's Trisakti University. This triggered further protests calling for reforms of the political system and eventually escalated into widespread riots and looting of ethnic Chinese businesses, in which hundreds of people died. On 21 May the events culminated in the end of the 32-year Suharto era and the installation of Vice President B.J. Habibie as the Republic's third president.

At that point the economy was in a freefall, with GDP declining at a rate of 20 per cent year-on-year, the foreign exchange rate having collapsed from Rp.8,000 in early May to over Rp.16,000 by mid-June, and inflation being close to 100 per cent, with even higher price increases for rice and other staples for the poor, resulting in a doubling of the poverty headcount to 27 per cent (Hofman *et al.* 2004: 54).

Causes of the crisis

The question remains why the Indonesian crisis was so severe. Hill (1999: 48) argues that 'in Indonesia practically everything went wrong at once over the period 1997–98'. Economic factors were undoubtedly at the core of the crisis, but underlying institutional weaknesses are key to understanding the severity of the Indonesian crisis. Two (probably interacting) economic explanations for the Asian crisis are the following (Booth 2001: 20).

The 'fundamentalist explanation' asserts that the Asian crisis was caused by basic economic weaknesses within the countries (Radelet and Sachs 1998: 3). The problems included: 1) large and rising private capital, much of which was short-term and unhedged; 2) the rapid buildup and volatility of private capital inflows; 3) major shortcomings in macroeconomic management by running a fixed or quasi-fixed exchange rate while experiencing large inflows of mobile capital (Thee 2003a: 185; Hill 1999: 50).

These factors were all present in Indonesia. Prospects of the booming Southeast Asian economies, which were boosted by the favourable assessments of the World Bank, the IMF and credit-rating agencies such as Moody's and Standard and Poor's, resulted in a rapid increase in private investments. And although Indonesia did not have a pegged exchange rate to the dollar, it did maintain a quasi-fixed exchange rate implicitly guaranteed by the government (Hill 1998: 96, Dick *et al.* 2002: 235). These circumstances, combined with domestic nominal interest rates which were about three times above international levels, caused external debt to double between 1991 and mid-1997. About half of this was private debt and much of it both short-term and unhedged (see Table 9.2).

A second explanation is that international financial markets are inherently unstable (Radelet and Sachs 1998: 4–5). This view holds that a crisis erupts as a result of large shifts in sentiment, causing panic to spread to other countries through a process of contagion. This explains the characterization of the Asian crisis as a situation in which 'irrational exuberance suddenly became irrational pessimism' (Hill 1999: 48). Once foreign exchange markets perceived that a serious problem was emerging in Indonesia, 'herding' behaviour led to a massive flight out of the rupiah. And although this behaviour by creditors was rational, 'market outcomes produced sharp, costly and *fundamentally unnecessary* panicked reversals in capital flows' (Radelet and Sachs 1998: 5; see also Kindleberger 1978).

The two economic explanations above do elucidate why the Asian crisis occurred. Yet they do not explain why the crisis hit Indonesia so much harder than other Southeast Asian countries. Indonesia was the only Asian country where the initial currency crisis subsequently turned into a financial crisis, an economic crisis

Table 9.2 Indonesia's external debt, 1991–1998 (in US$ billion, year-end)

	1991	1992	1993	1994	1995	1996	1997	1998
Total	65.7	73.3	80.6	96.5	107.8	110.1	136.1	142.0
Medium- to long-term	56.5	65.0	71.8	88.8	98.4	98.8	117.3	128.4
Government	49.1	53.3	57.5	63.6	64.4	60.0	57.8	62.5
Private	7.4	11.8	14.3	25.2	34.0	37.8	57.6	64.4
Securities							2.0	1.5
Short-term	9.2	8.3	8.8	7.7	9.5	13.4	18.8	13.6
Government			0.1	0.1		0.1	0.1	
Private	9.2	8.3	8.7	7.6	9.4	13.3	10.4	9.3
Securities							8.3	4.2

Source: Hill 1999: 63.

Note
Short-term is defined as one year maturity or less. Government includes state enterprises.

and a political crisis. The explanation for this lies in the institutional weaknesses, which were more apparent in Indonesia (see also MacIntyre 1999; Sadli 1999).

First of all, institutional weaknesses played an especially important role in the financial sector (Johnson *et al.* 2000; Hofman *et al.* 2004). As Krugman (1998) stated, the Indonesian financial sector was 'over-guaranteed but under-regulated'. This leads to the problem of moral hazard: agents behave differently because they do not bear the full risk. According to Hill (1999: 51), such reckless lending behaviour occurred especially among the politically well-connected. The 'Suharto connection' became the guarantee or collateral underlying the viability of many enterprises and financial institutions. Fisman (2001), in a study of the interrelationship between Suharto and corporate performance on the Jakarta Stock Exchange, found that political connectedness, rather than fundamentals such as productivity, was the primary determinant of profitability, and that this had led to distorted investment decisions. At the same time, any financial regulator who attempted to apply prudential rules to such connected financial institutions was removed from office (Cole and Slade 1998: 65). 'Crony capitalism' was thus widespread, as is also reflected by the many questionable loans in the portfolios of the banks that were closed in November 1997 (Cassing 2000: 165; Pomerleano 1998). Such a financial system proliferates in an environment of high growth, but the shock that the Asian crisis caused uncovered the weaknesses of the system. Cole and Slade had already expressed their concerns about these weaknesses in 1996:

> Given all the uncertainties surrounding the political leadership and the influence of different power groups in Indonesia in the coming years, it is difficult to predict whether the foundations and institutions of the financial system that have so far been established will be strong enough to continue evolving in a healthy and productive fashion.
>
> (Cole and Slade 1996: 344)

And they continue:

> Increasing politicization of major investment and financial decisions raises the level of risk. Most financial systems do experience crises sooner or later, and Indonesia is not likely to be an exception. If and when such a crisis arises, its handling will provide an important test of how sound a structure has been created.
>
> (Cole and Slade 1996: 357)

As it turned out, not long after the publication of their book, the proof of the pudding was indeed in the eating, and the financial system more or less collapsed. The above quote brings us to the second institutional weakness: the political system was weak, too dependent on President Suharto and based on corruption, collusion and nepotism (KKN – *korupsi, kolusi dan nepotisme* – in Indonesian). Suharto's perception that political competition and open policy discourse had led to chaos in the 1960s, led him to create an all-powerful presidency guided by a small inner circle of policy advisors (MacIntyre 1999: 149). According to Cassing (2000: 164):

> All policies were formed in a vacuum, not subject to scrutiny or comment by the public or political rivals, and immune from legal challenges in the courts. The ultimate arbiter was Suharto.

Schwarz (2000: 91) adds to this:

> Indonesia's government is noted for the extreme concentration of power at the very top and the close relationships between government officials and leading business actors. In such an environment, government intervention is not likely to be based on strictly economic criteria and is not, therefore, likely to be of much benefit to the economy.

The lack of political competition created an environment in which the returns to rent-seeking were high. At the same time the Suharto government did not tolerate opposition from, for example, students, the urban elite, organized social groups and the press (Hofman *et al.* 2004: 39). In this way civil society, which in a well-functioning democracy acts as checks and balances on those in power, was suppressed. In other words, the political fundamentals were extremely weak in Indonesia, undermining investor confidence (Sadli 1999: 18).

A third factor where institutional weaknesses aggravated the crisis was arguably the role of the IMF. The demand for tighter fiscal and monetary policies, while budgets were broadly in balance and the economy was already beginning to contract, was clearly a mistake. In addition, the attempt to resolve banking sector distress by suddenly closing 16 banks aggravated the general loss of confidence. Hill (1999: 78) even speculates that the Fund used the opportunity 'to push through practically every conceivable item on its Indonesian reform agenda'. However, the Indonesian government's resistance, but also its incompetence, to implement such an ambitious agenda had a negative effect on market confidence. Soesastro (2003: 168) argues that these 'structural reforms' became the Achilles heel in the IMF involvement in Indonesia.

Reformasi *and recovery*

> The first president (Sukarno) was crazy about women. The second president (Soeharto) was crazy about fortune. The third president (Habibie) was truly crazy.
>
> (Abdurrahman Wahid, 1999 (cited in Schwarz 2000: 367))

When B.J. Habibie, a long-time protégé of Suharto, assumed power, this was felt as a bittersweet victory for the pro-democracy movement. Prior to Suharto's resignation, Habibie had never publicly voiced a political vision other than endorsement of Suharto's authoritarian rule (Schwarz 2000: 372). However, Habibie was not as crazy as the quote above, by his successor Abdurrahman Wahid, suggests. When he became president he called for new parliamentary elections in mid-1999 and the selection of a new president by the end of 1999. Habibie was aware that economic recovery offered him the best chance for a re-election (Boediono 2002: 387). Therefore he appointed Ginanjar Kartasamita as senior economics minister and Wijoyo Nitisastro and Ali Wardhana, two long-time technocrats, as economic advisers. All three men had good relations with the international financial community (Schwarz 2000: 373). This resulted in resumed disbursement of the rescue package by the IMF and the World Bank as well as new humanitarian assistance programmes.

By October 1998 the rupiah had strengthened to around 8,000 to the dollar and inflation dropped dramatically. Moreover, several key non-oil exports began to show signs of recovery. Thus, Habibie succeeded in preventing the imminent collapse of the economy, stabilized it and partially reversed the downward slide (Boediono 2005: 314). Yet, as had been the case since the crisis had begun, Indonesia's economic prospects were inextricably tied to the political process. As long as the political situation was uncertain and investors had no idea who would be in charge of economic policy, the economy muddled along (Schwarz 2000: 409). The political situation and its social and legal problems were thus crucial to economic recovery because of the impact on investor confidence (Fane 2000: 18). But the unfolding of a high-profile corruption scandal (the Bank Bali case, see Booth 1999: 4–8) and violent clashes in East Timor hampered further recovery. This is also shown in Figure 9.2, where we see that gross fixed capital formation growth remained negative under Habibie.

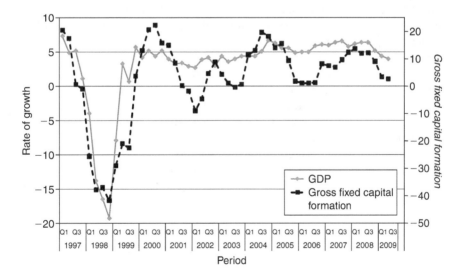

Figure 9.2 Quarterly growth (year-on-year) of GDP and gross fixed capital formation, 1997–2009 (sources: *The Indonesian Quarterly*, various issues; 'Survey of Recent Development', *BIES*, various issues; BPS 2000).

In October 1999, Abdurrahman Wahid was elected as president after the first free elections since 1955. When Wahid (colloquially known as Gus Dur) took office, there were high hopes for a calmer social and political climate. Yet economic recovery remained hostage to politics (McLeod 2000: 5). Wahid failed to manage his cabinet and economic team, which were the product of political compromises. This resulted in a high turnover of ministers (among the replaced ministers were the later president Susilo Bambang Yudhoyono, the later vice presidents Hamzah Haz and Jusuf Kalla, and General Wiranto). Regional unrest (in the Moluccas and Irian Jaya) and his alleged involvement in two corruption scandals (Buloggate and Bruneigate) undermined not only his position as president, but also economic stability. Wahid, however, refused to compromise, let alone resign. In January 2001 the Indonesian Parliament (DPR)[1] passed a memorandum of censure. This led to sometimes-violent mass demonstrations as well as internal political power struggles. Vice President Megawati Soekarnoputri, the eldest daughter of Sukarno, supported the censure, but opposed a possible impeachment. A carefully worded reply in late April initially gave Wahid some breathing room, but after continued political instability the DPR voted on 30 May, by a large majority, to request to the People's Consultative Assembly (MPR) to hold a special session to review the mandate it had given the president. On 23 July, the MPR unanimously voted to impeach Wahid and to replace him with Megawati as president. Illustrative for Wahid's erratic behaviour, he continued to insist that he was the president and stayed for some days in the Presidential Palace.

Megawati Soekarnoputri, then vice president, was sworn in as president for the remainder of Wahid's five-year term. Her start in office was promising, as she appointed prominent, qualified and professional ministers (Siregar 2001: 280; CSIS 2002: 13; Hill and Shiraishi 2007: 128). This mood started to change, however, when the feeling gained ground that the government was muddling along, but not sufficiently vigorously attacking the issues facing the country (Deuster 2002: 15). This is also reflected in the lack of investor confidence. Gross fixed capital formation growth was low during Megawati's presidency, while GDP growth was mediocre. It was mainly household and government consumption that drove this growth (Kenward 2004: 12).

Under Megawati the process of democratic reform continued, albeit slowly and erratically. Moreover, in its 39 months in office, the Megawati government did succeed in re-establishing economic stability, but was less successful in accelerating growth, largely because it lacked a solid and focused programme to achieve this goal (Boediono 2005: 315). Moreover, unemployment and poverty remained high.

It seems that 2004 was a turning point. The general election of 5 April already reflected widespread discontent with the leadership of Megawati. The share of the national vote for her party fell from 33.7 per cent in 1999 to 18.5 per cent in 2004 (Marks 2004: 152). In the subsequent presidential election Megawati was defeated in a second round by Susilo Bambang Yudhoyono (commonly known by his initials, SBY), who won convincingly by 61 to 39 per cent of the votes. On 23 October 2004, SBY was installed as Indonesia's sixth president.

The election of SBY gave a boost to investor confidence, resulting in an increase in investment, while at the same time exports were picking up. This moved the Indonesian economy to a higher growth path and at the end of 2004 GDP per capita finally reached pre-crisis levels. But in December 2004, Indonesia suffered another crisis in the form of the tsunami that hit Aceh. While this caused massive social and human capital losses, it had little impact on the national economy. Ironically, it may even have contributed positively to economic growth, because of the large inflows of humanitarian assistance for the reconstruction of Aceh (Ananta and Riyanto 2006: 3).

The global financial crisis, which started to unfold in late 2008 after the bankruptcy of Lehman Brothers, has had a relatively modest impact on the domestic economy. At least the decline in Indonesia's growth rate was less severe than that of several other Asian economies. This can be explained by the fact that the Indonesian economy is still less closely connected to the global economy than, for example, Singapore. The impact of the crisis has indeed been limited mainly to foreign trade and a severe decline in exports. But since many exports have a high import content, there have been similar declines in imports, tending to offset the impact on the level of output (Patunru and von Luebke 2010: 14). Moreover, the government and the central bank have reacted effectively with a fiscal stimulus package, combined with prudent monetary policies (Resosudarmo and Yusuf 2009: 289).

In 2009 SBY was re-elected as president with Boediono as his vice president, who had been Minister of Finance under Megawati and Coordinating Minister of the Economy under Yudhoyono before becoming Governor of Bank Indonesia in 2008. With this background it is unsurprising that SBY and his vice president announced ambitious economic targets to be achieved during SBY's second term in office. These included a rate of economic growth rising to approximately 7 per cent, a fall in unemployment to 5–6 per cent, and a reduction of the proportion of people living in poverty to 8–10 per cent. Nevertheless, changes to the policy and institutional framework will be necessary if Indonesia is to achieve these objectives; yet observers have been especially disappointed with the progress in this respect. Moreover, it appears that economic growth has stabilized rather than continuing to accelerate (Thee and Dharma Negara 2010). In a book about the long-term economic development of Indonesia it is, however, too early to judge whether this is just a short deviation from the trend, or indeed a more persistent change in the growth trajectory.

Institutional change?

> The institutional foundations are in place for economic policy-making. But how these institutions perform ultimately depends on who runs them.
>
> (Hill and Shiraishi 2007: 139)

The importance of institutions for economic growth has been reiterated in this book, further demonstrating that the depth of the crisis in Indonesia can for a large part be attributed to institutional weaknesses (see also Hofman *et al.* 2004). As the quote above shows, the common belief is that institutions in Indonesia have indeed improved in quality. This belief is based on largely qualitative evidence. Statistics by the World Bank do, however, make it possible to assess this claim with quantitative evidence.

Since 1999 the World Bank has been publishing the Worldwide Governance Indicators (WGI) (Kaufmann *et al.* 2009). These indicators measure six dimensions of governance:

1   Voice and accountability – capturing perceptions of the extent to which a country's citizens are able to participate in selecting their government, as well as freedom of expression, freedom of association and a free media.
2   Political stability and absence of violence – capturing perceptions of the likelihood that the government will be destabilized or overthrown by unconstitutional or violent means, including politically motivated violence and terrorism.
3   Government effectiveness – capturing perceptions of the quality of public services, the quality of the civil service and the degree of its independence from political pressures, the quality of policy formulation and implementation, and the credibility of the government's commitment to such policies.
4   Regulatory quality – capturing perceptions of the ability of the government to formulate and implement sound policies and regulations that permit and promote private sector development.
5   Rule of law – capturing perceptions of the extent to which agents have confidence in and abide by the rules of society, and in particular the quality of contract enforcement, property rights, the police and the courts, as well as the likelihood of crime and violence.
6   Control of corruption – capturing perceptions of the extent to which public power is exercised for private gain, including both petty and grand forms of corruption, as well as 'capture' of the state by elites and private interests.

These WGI are based on a wide variety of sources, such as surveys of firms and individuals, and assessments by commercial risk rating agencies, NGOs, a number of multilateral aid agencies and other public sector organizations. The aggregate governance indicators for Indonesia between 1996 and 2008 have been graphed in Figure 9.3. The scores of the indicators can range between –2.5 and 2.5 with higher scores corresponding to better outcomes. Kaufmann *et al.* (2009) insist on taking the margins of error into account when making comparisons over time.

Kaufmann *et al.* (2010) show that between 1996 and 2005, Indonesia has improved on one governance indicator (voice and accountability), but relapsed on five other indicators (political stability and absence of violence, government effectiveness, regulatory quality, rule of law and control of corruption). The improvement on voice and accountability is a clear virtue of the *reformasi* movement and the resulting democratization that has taken place since the fall of Suharto. On all

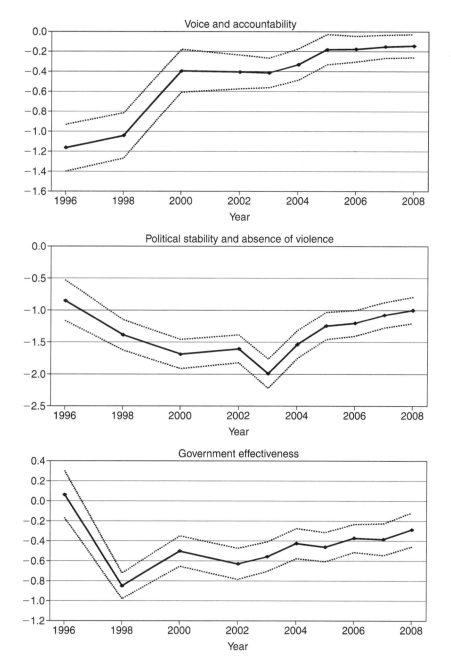

Figure 9.3 Indonesia's governance indicators, 1996–2008 (source: Kaufmann *et al.* 2009).

continued

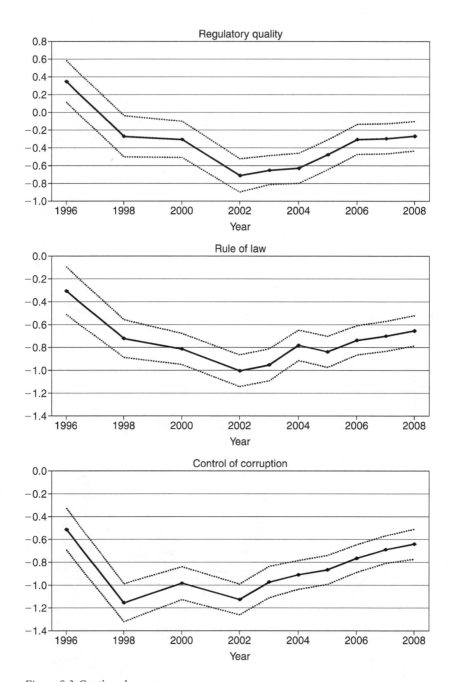

Figure 9.3 Continued.

of the five other indicators, however, Indonesia initially relapsed, before returning to a level of governance comparable to that at the end of the New Order.

Is this a surprising finding? Actually it is not. An authoritarian regime is better able to control the government, albeit at the expense of (democratic) freedom. Perhaps it is striking that, according to these estimates, control of corruption was actually better under Suharto than in the post-Suharto era. The reason for this deterioration is probably the decentralization that has since taken place. In Suharto's Indonesia, corruption was centralized and predictable. Corruption was controlled by the first family and the top military leadership, in partnership with ethnic Chinese conglomerates. Although business complained about it, investors could accurately predict the costs associated with corruption and bureaucratic red tape and factor it into the cost of doing business (Henderson and Kuncoro 2006).

Decentralization has brought about shifts in power relations not only between the centre and the regions, but also between the branches of government at the regional level. Some of these changes have given rise to rampant 'money politics' – by district heads seeking to gain and maintain support from the legislature, and by legislators exploiting their newly acquired power over local budgets to secure financing for their political parties. But, most commonly, all sides have taken the chance to embezzle funds for self-enrichment (World Bank 2007).

We do, however, see that the five indicators that initially relapsed all show an upward trend since the election of SBY, and this trend has continued and even accelerated since the re-election of SBY in 2009. Most indicators had already started to turn around in 2002. This is a promising sign, but in a comparative perspective Indonesia still has a long way to go.

Evolution of living standard since independence

We concluded the chapter on the colonial economy by assessing the effects that colonial rule had on the standard of living of the population of Indonesia. Did their real income rise – and what happened to income inequality? Did they improve their position in terms of education? We want to draw up a similar balance sheet here: what happened to the standard of living of the Indonesians during the period of independence?

As we saw in the preceding chapters, in the more than 60 years since Indonesia became officially independent, a profound economic and political transition has taken place. GDP per capita has grown by nearly 500 per cent, or, on average, by 3.1 per cent annually, between 1949 and 2007. And whereas in 1949 nearly 70 per cent of the population was employed in agriculture, this fell to 45 per cent in 2007. These changes went hand in hand with strong demographic growth, from roughly 80 million in 1950 to more than 230 million in 2010, and extensive rural–urban migration and hence urbanization, from roughly 17 per cent in 1970 to more than 40 per cent in 2000. Meanwhile Indonesia went through an experiment with parliamentary democracy and two phases of authoritarian rule, followed by a return to democracy. The following paragraphs aim to put together a balance sheet of these developments by assessing their effects on changes in living standards in Indonesia in this period. Specifically we will look at four indicators of the standard of living; namely real wages, numeracy, human stature and inequality.

Real wages

Whereas GDP per capita is the probably the best measure of the success of the productive capacity of the economy, it does not capture distributional dimensions. GDP per capita and real wages can be expected to diverge when the share of national income allocated to labour changes (Angeles 2008).

Figure 9.4 presents series for both GDP per capita and unskilled real wages. It shows that while GDP per capita more or less stagnated in the long run between 1950 and 1967, unskilled real wages fell sharply, suggesting a decline in the standard of living for labourers. This finding is not surprising given the rapid inflation, for which labourers were apparently not sufficiently compensated. In this period the price of a kilogram of medium-quality rice increased from around 1 rupiah in January 1950 to around 8 rupiah in January 1960 to nearly 300 rupiah in December 1964. In the meantime the nominal wage increased only from 3.6 rupiah in 1950 to 8.6 rupiah in 1960 to 127 rupiah in 1964. This is in line with data on per capita rice availability, which falls from 109 kilogram in 1960 to only 92 kilogram in 1965 (Booth 1998: 117; Mears 1984: 126).

From 1965 onwards we see unskilled real wages rising again, although they drop in the second half of the 1970s, due to inflationary pressures fuelled by the oil boom and a number of harvest failures. But what stands out is that overall unskilled real wages grew rapidly during the New Order era.

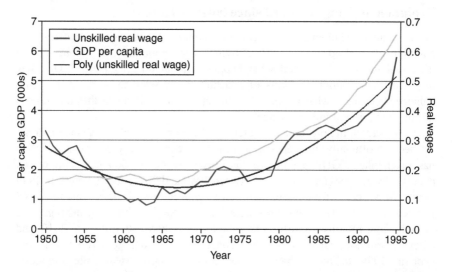

Figure 9.4 GDP per capita and unskilled real wages, 1950–1995 (sources: unskilled wage series: Van Leeuwen 2007: 241–242; GDP per capita: Van der Eng 2002: 172–173).

Height

Historical data on (human) height are an important complementary measure of living standard (Fogel 1994; Komlos 1994; Steckel 1995, 2009; Komlos and Baten 1998). It is believed that, although height does not measure the purchasing power aspect of the living standard, it is better at capturing the 'biological' component of welfare such as health, life expectancy and the quality of nutrition. The development of human stature in Indonesia is shown in Figure 9.5, based on a general study by Baten *et al.* (2009b) and on a study by Földvari *et al.* (2010), who use military data on an individual level, which makes it possible to

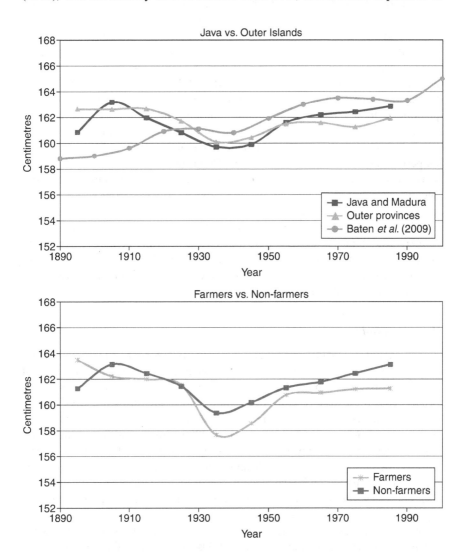

Figure 9.5 Trends in height, Java vs Outer Islands (source: Földvari *et al.* 2010).

disaggregate developments in height by different categories, for example by province, or by farmers as opposed to non-farmers. Three issues stand out.

First, we see a downward trend in human stature for people born in the 1930s and the early 1940s. Apparently, the Great Depression in the early 1930s had affected the biological standard of living. And of course the war and revolution left their mark on human development. From 1950 onwards an upward trend can be discerned.

Second, until 1955 people born in the Outer Islands tended to be taller than those born in Java. From 1955 onwards this trend reverses. This might be due to the fact that, being the economic core of the Archipelago, Java is in general better developed, resulting in better health care facilities and a higher biological standard of living. It also seems to confirm the strong redistributive impact of economic policies after independence, from which Java in particular profited (see Chapter 7). Another argument is that in the initial phase of development a drop in average height often occurs (Komlos 1989). The reason for this is that the shadow price of food is lower for a farmer than the market price of the same quantity of food for an urban labourer. Initially the earnings of the labourer might not match this difference, resulting in a decline of average food intake, and therefore, of the average height. This can explain why Java first fell behind, but perhaps also the drop in height for the Outer Islands in the late 1960s.

Third, non-farmers were on average taller than farmers. This might seem conspicuous, because in general farmers are believed to have better access to food and therefore to often be taller than non-farmers. This deviant finding can probably be attributed to the fact that the underlying data are military recruits. Farmers who joined the army were in general peasants and not landowners. Moreover, it is interesting to see that farmers especially suffered in the 1930s, probably because they were the worst affected by the declining agricultural prices as a result of the Great Depression.

Human capital formation

Human capital is considered a crucial factor in modern economic growth theory (Romer 1989; Galor and Weil 2000). Unfortunately, the paucity of data makes it difficult to study human capital formation, especially for LDCs. Economic historians have tried to solve this by adapting other measures to proxy human capital. In the economic history literature, age heaping is used as an indicator of human capital (Mokyr 1983; A'Hearn et al. 2009; Crayen and Baten 2010) (see also Chapter 6 for an analysis of age heaping during the colonial period). The rationale behind this is that age heaping, as a proxy for numeracy, contains important information on human capital. According to Crayen and Baten (2010: 83), 'numeracy goes hand-in-hand with technological abilities, and it is a necessity for modern commercial economies'.

Based on census data we have been able to calculate the Whipple Index for Indonesia for the birth cohorts from the 1900s to the 1970s, for both males and females, as well as for the urban and the rural population. Figure 9.6 shows that

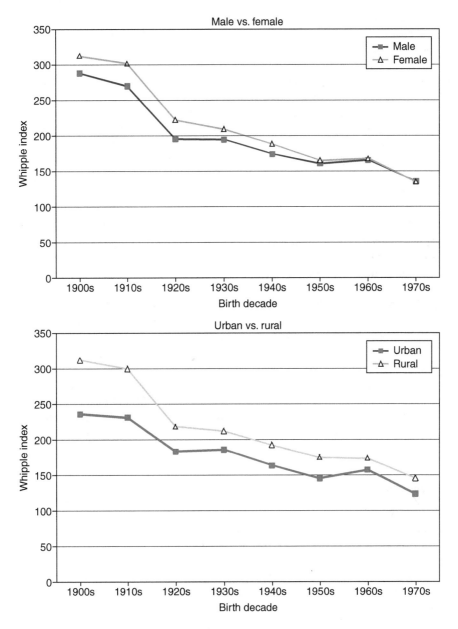

Figure 9.6 Age heaping in Indonesia, male vs female, urban vs rural (source: population census, 1971, 1981, 1990 and 2000.

Note
Age heaping for different birth cohorts (people born in the decades indicated).

in general age heaping declined rapidly, albeit from a comparatively high level. In Western Europe age-heaping levels between 100 and 150 were already normal in the early nineteenth century – and in a few cases, such as the Low Countries, such low levels were already reached in the early modern period (De Moor and van Zanden 2010). Strikingly, Baten *et al.* (2010) find that age heaping in China more or less disappears from the 1860s onwards. Levels comparable to Indonesia in the early twentieth century are found in Africa and the Middle East (Crayen and Baten 2010: 85–86). The most significant decline seems to have occurred during the 1920s, or to be more precise, when the birth cohort of the 1920s went to (primary) school, during the late 1920s and 1930s. It points to the relative success of this part of the Ethical Policy. But despite the rapid improvement and the clear downward trend in age heaping, numeracy in Indonesia is still rather low for those born in the 1970s.

Figure 9.6 also shows that an initial, limited, difference in numeracy between males and females has disappeared over time. Moreover, the rural–urban disparity has remained over time, with those in rural areas having, on average, lower levels of numeracy.

The age-heaping story is broadly in line with developments in education. From the late 1940s onwards there was an explosion in primary education, backed by increasing government expenditure on education. In the mid-1980s the gross enrolment ratio peaked at around 137 per cent (Van Leeuwen 2007: 86). A gross enrolment ratio above 100 per cent occurs in countries when they try to achieve universal primary education. To this end, all older persons follow primary education as well. Changes were even more pronounced in secondary education. Gross enrolment in secondary education increased from around 3 per cent in 1950 to 12.5 per cent in 1970, and to around 55 per cent in 1990 and roughly 60 per cent in 2000 (Van Leeuwen 2007: 265–266). Nevertheless, it seems that progress in education has not yet fully erased the incidence of age heaping, possibly signalling that that the quality of education remains limited.

Inequality

Growth with equity was the key of the message by the World Bank in its famous study of the East Asian Growth Miracle (World Bank 1993). In many publications on the success of the Suharto period, the same gospel was spread: that its most striking characteristic was the combination of rapid growth from which all segments of the population seem to have profited (Booth 1992, 2000). This idea is, however, based on rather limited and perhaps even problematic data: the consumer expenditure data from the *Susenas* became the main source for inequality studies in Indonesia. The Gini coefficients derived from the BPS elaboration of *Susenas* data, as presented in Figure 9.7, have become the most important source for conclusions regarding the inequality trend during Suharto's presidency.[2] The graph shows that during the Suharto era (1966–1998), the Gini coefficient of the national consumption expenditure distribution fluctuated between 0.33 and 0.38, suggesting that Indonesian inequality was relatively modest as compared to

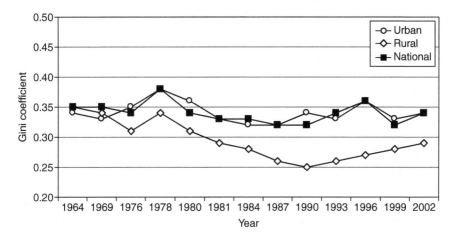

Figure 9.7 Gini coefficients of Indonesian household consumption expenditure, 1964–2002 (source: BPS, *Statistical Yearbook of Indonesia*, various issues).

international standards, and has also been fairly stable over time. On the basis of these data, Boediono (1990) concludes that high growth rates in Indonesia have been associated with a slight overall decline in total inequality, affirming the success of Suharto's development trilogy. Yet Dick *et al.* (2002: 227) argue that contrary to this statistical evidence, people held the view that economic disparities were widening, because of the excessive self-enrichment of the elite circles around the Suharto family, as well as increasing income gaps between urban and rural areas. The occurrence of such opposite views can be partly explained by some specific peculiarities concerning Indonesia's income distribution data.

In most literature on income distribution in Indonesia expenditure Gini coefficients are cited. However, Atkinson and Brandolini (2001) argue that expenditure distributions tend to reveal lower levels of inequality, since the better off are likely to save part of their income, whereas the household expenses of the poor are usually equal to or above net income. Moreover, since especially poor households tend to smooth their expenditure in response to income shocks, the effects of economic crises on the distribution of income are less likely to be picked up adequately.[3] Hence it is not surprising that some authors have found that in the mid- to late 1980s income Gini coefficients based on the *Susenas* data for a few benchmark years suggest a rise in inequality, which is not captured by the expenditure Gini coefficients (Asra 2000: 102; Cameron 2002: 12).[4]

Although the income approach seems a promising venue for a better understanding of Indonesian inequality, some of the problems of the *Susenas* expenditure data are equally valid for the *Susenas* income data. Sudjana and Mishra (2004: 5) suggest that the *Susenas* survey tends to exclude the very wealthy since they are the least likely to be reached by the enumerators, and if they are, they are often excluded from the data as outliers. The World Bank also refers to this perceived selection bias stating that 'BPS indicated that often their interviewers were not received at the houses of the very wealthy, resulting in a selective non-response' (World Bank 2003: 52, endnote 5).

Hofman *et al.* (2004) illustrate the possible implications of selection bias. They show that according to the *Susenas* data of 2002, the upper one percentile of households earns an improbably low average monthly income of *c.* $300 per household, which corresponds with an income Gini of 0.41. This is without doubt a severe underestimation. Assuming that the upper one percentile of households earns a monthly income ten times as large as the actually reported amount of 2.5 million rupiahs (hence, *c.* $3,000 in 2002 prices), the Gini coefficient would rise to 0.68 (Hofman *et al.* 2004: 35).

Further evidence of a selection bias in the *Susenas* data is provided by Van der Eng (2001). He shows that estimates of private consumption based on the *Susenas* data are significantly lower than those in the national accounts, deviating by more than 50 per cent on average. Van der Eng attributes this underestimation to the exclusion of non-food expenditures, and particularly such consumer durables as televisions and cars. In support of this argument, Sudjana and Mishra (2004) argue that the list of consumption items of the survey is too confined to accurately capture the consumption bundle of the very rich, consisting of high quality products and luxury goods.[5] Yusuf (2006) further supports this notion, showing that food expenditure in the input-output table is a factor 1.74 higher than in the corresponding *Susenas*, whereas non-food expenditure is a factor 3.27 higher. This suggests that the *Susenas* especially underreports expenditure on non-food items. The reason for this can be either underreporting of non-food consumption by higher income groups or a misrepresentation of these groups themselves. In both cases the outcome is the same: underestimated inequality levels. The problem of underreporting also affects the reliability of the time-series, since the amount of underreporting is likely to be positively correlated with the relative expenditure share of the top income groups.

Leigh and Van der Eng (2006) recently adopted a new approach. Following the seminal work of Piketty (2003) and Piketty and Saez (2003, 2006), they trace the evolution of top incomes in Indonesia on the basis of tax registers and household income data from *Susenas*. The authors conclude that the income share of the richest 10 per cent of income earners remained quite stable throughout the twentieth century. Moreover, they find that top income shares in Indonesia were higher than in China or India, and similar to levels prevailing in the US. Yet Van der Eng and Leigh also explicitly admit the problems they encountered with the *Susenas* data they used for the years 1982–2002 (Leigh and Van der Eng 2006: 16).

The *Susenas* data are clearly not a reliable guide to what happened to income inequality in Indonesia in the New Order period. Therefore, we have tried to collect other sources of data, following Frankema and Marks (2009, 2010), which can inform us about the determinants of the income distribution in Indonesia. Frankema and Marks focus on three important constituents of income inequality:

1   The ratio of unskilled wages to GDP per worker, which provides informa-
     tion about the relative degree of earnings of a large category of unskilled
     wage-workers vis-á-vis the combined incomes of skilled workers and capital
     owners. As Williamson pointed out in constructing this indicator, trends in
     the wage–GDP per worker ratio provide a good indication of whether the
     relative position of the low-income groups improves or worsens (William-
     son 1997, 2002, 2006; Prados de la Escosura 2006).
2   The Theil coefficient of the inter-industry wage distribution in the manufac-
     turing sector. Given its size and variation in relative skill, capital and
     technology-intensity, the manufacturing sector wage distribution sheds light
     on the relative earnings gaps between typically labour-intensive and capital-
     or skill-intensive industries. Hence, trends in the Theil coefficient are likely
     to reflect changes in skill-premium or the diffusion of monopoly profits in
     sectors facing reduced competition (Conceiçao and Galbraith 2001; Gal-
     braith and Kum 2005). Moreover, since the manufacturing sector has played
     a leading role in the economic transition in Indonesia since the late 1960s,
     the effects of structural change on the earnings distribution have become
     readily observable.
3   The development of the relative size of the urban informal sector, approxi-
     mated by the percentage share of self-employed in total non-agricultural
     employment. Although the urban informal sector is not a direct income dis-
     tribution component, it reveals how structural change had an impact on the
     composition of the urban labour force. Since the urban informal sector
     workers in developing countries constitute one of the least productive and,
     on average, poorest segments of the labour force, the comparative magni-
     tude of the informal sector is an important indicator of comparative inequal-
     ity levels (PREALC 1982; Bhattacharya 2007).

A comparison of the unskilled wage–GDP per worker in the US, Indonesia,
Brazil and Mexico for the period 1960–2003 is presented in Figure 9.8. The graph
confirms the expectation that the unskilled wage share in the US is higher than in
Indonesia, Brazil and Mexico. The US series reveal a turning point around 1982,
when a gradual but sustained decline of the wage share sets in. This observation
is in line with a large literature studying the causes of the declining relative position of wage earners at the bottom of the wage distribution.[6] A comparable
turning point can be found in the Mexican series in the year 1976. Both the
Mexican and Brazilian series reveal a notable decline of the unskilled wage share
towards the end of the century, with rates dropping below 10 per cent.

The development of the unskilled wage share in Indonesia shows some similarities, but also some important differences with the three benchmark countries.
On the whole, a notable decline can be observed from the early 1970s until 1998,
the year of the economic crises and the stepping-down of Suharto as president of
Indonesia. But the ratio does not become as low as in Mexico and Brazil, and
stabilizes around 20 per cent in the aftermath of the crises. Hence, Indonesian
unskilled rural labourers obtained a higher relative share of total national income

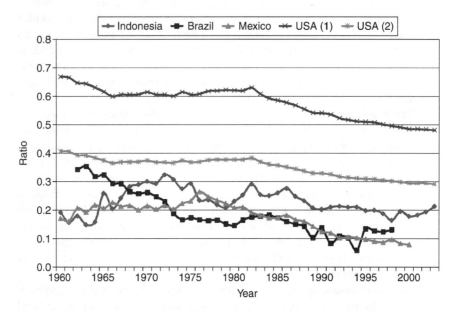

Figure 9.8 The ratio of unskilled labour wages over GDP per person employed in Indonesia, Brazil, Mexico and the US (lower bound and upper bound estimate), 1960–2003 (source: Frankema and Marks 2010).

than their counterparts in Mexico and Brazil during most of the period 1966–1998. The unskilled wage workers in the US were relatively better off than in Indonesia during the entire period.

The second measure adopted by Frankema and Marks (2010) to analyse income distribution in Indonesia is the Theil coefficient of manufacturing labour income. This measure not only has the advantage that data are comparatively well standardized, but it is also believed that it tends to pick up broader movements in the direction of wage disparities in the urban economy.[7] The result is presented in Figure 9.9. The graph reveals that wage differentials have been rather volatile during the last decades, but again a long-term upward or downward trend can hardly be discerned. A more detailed analysis of the changes over time leads to some interesting observations. The steep decline during the period 1958–1963 and the continuation of low wage inequality during the 1960s corresponds with the start of a period of profound state intervention in the industrial sector. The nationalization of key industrial sectors and the supervision of private enterprises by publicly controlled industry associations was a key feature of Sukarno's socialist programme of 'Guided Democracy and Guided Economy' implemented during the late 1950s (Thee 2003b: 9). Sukarno's idea of *Socialism à la Indonesia* appears to have entailed a policy of wage equalization – or perhaps this was the consequence of the strong decline in real wages in this period, which apparently compressed the wage structure.

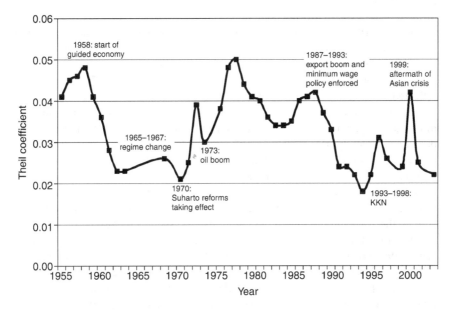

Figure 9.9 Theil coefficient of inter-industry manufacturing wage inequality (source: Frankema and Marks 2010).

As pointed out earlier, the regime change during the years 1965–1967 marked a reversal in many aspects of economic life. Suharto started to privatize the industries that were nationalized under Sukarno, and inter-industry wage differentials rose in response to the abolishment of Sukarno's guided economy programme. During the 1970s a steep increase of the Theil index can be observed, with a peak in 1977. The oil boom in 1973 enhanced the increase of wage differentials, as the sectors benefiting from the oil boom, such as the refining and chemical industries, transferred part of their increasing revenues to their employees, while the appreciation of the rupiah as a result of the oil boom harmed the competitiveness of the non-oil export sectors. Although wage inequality declined after a peak in 1977, it remained at fairly high levels until 1987.

The steep decline from around 0.04 in 1987 to around 0.02 in 1993 corresponded with a new phase in economic policy.[8] Since 1981 rates of economic growth had been disappointing, and around the mid-1980s a renewed sense of urgency arose to undertake a decisive reorientation of the economy. The main goal was to diminish Indonesia's economic dependence on oil revenues. Firms exporting at least 85 per cent of their output were exempted from all import duties and corresponding import regulations (Dick *et al.* 2002: 212). In addition, the government implemented exchange rate policies tailored to the non-oil export sector.[9] During the years following these reforms the export of manufacturing products boomed (Hill 2000: 17). These impressive growth rates went along with a sharp decline in wage inequality in manufacturing. A combination of factors can explain this phenomenon.

The post-1987 export boom was based on an expansion of labour-intensive manufactures such as textiles, clothing, footwear and basic electronic equipment. The shift from resource-intensive industries to labour-intensive industries supported the convergence of unskilled and skilled labour wages. This tendency is reflected by the relative sector movements in the Theil index. A second cause of the notable decline in wage inequality after 1987 is the re-enhancement of minimum wage policies by the Suharto administration. Although already introduced in the early 1970s, it was only in the late 1980s that the government undertook serious measures to enforce the payment of minimum wages. In the first half of the 1990s minimum wages tripled in nominal terms and more than doubled in real terms (Suryahadi *et al.* 2003). Minimum wage policies are likely to have supported wage convergence, especially since they placed upward pressure on the wages in the lowest paying industries, such as the textile sector.

The rise of wage inequality in the last years of the Suharto administration (1993–1998) may also be attributed in part to policies that strongly favoured the growth of large business groups (conglomerates) and prestigious industrial 'high-tech' projects, owned and controlled by the president's relatives and their crony network, together with a range of restrictions (including cartels, price controls, entry and exit controls, exclusive licensing, dominance of SOEs in certain industries and ad hoc government interventions) that artificially raised the costs of doing business for small- and medium-scale enterprises (Dick *et al.* 2002: 214–215). These policies encouraged structural change of a kind that increased employment opportunities for more highly skilled labour at the expense of unskilled labour, thus further skewing the distribution of labour incomes.

Figure 9.10 presents the Indonesian Theil coefficient of inter-industry labour earnings inequality in a comparative perspective, yielding two further insights. First, the average levels of wage inequality in Indonesia appear to be comparable with Brazil and are, at any point in our time period, higher than in Mexico and the US. Although the large volatility of the Indonesian trend makes cross-country comparisons at a specific point in time somewhat arbitrary, the average Theil coefficient of Indonesia is 0.034, which compares to 0.033 for Brazil, 0.014 for Mexico and 0.010 for the US. The major difference between Indonesia and Brazil is that the latter has witnessed an almost uninterrupted increase of its Theil index since the 1950s, whereas in Indonesia the distribution of labour earnings since the late 1970s shows a long-run declining tendency. Second, manufacturing wage inequality in Indonesia appears to be much more volatile than in all of the three comparison countries. Similar to the trends observed in unskilled wage–GDP per worker ratios, the period 1966–1998 is characterized by large volatility, but a net increase or decline in manufacturing wage inequality is hardly noticeable.

The last measure to study income inequality adopted by Frankema and Marks (2010) is the expansion of the urban informal sector. Ample literature has established a direct relationship between the high levels of asset and income inequality

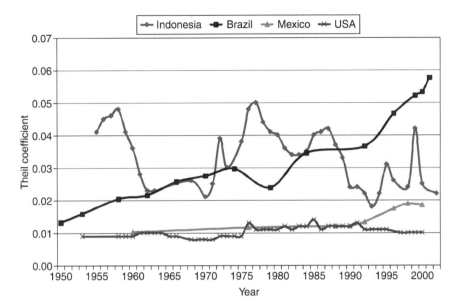

Figure 9.10 Theil index of inter-industry manufacturing wage for selected countries, 1950–2002 (source: Frankema and Marks 2010).

and the explosion of the urban informal sectors in the second half of the twentieth century (Cardoso and Helwege 1992; Thorp 1998; Birdsall *et al.* 1997; De Soto 2000; Morley 2001). Figure 9.11 compares the share of urban self-employed in Indonesia with Brazil, Mexico and the US. For Brazil the various changes in the statistical conceptualization of employment status made it impossible to construct a consistent series for the post-1990 years.[10] Figure 9.11 shows that the share of urban self-employed in Indonesia since the early 1960s compares quite well with the developments in Brazil and Mexico. It started out at a slightly lower level than Mexico during the 1970s before rapidly catching up, fell behind since the early 1980s and caught up again after 1992. In 2003 the shares were 22 per cent for Indonesia and 23.5 per cent for Mexico in 2001. These levels clearly deviated from present OECD countries as exemplified by the United States.

In the discussion about inequality in Indonesia, two other issues require some consideration: land distribution and regional inequality.

The Indonesian agricultural sector is composed of a large group of smallholders, primarily engaged in rice cultivation, and a more confined group of medium- and large-scale farmers involved in the production of tropical cash crops such as rubber, palm oil, coffee and tea. From a global comparative perspective, the distribution of land in Indonesia is moderate, with land Gini's ranging around 0.52 to 0.45 (Frankema 2009). In Table 9.3 the available land inequality figures are presented as a Theil index for the period 1963–2003. The estimates are based on decennial agricultural censuses carried out since 1963.

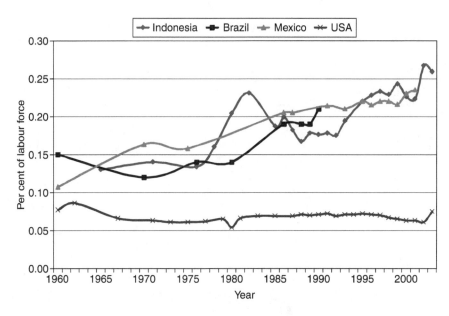

Figure 9.11 Urban self-employed as a share of total labour force (sources: for Indonesia BPS, *Statistical Yearbook of Indonesia* (*Statistik Indonesia*), various issues 1975–2003; ILO, *Yearbook of Labour Statistics*, various issues 1966–2005).

Table 9.3 A Theil index of land distribution among agricultural households, 1963–2003

	1963	1973	1983	1993	2003
Theil land distribution	0.290	0.278	0.230	0.228	0.256
Gini coefficient land distribution	52.7	47.1		54.4	

Source: Theil: authors' calculations from BPS, Agricultural censuses; Gini coefficients: Frankema 2009.

Note
Large estates not included.

Table 9.3 shows that levels of land inequality declined until 1993, and then increased up to the year 2003; yet the changes remained confined. According to the census data, the size of land holdings declined from an average of 1.2 hectare in 1963 to 0.81 hectare in 2003, which indicates that the intensification of land use has continued throughout the period under consideration. In the meantime, total output and, consequently, output per hectare have increased considerably. The distribution of land gives us an indication of trends in agricultural income inequality, but there is no linear relation between land and income distribution. In fact, several studies show that land productivity is consistently inversely related to land size (see, for instance, Booth 2002). Decreasing marginal returns to scale reflect the fact that smallholdings generally dispose of plots of higher quality that are used more intensively. In other words, the Theil index of land distribution will probably overestimate the agricultural income Theil. Therefore the conclusion that land distribution in Indonesia had a mitigating effect on income inequality seems to be justified.

Regional income inequality, as measured by the coefficient of variation, is a different story, however. Using data on provincial GDP per capita, which have been available since the early 1970s and which are considered relatively reliable (Resosudarmo and Vidyattama 2006: 33), shows that it has been fairly constant between 1971 and 2000. We do see that in the 1970s income disparity between regions increased significantly, if we look at GDP per capita including oil and gas, but it decreased if we look at GDP per capita without oil and gas (Figure 9.12). This is of course the result of the two oil booms during the 1970s.

Overall, East Kalimantan, Riau, Jakarta and Aceh have always been among the richest provinces, whereas East and West Nusa Tenggara were considered to have always been among the poorest. Yet while regional income disparity might have been stable, it should be stressed that it was also highly unequal. GDP per capita of provinces in the richest group were typically around ten times those of provinces in the poorest group (Resosudarmo and Vidyamatta 2006: 36). Also, when comparing the coefficient of variation (CV) of provincial per capita GDP in Indonesia with several other developing countries in Asia, Africa, Europe and Latin America, Indonesia stands out as spatially highly unequal (Table 9.4).

The discussion above shows that there is no evidence that economic growth in Indonesia also entailed *increasing* inequality. But the current view on this

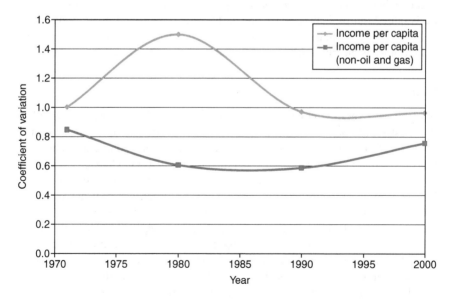

Figure 9.12 Regional GDP per capita inequality, 1971–2000 (source: authors' calculations from BPS's provincial per capita GDP in current prices).

Table 9.4 Regional income disparity in Indonesia in comparative perspective (coefficient of variation)

Country	1996	1997
Brazil		0.563
China		0.692
India		0.387
Indonesia	0.840	
Mexico		0.473
Nepal	0.157	
Pakistan		0.186
Philippines		0.530
Poland	0.206	
Rumania	0.189	
Russia		0.625
Thailand		0.797
Uganda		0.274
Uzbekistan		0.353
Vietnam		1.067

Source: Resosudarmo and Vidyattama (2006: 36); see also Shankar and Shah (2003).

link, that the New Order regime was characterized by 'growth with equity', and that income and wealth inequality in Indonesia were rather low by international standards, is not based on entirely convincing evidence. Some of the major determinants of income inequality (wage inequality, the share of the self-employed in labour force) appear similar to those in countries that display some of the highest levels of income inequality in the world. Regional income inequality is quite high by international standards, whereas the land distribution seems to be relatively egalitarian. It is unclear what the net results of these forces are, but the story is clearly much more complex than the official version suggests.

Conclusion

A historical overview covering more than 200 years is necessarily brief about the most recent period, because it is much more difficult to evaluate what is going on at the moment. The danger is that one may draw conclusions about the recent past that are untenable due to coming events that will change our perspective on these developments. Nevertheless, it seems justified to say that Indonesia has made slow but significant progress since the Asian crisis. It has made the transition from authoritarian rule to democracy in less than a decade, and growth has returned, backed by prudent macroeconomic management. The total of five presidents within the space of just eight years reflects the political changes caused by Indonesia's economic crisis, but the re-election of SBY, who is widely respected and liked, suggests that the political and economic turbulence has eased. The main challenge is now to recover its pre-crisis growth performance and tackle unemployment and poverty. At the same time, the road ahead is still long.

Finally, our overall assessment of the evolution of living standards in the post-independence period turns out positive. Not surprisingly, growth was uneven throughout the whole period, with more favourable developments during the Suharto presidency than during Sukarno's reign. Keeping this in mind, however, we see an impressive growth in real wages, a significant improvement in numeracy and a clear upward trend in height, while inequality was rather stable, although probably higher than usually portrayed. Since the late 1960s, Indonesia has really been experiencing 'modern economic growth', and its recent political development seems to have created a solid basis for its continuation in the future.

Notes

1 Introduction: Indonesia between drama and miracle

1 Recent literature on 'poverty traps' refers to the same idea: see Collier 2007.

2 Exploring the proximate and ultimate causes of 200 years of economic growth in Indonesia, 1800–2000

1 There are insufficient data for reconstructing the national accounts for the 1800–1815 period; the analysis of the growth record therefore only starts in 1815.
2 We assume perfect competition, so that wages and the interest rate equal the marginal product of labour and capital respectively. In that case α is the share of income of capital in national income and β is the share of wages in national income.
3 Capital deepening is an increase in capital intensity, i.e. an increase in the amount of capital per unit of labour input.

3 Colonial state formation, 1800–1830

1 See *Koloniaal Verslag* 1882, which contains the first attempt to measure the extent of communal and private property in those parts of Java that were under direct Dutch rule.
2 According to notes in the National Archive The Hague, Ministry of Colonial Affairs (No. 3055), Yogyakarta had 60,000 inhabitants before the Java War, and 30,697 in 1832; a related source (No. 3043) states that Batavia had about 118,000 inhabitants, although the official figure was 55,000.
3 When the Portuguese arrived in the Indonesian Archipelago they found that in order to procure the desired Moluccan spices they had to offer high-quality Indian textiles in return; the Dutch took over this trade after 1600 – it had been one of the reasons for also establishing factories in India.

4 The Cultivation System, 1830–1870

1 Van den Bosch (1829: 313): 'trouwens, zolang de Javaan met meer voordeel rijst dan andere producten verbouwen kan, zal hij in zijn belang wel geene aansporing vinden, om zich op die andere kultures toe te leggen' [as long as the Javanese grow rice with much more profit than other crops, they will not be stimulated to cultivate those other crops].
2 He also made the point that in Europe this kind of 'coercion' of the labour force was the result of the fact that capital was concentrated in the hands of few (p. 316) and argued that the kind of coercion he wanted to (re)introduce in Java was basically similar.
3 His estimates of the daily wage of an agricultural labourer – 6 to 7 stivers – were

much too high; in reality it was only 2 to 3 stivers, which has important consequences for his estimates of cost prices of Javanese cash crops.

4 The classic example of this conflict is of course the story of Eduard Douwes Dekker, written down in the most famous Dutch novel of the nineteenth century, *Max Havelaar*, the publication of which in 1860 had important consequences for the public debate about the failure of the Cultivation System and the future course of colonial policy (Fasseur 1975).

5 The reasons why the official figures of net transfers are underestimates are discussed in van Zanden and Van Riel (2000: 222–224). Van der Eng (1993b) argues that the deficit on the merchandise account exaggerates the size of the colonial drain because it, for example, includes payments for services rendered by the colonial state.

6 van Zanden (2007); Boomgaard (2002), by stressing the external (weather-related) causes of the harvest failures of the 1840s, appears to ignore the economic and socio-political circumstances that made these harvest failures into relatively large-scale famines; it is striking that similar famines did not re-occur on Java during the rest of the nineteenth century (see the overview of fluctuations in rice production in *Changing Economy in Indonesia*, Vol. 10: 45).

7 This assessment of the consequences of the Cultivation System is rather pessimistic and critical of the optimistic assessment by Elson (1994), who emphasizes the positive effects during the 1830s rather than the negative outcomes that surfaced during the 1840s.

8 Timmer (1996: 45–74) discusses the same issues in relation to contemporary rice markets in Indonesia.

9 In 1846 the price lists discussed in the next section distinguish, for example, between a *koyang* of 27 *picul* (125 pounds) in Batavia, of 28 *picul* in Semarang and of 30 *picul* in Surabaya.

10 This method to quantify seasonal fluctuations was applied to make my results comparable to those of Van der Eng (1993: 173); the same method was applied to estimate seasonality in Figure 4.7.

11 Figure 3 from Chuan and Kraus gives the example of Soochow in the early eighteenth century (1975: 108).

12 See Mears (1961: 81–85), who, however, describes the situation in the 1950s.

13 Calculation based on Van der Kemp (1894: 346); storing rice in the warehouses of the state near the docks was much more expensive: in 1832 the monthly rate was 5 cents per *picul* (about 1/30 of a *koyang*) per month, 1 to 2 per cent of its value (or 12 to 24 per cent on an annual basis); official storage rates are quoted in Archives Ministry of Colonial Affairs 1814–1849 (in National Archive The Hague) No. 3042.

14 Translated and reprinted in Fernando and Bulbeck (1992: 23–25).

15 The best introduction is the collection of essays in Gonggrijp and Boeke (1966).

16 He stressed, for example, the backward bending supply curve, not only of labour, but also of agricultural produce, and that peasants did not produce for profit, but instead to satisfy their basic needs (Boeke 1947: 49). His views were strongly criticized by other colonial experts – see the papers in Gonggrijp and Boeke (1966); this debate can be seen as a precursor of the debate on peasant rationality in the late 1970s, see Scott (1977) and Popkin (1979).

17 In the planned economies of the twentieth century the preferred sector was of course the capital goods industry; see for example Allen 2003.

5 Liberalism and ethical policies, 1870–1914

1 The view that the opium *regie* led to less consumption has been criticized by Chandra (2000; 2002).

2 For the magnitude of these transactions, see Smits *et al.* (2000), Korthals Altes (1986) and Van der Eng (1998); as Van der Eng (1998) has argued, the net capital flows to

Indonesia were quite small, and the large sums 'invested' in the colony to a large extent consisted of reinvested profits and earnings made locally by Dutch entrepreneurs.

3 See Houben (1999) and the other contributions to Lindblad and Houben (1999) for a detailed assessment of this problem.

4 A slightly different calculation carried out by Bosch for the Dutch East Indies arrived at 11.5 per cent for 1900–1909 and no less than 18.4 per cent for 1910–1919 (Bosch 1947: 605).

5 In 1865/1866 one-sixth of the Chinese workers still died, but this incredibly high mortality was brought down to 10 per cent in the next year, and less than 2 per cent in the early 1870s (Mollema 1927: appendix 5).

6 The coffee industry on Java did not manage to do something similar, and more or less went down with the decline of the Cultivation System; other factors, such as international competition and coffee rust, a disease that destroyed the crop, played a role as well.

7 Similar stories can be told about the expansion of tobacco cultivation in Sumatra and other parts of the Archipelago.

8 Another reason why seasonal fluctuations in rice prices declined was that Java became increasingly dependent on imported rice (whereas before the 1860s it was a net exporter of that commodity); the harvest season in Southeast Asia (Thailand, Vietnam) preceded harvests in Indonesia, as a result of which prices during the *paceclik* could be lowered thanks to these imports, which helped to reduce seasonal variation (we thank Pierre van der Eng for pointing this out to us).

6 The constraints of a colonial economy, 1914–1942

1 Van der Eng (1996): 52–59 demonstrates that the increase in investment in irrigation already started in the 1890s, and that the interests of the sugar industry did not dominate this policy.

2 The problem is that we have no statistics for the activities of the private pawnshops before 1901, except for in the 1870s when they were liberalized, but were also obliged to report their activities to the colonial government; from the statistics published in the *Koloniaal Verslag* of 1874 it can be established that total lending by these pawnshops was about 11 million guilders (data for a few residencies are missing, so this is probably still an underestimate), or about 50 cents per capita; only in 1909 did the government monopoly pass this threshold when a total of 19.8 million was borrowed – the population had increased to almost 34 million in the meantime.

3 Source (Van Laanen 1980: Tables 6 and 7); for a few years, estimates had to be made by interpolation, and the value of the credit supplied by the *lumbungs* had to be estimated using rice prices as a conversion factor; value added in agriculture (Van der Eng 1996), and additional estimates by the author (see van Zanden 2002).

4 This was the term used by the colonial administration; we use these 'colonial' terms, but realize that 'Foreign Orientals' of 'Foreign Asiatics' were also Indonesians, and that also a large part of the 'Europeans' were born in the colony.

5 In other Asian and European budgets soap was also included, but we could not find the right price data for this and therefore included salt instead; nor could we find price data for candles and lamp oil, so it was assumed that these two items were 5 per cent of the total budget (the same assumption was used for rent); see Allen *et al.* 2011 for a detailed exposition of the methodology. Actual consumption of rice per capita was much lower than the 175 kg assumed here (in the order of 90–100 kg).

6 Perhaps we somewhat underestimate the real wage here, because we assume that the budget is dominated by rice only; in particular the inclusion of maize (which became increasingly important as a staple crop) may lower the costs of the subsistence budget a bit; see Boomgaard and van Zanden 1990: pp. 50–51.

7 Data for females are much more limited, but show more or less the same patterns:

about 150 cm in the 1860s, declining to 148 cm in the 1880s and 1910s, before recovering to 150 cm in the 1940s and 1950s, but still only 151–152 cm in the 1970s and 1980s (Baten *et al.* 2009b).

8 Note the huge gap between men and women within this group In 1930, when we have more data about the different subgroups, it is clear that the level of literacy of Chinese women is higher than of 'other foreign Asiatics' (12.4 versus 3.9 per cent) (Census 1930, VIII, p. 29).

9 The number of observations is in all these cases is more than 1,600, with the exception of the data from Talaud, where we only have about 500 observations for each sex.

10 Colijn was prime minister between 1933 and 1939, but he also combined this position with that of minister of colonial affairs, showing the importance he attached to the relationship with Indonesia (see Langeveld 1998).

11 In 1933 there was a rebellion by Dutch sailors and soldiers of the *Zeven Provincien*, but that 'incident' was unrelated to the colonial situation (Blom 1975).

7 The lost decades?: from colony to nation-state, 1942–1967

1 This estimate contained 814 million for rehabilitation of the mining industry, 814 million for rehabilitation of the agricultural sector, 140 million for rehabilitation of the manufacturing industry, 172 million for reparation of railways and tramways, 150 million for replacing ships, 80 million for rehabilitation of ports and 85 million for replacing cars.

2 Based on a re-calculation of Van der Eng's constant price estimates into current price estimates using his GDP reflator (Van der Eng 2002: 172).

3 In such a district system, or single winner voting system, a relatively small majority, or even a share in the vote of more than say 40 per cent, can lead to a large, absolute majority in Parliament; this can be a source of stability, because after elections it is relatively easy to form a government, which then has a clear mandate from Parliament.

4 Indicative is the rating of Indonesia in the Polity IV dataset, which measures the quality of democratic institutions (see www.systemicpeace.org/inscr/inscr.htm): in the early 1950s the rating is 0 (–10 is the minimum, +10 the maximum), declining to –5 in 1959, to –6 in 1966 and –7 in 1967, after which it remains at this level until 1998.

5 The share of education in the budget of the central government remained relatively small however – it was not more than 4–5 per cent in the late 1950s and early 1960s – against almost 10 per cent in the 1930s; local and provincial government was mainly responsible for the strong increase in spending on this item.

6 The Indonesian case is peculiar in this respect. In the 1950s the Indonesian military went into business and had extensive off-budget income sources (Purwanto 2009).

7 Suharto raised petroleum prices from 4 to 1,000 rupiah per litre in 1967/1968 (Bevan *et al.* 1999: 328).

8 At the same time it should be realized that fertility increased and mortality fell after 1950, which of course slowed per capita GDP growth. Similarly, fertility increased beginning in Java and Bali in the 1970s, gathering pace over the 1980s, which of course accelerated per capita GDP growth (see Hugo *et al.* 1987). Yet the relationship between population and economic growth is not straightforward. Population growth could be beneficial or detrimental to economic growth and economic growth could have an impact on population growth.

9 Because for the post-war period we have a much larger dataset at our disposal than could be used in Chapter 2 where we cover the whole period from 1800–2000, we present these results in more detail here.

10 Compare the same statistics for the colonial period: in 1939 there were 574 cooperatives with 52,216 members (Hatta 1957: 108–109).

11 In fact, farmers hardly used them at all. Fertilisers were mainly used in the sugar industry (Van der Eng 1996).
12 They rose from 24,000 tonnes in 1965/1966 to 55,000 tonnes in 1966/1967; domestic production of fertilizers also fell in these years (Bank Indonesia 1966–1967: 159).
13 This section is largely based on Marks (2009b) and Marks (2010b).
14 See Bertocchi 1994, Acemoglu *et al.* 2001, and Bertocchi and Canova 2002 for the relation between decolonization and economic growth.
15 Divergent opinions in Lindblad 2006, Sulistiyono 2003: 251–252 and Sulistiyono 2006: 123. They conclude that economic slowdown only started to gain ground in the early 1960s, while the take-over and nationalization of Dutch firms took place in 1957/1959.
16 Feith's (1962) seminal study still leaves many questions unanswered, as he admits himself.

8 Success and failure of the 'new order', 1967–1998

1 Since several of these economists had followed postgraduate study in economics at the University of California, Berkeley, they are sometimes referred to as the Berkeley Mafia.
2 It should be noted that the system of production sharing, which was actually introduced in the 1960s, allowed the Indonesian government (and of course Pertamina) to benefit hugely from the oil windfall.
3 The riots have become known as the Malari riots, from its Indonesian acronym *Malapetaka Limabelas Januari*, which can be translated as 'Disaster of 15 January'.
4 As we argued in Chapter 4, the real break in this respect was in the late 1950s, with the ending of the democratic experiment and the transition towards Guided Democracy; the replacement of the democratic constitution of 1950 by the presidential constitution in 1959 was emblematic of this change.
5 Typically, the first massive protests in spring 1998 against the Suharto regime were directed at the policy move to increase petrol prices (Suharto was pressured into this by the IMF); the measure was almost immediately withdrawn as a result.
6 Among the ancestors of these new varieties of rice were varieties that had been developed in Indonesia during the 1920s and 1930s (Van der Eng 1993: 90).
7 When, in the 1990s, the banking industry would be liberalized, it resulted in the setting up of many banks that tried to profit from the large interest rate gaps within the country (and with international capital markets). This development, however, would not be successful in the long run because the regulation of the banking industry was poorly organized (many new banks did not survive the 1998 backlash).
8 Bank Indonesia, *Annual Report*, 1976/1977: 121.
9 Actually the institutions to that end had been put in place just in time in the 1960s: a product-sharing contract system. Without that the oil bonanza would have only benefited foreign oil firms.

9 Crisis, recovery and the evolution of living standards since independence

1 The highest state institution is the People's Consultative Assembly (*Majelis Permusyawaratan Rakyat*, MPR), whose functions included electing the president and vice president (since 2004 the president has been elected directly by the people), establishing broad guidelines of state policy, and amending the constitution. The 695-member MPR includes all 550 members of the People's Representative Council (DPR) (*Dewan Perwakilan Rakyat*, DPR, the House of Representatives) plus 130 'regional representatives' elected by the 26 provincial parliaments and 65 appointed members from societal groups.

2 See for example Booth 1992: 335; Hill 2000: 197; Booth 2000: 75; and Dick *et al.* 2002: 227. See also the discussion of the inequality literature by Cameron 2002.

3 For a more extensive discussion on the advantages and disadvantages of the income and expenditure approach see also Deininger and Squire (1996), and François and Rojas-Romagosa (2005).

4 Income inequality Gini coefficients calculated from the raw *Susenas* income data were 0.42 for 1984 and 0.43 for 1990 (Cameron 2002: 12).

5 Nyberg (1976) addresses another weakness of the *Susenas* data, namely the timing of the survey. In some years the Islamic feast, called *Lebaran*, at the end of the fasting period is included, while in others it is not, possibly affecting expenditure patterns. This makes these *Susenas* data difficult to compare between years.

6 For a concise overview see Helpman (2004: 94–105).

7 Williamson (1980, 1982) has argued that wage differentials parallel broader trends in income distribution and can be considered as a simplified phenomenon of the evolution of overall inequality. Acemoglu (1997) found that wage inequality was the main component of rising income inequality in the USA, and Atkinson (1997) found close similarities in the movements of household income inequality and individual labour earnings inequality over the 1970s and 1980s in the UK. More recently the use of wage dispersion as an alternative for the widely-used Deininger and Squire database of Gini coefficients has been advocated by the University of Texas Inequality Project (UTIP) (see for example Conceiçao and Galbraith 2001; Galbraith and Kum 2005).

8 It should be noted that trends in the Theil coefficient cannot be linearly interpreted. For example, a decline from 0.04 to 0.02 does not reveal a reduction of inequality by 50 per cent.

9 In September 1986 the government substantially devalued the rupiah.

10 One of the main problems in assessing Latin American countries relates to the fact that labour-force surveys were often confined to urban areas in the 1990s.

References

Aass, S. (1982), 'The Relevance of Chayanov's Macro Theory to the Case of Java', in E.J. Hobsbawm (ed.), *Peasants in History: Essays in Honour of Daniel Thorner*, Calcutta: Oxford University Press, pp. 221–248.

Acemoglu, D. (1997), 'Matching, Heterogeneity, and the Evolution of Income Distribution', *Journal of Economic Growth*, Vol. 2, No. 1, pp. 61–92.

Acemoglu, D., S. Johnson and J.A. Robinson (2001), 'The Colonial Origins of Comparative Development: An Empirical Investigation', *American Economic Review*, Vol. 91, No. 5, pp. 1369–1401.

Ades, Alberto F. and Edward L. Glaeser (1992), 'Trade and Circuses: Explaining Urban Giants', *The Quarterly Journal of Economics*, Vol. 110, No. 1, pp. 195–227.

A'Hearn, Brian, Joerg Baten and Dorothee Crayen (2009), 'Quantifying Quantitative Literacy: Age Heaping and the History of Human Capital', *Journal of Economic History*, Vol. 69, No. 3, pp. 783–808.

Alexander, J. and A. Booth (1992), 'The Service Sector', in A. Booth (ed.) *The Oil Boom and After: Indonesian Economic Policy and Performance in the Soeharto Era*, Singapore: Oxford University Press, pp. 283–319.

Ali, Shamsher (1966), 'Interisland Shipping', *Bulletin of Indonesian Economic Studies*, Vol. 2, No. 3, pp. 27–51.

Alisjahbana, Armida and Arief Anshory Yusuf (2003), 'Assessing Indonesia's Sustainable Development: Long-Run Trend, Impact of the Crisis, and Adjustment During the Recovery Period,' Department of Economics, Padjadjaran University.

Allen, Robert C. (2001), 'The Great Divergence in European Wages and Prices from the Middle Ages to the First World War', *Explorations in Economic History*, Vol. 38, pp. 411–447.

Allen, Robert C. (2003), *Farm to Factory: A Reinterpretation of the Soviet Industrial Revolution*, Princeton: Princeton University Press.

Allen, Robert C., Jean-Pascal Bassino, Debin Ma, Christine Moll-Murata and Jan Luiten van Zanden (2011), 'Wages, Prices and Livings Standards in China, Japan and Europe, 1739–1925', *Economic History Review*, Vol. 64, No. 1, pp. 8–38.

Ananta, Aris and Yohanes Eko Riyanto (2006), 'Riding Along a Bumpy Road: Indonesian Economy in an Emerging Democratic Era', *ASEAN Economic Bulletin*, Vol. 23, No. 1, pp. 1–10.

Anderson, B.R.O'G (1966), 'The Problem of Rice', *Indonesia*, Vol. 1, No. 2, pp. 77–123.

Anderson, James E. and Douglas Marcouiller (1999), 'Trade, Insecurity, and Home Bias: An Empirical Investigation', NBER Working Paper No. 7000.

Angeles, Luis (2008), 'GDP per Capita or Real Wages? Making Sense of Conflicting

Views on Pre-Industrial Europe', *Explorations in Economic History*, Vol. 45, No. 2, pp. 147–163.

Anonymous. (1848), 'Algemeen overzigt van de toestand van Nederlandsch Indië gedurende het jaar 1846', *Tijdschrift voor Nederlandsch Indië*, Vol. 10, pp. 24–60.

Arndt, Heinz W. (1969), 'Survey of Recent Developments', *Bulletin of Indonesian Economic Studies*, Vol. 5, No. 2, pp. 1–16.

Arndt, Heinz W. (1971), 'Banking in Hyperinflation and Stabilization', in B. Glassburner (ed.), *The Economy of Indonesia: Selected Readings*, Ithaca, NY: Cornell University Press, pp. 359–395.

Arndt, Heinz W. (1975), 'Development and Equality: The Indonesian Case', *World Development*, Vol. 3, No. 2/3, pp. 77–90.

Artadi, Elsa V. and Xavier Sala-i-Martin (2003), 'The Economic Tragedy of the XXth Century: Growth in Africa', NBER Working Paper No. 9865.

Asicahyono, Haryo (1997), 'Transformation and Structural Change in Indonesia's Manufacturing Sector', in Mari E. Pangestu and Yuri Sato, *Waves of Change in Indonesia's Manufacturing Industry*, Tokyo: Institute of Developing Economies, pp. 1–28.

Asra, A. (2000), 'Poverty and Inequality in Indonesia: Estimates, Decomposition and Key Issues', *Journal of the Asia Pacific Economy*, Vol. 5, No. 1/2, pp. 91–111.

Athukorala, P. and B. Santosa (1997), 'Gains from Indonesian Export Growth: Do Linkages Matter?', *Bulletin of Indonesian Economic Studies*, Vol. 33, No. 2, pp. 73–95.

Atkinson, A.B. (1997), 'Bringing Income Distribution in from the Cold', *Economic Journal*, Vol. 107, No. 442, pp. 297–321.

Atkinson, A.B. and A. Brandolini (2001), 'Promise and Pitfalls in the Use of "Secondary" Data-Sets: Income Inequality in OECD Countries as a Case Study', *Journal of Economic Literature*, Vol. 34, No. 3, pp. 771–799.

Badhuri, A (1977), 'On the Formation of Usurious Interest Rates in Backward Agriculture', *Cambridge Journal of Economics*, Vol. 1, No. 4, pp. 431–450.

Bank Indonesia (1960–65), *Annual Report*, various issues, Jakarta: Bank Indonesia.

Bank Indonesia (1966–67), *Annual Report*, various issues, Jakarta: Bank Indonesia.

Barro, Robert J and Xavier Sala-i Martin (1995), *Economic Growth*, New York: McGraw Hill.

Basri, M.C. (2001), 'The Political Economy of Manufacturing Protection in Indonesia 1975–1995', PhD dissertation, ANU, Canberra.

Basri, M.C. and H. Hill (1996), 'The Political Economy of Manufacturing Protection in LDCs: An Indonesian Case Study', *Oxford Development Studies*, 24, pp. 241–259.

Bastin, J. (1954), *Raffles' Ideas on the Land Rent System in Java and the Mackenzie Land Tenure Commission*, 's-Gravenhage: Martinus Nijhoff.

Bataviasche Courant (1823–1827), Batavia: Landsdukkerij.

Baten, Joerg, Peter Foldvari, Bas van Leeuwen and Jan Luiten van Zanden (2009a), 'World Income Inequality, 1820–2000', paper for the XVth World Economic History Congress, Utrecht.

Baten, Joerg, Mojgan Stegl and Pierre van der Eng (2009b), 'Long-Term Changes in the Biological Standard of Living in Indonesia: New Anthropometric Evidence, 1770s–2000s', paper presented during the XVth World Economic History Conference, 3–7 August, Utrecht, the Netherlands.

Baten, Joerg, Debin Ma, Stephen Morgan and Qing Wang (2010), 'Evolution of Living Standards in the 18th–20th Centuries: Evidences from Real Wages, Age-Heaping, and Anthropometrics', *Explorations in Economic History*, Vol. 46, No. 1, pp. 53–69.

Bates, Robert H., John H. Coatsworth and Jeffrey G. Williamson (2007), 'Lost Decades:

Postindependence Performance in Latin America and Africa', *The Journal of Economic History*, Vol. 67, No. 4, pp. 917–943.

Baudet, H. and M. Fennema (1983), (eds) *Het Nederlands Belang bij Indië*, Utrecht: Het Spectrum.

Bell, C. (1988), 'Credit Markets and Interlinked Transactions', In H. Chenery and T.N. Srinivasan (eds), *Handbook of Development Economics*, Vol. I, Amsterdam: North Holland, pp. 763–830.

Berktay, Halil (1987), 'The Feudalism Debate: The Turkish End', *Journal of Peasant Studies*, 14, 291–313.

Bertocchi, Graziella (1994), 'Colonialism in the Theory of Growth', Working Paper, Brown University, No. 94–14.

Bertocchi, Graziella and Fabio Canova (2002), 'Did Colonization Matter for Growth? An Empirical Exploration into the Historical Causes of Africa's Underdevelopment', *European Economic Review*, Vol. 46, No. 10, pp. 1851–1871.

Bevan, David L., Paul Collier and Jan Willem Gunning (1999), *The Political Economy of Poverty, Equity, and Growth: Nigeria and Indonesia*, Oxford: Oxford University Press.

Bhagwati, J. and T.N. Srinivasan (2002), 'Trade and Poverty in the Poor Countries', *American Economic Review*, Vol. 92, No. 2, pp. 180–183.

Bhargawa, M. and J.F. Richards (2002), 'Defining Property Rights in Land in Colonial India: Gorakhpur Region in the Indo-Gangetic Plain', in J.F. Richards (ed.), *Land, Property, and the Environment*, Oakland: Institute for Contemporary Studies, pp. 235–263.

Bhattacharya, P.C. (2007), 'Informal Sector, Income Inequality and Economic Development', Center for Economic Reform and Transformation (CERT) Discussion Paper 2007/09.

Bird, K. and C. Manning (2003), 'Economic Reform, Labour, Markets and Poverty: The Indonesian Experience', in K. Sharma (ed.) *Trade Policy, Growth and Poverty in Asian Developing Countries*, London/New York: Routledge, pp. 74–94.

Birdsall, N., D. Ross and R. Sabot (1997), 'Education, Growth and Inequality', in N. Birdsall and F. Jaspersen (eds), *Pathways to Growth: Comparing East Asia and Latin America*, Washington: Inter-American Development Bank.

Blom, J.C.H. (1975), *De muiterij op de Zeven Provinciën*, Bussum: Fibula.

Blumberger, J.Th. Petrus (1987), *De nationalistische beweging in Nederlandsch-Indië*. Dordrecht: Foris Publications (original publication in 1931).

Blussé, L. (1986), *Strange Company: Chinese Settlers, Mestizo Women and the Dutch in VOC Batavia*, Dordrecht: Foris.

Boediono (1990), 'Growth and Equity in Indonesia', *Singapore Economic Review*, Vol. 35, No. 1, pp. 84–101.

Boediono (2002), 'The International Monetary Fund Support Program in Indonesia: Comparing Implementation under Three Presidents', *Bulletin of Indonesian Economic Studies*, Vol. 38, No. 3, pp. 385–391.

Boediono (2005), 'Managing the Indonesian Economy: Some Lessons from the Past', *Bulletin of Indonesian Economic Studies*, Vol. 41, No. 3, pp. 309–324.

Boediono and Mari Pangestu (1986), 'Indonesia: The Structure and Causes of Manufacturing Protection', in C. Findlay and Ross Garnaut (eds), *The Political Economy of Manufacturing Protection: Experiences of ASEAN and Australia*, Sydney: Allen and Unwin, pp. 1–47.

Boeke, J.H. (1910), *Tropisch-koloniale staathuishoudkunde*, Amsterdam: De Bussy.

Boeke, J.H. (1947), *Indische Economie, I, The Theorie der Indische Economie*, Haarlem: Tjeenk Willink.

Boomgaard, P. (1986a), 'Buitenzorg in 1805: The Role of Money and Credit in a Colonial Frontier Society', *Modern Asian Studies*, Vol. XX, No. 1, pp. 33–58.

Boomgaard, P. (1986b), 'The Welfare Services in Indonesia, 1900–1942', *Itinerario*, Vol. 10, No. 1, pp. 57–81.

Boomgaard, P. (1987), *Children of the Colonial State: Population Growth and Economic Development in Java, 1795–1880*, Amsterdam: Free University Press.

Boomgaard, P. (1990), 'Why Work for Wages? Free Labour in Java, 1600–1900', *Economic and Social History in the Netherlands*, Vol. 2, pp. 37–57.

Boomgaard, P. (1996), 'Geld, krediet, rente en Europeanen in Zuid- en Zuidoost-Azië in de zeventiende eeuw', in C.A. Davids, W. Fritsch and L.A. van der Valk (eds), *Kapitaal, ondernemerschap en beleid*, Amsterdam: Neha, pp. 483–511.

Boomgaard, P. (2002), 'From Subsistence Crises to Business Cycle Depressions, Indonesia 1800–1940', *Itinerario*, Vol. XXVI, 3/4, pp. 35–51.

Boomgaard, P. and A.J. Gooszen (1991), 'Population Trends 1795–1942', *Changing Economy in Indonesia*, Vol. 11, Amsterdam: Royal Tropical Institute.

Boomgaard, P. and D. Henley (eds) (2009) *Credit and Debt in Indonesia, 860–1930*, Singapore: KITLV Press/Institute of SouthEast Asian Studies.

Boomgaard, P. and J.L. van Zanden (1990), 'Foodcrops and Arable Land', *Changing Economy in Indonesia*, Vol. 10, Amsterdam: Royal Tropical Institute.

Booth, Anne (1989), 'Indonesian Agricultural Development in Comparative Perspective', *World Development*, Vol. 17, No. 8, pp. 1235–1254.

Booth, Anne (1992), 'Income Distribution and Poverty', in A. Booth (ed.), *The Oil Boom and After: Indonesian Economic Policy and Performance in the Soeharto Era*, Singapore: Oxford University Press.

Booth, Anne (1998), *The Indonesian Economy in the Nineteenth and Twentieth Centuries: A History of Missed Opportunities*, London: Macmillan.

Booth, Anne (1999), 'Survey of Recent Developments', *Bulletin of Indonesian Economic Studies*, Vol. 35, No. 3, pp. 3–38.

Booth, Anne (2000), 'Poverty and Inequality in the Soeharto Era: An Assessment', *Bulletin of Indonesian Economic Studies*, Vol. 36, No. 1, pp. 73–104.

Booth, Anne (2001), 'The Causes of South East Asia's Economic Crisis: A Sceptical Review of the Debate', *Asia Pacific Business Review*, Vol. 8, No. 2, pp. 19–48.

Booth, Anne (2002), 'The Changing Role of Non-Farm Activities in Agricultural Households in Indonesia: Some Insights from the Agricultural Censuses', *Bulletin of Indonesian Economic Studies*, Vol. 38, No. 2, pp. 179–200.

Booth, A. and R.M. Sundrum (1981), 'Income Distribution', in A. Booth and P. McCawley (eds), *The Indonesian Economy during the Soeharto Era*, Kuala Lumpur: Oxford University Press.

Bosch, K.D. (1947), *Nederlandse Beleggingen in de Verenigde Staten*, Amsterdam: Elsevier.

BPS (1961–1963), *Statistical Pocketbook*, various issues, Jakarta: BPS.

BPS (1975–2003), *Statistical Yearbook of Indonesia (Statistik Indonesia)*, various issues, Jakarta: BPS.

BPS (1995), *Statistik Dalam 50 Tahun Indonesia Merdeka*, Jakarta: BPS.

Braverman, A. and T.N. Srinivasan (1984), 'Agrarian Reforms in Developing Rural Economy Characterized by Interlinked Credit and Tenancy Markets', in H.P. Binswanger and M.R. Rosenzweig (eds), *Contractual Arrangements, Employment, and Wages in Rural Labor Markets in Asia*, New Haven and London: Yale U.P., pp. 63–81.

Breman, Jan (1980), *The Dessa on Java and the Early Colonial State*, Rotterdam: Erasmus University.

Breman, Jan (1983), *Control of Land and Labour in Colonial Java*, Leiden: KITLV.

Breman, Jan (1987), *Koelies, Planters and Koloniale Politiek*, Leiden: KITLV.

Brugmans, I.J., H.J. de Graaf, A.H. Joustra and A.G. Vromans (1960), *Nederlandsch-Indië onder Japanse Bezetting: Gegevens en Documenten over de Jaren 1942–1945* [The Netherlands-Indies under Japanese Occupation: Information and Documentation over the Years 1942–1945], Franeker: Wever (2nd edition).

Burger, D.H. (1975), *Sociologisch-economische geschiedenis van Indonesia*, Wageningen: Landbouwhogeschool.

Buringh, P., H.D.J. van Heemst and G. Staring (1975), *Computation of the Absolute Maximum Food Production of the World*, Wageningen: Agricultural University.

Burke, Paul, J. and Fredoun Z. Ahmadi-Esfahani (2006), 'Aid and Growth: A Study of South East Asia', *Journal of Asian Economics*, Vol. 17, No. 2, pp. 350–362.

Butzer, R., Y. Mundlak and D.F. Larson (2003), 'Intersectoral Migration in Southeast Asia: Evidence from Indonesia, Thailand, and the Philippines', *World Bank Policy Research Paper Series*, No. 2949.

Cain, P.J. and A.G. Hopkins (1993), *British Imperialism: Innovation and Expansion 1688–1914*, London: Longman.

Cameron, L. (2002), 'Growth With or Without Equity? The Distributional Impact of Indonesian Development', *Asian-Pacific Economic Literature*, Vol. 6, No. 2, pp. 1–17.

Campo, J.N.F.M. à (1992), *Koninklijke Paketvaart Maatschappij: Stoomvaart en staatsvorming in de Indonesische Archipel, 1888–1914* [Engines of Empire: Steamshipping and State Formation in Colonial Indonesia, 1888–1914], Hilversum: Verloren.

Campo, J.N.F.M. à (1998), 'Business Not as Usual: Dutch Shipping in Independent Indonesia, 1945–1958', *International Journal of Maritime History*, Vol. 10, No. 2, pp. 1–39.

Cardoso, E. and A. Helwege (1992), *Latin America's Economy: Diversity, Trends, and Conflicts*, Cambridge, MA: MIT Press.

Carey, P.B.R. (1975), 'Pangeran Dipanagara and the Making of the Java War', PhD thesis, Oxford, Magdalen College.

Carey, P.B.R. (2007), *The Power of Prophecy: Prince Dipanagara and the End of an Old Order in Java, 1785–1855*, Leiden: KITLV Press.

Cassing, John H. (2000), 'Economic Policy and Political Culture in Indonesia', *European Journal of Political Economy*, Vol. 16, pp. 159–171.

CBS (1947), 'De Economische Toestand van Nederlandsch-Indië tijdens de Japanse Bezetting, 1942–45' [The Economic Situation in the Netherlands-Indies during the Japanese Occupation, 1942–1945], *Statistische en Econometrische Onderzoekingen*, Vol. 2, No. 4, pp. 118–127.

Chandra, S. (2000), 'What the Numbers Really Tell Us about the Decline of the Opium Regie', *Indonesia*, Vol. 70, pp. 101–23.

Chandra, S. (2002), 'The Role of Government Policy in Increasing Drug Use: Java, 1875–1914', *Journal of Economic History*, Vol. 62, pp. 1116–21.

Chen, E. (1997), 'The Total Factor Productivity Debate: Determinants of Economic Growth in East Asia', *Asian-Pacific Economic Literature*, Vol. 11, No. 1, pp. 18–39.

Christanty, Linda and Raymond Atje (2004), 'Policy and Regulatory Developments in the Forestry Sector Since 1967', CSIS Working Paper, Jakarta.

Chuan, H. and R.A. Kraus (1975), *Mid-Ch'ing Rice Markets and Trade: An Essay in Price History*, Cambridge, MA: East Asian Research Center.

Clark, Gregory (1988), 'The Cost of Capital and Medieval Agricultural Technique', *Explorations in Economic History*, Vol. 25, pp. 265–294.

Cole, David C. and Betty F. Slade (1996), *Building a Modern Financial System: The Indonesian Experience*, Cambridge: Cambridge University Press.

Cole, David C. and Betty F. Slade (1998), 'Why Has Indonesia's Financial Crisis Been So Bad?', *Bulletin of Indonesian Economic Studies*, Vol. 34, No. 2, pp. 61–66.

Collier, Paul (2007), *The Bottom Billion: Why the Poorest Countries are Failing and What Can Be Done About It*, Oxford: Oxford University Press.

Collins, S.M. and B.P. Bosworth (2003), 'The Empirics of Growth: An Update', *Brooking Papers on Economic Activity*, No. 2, pp. 113–206.

Conceiçao, P. and J.K. Galbraith (2001), 'Constructing Long, Dense Time Series of Inequality Using the Theil Index', in J.K. Galbraith and M. Berner (eds), *Inequality and Industrial Change: A Global View*, Cambridge, New York and Melbourne: Cambridge University Press.

Crafts, N. and A.J. Venables (2003), 'Globalization in History: A Geographical Perspective', in M. Bordo, A.M Taylor and J.G. Williamson (eds), *Globalization in Historical Perspective*, Chicago: University of Chicago Press, pp. 323–364.

Cramer, J.C.W. (1929), *Het volkscredietwezen in Nederlandsch-Indië*, Paris, Amsterdam: H.J.

Crayen, Dorothee and Joerg Baten (2010), 'Global Trends in Numeracy 1820–1949 and its Implications for Long-Run Growth', *Explorations in Economic History*, Vol. 47, No. 1, pp. 82–99.

Creutzberg, P. and P. Boomgaard (1975–1996) (eds), *Changing Economy in Indonesia*, 16 volumes, Amsterdam: Royal Tropical Institute.

Cribb, Robert and Colin Brown (1995), *Modern Indonesia: A History Since 1945*, London: Longman.

CSIS (2002), 'Review of Political Development: The First 100 Days of Megawati's Administration: A Question of Willingness and Capability', *The Indonesian Quarterly*, Vol. 30, No. 1, pp. 12–19.

De Bree, L. (1928), *Gedenkboek van de Javasche Bank 1828–24 januari–1928*, 2 vols, Weltevreden: Kolff.

De Bruin, Jan (2003), *Het Indische Spoor in Oorlogstijd. De Spoor- en Tramwegmaatschappijen in de Vuurlinie, 1873–1949* [The Netherlands-Indies Railway during Wartime: The Rail- and Tramways in the Line of Fire, 1873–1949], Rosmalen: Uquilair.

De Bruyn Kops, G.F. (1857), *Statistiek van den Handel en de Scheepvaart op Java en Madura*, Batavia: Lange & Co.

De Groot, H.A. (1888), *Studie over rijstprijzen*, Soerabaija: Fuhri.

Deininger, K. and L. Squire (1996), 'A New Data Set Measuring Income Inequality', *The World Bank Economic Review*, Vol. 10, No. 3, pp. 565–591.

De Moor, T. and J.L. van Zanden (2010), 'Girlpower: The European Marriage Pattern (EMP) and Labour Markets in the North Sea Region in the Late Medieval and Early Modern Period', *Economic History Review*, Vol. 63, No. 1, pp. 1–33.

De Soto, H. (2000), *The Mystery of Capital: Why Capitalism Triumphs in the West and Fails Everywhere Else*, New York: Basic Books.

Deuster, Paul R. (2002), 'Survey of Recent Developments', *Bulletin of Indonesian Economic Studies*, Vol. 38, No. 1, pp. 5–37.

De Waal, E. (1865), *Aanteekeningen over koloniale onderwerpen*, 's-Gravenhage: Martinus Nijhoff.

Diamond, J. (1997), *Guns, Germs, and Steel*, New York: W.W. Norton & Co.

Dick, Howard W. (1985), 'Interisland Shipping: Progress, Problems and Prospects', *Bulletin of Indonesian Economic Studies*, Vol. 21, No. 2, pp. 95–114.

Dick, Howard W. (1987), *The Indonesian Interisland Shipping Industry: An Analysis of Competition and Regulation*, Singapore: Institute of Southeast Asian Studies.

Dick, Howard W. (2000), 'Representations of Development in 19th and 20th Century Indonesia', *Bulletin of Indonesian Economic Studies*, Vol. 36, No. 1, pp. 185–207.

Dick, Howard W. (2001), 'The Challenges of Sustainable Development: Economic, Institutional and Political Interactions, 1900–2000', in Grayson Lloyd and Shannon Smith (eds), *Indonesia Today: Challenges of History*, Singapore: ISEAS, pp. 200–215.

Dick, Howard W. (2002), 'The Frmation of the Nation State', in Howard Dick, Vincent Houben, J. Thomas Lindblad and Thee Kian Wie (eds), *The Emergence of a National Economy: An Economic History of Indonesia, 1800–2000*, St. Leonard: Allen & Unwin, 2002, pp. 153–194.

Dick, H.W. and D. Forbes (1992), 'Transport and Communications: A Quiet Revolution', in Anne Booth (ed.) *The Oil Boom and After: Indonesian Economic Policy and Performance in the Soeharto Era*, Singapore: Oxford University Press, pp. 258–282.

Dick, H.W., V.J. Houben, J. Th. Lindblad and Thee Kian Wie (2002), *The Emergence of a National Economy: An Economic History of Indonesia, 1800–2000*, Crows Nest, NSW: Allen & Unwin.

Diehl, F.W. (1993), 'Revenue Farming and Colonial Finances in the Netherlands East Indies, 1816–1925', in J. Butcher and H. Dick (eds), *The Rise and Fall of Revenue Farming in Southeast Asia*, Basingstoke: Macmillan, pp. 196–232.

Djojohadikoesoemo, Soemitro (1943), *Het volkscredietwezen in de depressie*, Haarlem: de erven F Bohn.

Dollar, David and Aart Kraay (2004), 'Trade, Growth, and Poverty,' *Economic Journal*, Royal Economic Society, Vol. 114(493), pp. F22–F49, 02.

Dowling, J. Malcolm and Peter Summers (1998), 'Total Factor Productivity and Economic Growth: Issues for Asia', *The Economic Record*, Vol. 74, No. 225, pp. 170–185.

Dros, N. (1992), 'Wages 1820–1940', *Changing Economy in Indonesia*, Vol. 13, Amsterdam: Royal Tropical Institute.

Easterly, William and Ross Levine (1997), 'Africa's Growth Tragedy: Policies and Ethnic Divisions', *Quarterly Journal of Economics*, Vol. 112, No. 4, pp. 1203–1250.

Elson, Robert E. (1979), 'Cane Burning in the Pasaruan Area: An Expression of Social Discontent', in F. van Anrooij, D. Kolff and J.Th. van Laanen (eds) *Between People and Statistics*, The Hague: Martinus Nijhoff, pp. 219–234.

Elson, Robert E. (1985), 'The Famine in Demak and Grobogan in 1849–50: Its Causes and Circumstances', *Review of Indonesian and Malaysian Affairs*, Vol. 19, No. 1, pp. 39–85.

Elson, Robert E. (1994), *Village Java under the Cultivation System*, Sydney: Allen & Unwin.

Elson, Robert E. (2001), *Suharto: A Political Biography*, Cambridge: Cambridge University Press.

Epstein, Stephen R. (2000), *Freedom and Growth: The Rise of States and Markets in Europe 1300–1750*, London: Routledge.

Fabricant, Solomon (1942), *Employment in Manufacturing, 1899–1939: An Analysis of its Relation to the Volume of Production*, Cambridge, MA: NBER.

Fane, G. (2000), 'Survey of Recent Developments', *Bulletin of Indonesian Economic Studies*, Vol. 36, No. 1, pp. 13–44.

Fane, G. and Condon, T. (1996) 'Trade Reform in Indonesia, 1987–1995', *Bulletin of Indonesian Economic Studies*, Vol. 32, No. 3, December, pp. 33–54.

Fasseur, C. (1975), *Kultuurstelsel en Koloniale Baten. De Nederlandse exploitatie van Java 1840–1860*, Leiden: Universitaire Pers.

Feeney, David (1989), 'The Decline of Property Rights in Thailand, 1800–1913', *Journal of Economic History*, Vol. 49, No. 2, pp. 285–296.

Feith, Herbert (1962), *The Decline of Constitutional Democracy in Indonesia*, Ithaca, NY: Cornell University Press.

Feith, Herbert (1964), 'Indonesia', in George McTurnan Kahin (ed.), *Governments and Politics of Southeast Asia*, Ithaca, NY: Cornell University Press.

Fernando, M.R. (1993), 'Growth of Non-Agricultural Indigenous Economic Activities in Java, 1820–1880', in J. Th. Lindblad (ed.), *New Challenges in the Modern Economic History of Indonesia*, Leiden: Programme of Indonesian Studies, pp. 89–109.

Fernando, M.R. and D. Bulbeck (eds) (1992), *Chinese Economic Activity in Netherlands India: Selected Translations from the Dutch*, Singapore: Institute of Southeast Asian Studies.

Fisman, Raymond (2001), 'Estimating the Value of Political Connections', *The American Economic Review*, Vol. 91, No. 4, pp. 1095–1102.

Fogel, Robert W. (1994), 'Economic Growth, Population Theory, and Physiology: The Bearing of Long-Term Processes on the Making of Economic Policy', *American Economic Review*, Vol. 84, No. 3, pp. 369–394.

Földvari, P., J. Gall, D. Marks and B. Van Leeuwen (2010), 'Indonesia's Regional Welfare Development, 1900–1990: New Anthropometric Evidence', paper presented at the Asian Historical Economics Congress, Beijing, May 2010.

François, J.F. and H. Rojas-Romagosa (2005), 'The Construction and Interpretation of Combined Cross Section and Time-Series Inequality Datasets', World Bank Policy Research Working Paper 3748.

Frankel, Jeffrey A. and David Romer (1999), 'Does Trade Cause Growth?', *American Economic Review*, Vol. 89, No. 3, pp. 379–399.

Frankema, E. (2008), 'The Historical Evolution of Inequality in Latin America: A Comparative Analysis, 1870–2000', PhD thesis, University of Groningen.

Frankema, E. (2009), *Has Latin America Always Been Unequal? A Comparative Study of Asset and Income Inequality in the Long Twentieth Century*, Global Economic History Series 3, Brill: Leiden.

Frankema, E. and D. Marks (2009), 'Was It Really "Growth with Equity" under Soeharto? A Theil Analysis of Indonesian Income Inequality, 1961–2002', *Economics and Finance in Indonesia*, Vol. 57, No. 1, pp. 48–80.

Frankema, E. and D. Marks (2010), 'Growth, Stability, and Equity? Re-assessing Indonesian Inequality from a Comparative Perspective', *Economic History of Developing Regions*, Vol. 25, No. 1, pp. 75–104.

Fruin, Thomas A. (1947), *Het Economische Aspect van het Indonesische Vraagstuk* [The Economic Aspect of the Indonesian Issue], Amsterdam: Vrij Nederland.

Fujita, M., P. Krugman and A.J. Venables (1999), *The Spatial Economy*, Cambridge, MA: MIT Press.

Gaastra, F.S. (2006), 'De amfioensocieteit. Een gepriviligeerde handelsonderneming onder de vleugels van de VOC, 1745–1794', in M. Ebben and P. Wagenaar (eds) *De Cirkel Doorbroken*, Leiden: Instituut voor Geschiedenis, pp. 101–116.

Galbraith, J.K. and H. Kum (2005), 'Estimating the Inequality of Household Incomes: A Statistical Approach to the Creation of a Dense and Consistent Global Data Set', *Review of Income and Wealth*, Vol. 51, No. 1, pp. 115–143.

Galiani, Sebastian and Sukkoo Kim (2008), 'Political Centralization and Urban Primacy:

Evidence from National and Provincial Capitals in the Americas', in *Understanding Long-Run Economic Growth: Essays in Honor of Kenneth L. Sokoloff*, Cambridge, MA: NBER.

Gallup, J.L., J.D. Sachs and A.D. Mellinger (1998), 'Geography and Economic Development', NBER Working Paper No. 6849.

Galor, Oded and David N. Weil (2000), 'Population, Technology and Growth: From the Malthusian Regime to the Demographic Transition', *American Economic Review*, Vol. 110, No. 4, pp. 806–828.

Glasburner, Bruce (1971), 'Economic Policy-Making in Indonesia, 1950–1963', in B. Glasburner (ed.), *The Economy of Indonesia: Selected Readings*, Ithaca, NY: Cornell University Press, pp. 70–98.

Gonggrijp, G. and J.H. Boeke (1966), *Indonesian Economics: The Concept of Dualism in Theory and Practice*, The Hague: W. van Hoeve.

Gooszen, H. (1999), *A Demographic History of the Indonesian Archipelago, 1880–1942*, Leiden: KITLV Press.

Gouka, N.G.B. (2001), *De petitie-Soetardjo: een Hollandse misser in Indië? (1936–1938)*, Amsterdam: Rozenburg Publishers.

Hageman, J. (1859), 'Aanteekeningen nopens de industrie, handel en nijverheid van Soerabaja', *Tijdschrift voor nijverheid en landbouw in Nederlandsch Indie*, Vol. 5, pp. 137–152.

Hall, R. and C.I. Jones (1999), 'Why Do Some Countries Produce So Much More Output per Worker than Others?', *Quarterly Journal of Economics*, Vol. 114, No. 1, pp. 83–116.

Hanson, J.R. (1980), *Trade in Transition: Exports from the Third World, 1840–1900*, New York: Academic Press.

Hasselman, C.J. (1914), *Algemeen overzicht van de uitkomsten van het welvaartsonderzoek, gehouden op Java en Madoera in 1904/05*, 's-Gravenhage: Nijhoff.

Hatta, M. (1957), *The Co-operative Movement in Indonesia*, Ithaca: Cornell University Press.

Head, K. and Th. Mayer (2004), 'The Empirics of Agglomeration and Arade', in V. Henderson and J.-F. Thisse (eds), *Handbook of Regional and Urban Economics, Volume IV*, Amsterdam: North Holland, pp. 2609–2665.

Helpman, E. (2004), *The Mystery of Economic Growth*, Cambridge, MA: Harvard University Press.

Henderson, J. Vernon and Ari Kuncoro (2006), 'Sick of Local Government Corruption? Vote Islamic', NBER Working Paper No. 12110.

Henderson, Vernon (2003), 'The Urbanization Process and Economic Growth: The So-What Question', *Journal of Economic Growth*, Vol. 8, pp. 47–71.

Henley, David (2004), 'Custom, Culture, and Koperasi: The Ideological Appropriation of the Cooperative Ideal in Indonesia', paper prepared for the workshop on Adat Revivalism in Indonesia's Democratic Tradition, Batam.

Hertzmark, Donald I. (2007), 'Pertamina: Indonesia's State-Owned Oil Company', The Baker Institute for Public Policy, Rice University.

Higgins, Benjamin (1957), *Indonesia's Economic Stabilization and Development*, New York: Institute of Pacific Relations.

Hill, Hal (1992), 'Manufacturing Industry', in Anne Booth (ed.), *The Oil Boom and After: Indonesian Economic Policy and Performance in the Soeharto Era*, Oxford: Oxford University Press, pp. 204–257.

Hill, Hal (1998), 'The Indonesian Economy: The Strange and Sudden Death of a Tiger', in Geoff Forrester and R.J. May (eds), *The Fall of Soeharto*, Bathurst: Crawford House, pp. 93–103.

Hill, Hal (1999), *The Indonesian Economy in Crisis: Causes, Consequences and Lessons*, Singapore: ISEAS.

Hill, Hal (2000), *The Indonesian Economy*, Cambridge: Cambridge University Press.

Hill, Hal and Takashi Shiraishi (2007), 'Indonesia after the Asian Crisis', *Asian Economic Policy Review*, Vol. 2, No. 1, pp. 123–141.

Hobson, J.A. (1902) *Imperialism: A Study*, London: Cosimo.

Hofman, Bert, Ella Rodrick-Jones and Thee Kian Wie (2004), *Indonesia: Rapid Growth, Weak Institutions*, Jakarta: World Bank. [A case study from: 'Scaling Up Poverty Reduction: A Global Learning Process and Conference', Shanghai, 25–27 May 2004.]

Horlings, E. (1995), *The Economic Development of the Dutch Service Sector 1800–1850: Trade and Transport in a Premodern Economy*, Amsterdam: NEHA.

Houben, Vincent J.H. (1999), 'Introduction: The Coolie System in Colonial Indonesia', in Vincent J.H. Houben and J. Thomas Lindblad (eds), *Coolie Labour in Colonial Indonesia*, Wiesbaden: Harroassowitz Verlag, pp. 1–25.

Hugenholtz, W.R. (1986), 'Famine and Food Supply in Java 1830–1914', in C.A. Bayly and D.H.A. Kolff (eds), *Two Colonial Empires*, Dordrecht: Martinus Nijhoff, pp. 155–88.

Hugo, Graeme, Terence H. Hull, Valerie J. Hull and Gavin W. Jones (1987), *The Demographic Dimension in Indonesian Development*, Singapore: Oxford University Press.

Hulten, C.R. (2001), 'Total Factor Productivity: A Short Biography', in C.R. Hulten, E.R. Dean and M.J. Harper (eds), *New Developments in Productivity Analysis*, Chicago: University of Chicago Press.

Hunter, Guy (1966), *South-East Asia: Race, Culture, and Nation*, London: Institute of Race Relations.

ILO (1966–1995), *Yearbook of Labour Statistics*, various issues, Geneva: ILO.

ILO (1993), *Statistics of Employment in the Informal Sector: Report of the XVth International Conference of Labour Statisticians*, 19–28 January, Geneva.

Jacob, Jojo (2005), 'Late Industrialization and Structural Change: Indonesia, 1975–2000', *Oxford Development Studies*, Vol. 33, No. 3–4, pp. 427–451.

Javasche Courant, officieel nieuwsblad (1828–1853), Batavia: Landsdrukkerij.

Johnson, Simon, Peter Boone, Alasidir Breach and Eric Friedman (2000), 'Corporate Governance in the Asian Financial Crisis', *Journal of Financial Economics*, Vol. 58, pp. 141–186.

Jomo, K.S. (1997), *Southeast Asia's Misunderstood Miracle: Industrial Policy and Economic Development in Thailand, Malaysia and Indonesia*, Boulder: Westview Press.

Jones, Gavin W. (2001), 'Which Indonesian Women Marry Youngest and Why?', *Journal of Southeast Asian Studies*, Vol. 32, No. 1, pp. 67–78.

Jonker, Joost and Jan Luiten van Zanden (2007), *From Challenger to Industry Leader, 1890–1939: A History of Royal Dutch Shell*, Vol. 1, Oxford: Oxford University Press.

Kahin, George M (1952), *Nationalism and Revolution in Indonesia*, Ithaca: Cornell University Press.

Kaufmann, Daniel, Aart Kraay and Massimo Mastruzzi (2009), 'Governance Matters VIII: Aggregate and Individual Governance Indicators 1996–2008', World Bank Policy Research Paper, No. 4978.

Kaufmann, Daniel, Aart Kraay and Massimo Mastruzzi (2010), 'The Worldwide Governance Indicators: Methodology and Analytical Issues', Brookings Institution, Working Paper.

Kenward, Lloyd R. (2004), 'Survey of Recent Developments', *Bulletin of Indonesian Economic Studies*, Vol. 40, No. 1, pp. 9–35.

Kindleberger, Charles P. (1978), *Manias, Panics, and Crashes: A History of Financial Crises*, London/Basingstoke: Macmillan Press.

'Koloniaal Verslag' (1880–1882), report on the state of the colonies included in *Handelingen der Staten Generaal*, Den Haag: Landsdrukkerij.

Komlos, John (1989), *Nutrition and Economic Development in the Eighteenth-Century Habsburg Monarchy: An Anthropometric History*, Princeton: Princeton University Press.

Komlos, John (1994), *Stature, Living Standards and Economic Development: Essays in Anthropometric History*, Chicago: University of Chicago Press.

Komlos, John and Joerg Baten (1998), *Studies on the Biological Standard of Living in Comparative Perspective*, Stuttgart: Franz Steiner Verlag.

Korthals Altes, W.L. (1986), *De betalingsbalans van Nederlandsch-Indië 1822–1939*, Rotterdam: Erasmus.

Korthals Altes, W.L. (1994), 'Prices (Non-rice) 1814–1940', *Changing Economy in Indonesia*, Vol. 15, Amsterdam: Royal Tropical Institute.

Krugman, P. (1994), 'The Myth of Asia's Miracle', *Foreign Affairs*, Vol. 73, No. 6, pp. 62–78.

Krugman, P. (1998), 'What Happened to Asia?', mimeo, MIT.

Krugman, P. and R. Livas (1992), 'Trade Policy and Third World Metropolis', NBER Working Paper No. 4238.

Kuitenbrouwer, M. (1985), *Nederland en de opkomst van het moderne Imperialisme*, Amsterdam: De Bataafsche Leeuw.

Kuitenbrouwer, M. (1994), 'Drie omwentelingen in de historiografie van het imperialisme in Engeland en Nederland', *Tijdschrift voor geschiedenis*, Vol. 107, pp. 559–85.

Kurasawa, Aiko (1997), 'Rice Shortage and Transportation', in Peter Post and Elly Touwen-Bouwsma (eds), *Japan, Indonesia and the War: Myths and Realities*, Leiden: KITLV Press, pp. 111–133.

Kuznets, S. (1966), *Modern Economic Growth*, New Haven: Yale University Press.

Kuznets, S. (1971), *Economic Growth of Nations: Total Output and Production*, Cambridge, MA: Harvard University Press.

Kymmell, J. (1992), *Geschiedenis van de Algemene Banken in Nederland, 1860–1914*, Amsterdam: NIBE.

Lains, P. (2004), 'Structural Change and Economic Growth in Portugal, 1950–1990', in S. Heikkinen and J.L. van Zanden (eds), *Explorations in Economic Growth*, Amsterdam: Aksant, pp. 321–340.

Langeveld, H. (1978), 'Arbeidstoestanden op de ondernemingen ter Oostkust van Sumatra tussen 1920 en 1940', *Economisch- en sociaal-historisch jaarboek*, No. 41, pp. 294–368.

Langeveld, Herman J. (1998), *Hendrikus Colijn, 1869–1944*, Amsterdam: Balans.

Lankaster, Tom (2004), 'Asian Drama: The Pursuit Of Modernization In India And Indonesia', *Asian Affairs*, Vol. XXXV, No. III, pp. 291–304.

Lau, L.J. and J. Park (2003), 'The Sources of East Asian Economic Growth Revisited', paper prepared for the Conference on International and Development Economics, Cornell University, Ithaca, September 2003.

Legge, J.D. (1972), *Sukarno: A Political Biography*, London: Lane.

Leigh, A. and P. van der Eng (2006), 'Top Incomes in Indonesia, 1920–2003', paper presented at the XIV International Economic History Congress, Helsinki, Finland, 21–25 August 2006.

Leigh, Andrew and Pierre van der Eng (2009), 'Inequality in Indonesia: What Can We Learn from Top Incomes?', *Journal of Public Economics*, Vol. 93, No. 1–2, pp. 209–212.

Leinbach, Th.R. (1986), 'Transport Development in Indonesia: Progress, Problems and Policies under the New Order', in Colin Mac Andrew (ed.) *Central Government and Local Development in Indonesia*, Singapore: Oxford University Press, pp. 190–220.

Leinbach, Th.R. (1989), 'Transport Policies in Conflict: Deregulation, Subsidies, and Regional Development in Indonesia', *Transportation Research*, Vol. 23A, No. 6, pp. 467–475.

Leinbach, Th.R. and Chia Lin Sien (1989), *South-East Asian Transport: Issues in Development*, Singapore: Oxford University Press.

Lewis, Peter M. (2007), *Growing Apart: Oil, Politics, and Economic Change in Indonesia and Nigeria*, Ann Arbor: University of Michigan Press.

Lindblad, J. Thomas (1988), 'De handel tussen Nederland en Nederlands-Indië, 1874–1939', *Economisch- en sociaal-historisch jaarboek*, Vol. 51, pp. 240–298.

Lindblad, J. Thomas (1989), 'De opkomst van de buitengewesten', in A.H.P. Clemens and J.Th. Lindblad (eds), *Het belang van de Buitengewesten 1870–1942*, Amsterdam: NEHA, pp. 1–39.

Lindblad, J. Thomas (1991), 'Foreign Investment in Late-Colonial and Post-Colonial Indonesia', *Economic and Social History in the Netherlands*, Vol. 3, pp. 183–208.

Lindblad, J. Thomas (1999), 'Conclusion', in Vincent J.H. Houben and J. Thomas Lindblad (eds), *Coolie Labour in Colonial Indonesia*, Wiesbaden: Harroassowitz Verlag, pp. 231–241.

Lindblad, J. Thomas (2006), 'Macroeconomic Consequences of Decolonization in Indonesia', paper presented at the XIVth Conference of the International Economic History Association, Helsinki, 21–25 August 2006.

Lindblad, J. Thomas (2008), *Bridges to New Business; The Economic Decolonization of Indonesia*, Leiden: KITLV Press.

Lucas, Robert E. (1988), 'On the Mechanics of Economic Development', *Journal of Monetary Economics*, Vol. 22, No. 1, pp. 3–42.

Maat, Harro (2001), *Science Cultivating Practice: A History of Agricultural Science in the Netherlands and its Colonies 1863/1986*, Wageningen: Ponsen & Looijen.

McCawley, Peter (1981), 'The Growth of the Industrial Sector', in Anne Booth and Peter McCawley (eds) *The Indonesian Economy During the Soeharto Era*, Kuala Lumpur: Oxford University Press, pp. 61–101.

McCloskey, D. and J. Nash (1984), 'Corn at Interest: The Extent and Cost of Grain Storage in Medieval England', *American Economic Review*, Vol. 74, pp. 174–187.

MacIntyre, Andrew (1999), 'Political Institutions and the Economic Crisis in Thailand and Indonesia', in H.W. Arndt and H. Hill (eds), *Southeast Asia's Economic Crisis: Origins, Lessons, and the Way Forward*, Singapore: ISEAS, pp. 16–27.

McLeod, Ross (1997), 'Postscript to the Survey of Recent Developments: On Causes and Cures for the Rupiah Crisis,' *Bulletin of Indonesian Economic Studies*, Vol 33, No. 3, pp. 35–52.

McLeod, Ross H. (2000), 'Survey of Recent Developments', *Bulletin of Indonesian Economic Studies*, Vol. 36, No. 2, pp. 5–41.

Maddison, A. (1987), 'Growth and Slowdown in Advanced Capitalist Countries: Techniques of Quantitative Assessment', *Journal of Economic Literature*, Vol. 25, No. 2, pp. 649–698.

Maddison, A. (1988), 'Ultimate and Proximate Growth Causality: A Critique of Mancur

Olson on the Rise and Decline of Nations', *Scandinavian Economic History Review*, Vol. 36, No. 2, pp. 25–29.

Maddison, A. (1989a), 'Dutch Income in and from Indonesia', in A. Maddison and G. Prince (eds), *Economic Growth in Indonesia*, Dordrecht: Foris Publications, pp. 15–41.

Maddison, A. (1989b), *The World Economy in the 20th Century*, Paris: OECD.

Maddison, A. (2001), *The World Economy: A Millennial Perspective*, Paris: OECD.

Maddison, A. (2003), *The World Economy: Historical Statistics*, Paris: OECD.

Manning, C. (1998), *Indonesian Labour in Transition: An East Asian Success Story?*, Cambridge: Cambridge University Press.

Mansvelt, W.M.F. (1924–1926), *Geschiedenis van de Nederlandsche Handelmaatschappij*, Vol. 2, Haarlem: Enschede & Zn.

Marks, Daan (2009a), *Accounting for Services: The Economic Development of the Indonesian Service Sector, ca. 1900–2000*, Amsterdam: Aksant Academic Publishers.

Marks, Daan (2009b), 'The Economic Consequences of Decolonization: The "Special Case" of Indonesia', in: J.Th. Lindblad and P. Post (eds), *Indonesian Economic Decolonization in Regional and International Perspective*, Leiden: KITLV Press.

Marks, Daan (2010a), 'Unity or Diversity? On the Integration and Efficiency of Rice Markets in Indonesia, c. 1920–2006', *Explorations in Economic History*, Vol. 47, No. 3, pp. 310–324.

Marks, Daan (2010b), 'The Lost Decades? Economic Disintegration in Indonesia's Early Independence Period', *Itinerario, International Journal on the History of European Expansion and Global Interaction*, Vol. 34, No. 1, pp. 77–95.

Marks, D. and J. van Lottum (2010), 'The Determinants of Internal Migration in a Developing Country: Quantitative Evidence for Indonesia, 1930–2000', Cambridge Working Papers in Economics, No. 1013.

Marks, Stephen V. (2004), 'Survey of Recent Developments', *Bulletin of Indonesian Economic Studies*, Vol. 40, No. 2, pp. 151–175.

Mayer, Th. (2008), 'Market Potential and Development', CEPR Discussion Paper, No. 6798, CEPR: London.

Mears, Leon A. (1961), *Rice Marketing in the Republik of Indonesia*, Djakarta: University of Indonesia.

Mears, Leon A. (1981), *The New Rice Economy of Indonesia*, Yokyakarta: Gadjah Mada University Press.

Mears, Leon A. (1984), 'Rice and Food Self-Sufficiency in Indonesia', *Bulletin of Indonesian Economic Studies*, Vol. 20, No. 2, pp. 122–138.

Meijer Ranneft, J.W. and W. Huender (1926), *Belasting Inlandsche Bevolking*, Weltevreden: Landsdrukkerji.

Mellegers, Joost (2004), *Public Finance of Indonesia 1817–1940*. Website containing datasets of public finance at www.iisg.nl/indonesianeconomy/publicfinance.html. Accessed 15 May 2010.

Milanovic, Branko, Peter Lindert and Jeffrey G. Williamson (2007), 'Measuring Ancient Inequality', NBER Working Paper No. 13,550.

Ministry of Colonial Affairs 1814–49, National Archive, The Hague.

Mokyr, Joel (1983), *Why Ireland Starved*, London: Allen & Unwin.

Mollema, J.C. (1927), *Gedenkboek Billiton 1852–1927*, Den Haag: Nijhoff.

Morley, S. (2001), *The Income Distribution Problem in Latin America and the Caribbean*, Santiago de Chile: UN, ECLAC.

Mulder, N. (1999), *The Economic Performance of the Service Sector in Brazil, Mexico and the USA*, No. 4, Groningen Growth and Development Centre Monographs Series: Groningen.

Myrdal, Gunnar (1968), *Asian Drama: An Inquiry into the Poverty of Nations*, 3 vols, Harmondsworth, Middlesex: Penguin Books.

Nagtegaal, L. (1996), *Riding the Dutch Tiger: The Dutch East Indies Company and the Northeast Coast of Java, 1680–1743*, Leiden: KITLV Press.

Nieboer, H.J. (1910), *Slavery as an Industrial System: Ethnological Researches*, The Hague: Nijhoff.

Nishijima Shigetada and Kishi Koicho (eds) (1963), *Japanese Military Administration in Indonesia* [Translation of the Japanese-language book *Indonesia ni Okeru Nihon Gunsei no Kenyuku*, edited by the Okuma Memorial Social Sciences Research Institute, Waseda University], Washington DC: US Department of Commerce.

North, Douglass C. (1981), *Structure and Change in Economic History*, New York: Norton.

North, Douglass C. (1990), *Institutions, Institutional Change and Economic Performance*, Cambridge: Cambridge University Press.

North, Douglass C. and Robert Paul Thomas (1973), *The Rise of the Western World: A New Economic History*, New York: Cambridge University Press.

North, Douglass C. and Barry Weingast (1989), 'Constitutions and Commitment: Evolution of Institutions Governing Public Choice in Seventeenth Century England', *Journal of Economic History*, Vol. 49, No. 4, pp. 803–832.

Nyberg, A.J. (1976), 'A Bias in Susenas Data', *Bulletin of Indonesian Economic Studies*, Vol. 12, No. 1, pp. 110–111.

Paauw, Douglas S. (1960), *Financing Economic Development: The Indonesian Case*, Glencoe, Illinois: Free Press of Glencoe.

Paauw, Douglas S. (1963), 'From Colonial to Guided Economy', in Ruth McVey (ed.) *Indonesia*, New Haven: Hraf Press.

Pack, Howard and Janet Rothenberg Pack (1990), 'Is Foreign Aid Fungible? The Case of Indonesia', *The Economic Journal*, Vol. 100, No. 399, pp. 188–194.

Pangestu, Mari (1991), 'The Role of the Private Sector in Indonesia: Deregulation and Privatisation', *The Indonesian Quarterly*, Vol. 19, No. 1, pp. 27–52.

Parenti, A. (1942), *Prezzi e mercato del grano a Siena, 1546–1785*, Firenze: Pubblicazioni della r. università degli studi di Firenze. Facoltà di economia e commercio XIX, Scuola di statistica.

Patten, Richard H., Jay K. Rosengard and Don E. Johnston, Jr. (2001), 'Microfinance Success Amidst Marcoeconomic Failure: The Experience of Bank Rakyat Indonesia during East Asian Crisis', *World Development*, Vol. 29, No. 6, pp. 1057–1069.

Patunru, Arianto A. and Christian von Luebke (2010), 'Survey of Recent Developments', *Bulletin of Indonesian Economic Studies*, Vol. 46, No. 1, pp. 7–31.

Penders, C.L.M. (1984), 'The "Ethical" Policy in Action: The Effect of Cheaper Credit Facilities and Agricultural Extention in Bojonegoro and Tulungagung', paper presented at the Conference on Economic Growth and Structural Change in Indonesia 1820–1940, Groningen.

Penny, David H. (1969), 'Indonesia', in R.T. Shand (ed.), *Agricultural Development in Asia*, Canberra: Australian National University Press, pp. 251–279.

Piketty, T. (2003), 'Income Inequality in France, 1901–1998', *Journal of Political Economy*, Vol. 111, No. 5, pp. 1004–1042.

Piketty, T. and E. Saez (2003), 'Income Inequality in the United States, 1913–1998', *Quarterly Journal of Economics*, Vol. 118, No. 1, pp. 1–39.

Piketty, T. and E. Saez (2006), 'The Evolution of Top Incomes: A Historical and International Perspective,' NBER Working Paper No. 11955.

Pomerleano, Michael (1998), 'Corporate Finance Lessons from the East Asian Crisis', *Public Policy for the Private Sector*, Note No. 155.

Popkin, S.L. (1979), *The Rational Peasant: The Political Economy of Rural Society in Vietnam*, Berkeley: University of California Press.

Poynder, Nick (1999), 'Grain Storage in Theory and History', paper presented at the Third Conference of European Historical Economics Society, Lisbon.

Prados de Escosura, L. (2006), 'Growth, Inequality and Poverty in Spain, 1850–2000: Evidence and Speculation', Working Papers in Economic History wp06–06, Universidad Carlos III, Departamento de Historia Económica e Instituciones.

Prawiro, R. (1998), *Indonesia's Struggle for Economic Development: Pragmatism in Action*, Kuala Lumpur: Oxford University Press.

PREALC (1982), *Mercado de Trabajo en Cifras, 1950–1980* [Labour Market in Numbers, 1950–1980], Santiago de Chile: ILO, ECLAC.

Prince, Ge (1989), 'Dutch Economic Policy in Indonesia, 1870–1942', in Angus Maddison and Ge Prince (eds), *Economic Growth in Indonesia, 1820–1940*, Dordrecht: Foris Publications, pp. 200–230.

Purwanto, Bambang (2009), 'Economic Decolonization and the Rise of Indonesian Military Business', in J.Th. Lindblad and P. Post (eds) *Indonesian Economic Decolonization in Regional and International Perspective*, Leiden: KITLV Press.

Radelet, Steven and Jeffrey Sachs (1998), 'The East Asian Crisis: Diagnosis, Remedies, Prospects', *Brookings Papers on Economic Activity*, No. 1.

Redding, S. and A.J. Venables (2004), 'Economic Geography and International Inequality', *Journal of International Economics*, Vol. 62, No. 1, pp. 53–82.

Reid, Anthony (1980), 'Indonesia: From Briefcase to Samurai', in Alfred W. McCoy (ed.) *Southeast Asia under Japanese Occupation*, New Haven: Yale University, pp. 16–32.

Reid, A.J.S. (1988–93), *Southeast Asia in the Age of Commerce, 1450–1680*, 2 vols, New Haven: Yale University Press.

Repetta, R. (1989), *Wasting Assets: Natural Resources in the National Accounts*, Washington: World Resources Institute.

Resosudarmo, Budy P. and Yogi Vidyattama (2006), 'Regional Income Disparity in Indonesia: A Panel Data Analysis', *ASEAN Economic Bulletin*, Vol. 23, No. 1, pp. 31–44.

Resosudarmo, Budy P. and Arief A. Yusuf (2009), 'Survey of Recent Developments', *Bulletin of Indonesian Economic Studies*, Vol. 45, No. 3, pp. 287–315.

Ricklefs, M.C. (2001), *A History of Modern Indonesia Since c. 1200*, Basingstoke: Palgrave.

Robertson, P. (2000), 'Diminished Returns? Growth and Investment in East Asia', *The Economic Record*, Vol. 76, No. 235, pp. 343–353.

Robison, Richard (1986), *Indonesia: The Rise of Capital*, Sydney: Allen and Unwin.

Rock, Michael T. (2003), 'The Politics of Development Policy and Development Policy Reform in New Order Indonesia', William Davidson Institute Working Paper Series No. 632.

Rodrigo, G. and E. Thorbecke (1997), 'Sources of Growth: A Reconsideration and General Equilibrium Application to Indonesia', *World Development*, Vol. 25, No. 10, pp. 1609–1625.

Rodrik, D. (1997), 'TFPG Controversies, Institutions, and Economic Performance in East Asia', NBER Working Paper No. 5914.

Rodrik, Dani (2003), *In Search of Prosperity: Analytic Narratives on Economic Growth*, Princeton, NJ: Princeton University Press.

Rodrik, D., A. Subramanian and F. Trebbi (2004), 'Institutions Rule: The Primacy of Institutions over Geography and Integration in Economic Development', *Journal of Economic Growth*, Vol. 9, No. 2, pp. 131–165.

Romer, Paul (1989), 'Human Capital and Growth: Theory and Evidence', NBER Working Paper No. 3173.

Rostow, W.W. (1960), *The Stages of Economic Growth: A Non-Communist Manifesto*, Cambridge: Cambridge University Press.

Rush, J. (1990), *Opium to Java: Revenue Farming and Colonial Enterprise in Colonial Indonesia, 1860–1910*, Ithaca: Cornell University Press.

Sachs, J.D. (2001), 'Tropical Underdevelopment', NBER Working Paper No. 8119.

Sachs, Jeffrey D. and Andrew Warner (1995), 'Natural Resource Abundance and Economic Growth', NBER Working Paper No. 5398, Cambridge, MA: National Bureau of Economic Research.

Sadli, Mohammad (1999), 'The Indonesian Crisis', in H.W. Arndt and H. Hill (eds), *Southeast Asia's Economic Crisis: Origins, Lessons, and the Way Forward*, Singapore: ISEAS, pp. 16–27.

Sato, Shigeru (1994), *War, Nationalism and Peasants: Java under the Japanese Occupation, 1942–1945*, Armonk, NY: Sharpe.

Schmitt, L. Th. (1991), *Rural Credit between Subsidy and Market: Adjustments of the Village Units of Bank Rakyat Indonesia in Sociological Perspective*, Leiden: Leiden Development Studies.

Schultz, T. Paul (1997), 'Demand for Children in Low Income Countries', in M.R. Rosenzweig and O Stark (eds), *Handbook of Population and Family Economics*, Amsterdam: Elsevier, pp. 350–430.

Schwarz, Adam (2000), *A Nation in Waiting: Indonesia's Search for Stability*, 2nd edition, Boulder, CO: Westview Press.

Scott, James C. (1977), *The Moral Economy of the Peasant: Rebellion and Subsistence in Southeast Asia*, Yale: Yale University Press.

Shankar, Raja and Anwar Shah (2003), 'Bridging the Economic Divide within Countries: A Scorecard on the Performance of Regional Policies in Reducing Regional Income Disparities', *World Development*, Vol. 31, No. 8, pp. 1421–1442.

Shiue, C.H. and W. Keller (2004), 'Markets in China and Europe on the Eve of the Industrial Revolution', NBER Working Paper No. 10778.

Siregar, Reza Y. (2001), 'Survey of Recent Developments', *Bulletin of Indonesian Economic Studies*, Vol. 37, No. 3, pp. 277–303.

Sluyterman, Keetie, Joost Dankers, Jos van der Linden and Jan Luiten van Zanden (1998), *Het Coöperatieve Alternatief: Honderd Jaar Rabobank 1898–1998*, Den Haag: SDU.

Smits, J.P. (1990), 'The Size and Structure of the Dutch Service Sector in International Perspective, 1850–1914', *Economic and Social History in the Netherlands*, Vol. 2, pp. 81–98.

Smits, J.P.H., E. Horlings and J.L. van Zanden (2000), *The Measurement of Gross National Product and its Components: The Netherlands 1800–1913*, Groningen: Groningen Growth and Development Centre.

Soehoed, A.R. (1967), 'Manufacturing in Indonesia', *Bulletin of Indonesian Economic Studies*, Vol. 3, No. 8, pp. 65–84.

Soesastro, Hadi (2003), 'The IMF and the Political Economy of Indonesia's Economic Recovery', *The Indonesian Quarterly*, Vol. 31, No. 2, pp. 165–179.

Solow, R. (1956), 'A Contribution to the Theory of Economic Growth', *Quarterly Journal of Economics*, Vol. 70, No. 1, pp. 65–94.

Srinivasan, T.N. and J. Bhagwati (1999), 'Outward-Orientation and Development: Are Revisionists Right?', Center Discussion Paper No. 806, Yale University.

Steckel, Richard H. (1995), 'Stature and the Standard of Living', *Journal of Economic Literature*, Vol. 33, No. 4, pp. 1903–1940.

Steckel, Richard H. (2009), 'Height and Human Development: Recent Developments and New Directions', *Explorations in Economic History*, Vol. 46, No. 1, pp. 1–23.

Stevens, Th. (1982), *Van der Capellen's koloniale ambitie op Java*, Amsterdam: Historisch Seminarium.

Stiglitz, Joseph E. (1988), 'Economic Organization, Information, and Development', in H. Chenery and T.N. Srinivasan (eds), *Handbook of Development Economics*, Vol. I, Amsterdam: North Holland, pp. 93–160.

Studer, R. (2008), 'India and the Great Divergence: Assessing the Efficiency of Grain Markets in Eighteenth- and Nineteenth-Century India', *The Journal of Economic History*, Vol. 68, No. 2, pp. 393–437.

Sudjana, B.G. and S. Mishra (2004), 'Growth and Inequality in Indonesia Today: Implication for Future Development Policy', United Nations Support Facility for Indonesia Recovery (UNSFIR) Working Paper, Jakarta, August 2004.

Sulistyono, Singgih Tri (2003), *The Java Sea Network: Patterns in the Development of Interregional Shipping and Trade in the Process of National Economic Integration in Indonesia, 1870s–1970s*, Leiden: KITLV Press.

Sulistyono, Singgih Tri (2006), 'The Expulsion of KPM and its Impact on the Inter-island Shipping and Trade in Indonesia, 1957–1964', *Itinerario*, Vol. 30, No. 2, pp. 104–128.

Sumitro Djojohadikusumo (1986), 'Recollections of My Career', *Bulletin of Indonesian Economic Studies*, Vol. 22, No. 3, pp. 27–39.

Suradisastra, Kedi (2006), 'Agricultural Cooperatives in Indonesia', paper for the 2006 FFTC–NACF International Seminar on Agricultural Cooperatives in Asia, Seoul, Korea.

Suryahadi, A., W. Widyanti, D. Perwira and S. Sumarto (2003), 'Minimum Wage Policy and Its Impact on Employment in the Urban Formal Sector', *Bulletin of Indonesian Economic Studies*, Vol. 39, No. 1, pp. 29–50.

Sutherland, H. (1979), *The Making of a Bureaucratic Elite: The Colonial Transformation of the Javanese Priyayi*, Singapore: Heinemann.

Syrquin, M. (1984), 'Resource Allocation and Productivity Growth', in M. Syrquin, L. Taylor and L.E. Westphal (eds) *Economic Structure Performance: Essays in Honor of Hollis B. Chenery*, New York: Academic Press.

Szirmai, A. (1993), 'Introduction', in A. Szirmai, B. van Ark and D. Pilat (eds), *Explaining Economic Growth: Essays in Honour of Angus Maddison*, Amsterdam: Elsevier.

Tabor, S.T. (1992), 'Agriculture in Transition', in A. Booth (ed.), *The Oil Boom and After: Indonesian Economic Policy and Performance in the Suharto Era*, Singapore: Oxford University Press, pp. 161–196.

Talens, J. (1999), *Een Feodale Samenleving in Koloniaal Vaarwater. Staatsvorming, Koloniale Expansie en Economische Onderontwikkeling in Banten, West-Java (1600–1750)* [A feudal society in colonial waters: Economic development, state formation and colonialism in Banten, West Java (1600–1750)], Hilversum: Verloren.

Taselaar, A. (1998), *De Nederlandse koloniale lobby*, Leiden: Research School CNWS.

Taylor, Norman (1945), *Cinchona in Java: The Story of Quinine*, New York: Greenberg.

Temple, Jonathan (2003), 'Growing into Trouble: Indonesia after 1966', in Dani Rodrik (ed.), *In Search of Prosperity: Analytic Narratives on Economic Growth*, Princeton: Princeton University Press.

The Indonesian Quarterly, various issues.

Thee Kian Wie (1987), 'Industrial and Foreign Investment Policy in Indonesia Since 1967', *Southeast Asian Studies*, Vol. 25, No. 3, pp. 383–396.

Thee Kian Wie (1991), 'The Surge of Asian NIC Investment into Indonesia', *Bulletin of Indonesian Economic Studies*, Vol. 27, No. 3, pp. 55–88.

Thee Kian Wie (1996), 'Foreign Direct Investment in Indonesia Since Independence', *Jurnal Ekonomi dan Pembangunan*, Vol. 4, No. 2, pp. 1–26.

Thee Kian Wie (2002), 'The Impact of the Asian Economic Crisis on the Prospects for Foreign Direct Investment in Indonesia', in J.Th. Lindblad (ed.) *Asian Growth and Foreign Capital: Case Studies from Eastern Asia*, Amsterdam: Aksant, pp. 37–58.

Thee Kian Wie (2003a), 'The Indonesian Economic Crisis and the Long Road to Recovery', *Australian Economic History Review*, Vol. 43, No. 2, pp. 183–196.

Thee Kian Wie (2003b), *Recollections: The Indonesian Economy, 1950s–1990s*, Singapore: ISEAS.

Thee Kian Wie (2009), 'Indonesia's Two Deep Crises: The Mid 1960s and Late 1990s', *Journal of the Asia Pacific*, Vol. 14, No. 1, pp. 49–60.

Thee Kian Wie and Siwage Dharma Negara (2010), 'Survey of Recent Developments', *Bulletin of Indonesian Economic Studies*, Vol. 46, No. 3, pp. 279–308.

Thorbecke, E. (1991), 'Adjustment, Growth and Income Distribution in Indonesia', *World Development*, Vol. 19, No. 11, pp. 1595–1614.

Thorp, R. (1998), *Progress, Poverty and Exclusion: An Economic History of Latin America in the 20th Century*, New York: Inter-American Development Bank, The Johns Hopkins University Press.

Timmer, C.P. (1991), 'Food Price Stabilization: Rationale, Design, and Implementation', in D.H. Perkins and M. Roemer (eds), *Reforming Economic Systems*, Cambridge: Harvard University Press, pp. 219–248.

Timmer, C. Peter (1996), 'Does Bulog Stabilise Rice Prices in Indonesia? Should it Try?', *Bulletin of Indonesian Economic Studies*, Vol. 32, pp. 45–74.

Timmer, M. and G. de Vries (2007), 'A Cross-Country Database for Sectoral Employment and Productivity in Asia and Latin America, 1950–2005', GGDC-Research Memorandum GD-94, University of Groningen.

Timmer, M. and A. Szirmai (2000), 'Productivity Growth in Asian Manufacturing: The Structural Bonus Hypothesis Examined', *Structural Change and Economic Dynamics* Vol. 11, pp. 371–392.

Touwen, Jeroen (2001), *Extremes in the Archipelago: Trade and Economic Development in the Outer Islands of Indonesia, 1900–1942*, Leiden: KITLV Press.

United Nations (2004), *World Urbanization Prospects: The 2003 Revision*, New York: United Nations Population Division, Department of Economic and Social Affairs.

Van Ark, Bart (1996), 'Sectoral Growth Accounting and Structural Change in Post-War Europe', in B. van Ark and N.F.R. Crafts (eds), *Quantitative Aspects of Post-War European Economic Growth*, Cambridge: CEPR/Cambridge University Press, pp. 84–164.

Van den Bosch, Joh. (1829), 'Advies van den Luitenant-Generaal van den Bosch over het stelsel van kolonisatie', in D.C. Steijn Parve, *Het koloniaal monopoliestelsel getoetst aan geschiedenis en staathuishoudkunde*, Zaltbommel: Joh. Noman en Zoon (published in 1851), pp. 294–328.

Van den Doel, H.W. (1994), *De stille macht. Het Europees binnenlands bestuur op Java en Madoera, 1808–1942*, Bert Bakker: Amsterdam.

Van der Eng, Pierre (1992), 'The Real Domestic Product of Indonesia, 1880–1989', *Explorations in Economic History*, Vol. 29, No. 3, pp. 343–373.

Van der Eng, Pierre (1993), 'The "Colonial Drain" from Indonesia, 1823–1990', Canberra: Research School of Pacific Studies, Economics Division Working Paper, Southeast Asia 93/2.

Van der Eng, Pierre (1994), *Food Supply in Java during War and Decolonisation, 1940–1950*, Hull: Centre for Southeast Asian Studies.

Van der Eng, Pierre (1996), *Agricultural Growth in Indonesia: Productivity Change and Policy Impact since 1880*, London: MacMillan Press.

Van der Eng, Pierre (1998), 'Regulation and Control: Explaining the Decline of Food Production in Java, 1940–6', in Paul H. Kratoska (ed.), *Food Supplies and the Japanese Occupation in South-East Asia*, London: Macmillan Press, pp. 187–207.

Van der Eng, Pierre (2000), 'Review of Anne Booth, *The Indonesian Economy in the Nineteenth and Twentieth Centuries: A History of Missed Opportunities*', *Bulletin of Indonesian Economic Studies*, Vol. 36, No. 1, pp. 243–245.

Van der Eng, Pierre (2001), 'Long-term Trends in Gross Domestic Expenditure in Indonesia and its Usage to Estimating the "Colonial Drain"', paper presented at the Modern Economic Growth and Distribution in Asia, Latin America and the European Periphery: A Historical National Accounts Approach Workshop, Hitotsubashi University, Tokyo.

Van der Eng, Pierre (2002), 'Indonesia's Growth Performance in the Twentieth Century', in Angus Maddison, D.S. Prasada Rao and William F. Shepherd (eds), *The Asian Economies in the Twentieth Century*, Cheltenham/Northampton: Edward Elgar, pp. 143–179.

Van der Eng, Pierre (2010), 'The Sources of Long-term Economic Growth in Indonesia, 1880–2008', *Exploration in Economic History*, Vol. 47, No. 3, pp. 294–309.

Van der Kemp, P.H. (1894), *Handboek tot de kennis van 's Lands Zoutmiddel in Nederlandsch-Indie*, Batavia: G. Kolff & Co.

Van der Kerkhof, Jasper (2005), 'Indonesianisasi of Dutch Economic Interests, 1930–1960: The Case of Internatio', *Bijdragen tot de Taal-, Land- en Volkenkunde*, Vol. 161, No. 2/3, pp. 181–209.

Van der Kraan, A. (1980), *Dutch Rule on Lombok, 1900–1940: The Development of Underdevelopment*, Townsville: James Cook University of North Queensland.

Van Doorn, J.A.A. (1994), *De laatste eeuw van Indië*, Amsterdam: Ooievaar.

Van Laanen, J.T.N. (1980), 'Money and Banking 1816–1940', *Changing Economy in Indonesia*, Vol. 6, Amsterdam: Royal Tropical Institute.

Van Leeuwen, Bas (2007), 'Human Capital and Economic Growth in India, Indonesia and Japan', PhD thesis, Utrecht University.

Van Luijk, Eric W. and Jan C. van Ours (2001), 'The Effects of Government Policy on Drug Use: Java, 1875–1904', *Journal of Economic History*, Vol. LXI, pp. 1–19.

Van Niel, Robert (1992), *Java under the Cultivation System*, Leiden: KITLV Press.

Van Oorschot, H.J. (1956), *De ontwikkeling van de nijverheid in Indonesië*, 's-Gravenhage/Bandung: W. van Hoeve.

Van Ours, Jan C. (1995), 'The Price Elasticity of Hard Drugs: The Case of Opium in the Dutch East Indies, 1923–1938', *The Journal of Political Economy*, Vol. 103, No. 2, pp. 261–279.

Van Roosmalen, J. and J.L. van Zanden (2001), 'Cooperatives: Their Economic Function and the Rise of Dutch Cooperatives', in W van Diepenbeek (ed.), *Cooperatives and Cooperative Banks: Their Contribution to Economic and Rural Development*, Utrecht: Rabobank International.

van Zanden, J.L. (1997), *Een Klein Land in de Twintigste Eeuw*. Utrecht: het Spectrum.

van Zanden, J.L. (2002), 'Economic Growth in Java 1815–1939: The Reconstruction of the Historical National Accounts of a Colonial Economy', Working Memorandum IISG, published at www.iisg.nl/research/jvz-reconstruction.pdf. Accessed 15 May 2010.

van Zanden, J.L. (2003), 'Rich and Poor before the Industrial Revolution: A Comparison between Java and the Netherlands at the Beginning of the 19th Century', *Explorations in Economic History*, Vol. 40, pp. 1–23.

van Zanden, J.L. (2004), 'On the Efficiency of Markets for Agricultural Products: Rice Prices and Capital Markets in 19th Century Java', *Journal of Economic History*, December.

van Zanden, J.L. (2007), 'Linking Two Debates: Money Supply, Wage Labour and Economic Development in Java in the Nineteenth Century', in Jan Lucassen (ed.), *Wages and Currency: Global Comparisons from Antiquity to the Twentieth Century*, International and Comparative Social History, Vol. 10, Bern: Peter Lang, pp. 169–193.

van Zanden, J.L. (2009a), 'Credit and the Colonial State: The Reform of Capital Markets on Java, 1900–1930', in David Henley and Peter Boomgaard (eds), *Credit and Debt in Indonesia, 1860–1930*, Singapore: KITLV Press/Institute of South East Asian Studies, pp. 160–178.

van Zanden, J.L. (2009b), 'The Skill Premium and the "Great Divergence"', *European Review of Economic History*, Vol. 13, No. 1, April, pp. 121–153.

van Zanden, J.L. and A. van Riel (2000), *Nederland 1780–1914. Staat, instituties en economische ontwikkeling*, Amsterdam: Balans.

Vitalis, L. (1851), 'Over de pachten in het algemeen, de onzedelijkheid van sommige, en de verdrukking waaraan de overmatige misbruiken van andere de Javaansche bevolking blootstellen', *Tijdschrift voor Nederlandsch Indië*, Vol. 13, pp. 365–386.

Wei, Shang-Jin (2000), 'Natural Openness and Good Government', NBER Working Paper No. 7765.

Widodo, Tri (2008), 'The Structure of Protection in Indonesian Manufacturing Sector', *ASEAN Economic Bulletin*, Vol. 25, No. 2, pp. 161–178.

Williamson, Jeffrey G. (1980), 'Earnings Inequality in Nineteenth-Century Britain', *Journal of Economic History*, Vol. 40, No. 3, pp. 457–475.

Williamson, Jeffrey G. (1982), 'The Structure of Pay in Britain, 1710–1911', *Research in Economic History*, Vol. 7, pp. 1–54.

Williamson, Jeffrey G. (1997), 'Globalization and Inequality, Past and Present', *World Bank Research Observer*, Vol. 12, No. 2, pp. 117–135.

Williamson, Jeffrey G. (2002), 'Land, Labor, and Globalization in the Third World, 1870–1940', *The Journal of Economic History*, Vol. 62, No. 1, pp. 55–85.

Williamson, Jeffrey G. (2006), *Globalization and the Poor Periphery before 1950*, Cambridge, MA: MIT Press.

Wolf, Eric R. (1966), *Peasants*, Engelwood Cliffs: Prentice Hall.

Woo Wing Thye (1991), 'Using Economic Methodology to Assess Competing Models of Economic Policy-Making in Indonesia', *ASEAN Economic Bulletin*, Vol. 7, No. 3, pp. 307–321.

World Bank (1993), *The East Asian Miracle: Economic Growth and Public Policy*, Oxford: Oxford University Press.

World Bank (1998), *Indonesia in Crisis: A Macroeconomic Update*, Washington DC: World Bank.

World Bank (2003), *Indonesia: Maintaining Stability, Deepening Reforms*, report No. 25330, Jakarta: World Bank.

World Bank (2007), *Fighting Corruption in Decentralized Indonesia: Case Studies on Handling Local Government Corruption*, Washington DC: World Bank.

Young, A. (1995), 'The Tyranny of Numbers: Confronting the East Asian Growth Experience', *The Quarterly Journal of Economics*, Vol. 110, No. 3, pp. 641–680.

Yusuf, Arief A. (2006), 'On the Re-Assessment of Inequality in Indonesia: Household Survey or National Account?', Working Paper in Economics and Development Studies No. 200605, Padjadjaran University, Bandung.

Zollinger, H. (1847), 'De Lampongsche districten en hun tegenwoordige toestand', *Tijdschrift Neêrlandsch Indie*, Vol. 9, pp. 1–38, 121–141, 249–320; cited from the English version 'The Lampong Districts and their Present Condition', *Journal of Indian Archipelago and Eastern Asia*, Vol. 5, 1851, pp. 625–641, 691–703.

Index

Page numbers in *italics* denote tables, those in **bold** denote figures.

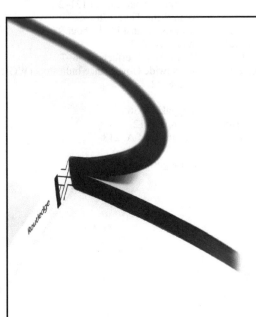